Law of Health and Safety at W

Law of Health and Safety at Work

Norman Selwyn

LLM, Dip Econ (Oxon), Barrister

Croner Publications Ltd
Croner House
London Road
Kingston on Thames
Surrey KT2 6SR
Telephone: 081–547 3333

First published 1982 by Butterworth & Co (Publishers) Ltd
Second edition published by Croner Publications Ltd 1993

Published by Croner Publications Ltd,
Croner House,
London Road,
Kingston upon Thames,
Surrey KT2 6SR
Telephone: 081–547 3333

While every care has been taken
in the writing and editing of this book,
readers should be aware that only Acts of Parliament
and Statutory Instruments have the force of law,
and that only the courts can authoritatively
interpret the law

A CIP Catalogue Record for this book is available
from the British Library

ISBN 1–85524–104–8

Typeset by Create, 11 Riverside Court, Bath BA2 3DZ
Index compiled by Indexing Specialists, 202 Church Road, Hove, East Sussex BN3 2DJ
Printed by Redwood Books, Kennet House, Kennet Way, Trowbridge, Wiltshire BA14 8RN

Contents

Preface

Although the subject of health and safety at work is of vital importance to every employer, employee and self-employed person, there is an apparent dearth of books which explain the complex legal requirements in a manner which can be readily understood and appreciated by those who are most affected. The aim of this book is to fill that gap. It should be of interest to employers, company secretaries, managers, trade unionists, safety officers, safety representatives, enforcement officers and lawyers, as well as to students who are seeking to be in employment in the future.

The book is intended to be a guide, not a bible. The aim is to promote knowledge, yet at the same time to give understanding. In other words, I have tried not only to state the law, but also to explain it. If the consequence has been a certain amount of oversimplification, I believe that this is a price well worth paying. However, the reader will appreciate that when legal problems arise in practice, it may be necessary to consult the actual statutory provisions, or, where necessary, seek expert legal advice.

Health and safety is an ubiquitous subject and it is not easy to draw boundaries. There is no obvious delineation between health and safety at work and health and safety generally. Road traffic, environmental issues, consumer protection, etc all overlap with health and safety at work. Thus I have included some material on "peripheral" matters, but if the line has been drawn somewhat arbitrarily, it is perhaps better to do so than not to draw one at all.

The *raison d'être* of the law on health and safety at work is not always easy to discover, for there are differing social objectives to be achieved. The law is intended to be partly preventative, partly punitive, and partly compensatory. The rules are an amalgam of contract, tort and criminal law. Statutory provisions are interwoven with judicial decisions, and, in recent years, Approved Codes of Practice have assumed a greater importance in giving practical guidance. Each industry has its own peculiar problems. Each firm has its own difficulties. Each incident has its own unique features. These variations make the task of preventing accidents difficult for those involved. But however complex these matters may be, ignorance of the legal requirements is the least excuse.

The law on health and safety at work is constantly changing, and readers and practitioners must always try to keep abreast of the latest developments. In this edition, I have included the new regulations recently introduced (Management of Health and Safety at Work, Personal Protective Equipment, Workplace, Work Equipment, Manual Handling Operations and Display Screen Equipment) which have been passed following the EC Framework Directive and first five daughter Directives, as well as a number of other changes which have occurred since the previous edition. In particular, attention should be paid to the new powers of punishment provided by the Offshore Safety Act 1992 and the Criminal Justice Act 1991, and the important amendments made to the Employment Protection (Consolidation) Act 1978 by the Trade Union Reform and Employment Rights Act 1993, although at the time of writing, Commencement Orders have not been made. New material has been added, and attention paid to a considerable number of recent legal decisions.

I would like to express my thanks to Sarah Tullett, of the Engineering Employers' Federation, for placing her encyclopaedic knowledge at my disposal, thus saving me from committing a number of errors of commission and omission. My thanks are also due to my colleague John Riley, Barrister, for reading the proofs of this book, and making some helpful suggestions.

I have tried to state the law according to the sources available to me at 1 July 1993.

Norman Selwyn

Solihull, West Midlands

1

Law and legal institutions

The background to health and safety law

1.1 Legislative intervention in pursuance of the cause of health and safety dates from the Health and Morals of Apprentices Act 1802. This Act was designed to protect young children working in cotton and woollen mills and other factories where more than twenty persons were employed. At that time it was the custom to put four children in a bed during the day and four more in the same bed at night while the day-time occupants were working. It was this type of abuse at which the Act was aimed. Other pieces of minor legislation were passed in the ensuing years, but the real breakthrough came in 1833 when the Factory Act was passed. It provided that four factory inspectors were to be appointed with powers of investigation and prosecution. From that time on the factory movement gathered momentum, although the motives of some of the protagonists were not always of high altruism. Sometimes the legislation was designed to restrict the hours of work of women and young children (indirectly benefiting adult male labour), while other enactments were concerned with establishing safe working conditions. Perhaps the worst feature was the multiplicity of legislation—in 1876 a Factory Commission reported that the law was in a complete state of chaos, with no less than nineteen different enactments to be considered. It was not until the Factory and Workshop Act of 1901 that a comprehensive piece of factory legislation was enacted, when all the previous law was consolidated into one statute. One of the more interesting innovations was to give the power to the Secretary of State to make regulations for particular industries, a power which was used extensively to control a large number of different industrial processes. In 1916 this power was extended to permit Welfare Orders to be made dealing with washing facilities, first aid provisions, and so on. A further major breakthrough came in 1937 when the Factories Act was passed. It swept away the old distinctions between the different types of premises (textile factories, workshops, etc) and made detailed provisions for health, safety and welfare. Minor amendments were made in 1948 and 1959, and the various statutes were consolidated once more by the Factories Act 1961, which is still in force today, although it is in the process of being progressively repealed, and replaced by new Health and Safety Regulations and Approved Codes of Practice.

1.2 The mining industry was an obvious subject for protective legislation, and in 1842 a Mines and Collieries Act was passed, which was mainly concerned with regulating hours and working conditions of women and children. Work in quarries was brought within the scope of the law by the Metalliferous Mines Regulations Act 1872, and a further major reform took place in 1911, with the passing of the Coal

Mines Act. These provisions were strengthened and brought up to date in the Mines and Quarries Act 1954 which, together with regulations made, lays down a comprehensive protective code of legislation for these industries.

1.3 Health and safety legislation for the non-industrial worker came somewhat later. In 1886, the Shop Hours Regulation Act restricted the hours of work of young persons, and the Seats for Shop Assistants Act 1899 may be regarded as an important welfare statute. After many attempts had been made to give legislative cover to office workers, an Offices Act was passed in 1960, but this (and other legislation) was superseded by the Offices, Shops and Railway Premises Act 1963 (for which see chapter 5). Other statutes which regulated hours of work include the Employment of Women, Young Persons and Children Act 1920, Hours of Employment (Conventions) Act 1936 and Young Persons (Employment) Act 1938.

1.4 The original intention of the framers of the legislation was that health and safety laws would be enforced through the use of criminal sanctions, but for two reasons this emphasis changed over the years. The first was the gradual realisation that a rigorous policy of enforcement by the factory inspectorate would probably lead to the shutdown of large sections of British industry, already fighting hard to maintain its position against competition from foreign countries which were not necessarily inhibited by such constraints. The policy would also clutter up the courts and require a massive expansion of the machinery for bringing prosecutions. The second and possibly more significant reason for the change in emphasis was the ability of injured workers to bring civil actions in respect of injuries suffered as a result of their employers' failure to observe the statutory duties. This action—for breach of statutory duty—was first successful in the case of *Groves v Lord Wimborne* in 1898, and, because of the absolute nature of many of the statutory duties, became a fruitful source of financial solace. But the result was to divert the objects of the law away from prosecution and prevention towards a system of civil compensation. As Goddard LJ stated in *Hutchinson v London and North Eastern Rly Co.*, "The real incentive for the observance by employers of their statutory duties . . . is not their liability to substantial fines, but the possibility of heavy claims for damages". Even this, however, was not entirely correct, for most employers realised the value of taking out insurance policies against such claims (a requirement which was made compulsory in 1969) with the result that both the civil and criminal law ceased to be major deterrents.

1.5 At the same time as these developments were taking place, the common law of the country was also becoming active. In a leading case decided in 1837 (*Priestley v Fowler*) a claim based on an allegation of negligence by an employer towards his employee failed, but a few years later, in 1840, a young girl successfully sued when she was seriously injured in a mill accident and was awarded damages (*Cottrell v Stocks*). From then on, common law claims were bogged down with problems arising from the doctrine of "common employment" (abolished in 1948 by the Law Reform (Personal Injuries) Act), the inability to sue at common law if the injured worker had also claimed under the Workman's Compensation Act (amended by the

National Insurance (Industrial Injuries) Act 1946), and the inability to claim if the employee had been contributorily negligent (amended by the Law Reform (Contributory Negligence) Act 1945). By 1970, the law on health and safety was largely concerned with issues of compensation.

1.6 In 1970 a committee on health and safety at work was appointed under the chairmanship of Lord Robens, which reported two years later. In their report, the Robens Committee reached some fundamental conclusions. First, although it was generally recognised that we had in this country the finest regulatory system of legal controls anywhere in the world, this did not prevent the annual carnage which took place, evidenced by the numbers who were killed or injured. Second, much of our law was obscure and unintelligible to those whose actions it was intended to influence. There was a haphazard mass, intricate in detail, difficult to amend and frequently out-of-date. Third, the various enforcement authorities had overlapping jurisdictions which caused some confusion.

1.7 But the main conclusion of the Robens Committee was that there was one single cause, above all else, for accidents and ill health at work. This was apathy. Apathy at the top, apathy at the bottom, apathy at all levels in between. True, there were a few dedicated people who worked hard at trying to influence people's attitudes, but these rarely had sufficient power or authority to override considerations of production, and in the main, health and safety had a low priority in almost all workplaces. In an attempt to overcome this attitude, the Robens Committee made a number of far-reaching proposals. The first was to devise a system whereby all employers and all employees became aware that health and safety was the concern of everyone, and not just a matter for the dedicated few. As the report stated, "Our present system encourages too much reliance on State regulation, and rather too little on personal responsibility and voluntary, self-generating effort." Next, it was suggested that there was a need for a single comprehensive framework of legislation which would cover all work activity, supported and supplemented by a series of controls to deal with specific problems, and assisted by voluntary standards and more flexible codes of practice. Finally, a more unified enforcement authority was needed, having overall responsibility for initiating legal proposals and giving assistance and advice, possessing stronger enforcement powers, and with the ability to delegate its enforcement functions when necessary.

1.8 The result was the passing of the Health and Safety at Work etc Act 1974 (HSWA), an important piece of legislation which adopts a fundamentally different approach to the whole subject. In the first place, the Act applies to all employed persons, wherever they work (except domestic servants in private households). This brought into the protective umbrella an estimated 8,000,000 "new entrants" who were not hitherto covered by previous legislation. Next, as well as laying down duties for employers and employees, the Act imposes certain legal requirements on those who manufacture, import, design or supply articles and substances which are to be used at work. Some of the provisions (eg safety policies, safety representatives) are designed to bring about a greater personal involvement of all concerned. New institutions were created, new enforcement powers were enacted, and new concepts, such as the use of Approved Codes of Practice, were introduced. The "old" law, eg Factories Act, Offices, Shops and Railway Premises Act, etc was intended to remain in force for the time being, although the ultimate objective is to gradually repeal and replace them by new regulations which will be supplemented by Approved Codes of Practice and guidance literature.

1.9 It must not be assumed that the Health and Safety at Work Act is the answer to all our problems, or that it is a perfect piece of legislation. On the contrary, despite the criticism levelled by the Robens Committee against the legalistic and unintelligible nature of the then existing law, the Act is turgid, soporific and in parts about as meaningful as medieval metaphysics. Further, it is basically a criminal statute, with appropriate penalties for breaches, and does not confer on anyone the right to make a claim for compensation. This means that most of the cases will start and finish in the magistrates' courts, with the result that there is very little opportunity for authoritative interpretations of the complex legal language. In the nineteen years since the Act was passed, there have been relatively few legal decisions from higher courts, thus problems and queries remain.

1.10 On the positive side, the Act has acted as a catalyst for considerable management activity, as a greater awareness of responsibility has brought about increased concern for the health and safety of employees. It is, perhaps, too early to judge the psychological impact of the Act, or to evaluate its success, for although it is possible to note some downward trends in the numbers of accidents, there are many other factors which need to be taken into account, and we can never know how many accidents did not happen as a result of a more safety-conscious approach. Whether the encouraging reduction in accident rates over the past decade has been due to a greater awareness of the legal requirements, to pro-active safety policies, to changes in manufacturing processes, or to a reduction in the numbers employed in those industries which were traditionally a major source of accidents and ill health, is always going to be a matter for debate. Meanwhile, if the propaganda which surrounds the Act brings about a greater awareness that health and safety is everyone's concern, and not merely a matter for those who have a specialised interest in the problem, nothing but good will be the result.

1.11 Since 1974, the Act has been amended by the Consumer Protection Act 1987 (in particular strengthening s.6), the Criminal Justice Act 1991 and the Offshore Safety Act 1992, which have increased the penalties which may be imposed for various breaches. The progressive repeal of the Factories Act and other primary legislation has continued, and, more recently, there has been a spate of new Health and Safety Regulations (supplemented by Approved Codes of Practice and Guidance Notes) consequent on our membership of the European Community. However, the basic principles of the Act remain.

1.12 The present situation, therefore, is that the law on health and safety at work is an amalgam of criminal law, civil law, and preventative measures. Breaches of the various statutory provisions (and regulations made thereunder) are capable of being criminal offences, in respect of which the wrongdoer may be fined or (in rare circumstances) imprisoned. Civil claims for compensation may arise in respect of injuries received as a result of a failure by the employer to observe the statutory requirements (other than HSWA), or a failure to carry out those duties imposed by the common law of the land. The preventative measures can be found in the new enforcement notices which may be issued, the greater involvement of the workforce by the appointment of safety representatives and the creation of safety committees, and the more detailed requirements of the new Health and Safety Regulations.

1.13 This mixture of legal objectives is reflected in the decided cases which explain and expand on the nature of the legal duties. For practical reasons, the majority of these cases stem from civil claims, although in recent years there has been an increasing number of rulings in the industrial tribunals which add to our understanding of the legal rules. Care must always be taken not to elevate all such decisions to absolute principles, for the statute is always paramount, and individual cases can only be decided on their own special facts. Legal interpretation is more of an art than a science.

Sources of law

Legislation

1.14 The prime source of law in the UK consists of Acts of Parliament. With the important exception noted below relating to the Treaty of Rome, an Act of Parliament is the supreme law of the land. Parliament, it is said, can make or unmake any law whatsoever. In strict theory, this could lead to severe problems, but in reality there are clearly political and practical limits on what Parliament in fact will do.

1.15 Statute law commences with the introduction of a Bill into either House of Parliament. This will receive a formal First Reading when it is published. The House will then hold a full debate on the general principles behind the proposed legislation, and a vote may be held on a proposal to give the Bill a Second Reading. If successful, the Bill will then be sent to a committee, where it is considered in detail, and amendments may be made. Next, the Bill is presented to a report stage of the full House, when the amendments are considered, and finally, the Bill will receive its Third Reading. It will then go to the other House, where a similar procedure is adopted. When both Houses have passed the Bill, it is presented to the Queen for the Royal Assent, which, by convention, is never refused.

1.16 However, although the Bill is now an Act, its implementation may be delayed in whole or in part. Modern legislation frequently contains powers which enable the appropriate Minister to bring the Act into force in various stages, often with transitional provisions. In those cases the law will not come into force until the date specified in a Commencement Order.

Regulations

1.17 An Act may confer upon a Minister the power to make new or additional law by means of regulations. Such subordinate legislative power has many advantages, for it enables technical proposals to be passed, it is speedier than the procedure adopted for an Act, and enables the law to be amended by a simpler procedure. Regulations must be laid before Parliament, and are considered by the Joint Committee on Statutory Instruments, which has members from both Houses. They are not concerned with the policy or merits of the regulations, only the technical competence of the Minister to make them. For example, the committee will ascertain whether the regulations are within the powers which are conferred by the parent Act, and whether they contain any unusual or unexpected use of that power. Some regulations will only become law after an affirmative vote by both Houses of Parliament, but the majority will become law when they are made. However, they can subsequently be vetoed by a negative vote within 40 days of laying. Regulations which are made under HSWA are of this type (see s.82(3)).

1.18 Regulations have the full force of law until they are repealed or amended in some way. It is possible for them to supersede specific provisions of the parent Act. In *Miller v William Boothman*, the plaintiff was injured while working on a circular saw, the fencing of which complied with the Woodworking Machinery Regulations 1922. It was argued on his behalf that the employers were still liable for his injury, as they were in breach of the requirements of s.14 of the Factories Act to fence every dangerous part of any machinery. The argument was rejected. The Minister had exercised the power vested in him to exclude the provisions of the Act by regulation, and the latter prevailed.

1.19 As has already been indicated, one of the main objects of HSWA is to replace the existing statutory provisions over a period of time with a more streamlined system in which regulations will play a major part. These will fall generally into different categories. First, there will be those regulations which will apply to most or all employment situations (for example, the Reporting of Injuries, Diseases and Dangerous Occurrences Regulations 1985); second, there will be those regulations which are designed to control a particular hazard in a particular industry (eg Agriculture (Threshers and Balers) Regulations 1960); third, there are those which will refer to a particular hazard or risk which may be found in a number of industries or processes, eg the Control of Lead at Work Regulations 1980); fourth, regulations may be introduced in order to further the streamlining process or because the old provisions were out of date (eg the First Aid Regulations 1981). Others may be introduced consequent upon the discovery of a loophole in the law which may have come to light because of some litigation (the Abrasive Wheels Regulations 1970 were made in order to nullify the decision of *Summers & Sons v Frost*). As a general rule, regulations are designed to supplement and strengthen the provisions of the various Acts of Parliament, spelling out the requirements in greater detail (eg Power Presses Regulations 1965).

1.20 Health and safety regulations made under HSWA, s.15 may be for any of the following purposes:

(a) repeal or modify any existing statutory provision
(b) exclude or modify in relation to any specific class of case any of the provisions of ss.2–9 (chapter 3) or any existing statutory provision
(c) make a specific authority responsible for the enforcement of any relevant statutory provision
(d) impose requirements by reference to the approval of the Commission or other specified body or person
(e) provide that any reference in a regulation to a specific document shall include a reference to a revised version of that document
(f) provide for exemptions from any requirement or prohibition
(g) enable exemptions to be granted by a specified person or authority
(h) specify the persons or class of persons who may be guilty of an offence
(i) provide for specified defences either generally or in specified circumstances
(j) exclude proceedings on indictment in relation to certain offences
(k) restrict the punishment which may be imposed in respect of certain offences.

1.21 In addition to the above, Schedule 3 to HSWA contains detailed provisions about the contents of such regulations, sufficient, it is thought, to completely replace the old law, and wide enough to enable the Secretary of State and the Commission to do almost anything in the interest of health and safety. In particular, however, we may note two further important provisions. The first is the power to prohibit the carrying on of any specified activity or the doing of any specified thing without a licence granted for that purpose, which may be subject to conditions. The second is contained in s.79 of the Act, which amends s.16 of the Companies Act 1967 (see now Companies Act 1985, s.235 and Schedule 10, Pt IV) so as to enable the Secretary of State to prescribe cases whereby directors' reports will contain such information about the arrangements in force for that year for securing the health, safety and welfare at work of the employees of that company (and any subsidiary company), and for protecting other persons against risks to health resulting from the activities at work of the employees. To date, no action has been taken to implement this provision.

1.22 A breach of a duty imposed by regulations is, of course, punishable as a criminal offence. Additionally, a breach may give rise to civil liability, except insofar as the regulations provide otherwise.

The making of regulations

1.23 Health and safety regulations are made by the Secretary of State as a result of proposals made to him by the Health and Safety Commission (HSC). He may also make them on his own initiative, but before doing so he must consult with HSC and with any other appropriate bodies. If HSC makes the proposals, it too must consult with appropriate Government departments and other interested bodies (HSWA, s.50). The normal practice is for HSC to initiate proposals in the form of a consultative document, which is given a wide circulation to interested bodies, such as employers' associations, trade unions, trade associations, and so on. Comments received are considered, and the proposals may be modified in the light of these. Draft regulations are then publicised, amended if necessary, and the regulations, in their final form, are presented to the Secretary for State, to be laid before Parliament.

1.24 Although regulations are usually made by the Secretary of State for Employment, some have emanated from other Government departments (eg Defence, Transport, Social Services).

Orders

1.25 Historically, Orders were promulgated by the Queen in her Privy Council, exercising the royal prerogative. This procedure was a convenient way of avoiding Parliamentary scrutiny, but since the Statutory Instruments Act 1946 this is no longer so, and Orders are now subject to annulment on a resolution of either House of Parliament (see HSWA, s.84(4)). Modern practice is to confer on the appropriate Minister the power to make Orders, which again can only be exercised within the powers conferred. For example, s.84 of HSWA empowers the Queen by order in council to extend the provisions of the Act outside Great Britain (see Health and Safety at Work etc Act 1974 (Application outside Great Britain) Order 1989), whereas s.85 enables the Secretary of State to make Commencement Orders.

1.26 As a rough guide, the distinction between a regulation and an Order is that the former is a means whereby the power to make substantive law is exercised, whereas the latter gives the force of law to an executive act.

By-laws

1.27 Local authorities have power to pass by-laws for the administration of their own area. These must be within the powers conferred by the parent Act of Parliament, and must also be reasonable. It is possible to challenge the validity of a by-law in the courts.

Judicial precedent

1.28 The bulk of British law is contained in the decisions made by the judges in cases which come before them in the courts. When a judge decides a case, he will state his reasons for that decision. Frequently, the case will be reported in one of the many series of law reports (official or commercial) which exist. From the report, it may be possible to cull the narrow reason for the decision, ie the *ratio decidendi*. Anything else uttered in the course of the decision is regarded as *obiter dicta*, ie things said by the way. Distilling the *ratio* of a case, and distinguishing it from *obiter dicta*, is a legal art.

1.29 Strictly speaking, it is only the decisions of the higher courts which become binding precedents. Other decisions are said to be "persuasive". Thus a decision of the House of Lords will bind all lower courts, and can only be changed by a further decision of the House of Lords itself (a rare occurrence) or by an Act of Parliament. A decision of the Court of Appeal will also bind lower courts, but not, of course, the House of Lords. All other lower courts only create persuasive precedents.

1.30 However, lawyers will attempt to avoid inconvenient precedents (when necessary) by using their legal ingenuity. Thus it may be possible to distinguish a previous decision on the ground that the facts are not identical, or that there are material differences sufficient to warrant not following an earlier decision. Since the *ratio* of a case is uncertain, inconvenient remarks may be brushed aside as being *obiter dicta*, on the ground that they were not essential for the actual decision. A court may be asked to refuse to follow a precedent because it was decided *per incuriam*, ie without a full and proper argument on the point in issue. Frequently, there will be an abundance of precedents, and each side will quote those which support its argument. Occasionally, the point may never have arisen for decision before, and the court must reach its conclusions on first principles, thus creating a precedent. It is because of these points that the vagaries, as well as the richness, of British law emerges, but it will also be seen why litigation is so uncertain.

Approved Codes of Practice

1.31 For the purpose of providing practical guidance, in recent years Parliament has authorised a number of organisations to issue Codes of Practice, which, though not having the force of law, may be taken into consideration by the courts and tribunals in appropriate circumstances. So far as this book is concerned, s.16 of HSWA conferred on the Health and Safety Commission power to approve and issue codes of practice for the purpose of providing practical guidance with respect to any of the general duties laid down in ss.2–7 of the Act, or any health and safety regulations or existing statutory provision. The Commission may also approve other codes which are drawn up by other persons or organisations (eg British Standards). The Commission cannot approve a code without first obtaining the consent of the Secretary of State, and prior to obtaining this, it must consult with Government departments and other appropriate bodies. Codes may be revised from time to time, and the Commission may, if necessary, withdraw its approval from a particular code.

1.32 A failure on the part of any person to observe the provisions contained in an Approved Code of Practice does not, of itself, render that person liable to any criminal or civil proceedings, but in any criminal proceedings, if a person is alleged to have committed an offence concerning a matter in respect of which an approved code is in force, the provisions of that code are admissible in evidence, and a failure to observe it constitutes proof of the breach of duty, or contravention of the regulation or statutory provision in question, unless the accused satisfies the court that he complied with the requirement of the law in some other equally efficacious manner. Approved codes, therefore, are guides to good safety practice. If a person follows the requirements of the codes it is unlikely that he will be successfully prosecuted for an offence. If he fails to follow the code, he may be guilty of an offence unless he can show that he observed the specific legal requirements in some other way (HSWA, s.17).

1.33 The purpose behind the making of increasing use of codes of practice is to avoid built-in obsolescence in legal requirements, and to give practical guidance for the benefit of those upon whom duties are placed by virtue of a statute or regulation. HSWA contains no guidance on the status of codes of practice in civil proceedings, but it is likely that a failure to observe their provisions could constitute *prima facie* evidence of negligence, which would have to be rebutted by evidence to the contrary.

Guidance Notes

1.34 The Commission and Executive frequently issue Guidance Notes, sometimes alongside codes and sometimes independently of them. Guidance Notes contain practical advice and sound suggestions, and are frequently more informative than the codes (see, for example, the Guidance Notes attached to the Safety Representative and Safety Committee Regulations, which are far more helpful than the actual code). Although the Guidance Notes have no legal standing, it is possible to use them as evidence of the state of knowledge at the time of issue. For example, in *Glyn Owen v Sutcliffe* an Environmental Health Officer (EHO) issued an improvement notice requiring a self-employed shoe repairer to install ventilation in his shop, following complaints about the strong smell of solvent fumes. At an appeal before an industrial tribunal, the EHO referred to an HSE Guidance Note, and also to one issued by the British Adhesive Manufacturers Association, both of which warned of the dangers of inhaling solvent vapour, and suggested suitable ventilation and vapour extraction. The industrial tribunal affirmed the improvement notice, for the shoe repairer was in breach of his duty under the Act to himself as well as to others (s.3(2)). In *Burgess v Thorn Consumer Electronics (Newhaven) Ltd* it was held that if employers do not warn employees of the dangers referred to in the Guidance Notes, they may be liable to employees for negligence, as the notes indirectly give rise to a duty of care.

The European Community

1.35 As from 1 January 1973, the UK became a member of the EC, and by the European Communities Act 1972 (s.2) all obligations arising out of the various treaties which set up the EC are to be given legal effect in this country without further enactment. European law is of particular importance to the study of domestic law on health and safety at work. First, since the object of the EC is economic harmonisation, it would distort market forces if one country could economise on health and safety matters to the disadvantage of others. Second, a number of changes have been brought about in our domestic law in order to conform to European standards. Third, the EC has recently introduced the "social dimension" whereby positive steps are to be taken to increase protections offered to workers from the risks of accidents and ill health at work, and generally raise standards of employment protection throughout the Community. Thus the impact of European law on domestic law is gathering momentum and cannot be ignored. In order to understand European law, we must examine the treaties, the institutions and the nature of European law.

Treaty of Rome

1.36 This Treaty was signed in 1957 by the original six founding States (France, West Germany, Italy, Belgium, The Netherlands and Luxembourg). The UK, Ireland and Denmark acceded to the Treaty in 1973, Greece in 1981, and Spain and Portugal became full members in 1992. The original Treaty required unanimity between all the Member States before laws could be passed. So far as is relevant, Article 118 of the Treaty stated that one of the objects of the Community was to harmonise laws relating to "employment, labour law and working conditions, basic and advanced training, social security, protection against occupational accidents and diseases, occupational hygiene, law of trade unions, and collective bargaining between workers and employers."

1.37 In 1986, the Single European Act was signed in The Hague and Luxembourg, making certain amendments to the Treaty of Rome. These amendments were given effect in this country by the European Communities (Amendment) Act 1986. One significant change made was the introduction of a system of "qualified majority voting" on certain issues. Each State has been allocated a certain number of votes (Germany, Italy, France and the UK have 10 votes each, Spain has 8, Belgium, The Netherlands, Portugal and Greece have 5, Denmark and Ireland have 3 and Luxembourg has 2). A qualified majority decision requires 54 out of the 76 votes available to pass a particular proposal. The significance is that qualified majority voting can be used to pass proposals relating to health and safety matters in the working environment under the new Article 118A of the Treaty (see chapter 10).

Community institutions

Council of Ministers

1.38 This is the supreme policy making body of the Community. Each meeting of the Council is attended by a minister from each Member State. Usually, this will be the respective foreign secretaries, but sometimes, when specific detailed proposals are being discussed, the respective "portfolio" ministers will attend. One member of the Council will hold the presidency for six months and then the position rotates. The Council is assisted by a Secretariat (comprising of a staff of some 2,000) and preparatory work for the meetings is undertaken by frequent meetings of senior civil servants from the respective countries, known as the Committee of Permanent Representatives (Coreper).

The Commission

1.39 This is sometimes described as being the "bureaucracy" of the Community, but perhaps a more accurate description would be the "engine room". There are 16 commissioners (Germany, France, Italy and the UK each appoint two commissioners, the other Member States each appoint one). However, although appointed by their respective countries, commissioners are totally independent of them. Each commissioner has certain departmental responsibilities and is assisted by a cabinet and directorate general. Decisions are taken on a collegiate basis.

1.40 The Commission has the responsibility of initiating and drafting proposals for approval by the Council. It acts as a mediator between States, and as a "watch dog" to ensure that Community rules are being observed. Indeed, if the commission consider that a Member State is failing to comply with a Community law, it can take enforcement action by referring the alleged breach to the European Court of Justice for a ruling (see below).

European Parliament

1.41 This body sits in Strasbourg and consists of 512 Members of the European Parliament (MEP) elected directly from each Member State. It can express an opinion to the Council of Ministers on proposals which emanate from the Commission, can submit questions to both institutions, and can, as a final sanction, dismiss the Commission on a vote of censure passed by a two-thirds majority. The Single European Act introduced a cooperation procedure, whereby the views of the Parliament must be established prior to the Council of Ministers reaching a common position on any particular proposal.

European Court of Justice

1.42 This court sits in Luxembourg, and comprises thirteen judges and six advocate generals. Appointments are made for six years. The court gives rulings on the interpretation of European law, either on a reference from the Commission, at the request of the courts of a Member State or on a claim brought by an individual person or corporation in a Member State. Once it has given its ruling the matter is then referred back to the courts of the Member State for compliance.

European law

The Treaty of Rome

1.43 The Treaty of Rome is the supreme law of all Member States. If an Article of the Treaty is clear, precise, requires no further implementation and does not give discretion to Member States, then it is directly applicable, and does not require the

Member States to pass domestic legislation to give it effect. The main significance of this rule relates to the way Article 119 of the Treaty—which requires that there should be equal pay for equal work—has been invoked by courts when national law has failed to ensure compliance (for example, see the recent case of *Secretary of State for Scotland v Wright*). Also significant is Article 48, which requires the free movement of workers within the Community without discrimination (*Van Duyn v Home Office (no. 2)*).

Regulations

1.44 Once a regulation has been passed by the Council of Ministers, it becomes part of the laws of Member States, and overrides any contrary domestic provision. No implementing legislation is needed. A number of regulations have been passed dealing with the transportation of goods, vehicle movements generally, etc. For example, EC Regulation 3820/85 controls the hours of work of drivers of goods and passenger vehicles throughout the Community. More recently, the Council of Ministers adopted the Existing Substances Regulation (EEC/793/93) establishing a framework for the notification and assessment of existing chemical substances.

Directives

1.45 A Directive passed by the Council of Ministers is binding on Member States as to the results to be achieved, but generally leaves a choice as to form and method. There are a number of problems relating to the precise legal effect of a Directive, but it is generally accepted that in the field of health and safety they are not directly applicable in Member States, and do not, by themselves, give rise to any enforceable Community right. Health and safety generally is a topic for considerable activity by the Community and a number of Directives have been passed which are either in force or due to come into force within the near future. Indeed, the Health and Safety Commission must keep a very close look at European Directives (a) to ensure that our existing laws comply, (b) to ensure that future changes do not conflict and (c) to consider ways in which European standards can be implemented.

Decisions

1.46 A decision may be given by the Commission on any particular case referred to them, either by a Member State, an individual or a corporate body. The decision is only applicable to that case and has no value as a binding precedent.

Recommendations

1.47 The Council of Ministers may make recommendations, which have no binding effect. However, they may be considered by national courts when dealing with a problem arising out of the interpretation of domestic law. For example, there is a Council Recommendation that all employees should have a minimum of four weeks' annual holiday, but this is in no way enforceable. However, in *Grimaldi v Fonds des Maladies Professionelles*, the European Court of Justice held that national courts should take recommendations into account when determining disputes before them, particularly when they purport to clarify the interpretation of laws passed to implement them, or when they are designed to supplement binding Community measures.

European Charter for Fundamental Social Rights

1.48 Following the amendment to the Treaty by the Single European Act, the Commission produced a Charter for Fundamental Social Rights. Some of these proposals are regarded as being controversial and it is not entirely clear whether they can be passed by the qualified majority voting system or require a unanimous vote. For example, a recent proposed Directive restricting working hours is to be challenged by the UK Government on the ground that it is not strictly a health and safety measure. Other proposals are generally accepted. Currently, draft Directives are being discussed concerning a number of matters raised by the Charter, including protection for young persons, pregnant women, and so on. Less controversial are the health and safety Directives, which are discussed in chapter 10. However, it is clear that the EC is now the major driving force behind health and safety legislation generally, as well as the impetus behind environmental protection and protection from major hazards.

The judicial system in England and Wales

Criminal courts

Magistrates' courts

1.49 These courts are presided over by Justices of the Peace, who are generally non-lawyers, appointed by the Lord Chancellor on the recommendation of a local advisory committee. The aim is to select magistrates from a wide cross-section of the local community, so that the bench is a balanced one. Magistrates are advised on points of law by a (usually) legally qualified clerk, but it is the responsibility of the bench to determine the facts and to make a decision. In certain large cities, full-time stipendiary magistrates may be found. These are qualified lawyers and are paid a stipend. A stipendiary magistrate will usually sit alone, whereas lay magistrates will normally sit in benches of three.

1.50 A magistrates' court has some civil jurisdiction (mainly concerned with matrimonial disputes) but the bulk of the work is criminal, and indeed, over 94 percent of all criminal cases start and finish in the magistrates' courts. True, the overwhelming majority of these are motoring offences, but a fair amount of petty crime is also dealt with. The powers of punishment are normally limited to imposing a maximum fine of £5,000 (£20,000 in certain circumstances), or to send someone to prison for up to six months, although the relevant statute will usually contain the maximum penalties. Sometimes, in respect of continuing offences, a fine may be imposed for each day in which the offence is continued.

1.51 Procedurally there are three types of offences. First, there is a summary offence, which can only be dealt with before a court of summary jurisdiction, ie the magistrates' court. Second, there is an indictable offence which results in a formal document, known as an indictment, being drawn up. An accused will be brought before the magistrates for them to determine whether or not there is sufficient evidence (or a *prima facie* case) to commit the accused to the Crown Court for trial (hence these are known as committal proceedings) where the case will be heard before a judge and jury. Third, there are those cases which are triable either way (ie summarily or on indictment) depending on the option exercised by the accused and the gravity of the case, which may cause the magistrates to decide to send the matter for trial or to hear it themselves.

1.52 So far as health and safety legislation is concerned, some offences under HSWA, Factories Act, Offices, Shops and Railway Premises Act, etc are summary, others are triable either before the magistrates or at the Crown Court, depending on the seriousness of the offence.

1.53 The overlap between certain statutory provisions may cause some problems. For example, an obligation under the Factories Act may be an absolute one (see below para 1.86), eg to securely fence a dangerous part of any machinery, whereas under HSWA, an offence may be committed only if the accused failed to take steps which were reasonably practicable. In the former case, a failure to do the thing required is an offence, and the fact that it was difficult, or even impossible, to carry out the obligation is no defence, whereas in the latter case, the accused may be able to show that it was not reasonably practicable to do more than he in fact did.

1.54 If a person wishes to appeal from the decision of the magistrates' court on a point of law, this is done by way of a "case stated" to the Queen's Bench Divisional Court. Either the prosecution or the defence may so appeal. Appeals against conviction and/or sentence may be made by the accused to the Crown Court, and will take the form of a re-hearing before a judge (without a jury).

Crown Court

1.55 This court will hear indictable offences and those cases (usually of a more serious nature) which the prosecution or defence have elected to have tried before the Crown Court. Such cases are heard before a judge and jury. It is the function of the judge to ensure that the trial is conducted fairly, and to sum up for the jury on points of law. The jury returns a verdict depending on the facts. Under HSWA, offences are punishable by an unlimited fine, and eight particular offences (see para 3.155) may be punished by a term of imprisonment of up to two years. In recent years there have been several instances of persons being convicted and given suspended prison sentences (for failure to comply with prohibition notices) and the highest fines recorded are £500,000 and £250,000 following a serious accident at an oil refinery. An appeal against conviction and/or sentence will lie to the Court of Appeal.

Divisional Court

1.56 The Queen's Bench Divisional Court is presided over by (usually) the Lord

Chief Justice, who will normally sit with two other judges. This court will hear appeals by way of "case stated" from the decisions of the magistrates' courts. The Divisional Court also hears appeals from decisions of industrial tribunals relating to prohibition and improvement notices (see para 3.103). The reason appeals against enforcement notices go to this court (instead, as one might expect, to the Employment Appeal Tribunal) is because a failure to comply with one of these enforcement notices is a criminal offence and the Divisional Court is basically a criminal appeal court, hearing appeals from inferior courts and tribunals.

Civil courts

County Court

1.57 This is a civil court, which formerly had limited jurisdiction. However, as a result of recent changes, the County Court now has concurrent jurisdiction with the High Court in all matters other than specified exceptions. In particular, personal injury claims which are likely to involve less than £50,000 must be started in the County Court. Cases will be heard by a County Court Judge or a Circuit Judge. "Small claims" of less than £1,000 may be heard by a District Judge in a special informal procedure.

High Court of Judicature

1.58 For all practical purposes, this is the major civil court, and is presided over by a High Court Judge, sitting in the Queen's Bench Division (there are other specialised courts at this level which deal with commercial matters, admiralty claims, divorce, probate, etc). Juries have long been abolished in all but the most exceptional civil cases and thus the judge will be the sole arbiter of law and fact. This court is based in the Strand in London, but will also hear cases in various parts of the country. So far as this book is concerned, civil claims for industrial accidents, etc are usually heard in this court.

Other courts, etc

Court of Appeal

1.59 This court acts as the appeal court from the decisions of the Queen's Bench in civil matters, the Queen's Bench Divisional Court in criminal matters, from the Crown Court and County Court and the Employment Appeal Tribunal. It is presided over by the Master of the Rolls who sits with two other Lord Justices of Appeal. Appeals may only be made on a point of law, and thus cases will consist entirely of legal argument.

House of Lords

1.60 In its legal capacity, the House of Lords is the highest court in the land. It consists of "Law Lords", ie judges who have been "promoted" from the lower courts. The Lord Chancellor (a political appointee) is entitled to sit, as is any ex-Lord Chancellor. Normally, the House will sit with five members present, but as in theory the House of Lords is part of the legislature, the judgments consist of "speeches". By convention, only the Law Lords and Lord Chancellors (past and present) will attend when the House is sitting in its legal capacity. Once a decision of the House of Lords is given on a point of law, it will bind all lower courts until the House gives a different ruling, or until the decision is changed by an Act of Parliament. But precedence must always be given to European law, as interpreted by the European Court or the House of Lords itself.

Industrial tribunals

1.61 These were created in 1964, and now have a wide jurisdiction relating to problems arising out of modern employment legislation. For the purpose of this book, industrial tribunals have three important functions, namely (a) to hear appeals from the decision of an inspector to impose a prohibition or improvement notice; (b) to hear claims for unfair dismissal; and (c) to hear other claims arising out of the Employment Protection (Consolidation) Act 1978, ie refusal to give time off work to safety representatives, a failure to pay for such time off work, protection in health and safety cases, and a refusal to pay medical suspension pay. An industrial tribunal consists of a legally qualified chairman, with two "wingmen" chosen from each side of industry. Decisions of industrial tribunals, though not regarded as precedents, are valued for their reasoning and guidance. Any person may represent a party before an industrial tribunal, costs are not normally awarded to the winner (but see para 3.148), and proceedings are generally more informal than in other courts. An appeal from a decision of an industrial tribunal on a point of law relating to cases concerning improvement and prohibition notices will go to the Queen's Bench Divisional Court, but appeals on all other matters will go to the Employment Appeal Tribunal.

Employment Appeal Tribunal

1.62 This is a specialised court whose main function is to hear appeals on points of law from the decisions of industrial tribunals. It will consist of a High Court judge and two wingmen chosen from each side of industry. Again, procedure is relatively more informal than in other courts, legal representation is not insisted upon, costs are not normally awarded to the winner, and the procedure is designed to hear cases with a maximum amount of simplicity and a minimum amount of delay. A further appeal may be made to the Court of Appeal.

The judicial system in Scotland

1.63 For historical reasons, Scotland has its own distinctive legal system, with its own procedure and, to some extent, legal rules. Acts of Parliament which apply to Scotland must be specifically stated to be so, and frequently Parliament will enact legislation which is parallel to English law.

District Court

1.64 Minor criminal offences are heard summarily by the District Court, which is presided over by justices of the peace or a stipendiary magistrate.

Sheriff Court

1.65 More serious criminal offences are heard by the sheriff or sheriff principal, who can impose a fine of up to £5,000 (£20,000 in certain circumstances) and/or impose a prison sentence of up to two years. Minor civil cases can also be heard.

High Court of Justiciary

1.66 This court only hears trials on indictment and has unlimited powers of punishment.

Court of Criminal Appeal

1.67 Appeals from the District Court, Sheriff's Court and the High Court of Justiciary are heard by the Court of Criminal Appeal which consists of three judges. A further appeal will lie to the House of Lords.

Court of Session

1.68 This is the major civil court in Scotland. The Outer House has originating jurisdiction and the Inner House acts as a court of appeal. A further appeal lies to the House of Lords.

1.69 So far as the subject of health and safety at work is concerned, there are no differences in the legal rules applied in England and Wales and Scotland. Insofar as cases from Scotland are cited in this book, certain terminology has been transposed into the English equivalent for the sake of consistency and simplicity.

The divisions of substantive law

1.70 All the laws of Great Britain may be found in the thousands of volumes of statutes and judicial decisions which line the shelves of law libraries. For convenience, we tend to subdivide subjects under different headings, each with their own special rules and application. Thus, if a person dies, interested parties will want to know something about the law of wills, or probate, or succession, as the case may be. If someone buys a house, he will get involved with land law, or conveyancing, and so on. In the field of occupational health, safety and welfare, we are mainly concerned with employment law, which is an amalgam of the law relating to contract, tort and crime. Each of these requires a brief examination.

Contract law

1.71 Most people enter into contracts almost every day of their lives. When they buy a newspaper, go on a train journey, eat a meal in a restaurant, etc they are entering into a contract. The law on this subject is made up largely of judicial decisions, supplemented by certain statutory provisions and can be found in any recognised textbook on the subject. Occupational health and safety is fundamentally based on the existence of a contract of employment, and certain aspects of this will be dealt with in chapter 9. There is some force in the view that the duties which employers owe to employees to ensure their safety and health at work are based on contract as well as tort (*Matthews v Kuwait Bechtel Corporation*, chapter 8).

Law of tort

1.72 A tort is a civil wrong, ie a wrongful act by one person which gives a right to the injured party to sue for a legal remedy, which is usually, but not exclusively, an action for damages. Torts are subclassified under a number of well-known headings; thus defamation, trespass, nuisance, negligence, etc are all torts each with their own special rules and legal requirements. We will be concerned to a large extent with the tort of negligence, which is the breach of a legal duty to take care not to cause damage or injury to another. Thus an employer owes a duty to take care in order to ensure the health and safety of the employees (see chapter 8), as well as to others who may be adversely affected by the work activities.

Crime

1.73 A crime is an act which is punishable by the State in the criminal courts. Parliament has taken the view that employers and others who fail to comply with certain minimum standards shall be punished, in order to deter others from breaking the law. It cannot be pretended that the actual amount of the fines imposed acts as a great deterrent, for these seldom reflect the hazard created, nor the ability of the employer to pay. Nonetheless, the adverse publicity and the tarnishing of reputation is regarded as being undesirable. Modern management will take the view that health and safety is an objective to be pursued for its own sake, not through fear of punishment.

1.74 It is clear that the object of the law must be prevention, not retribution, rectification of potential hazards, not punishment for indifference. The criminal law should always be a weapon of last resort, rather than an instant reaction when offences are discovered. Certainly, this is the philosophy behind the HSE inspectorate, for the number of prosecutions undertaken will represent only a small fraction of the number of breaches which may be discovered.

Criminal offences

1.75 As has been noted, a breach of health and safety legislation is generally a criminal offence. However, this does not imply that the only criminal offences are those which are in breach of the relevant statutory provisions, for the general criminal law is also capable of being invoked. In particular, in recent years the crime of manslaughter has been raised in cases where death has occurred due to recklessness or dangerous conduct which is itself an unlawful act. The first successful prosecution for manslaughter was brought in 1990, when a company director pleaded guilty following the death of an employee at his factory.

1.76 More difficult, and perhaps more controversial, have been recent instances of bringing charges of corporate manslaughter against companies. The problem is that in general, the crime of manslaughter requires the accused to have *mens rea*, ie a "guilty mind", which is an essential ingredient in the crime. Can a company have "a mind" of its own (irrespective of the minds of its employees and/or directors) so as to possess the necessary *mens rea*? An attempt to re-establish the offence of corporate manslaughter failed with the collapse of the prosecutions in 1991 arising out of the Zeebrugge disaster, and the difficulties inherent in such prosecutions may well inhibit further cases along these lines.

1.77 For the purpose of this book, the overwhelming number of criminal offences which may be committed are those specified in the various statutory provisions. It is quite possible for a single occurrence to give rise to more than one offence. For example, the HSE may decide to prosecute for a breach of HSWA at the same time as for a breach of the Factories Act or other regulation.

Defence of due diligence

1.78 A statutory provision may provide that it is a defence for an accused to show that he or she used due diligence to secure compliance with the law (eg OSRPA s.67). This is a question of fact, and the standard of proof is that of the balance of probabilities (*R v Carr-Briant*). If the accused is an incorporated association (eg a limited company) the prosecution would need to show that the failure to comply was due to the act or omission of a person who can be identified with the controlling mind and will of the company. The default by a subordinate will not necessarily be that of the company. In *Tesco Supermarkets v Natrass* a supermarket advertised a washing powder at a discount rate. A customer sought to purchase the item, but was told the special rate stock had been exhausted. The supermarket was prosecuted under the Trade Description Act. In its defence it was argued that the store manager had been responsible for the breach because his system of daily checks had broken down, and further argued that the company had done all it could to ensure that the offence would not be committed. It was held that the company was entitled to plead the defence of due diligence. The store manager did not act *as* the company, but *for* the company. The *mens rea* of the company could only be derived from the actions of those officers who represented the company's controlling mind. It is this "controlling mind" theory which make prosecutions for those offences which require *mens rea* (eg manslaughter) difficult to sustain.

The overlap of the law

1.79 Since there are no clear boundaries between legal concepts, an act may frequently have two or more legal implications. Thus an accident at work may result in a prosecution for a criminal offence; the same incident may result in a civil claim being brought for compensation. Indeed, in civil proceedings, the fact that there has been a criminal conviction in respect of the relevant incident is admissible in evidence (Civil Evidence Act 1968, s.11) for the purpose of proving that the defendant committed the offence, although it is not conclusive, and rebutting evidence may be given. The majority of legal decisions on health and safety which explain and interpret the various statutory provisions arise out of civil proceedings, a fact which indicates how the law on occupational health and safety tends to work in practice.

Statutory interpretation

1.80 It is the task of the courts to interpret the words used by Parliament, not to legislate, although there can be little doubt in practice that by doing the former they achieve the latter. In recent years, the courts have taken a broader view in respect of reforming legislation and sought to interpret the words by seeking the intentions of Parliament. Indeed, the House of Lords have recently held that when construing a statute, reference may be made to Parliamentary material (eg Hansard) where the legislation is ambiguous or obscure, or leads to an absurdity (see *Pepper v Hart*). An exploration of this aspect of judicial innovation is beyond the scope of this book.

1.81 All modern Acts of Parliament contain a section which deals with interpretation, and they will also define special terms where necessary. Thus, the meaning of the word "factory" is contained in an extremely lengthy section in the Factories Act 1961 (see s.175). The Health and Safety at Work Act contains four sections (ss.52–53, 76, 82) which are concerned with the meaning of words and phrases used in the Act, and this practice is to be found in other relevant statutes and regulations. It is to these that reference should be made in the first instance. Words used in health and safety regulations are generally construed in accordance with the parent Act.

1.82 The Interpretation Act 1978 can be looked to for assistance in some circumstances. By that Act, unless the contrary is intended, a reference to a male includes a reference to a female, and vice versa, and a reference to the singular includes the plural. A "person" includes a body of persons (whether corporate or unincorporate), "month" means calendar month, and so on.

1.83 There are a number of rules for statutory interpretation which are well known and used in legal circles, sometimes with Latin tags. There is the "literal rule", whereby the courts will look at the ordinary and grammatical sense of the words used. If this leads to absurdity or inconsistency, the "golden rule" may be applied, whereby a construction is given which leads to a sensible interpretation, taking into account the whole statute. The tag *ejusdem generis* (of the same species) may be used on occasions. For example, if a statute referred to "any car, van, bus or other vehicle'' it is doubtful if the latter phrase would include a bicycle, as the species is clearly motorised transport.

1.84 Sometimes, the courts may look to the interpretation already given to a particular word or phrase when used in another enactment, particularly when the two statutes are dealing with the same or similar subject matter. Thus words used in the Offices, Shops and Railway Premises Act may be construed on the same lines as identical words used (and judicially explained) in the Factories Act. This is known as construing in *pari materia* (in similar circumstances).

1.85 The following are some of the words and phrases which are to be commonly found in the law on health and safety generally.

"Shall"; "shall not"

1.86 These words impose an absolute obligation to do (or not to do) the act or thing in question, and it is not permissible to argue that it is impracticable, difficult or even impossible to do it (or not to do it). Thus, when the Factories Act, s.14 states that "Every dangerous part of any machinery shall be securely fenced", it imposes an absolute obligation to securely fence, and a failure to do so may result in criminal proceedings or, if someone is injured because of a failure to securely fence, a civil action for compensation. If it is impossible to use the machine when it is securely fenced, then the Act implicitly prohibits its use (*Summers & Sons v Frost*) or the occupier of the factory uses it at his peril.

"So far as is practicable"; "best practicable means"

1.87 This is a high standard, but not an absolute one because if it is impossible to do something, then clearly it is not practicable to do it (*Jayne v National Coal Board*). If something is practicable, it must be done; if the best practical means are required, then it is up to the person on whom the obligation is placed to find the best practicable means, and to constantly bring his knowledge up to date. However, it is not practicable to take precautions against a danger which is not known to exist, although once the danger is known, it becomes practicable to do something about it (*Cartwright v GKN Sankey Ltd*). The test is one of foresight, not hindsight (*Edwards v National Coal Board*). The standard of practicability is that of current knowledge and invention (*Adsett v K and L Steelfounders and Engineers Ltd*). Once something is found to be practicable, it is feasible, and it must be done, no matter how inconvenient or expensive it may be to do it. The burden of proof to show that it was not practicable to do something, or to do more than was in fact done, is on the person upon whom the obligation is placed (in civil proceedings) and upon the defendant or accused in criminal proceedings (HSWA, s.40). The Environmental Protection Act 1990 introduced a slight variant of this test, by laying down a standard of "best available technique not entailing excessive cost" (BATNEEC).

"Reasonably practicable"

1.88 This phrase causes more concern to practitioners than any other, although there is no magic or mystery about it. It should be looked at in the following way.

1.89 First, we start off with the presumption that if something is practicable, the courts will not lightly hold that it is not reasonably practicable (*Marshall v Gotham & Co.*).

1.90 Second, it is a somewhat lesser standard than "practicable". It is permissible to take into account on the one hand the danger or hazard or injury which may occur, and balance it, on the other hand, with the cost, inconvenience, time and trouble which would have to be taken to counter it. As Asquith LJ stated in *Edwards v National Coal Board*, "'Reasonably practicable' is a narrower term than 'physically possible' and seems to me to imply that a computation must be made by the owner in which the quantum or risk is placed in one scale and the sacrifice involved in the measures necessary for averting the risk (whether in money, time or trouble) is placed in the other, and that, if it be shown that there is a gross disproportion between them—the risk being insignificant in relation to the sacrifice—the defendants discharge the onus on them. Moreover, this computation falls to be made by the owner at a point in time anterior to the accident." By way of example, we may cite *Marshall v Gotham & Co.* where, although the roof of a mine had been tested in the usual way, it collapsed because of the existence of a rare geological fault. It was held that the employers were not liable for the injuries to the plaintiff which ensued. The court held that, "The danger was a very rare one. The trouble and expense involved in the use of precautions, while not prohibitive, would have been considerable. The precautions would not have afforded anything like complete protection against the danger . . .". In the circumstances, the employers had done all that was reasonable.

1.91 Third, in criminal proceedings, it shall be for the accused to prove that it was not reasonably practicable to do more than was in fact done to satisfy the duty or requirement (HSWA, s.40). However, this can be established by the defendant by the ordinary burden of proof, ie on the balance of probabilities.

1.92 Fourth, in the last analysis, it will be for the court to decide, as a question of fact, based on the evidence which can be adduced, whether or not something was reasonably practicable. In the last resort, therefore, the issue can only be determined after the event when it has been tested in court.

1.93 For example, in *Martin v Boulton & Paul Ltd*, an employee of the defendants was injured while erecting a steel beam, and the defendants were prosecuted for failing to provide, so far as was reasonably practicable, a safe system of work. The magistrate found that the method adopted by the defendants was a universal practice adopted in the steel erection industry and dismissed the charge. On appeal by way of "case stated", the Divisional Court held that the existence of a universal practice did not, by itself, lead to the conclusion that there was no other reasonably practicable way of doing something. There may be evidence to suggest that despite the universal practice, there were other ways of doing the work which were safer and therefore reasonably practicable. Thus evidence of a universal practice does not discharge the burden of proof which lies on the defendant, though it is a factual matter which can be taken into account, along with all the other evidence.

1.94 Indeed, it would not be impossible for different courts and tribunals to come to contrary conclusions on identical facts if perceptions differ. The passage of time, greater knowledge and experience, accident statistics, as well as the "inarticulate major premise" of those hearing cases, may account for a different end result. For example, an industrial tribunal in *International Stores Ltd v Johns* quashed a prohibition notice imposed on an unguarded meat-slicing band saw, whereas in *Gateway Foodmarkets Ltd v Eastwood*, a similar notice on an identical machine was upheld.

"Relevant statutory provisions"

1.95 This means the provisions of Part 1 of HSWA (including health and safety regulations made under the Act), plus the following provisions, which are contained in Schedule 1 of HSWA.

	Provisions which are relevant statutory provisions
The Explosives Act 1875	The whole Act except sections 30 to 32, 80 and 116 to 121
The Boiler Explosions Act 1882	The whole Act
The Boiler Explosions Act 1890	The whole Act
The Alkali, etc Works Regulation Act 1906	The whole Act
The Revenue Act 1909	Section 11
The Anthrax Prevention Act 1919	The whole Act
The Employment of Women, Young Persons and Children Act 1920	The whole Act
The Celluloid and Cinematograph Film Act 1922	The whole Act
The Explosives Act 1923	The whole Act
The Public Health (Smoke Abatement) Act 1926	The whole Act
The Petroleum (Consolidation) Act 1928	The whole Act
The Hours of Employment (Conventions) Act 1936	The whole Act
The Petroleum (Transfer of Licences) Act 1936	The whole Act
The Hydrogen Cyanide (Fumigation) Act 1937	The whole Act
The Ministry of Fuel and Power Act 1945	Section 1(1) so far as it relates to maintaining and improving safety, health and well-being of persons employed in and about mines and quarries in Great Britain
The Coal Industry Nationalisation Act 1946	Section 42(1) and (2)
The Radioactive Substances Act 1948	Section 5(1)(a)
The Alkali, etc Works Regulation (Scotland) Act 1951	The whole Act
The Fireworks Act 1951	Sections 4 and 7
The Agriculture (Poisonous Substances) Act 1952	The whole Act

	Provisions which are relevant statutory provisions
The Emergency Laws (Miscellaneous Provisions) Act 1953	Section 3
The Mines and Quarries Act 1954	The whole Act except section 151
The Agricultural (Safety, Health and Welfare Provisions) Act 1956	The whole Act
The Factories Act 1961	The whole Act except section 135
The Public Health Act 1961	Section 73
The Pipe-lines Act 1962	Sections 20 to 26, 33, 34 and 42, Schedule 5
The Offices, Shops and Railway Premises Act 1963	The whole Act
The Nuclear Installations Act 1965	Sections 1, 3 to 6, 22 and 24, Schedule 2
The Mines and Quarries (Tips) Act 1969	Sections 1 to 10
The Mines Management Act 1971	The whole Act
The Employment Medical Advisory Service Act 1972	The whole Act except sections 1 and 6 and Schedule 1
Offshore Safety Act 1992	The whole Act

1.96 Since the passing of HSWA, many of the above provisions have been repealed in whole or in part or superseded in some way.

"Prescribed"

1.97 If something is to be prescribed, it has to be specifically referred to at some future time. Thus, if a statute states that something shall be done "in prescribed cases" then the power exists for someone (eg the Secretary of State) to prescribe the cases where that thing shall be done, and until the power is exercised, nothing has happened. For example, s.2(7) of HSWA states that in prescribed cases an employer shall establish a safety committee, and the Safety Representatives and Safety Committee Regulations 1977 specify that this shall be done when at least two safety representatives request the employer, in writing, to establish such a committee. If something has to be prescribed under the Act, it will be done by regulations (s.53(1)).

"At work"

1.98 An employee is at work throughout the time when he is in the course of his employment, but not otherwise (s.52(1)(b)). The phrase "course of his employment" is not capable of precise definition and legal authorities based on civil cases have, as a matter of policy, given it a somewhat liberal construction. These authorities do not necessarily bind in criminal law. In *Coult v Szuba*, the defendant was employed to work at the Scunthorpe site of the British Steel Corporation. The site had 39 miles of roads. The defendant, who was due to start work at 6 am clocked in at 5.41 am and then drove along a road to the place where he was due to work. On the way, he was involved in an accident with another car due to the defendant's fault. He was prosecuted for an offence under s.7(a) of HSWA for failing to take reasonable care of the safety of himself and others while at work. The magistrates dismissed the charge, and their decision was upheld by the Divisional Court on appeal. On the facts of the case, it was not possible to say that the defendant was in the course of his employment at the time of the accident (this case may be contrasted with *Bolton Metropolitan Borough Council v Malrod Insulations Ltd*, para 3.20).

1.99 It will be noted that trainees and others on work experience are "at work" for the purpose of s.52(1)(b) even though they are not employees in the legal sense (see para 3.12).

"Competent person"

1.100 A number of legislative provisions require that certain types of work (inspections, testing, assessments, etc) shall only be done by a "competent person" but the phrase is rarely defined and little guidance is given as to the abilities or expertise which are required. Some help may be obtained from an Approved Code of Practice (eg see ACOP on Ionising Radiation Regulations, Control of Asbestos at Work Regulations, etc) but the provisions are usually in very general terms. The Management of Health and Safety at Work Regulations (see para 4.5) provide that a person shall be regarded as competent "... where he has sufficient training and experience or knowledge and other qualities to enable him properly ..." to do the task in question. However, the ACOP for Pressure Systems and Transportable Gas Container Regulations 1989 does contain a very detailed definition of a competent person. In practice, whether or not a person is competent will be determined by the courts retrospectively in any particular case (see *Brazier v Skipton Rock*).

1.101 It is clear that the obligation is on the employer to select a competent person and to ensure that either he is trained in the relevant tasks to be performed or that he receives the necessary training. Full information must be given of the tasks to be performed, and all necessary facilities. A competent person is one who has the necessary theoretical and practical knowledge and has the technical and practical experience to carry out the task, such experience being matched to the complexity of the work and the degree of the risk. The statutory provision itself may indicate what is required. Thus, if a statute requires an "inspection", this is something less than an "examination"; it may be that the latter should be carried out by someone with appropriate technical qualifications, whereas the former need not be (see *Gibson v Skibs*).

Burden of proof

1.102 In criminal cases, the general rule is that it is for the prosecution to prove its case—in the hallowed phrase—beyond reasonable doubt. However, in some circumstances, the burden of proof is on the defendant. For example, s.17 of HSWA requires the accused to show that he observed the specific statutory provision otherwise than by observing the Approved Code of Practice; s.40 of HSWA requires the accused to show that it was not practicable or not reasonably practicable to do more than in fact was done, etc. However, this burden can be discharged by proof on the balance of probabilities (*R v Carr-Briant*).

1.103 In civil cases, the rule is that the burden is upon the plaintiff to prove his case on the balance of probabilities. In this, he may be assisted by some principles of evidence.

(a) Res ipsa loquitor

1.104 If something is under the control of the defendant, and an accident occurs in circumstances such that it would not have happened unless there had been a want of care by the defendant, then a presumption is raised that the defendant has been negligent. The burden is then put on the defendant to explain the accident, and to show that there was no want of care on his part. In other words "the facts speak for themselves". However, the defendant may be able to show a convincing reason why he was not negligent (eg the accident was caused by the fault of a third party) in which case the burden of proof is thrown back to the plaintiff to prove his case in the usual manner.

(b) Shifting presumptions

1.105 Sometimes, the mere statement of facts will give rise to an inferential presumption which may cause the burden of proof to shift from one party to the other, requiring it to be rebutted by evidence. For example, in *Gardiner v Motherwell Machinery and Scrap Co. Ltd*, the plaintiff sued in respect of dermatitis which he alleged was contracted at work. Lord Reid said, "When a man who has not previously suffered from a disease contracts that disease after being subjected to conditions likely to cause it, and when he shows that it starts in a way typical of the disease caused by such conditions, he establishes a *prima facie* presumption that his disease was caused by those conditions." Thus if a person contracts bronchitis after working in dusty conditions, or suffers deafness after being exposed to excessively noisy conditions, an evidential presumption arises that those conditions caused the disease or injury in question.

The scope of the law

1.106 For historic reasons, the UK is made up of four countries, namely, England, Wales, Scotland and Northern Ireland. Although there is a general common law operating throughout the UK, there are some procedural differences. A reference to Great Britain excludes Northern Ireland.

1.107 England and Wales may be regarded as one country for legal purposes and no difference exists in the law or procedure (certain problems may arise over the use of the Welsh language, but this is irrelevant for our purposes). Scotland, on the other hand, retains its own legal system, which has certain distinctive terminology, procedure and sometimes different legal rules. As a general principle, the law on health and safety in Scotland is the same as in England and Wales and will be so treated throughout this book. Acts of Parliament will usually state whether or not they apply to Scotland, and if they do not, it is frequently necessary to enact further legislation in order to bring the countries into harmony. Some Acts apply to England, Wales and Scotland, and merely note the different terminology by reference to the appropriate Scottish words. Northern Ireland, however, has its own legal system, though at the present time it is governed direct from the UK Parliament and will usually follow the pattern already laid down for Great Britain. The Health and Safety at Work (Northern Ireland) Order 1978 created the Health and Safety Agency, with functions and responsibilities similar to those of the Health and Safety Commission. The Isle of Man and the Channel Islands are not part of the UK (Royal & Parliamentary Titles Act 1927).

1.108 By the Health and Safety at Work Act (Application outside Great Britain) Order 1989, the provisions of the Health and Safety at Work Act are extended to cover offshore oil and gas installations, pipeline work, offshore construction work, certain loading and unloading operations, and shipbuilding, repair work and diving operations which take place outside British territorial waters. This is additional to the provisions of the Mineral Workings (Offshore Installations) Act 1971, the Petroleum and Submarine Pipe-lines Act 1975 and regulations made thereunder. The Offshore Installations (Safety Representatives and Safety Committees) Regulations 1989 and the Offshore Installations and Pipeline Works (First Aid) Regulations 1989 also apply.

1.109 It may be noted at this stage that the Offshore Safety Act 1992 transferred responsibility for health and safety on offshore installations from the Department of Energy to the Health and Safety Executive, following recommendations made in the Cullen Report, which enquired into the Piper Alpha disaster.

2

The institutions of health and safety

The role of Government

2.1 The prime responsibility for overseeing health and safety legislation is a political function of the relevant Government department. The major role is played by the Department of Employment, the head of which is a Secretary of State (with a seat in the Cabinet) assisted by various junior ministers, one of whom will have been designated as having a special responsibility for occupational health and safety matters. Other problems of health and safety, which are partly concerned with the occupation and partly of general concern to the whole community are dealt with by other departments. Powers relating to the control of industrial pollution are now exercisable by the Secretary of State for the Environment and the former responsibility of the Department of Energy for occupational health and safety on offshore installations has now been assigned to HSE. Similarly, the Railway Inspectorate has been transferred from the Department of Transport to HSE.

2.2 The Secretary of State for Employment appoints the Chairman of the Health and Safety Commission and not less than six nor more than nine other members. As to three of these appointees, he must first consult with such organisations representing employers as he considers appropriate, as to a further three, he must consult with trade union organisations, and as to the remainder, he must consult with organisations representing local authorities and other bodies concerned with matters of health, safety and welfare. He must also approve the appointment by the Health and Safety Commission of the Director General of the Health and Safety Executive and of the two other members. He exercises a general control over the Commission by approving (with or without modifications) proposals submitted to him, and may give directions to the Commission with respect to its functions. He will make regulations and give his consent to the issue of Codes of Practice by the Commission.

Health and Safety Commission (HSC)

2.3 This body was created by the Health and Safety at Work etc Act 1974 (HSWA), s.10, and has the prime responsibility for administering the law and practice on occupational health and safety. As already noted, it consists of a chairman and up to nine members. Details of the terms of appointment and constitution of HSC can be found in Schedule 2 to HSWA.

General duties of HSC (HSWA, s.1(1))

2.4 The general duty of HSC is to do such things and make such arrangements as it considers appropriate for the general purposes laid down in s.1(1) of HSWA, which are:

(a) securing the health, safety and welfare of persons at work
(b) protecting persons other than persons at work against risks to health or safety arising out of or in connection with the activities of persons at work
(c) controlling the keeping and use of explosives or highly flammable or otherwise dangerous substances, and generally preventing the unlawful acquisition, possession and use of any such substance
(d) protecting the public from personal injury, fire, explosions and other dangers arising from the transmission and distribution of gas through pipes, or arising from the use of gas supplied through pipes (HSWA, s.1(1); Gas Act 1986, s. 18)
(e) applying HSWA to offshore activities and installations and to onshore pipeline activities, including construction and safe operation of pipelines (HSWA, s.1(1), as amended by the Gas Act 1986 (sch.8. pt.I), and Offshore Safety Act 1992, ss.1–3).

2.5 It should be noted that HSC will lose responsibility for controlling the emission into the atmosphere of noxious or offensive substances, as s.1(1)(d) of the Act will be repealed (Environmental Protection Act 1990, Schedule 16). Industrial pollution control is now the responsibility of HM Inspectorate of Pollution (HMIP) (which is under the Department of the Environment) or local authorities, depending on the type and size of process involved.

Particular duties of HSC (s.11(2))

2.6 Additionally, HSC has the following duties:

(a) assist and encourage persons concerned with matters relevant to any of the above general purposes to further them
(b) make such arrangements as it considers appropriate for the carrying out of research, the publication of results, the provision of training and information connected therewith, and to encourage research and the provision of training and information by others
(c) make arrangements for ensuring that Government departments, employers, employees, employers' organisations, trade unions and others concerned are provided with an information and advisory service and are kept informed and adequately advised

(d) submit proposals for the making of regulations by the appropriate authority (ie via the Minister responsible).

2.7 HSC shall also submit to the Secretary of State from time to time particulars of what it proposes to do for the purpose of performing its functions. It must ensure that its activities are in accordance with proposals approved by the Secretary of State, and give effect to any directions given by him.

Powers of HSC (s.13)

2.8 HSC may do anything (except borrow money) which is calculated to facilitate, or is conducive or incidental to, the performance of its functions, and in particular may:

(a) enter into agreements with any Government department or other person for that department or person to perform any function on behalf of HSC or the HSE. For example, HSC has made an "agency agreement" with the National Radiological Protection Board for the latter to perform certain functions relating to ionising and other radiations
(b) make agreements whereby HSC performs functions on behalf of any other Minister, Government department or other public authority, being functions which, in the opinion of the Secretary of State, can appropriately be performed by HSC (but not the power to make regulations or other legislative instruments)
(c) provide services or facilities which may be required by any Government department or public authority
(d) appoint persons or committees to provide HSC with advice (see para 2.17)
(e) pay travelling and/or subsistence allowances and compensation for loss of remunerative time in connection with any of the functions of HSC
(f) pay for any research connected with the functions of HSC and to disseminate (or pay for the dissemination of) information derived from such research
(g) make arrangements for the making of payments to HSC by other parties who are using facilities and services provided by HSC.

Investigations and enquiries (s.14)

2.9 If there is an accident, occurrence, situation or other matter which HSC thinks necessary or expedient to investigate in order to fulfil any of the general purposes of the Act (above) or with a view to the making of regulations for those purposes, it may direct HSE or any other person to carry out that investigation and make a report (s.14(2)(a)).

2.10 As an alternative, and with the consent of the Secretary of State, HSC may direct that an enquiry shall be held into the matter (s.14(2)(b)). The result of the investigation or enquiry may be made public, in whole or in part, as HSC thinks fit.

2.11 The distinction between an investigation and an enquiry is that an enquiry is a formal, public affair into a matter in which there is general public interest as to its outcome, whereas an investigation is more informal and may be carried out in a manner determined by the investigator, though he must still observe the rules of natural justice, and receive evidence from any person who may be able to contribute worthwhile information.

2.12 The Health and Safety Inquiries (Procedure) Regulations 1975 as amended, lay down the procedure for the conduct of enquiries under s.14(2)(b). The date, time and place shall be fixed (and may be varied) by HSC, who shall also give 28 days' notice to every person entitled to appear whose name and address is known. It must also publish a notice of the intention to hold the enquiry in one or more newspapers (where appropriate, circulating in the district in which the subject matter of the enquiry arose) giving the name of the person who has been appointed to hold the enquiry and of any assessors appointed to assist.

2.13 The following persons shall be entitled to appear at the enquiry as of right:

(a) the Commission
(b) any enforcing authority concerned
(c) in Scotland, the Procurator Fiscal
(d) any employers' association or any trade union representing employers or employees concerned
(e) any person who was injured or who has suffered damage as a result of the incident, or his personal representatives
(f) the owner or occupier of any premises in which the incident occurred
(g) any person carrying on the activity which gave rise to the incident.

Other persons may appear at the enquiry, but only at the discretion of the person appointed to hold it. Anyone wishing to appear at an enquiry may do so in person, or may be represented by a lawyer or by any other person.

2.14 The person appointed to conduct the enquiry may, either on his own volition or on the application of any person entitled or permitted to appear, require the attendance of any other person in order to give evidence or to produce any document, and it is an offence, punishable by a fine of up to £5,000 to fail to comply with such requirement.

2.15 The conduct of the enquiry will be the responsibility of the appointed person, and it will be held in public unless a Minister of the Crown directs that part or all of the enquiry shall be held in private because it would be against the interests of national security to allow certain evidence to be given in public. Also, a private session may be held if information is likely to be disclosed which relates to a trade secret, on an application made by a party affected. Otherwise, the procedure to be followed will be at the discretion of the appointed person, which he will state at the commencement of the proceedings, subject to any submissions made by any person appearing (or their representatives). He will also inform them as to any proposals he may have regarding an inspection of any site, will determine the order of the witnesses, permit opening statements, examination and cross-examination, hear evidence on oath, permit documents to be introduced as evidence and allow them to be inspected and copied. He may receive any written submissions, and if necessary, adjourn the proceedings from time to time.

2.16 After the enquiry has been concluded, a report, containing the findings of fact and any recommendations, will be made to HSC.

Advisory committees

2.17 A number of advisory committees have been created in order to provide HSC with specialised advice and information. These will usually consist of representatives from each side of industry, academic and industrial experts, and officials from HSE. They will report to HSC, and may make recommendations. Examples of existing Standing Advisory Committees are as follows.

Advisory Committee on Major Hazards

2.18 This committee was set up in order to investigate major hazards or actual disasters, and to make recommendations to minimise or eliminate the dangers from major incidents of the Flixborough type. It has invited views from various organisations on how to tackle the problems which arise from the existence of installations which represent potential major hazards, and issues reports for consideration. The Committee's last report was published in 1984.

Advisory Committee on Toxic Substances

2.19 This committee was set up to advise HSC on methods of controlling health hazards to persons at work (especially in connection with the COSHH Regulations, see para 6.135) and also to the general public consequent on or arising from the use of toxic substances. The committee has representatives from industry, local authorities and other expert advisers.

Advisory Committee on Dangerous Substances

2.20 This committee considers methods of securing the safety of persons at work and related risks to the general public arising from the manufacture, import, storage, conveyance and use of materials which are flammable or explosive, and the transportation of a wide range of dangerous substances. Its membership includes representatives from industry, local authorities and other experts.

Advisory Committee on the Safety of Nuclear Installations

2.21 This committee advises on all aspects of nuclear safety. It is chaired by an independent member and has scientific and industrial advisers.

Advisory Committee on Dangerous Pathogens

2.22 This committee will advise HSC and the Departments of Health and Agriculture on matters relating to all classes of pathogens which are dangerous to human beings. As well as representatives from both sides of industry it has a number of medical and scientific experts. It will advise HSC on the general standards of safe working to be observed in laboratories, point out any improvements necessary, consider new hazards, and make recommendations concerning proposed regulations, approved codes of practice and guidance generally.

Advisory Committee on Genetic Modification

2.23 This committee gives guidance on the planned release of genetically manipulated organisms for agricultural and environment purposes, including risk assessment and notification of proposals to carry out such work. It also deals with guidelines for the health surveillance of persons involved in genetic manipulation in laboratories, etc and the setting up of safety committees.

Industrial Advisory Committees (IACs)

2.24 A number of industry based advisory committees and joint standing committees have been set up with a view to stimulating action to promote the health and safety of workers within particular industries and to protect the general public from related hazards arising from such activities. As a general rule, HSE provides the secretariat and chairmen, with the rest of the membership drawn from the main organisations in the industry. Each IAC will draw up its own plan of work (short term and long term) reviewing specific problems which need to be tackled, which is submitted to HSC for approval. Proposals for action to be taken may also be placed before HSC for consideration.

2.25 IACs exist for the following industries: agriculture, ceramics, construction, cotton and textiles, education, foundries, health services, oil, paper and board, printing, railways and rubber.

Ad hoc committees

2.26 HSC will sometimes set up a committee to deal with a particular problem. For example, the Advisory Committee on Asbestos was created to consider and investigate the special hazards to health arising from the use of asbestos in industry. It issued several reports which, together with its final report contained a number of specific recommendations, and a new Approved Code of Practice (together with Guidance Notes) has been published giving practical advice on the precautions to be observed when working with asbestos insulation and asbestos coatings.

Health and Safety Executive (HSE)

2.27 HSE was established by s.10 of HSWA. It is headed by a director general appointed by HSC with the approval of the Secretary of State, and two other members appointed by HSC with like approval after consultation with the director general. HSE, which has its headquarters in London, controls the various branches of the Inspectorate.

2.28 HSE has recently undergone considerable organisational changes, with a view to increasing its efficiency and effectiveness. It has recently taken over responsibility for the Railway Inspectorate, and, from April 1991, offshore oil and gas safety. The basic work of inspections and field services is done by the new Field Operations Division (incorporating the former Factories, Agricultural and Quarries inspectorates and the Employment Medical Advisory Service (EMAS)), which comprises of nearly 50% of all HSE staff. There are seven regional directors, who control some 21 area offices. Other divisions (health policy, special hazards, safety and general policy, etc) provide essential back-up services and combine policy with operational responses.

2.29 In addition, HSE controls the activities of the Employment Medical Advisory Service (see below). Thus, although industry has to deal with one unified body, in practice specialists from the different branches may be encountered, as well as other enforcement bodies (eg fire authority, local authorities, see below). Each inspectorate will obviously deal with those matters in respect of which it has been assigned.

National Interest Groups (NIGs)

2.30 The internal organisation of HSE is designed to permit a greater degree of industrial specialisation. This is done by means of National Interest Groups, which exist for the following industrial activities: agriculture, ceramics, chemicals, construction, docks, food, footwear, molten metals, engineering, education, health services, paper, plastics, printing, rubber, shipbuilding, textiles (wool and cotton), woodworking. In all, some 30 NIGs are in existence, each attached to an HSE area office (see Appendix). Any inspector may approach the NIG specialist for assistance and information. In addition, a number of area offices have National Responsibility Groups (NRG) for certain processes in respect of which NIGs do not exist.

Duties of HSE

2.31 It is the duty of HSE to exercise on behalf of HSC such of the latter's functions as it may care to direct that HSE shall exercise, and to give effect to any directions given to it by HSC. However, except for the purpose of giving effect to directions given to HSC by the Secretary of State, HSC cannot give HSE any directions as to the enforcement of the relevant statutory provisions in any particular case (s.11(4)). In other words, HSE alone will decide when and how to enforce the law in individual cases.

2.32 HSE may also provide a Minister of the Crown with information in connection with any matter with which he is concerned and provide him with advice. HSE can do anything (except borrow money) which is calculated to facilitate, or is conducive or incidental to, the performance of any function within its statutory obligations. The duty of HSE to enforce the relevant statutory provisions is limited by the extent that some other authority is responsible for their enforcement (see Health and Safety (Enforcing Authority) Regulations 1989, below).

Enforcement by HSE (ss.20–26)

2.33 HSE has a number of actual and potential powers whereby it may seek to ensure compliance with the relevant statutory provisions. Primarily, however, it will seek to give advice and assistance to any employer or other person who is seeking ways of meeting the necessary standards. Persuasion, rather than compulsion, has always been the style adopted by the inspectorate, for the object has always been to establish high standards of health and safety rather than to punish offenders. Thus an inspector may give verbal or written advice as to the steps which need to be taken to ensure compliance with the statutory duties. For example, in 1989–90, local authority enforcement officers issued some 119,550 letters of compliance, requiring the persons to whom they were addressed to comply with the relevant legal requirements. If remedial steps are not taken, or where the dangers are so obvious or imminent that immediate action is necessary, the powers of issuing improvement or prohibition notices may be exercised. As a last resort, criminal proceedings may be brought by an inspector (see *Campbell v Wallsend Slipway & Engineering Co. Ltd*) which are usually instituted when there has been an incident, or after prior warnings have been given, or where the employer in question has a bad record of compliance. In other words, the inspectors will usually start off with advice, persuasion and encouragement. If these fail, resort may be had to compulsion or sanctions.

2.34 Every enforcement authority has the power to appoint as inspectors (under whatever title they may think fit) such persons having suitable qualifications as it thinks necessary for enforcing the relevant statutory provisions within its field of responsibility, and may also terminate the appointment (HSWA, s.19). However, it is submitted that this does not take inspectors outside the protection of the relevant provisions of the Employment Protection (Consolidation) Act 1978, particularly in respect of rights not to be unfairly dismissed.

Powers of inspectors (s.20)

2.35 When an inspector is appointed, he will be given a document specifying which of the powers conferred on him by the relevant statutory provisions are to be exercisable by him, and he may only exercise those powers within the area of the responsibility of the enforcing authority which appointed him (see *Laws v Keane*).

When seeking to exercise those powers, he must produce, on request, his instrument of appointment. The powers of inspectors are as follows:

(a) at any reasonable time, or, if there is a dangerous situation, at any time, to enter premises which he has reason to believe it is necessary to enter for the purpose of carrying into effect any relevant statutory provision
(b) to take with him a constable if he has reasonable cause to apprehend any serious obstruction in the execution of his duty
(c) to take with him any person duly authorised by the inspector's authority, and any equipment or materials required for any purpose for which the power of entry is being exercised
(d) to make such examination and investigation as may be necessary
(e) to direct that any premises or anything therein shall be left undisturbed so long as it is reasonably necessary for the purpose of examination or investigation
(f) to take such measurements and photographs and make such recordings as he considers necessary for the purpose of examination or investigation
(g) to take samples of any article or substance found in any premises and in the atmosphere in or in the vicinity of any such premises; the Secretary of State may make regulations concerning the procedure to be adopted in such cases
(h) in the case of any article or substance likely to cause danger to health or safety, to cause it to be dismantled or subjected to any process or test, but he may not destroy or damage it unless it is for the purpose of exercising his powers. If the person who has responsibilities in relation to those premises so requests, the inspector will exercise this power in that person's presence, unless he considers that it would be prejudicial to the safety of the State to do so. In any case, before exercising these powers, he must consult with appropriate persons for the purpose of ascertaining what dangers, if any, there may be in doing what he proposes to do
(i) in the case of any article or substance likely to cause danger to health or safety, to take possession of it, and detain it for so long as is necessary in order to examine it, to ensure that it is not tampered with before he has completed his examination, or to ensure that it will be available for use as evidence in any proceedings for an offence, or in respect of matters arising out of the issuing of an improvement or prohibition notice. He must leave a notice giving particulars of the article or substance, stating that he has taken possession of it, and, if it is practicable to do so, leave a sample with a responsible person
(j) if he is conducting an examination or investigation under (d) above, to require any person whom he has reasonable cause to believe to be able to give any information to answer such questions as the inspector thinks fit, and to sign a declaration of the truth of his answers. However, no answer given in response to an inspector's questions shall be admissible in evidence against that person or his husband or wife in any proceedings
(k) to require the production of, inspect, and take copies of, any entry in any books or documents which are required to be kept, and of any book or document which it is necessary for him to see for the purpose of any

examination or investigation under (d) above, but not if the production is refused on the ground of legal professional privilege

(l) to require any person to afford him such facilities and assistance within that person's control or responsibilities, as are necessary for him to exercise his powers

(m) any other power which is necessary for the purpose of exercising any of the above powers.

Obtaining information (s.27)

2.36 In order to discharge their functions, HSC, HSE or any other enforcing authority may need further information. To obtain this, s.27 gives power to the HSC, with the consent of the Secretary of State, to serve on any person a notice requiring him to furnish HSC, HSE or any other enforcing authority with such information about such matters as may be specified in the notice, and to do this in such form and manner, and within such time, as may be specified.

2.37 No information obtained under this power shall be disclosed without the consent of the person by whom it was furnished, but this does not prevent the disclosure:

(a) to HSC, or HSE, or Government department or any other enforcing authority

(b) by the recipient of the information to any person for the purpose of any function conferred on the recipient by any relevant statutory provision

(c) to an officer of a local authority, water authority, or river purification board, or to a constable, in each case to a person who is authorised to receive it

(d) by the recipient, as long as it is in a form which is calculated to prevent it from being identified as relating to a particular person or as a particular case

(e) of any information for the purpose of any legal proceedings or any investigation of enquiry held by virtue of s.14(2) (above) or any report made as a result thereof.

Disclosure of information by inspectors (s.28)

2.38 A person exercising powers of entry or inspection under s.14(4)(a), or general powers of inspection, etc under s.20 may not disclose any information obtained by him (including, in particular, any information with respect to any trade secret obtained by him in any premises into which he has entered by virtue of such powers) except:

(a) for the purpose of his functions, or

(b) for the purpose of any legal proceedings, or any investigation or inquiry held by virtue of s.14(2), or a report thereof, or

(c) with the consent of the person who furnished the information in pursuance of a requirement imposed under s.20, and with the consent of the person having responsibilities in relation to the premises where the information was obtained in any other case (s.28(7)).

2.39 However, an inspector is expressly authorised by s.28(8) to disclose information to employed persons or their representatives if it is necessary for him to do so for the purpose of assisting in keeping them adequately informed about matters affecting their health, safety or welfare. Normally, this information will be communicated to safety representatives, but in the absence of these, it can be to a shop steward, or to individuals or even their legal representatives, should this be necessary. The information which can be disclosed is:

(a) factual information obtained by him as a result of the exercise of any of his powers under s.20 (above) or as a result of a person who is holding an enquiry under s.14 (above) exercising his right to enter and inspect premises (see s.14(4)(a)), as long as the information relates to the premises where the employees are employed, or to anything which was or is in there, or was or is being done there, and
(b) information with respect to any action which he has taken or proposes to take in or in connection with those premises.

If the inspector does give such information to employees or their representatives, he must also give the like information to the employer.

Disclosure for civil proceedings (s.28(9))

2.40 Section 116 of the Employment Protection Act 1975 added a new subsection (s.28(9) to HSWA), which permits the disclosure by an inspector of information to a person who is likely to be a party to any civil proceedings arising out of an accident, occurrence or other situation. He will do this by providing a written statement of the relevant facts observed by him in the course of exercising any of his powers. Thus, in a civil action for damages (see chapter 8) either the plaintiff or the defendant may request the information from an inspector.

HSC has produced a Guidance Note on the subject.

Additional powers

2.41 As we shall see, an inspector may serve a prohibition notice, an improvement notice, and in England and Wales may prosecute offenders. He may seize and render harmless any article or substance likely to be a cause of danger, and is responsible for the enforcement of the employer's duty to display the certificate of insurance under the provisions of the Employers' Liability (Compulsory Insurance) Act 1969.

Power of an enforcing authority to indemnify inspectors (s.26)

2.42 A person who is aggrieved by any action of an inspector who has exceeded his powers may always bring a civil action against him. If the circumstances are such that the inspector cannot legally claim the right of indemnity from the appointing authority, the latter may nonetheless indemnify him in whole or in part against any damages, costs, or expenses ordered to pay or incurred if the authority is satisfied that he honestly believed that he was acting within his powers and that his duty as an inspector required or entitled him to do the act in question.

2.43 An aggrieved person may also pursue a complaint against an inspector, or HSE or HSC through the machinery laid down in the Parliamentary Commissioner Act 1967 (which created the investigatory role of the Ombudsman).

Local authorities

2.44 One of the problems disclosed by the Robens Committee was the overlapping jurisdiction of the different enforcement authorities. Thus, a shoe repair shop—since it was both a factory and a shop—could be visited by the factory inspector and a local authority inspector, each concerned with his own responsibilities. To prevent this happening, s.18 of HSWA enables the Secretary of State, by regulation, to make local authorities responsible for certain prescribed activities, to facilitate the transfer of responsibilities between HSE and local authorities, and to deal with uncertain areas.

2.45 For the purpose of enforcement of the relevant statutory provisions, a local authority is (in England and Wales) a district council, a London Borough Council, the Sub-Treasurer of the Inner Temple, the Under-Treasurer of the Middle Temple, or the Council of the Isles of Scilly. In Scotland the enforcing local authority is an islands or district council.

2.46 The enforcement functions are carried out by officials who have a number of different titles, although they are increasingly being known as Environmental Health Officers (EHOs). EHOs are usually members of the Institute of Environmental Health Officers (IEHO), the qualification for which is either passing the Institute's Diploma in Environmental Health, or obtaining a degree in Environmental Health from a recognised institution of higher education, or by obtaining a post-graduate diploma in environmental health. The Institute has over 7,000 members, most of whom are employed by local authorities throughout the country. EHOs have all the powers of an HSE inspector (see above).

2.47 The Health and Safety (Enforcing Authority) Regulations 1989 have drawn a clear line between the responsibilities of HSE and local authorities. The regulations basically apply three principles, namely (a) allocation of premises shall be based on the concept of the main activity carried on, (b) dual inspection is to be avoided, and (c) there shall be no self-inspection by enforcing authorities. Local authorities will be allocated responsibility for premises as specified in Schedule 1 of the regulations, below.

Main activities which determine whether LAs will be enforcing authorities

1. The sale or storage of goods for retail or wholesale distribution except:
   (a) where it is part of the business of a transport undertaking
   (b) at container depots where the main activity is the storage of goods in the course of transit to or from dock premises, an airport or a railway
   (c) where the main activity is the sale or storage for wholesale distribution of any dangerous substance
   (d) where the main activity is the sale or storage of water or sewage or their by-products or natural or town gas

   and for the purposes of this paragraph where the main activity carried on in premises is the sale and fitting of motor car tyres, exhausts, windscreens or sunroofs, the main activity shall be deemed to be the sale of goods.
2. The display or demonstration of goods at an exhibition for the purposes of offer or advertisement for sale.
3. Office activities.
4. Catering services.
5. The provision of permanent or temporary residential accommodation including the provision of a site for caravans or campers.
6. Consumer services provided in a shop except dry cleaning or radio and television repairs, and in this paragraph "consumer services" means services of a type ordinarily supplied to persons who receive them otherwise than in the course of a trade, business or other undertaking carried on by them (whether for profit or not).
7. Cleaning (wet or dry) in coin-operated units in launderettes and similar premises.
8. The use of a bath, sauna or solarium, massaging, hair transplanting, skin piercing, manicuring or other cosmetic services and therapeutic treatments, except where they are carried out under the supervision or control of a registered medical practitioner, a dentist registered under the Dentists Act 1984, a physiotherapist, an osteopath or a chiropractor.
9. The practice or presentation of the arts, sports, games, entertainment or other cultural or recreational activities except where carried on in a museum, art

gallery or theatre or where the main activity is the exhibition of a cave to the public.
10. The hiring out of pleasure craft for use on inland waters.
11. The care, treatment, accommodation or exhibition of animals, birds or other creatures, except where the main activity is horse breeding or horse training at a stable, or is an agricultural activity or veterinary surgery.
12. The activities of an undertaker, except where the main activity is embalming or the making of coffins.
13. Church worship or religious meetings.

Activities in respect of which the HSE is the enforcing authority

2.48 Where the main activity carried on in non-domestic premises is not covered by Schedule 1, HSE is the enforcing authority. This would cover factories, etc. In addition, HSE is the enforcing authority for local authorities premises, police and fire authorities, international organisations, the Crown, s.6 of HSWA (Manufacturers, etc, see para 3.71) and the following activities, set out in Schedule 2 of the regulations:

1. Any activity in a mine or quarry other than a quarry in respect of which notice of abandonment has been given under s.139(2) of the Mines and Quarries Act 1954.
2. Any activity in a fairground.
3. Any activity in premises occupied by a radio, television or film undertaking in which the activity of broadcasting, recording or filming is carried on, and the activity of broadcasting, recording or filming wherever carried on, and for this purpose "film" includes video.
4. The following activities carried on at any premises by persons who do not normally work in the premises:
   (a) construction work if:
      (i) s.127(6) of the Factories Act 1961 (which requires certain work to be notified to an inspector) applies to such work; or
      (ii) the whole or part of the work contracted to be undertaken by the contractor at the premises is to the external fabric or other external part of a building or structure; or
      (iii) it is carried out in a physically segregated area of the premises, the activities normally carried out in that area have been suspended for the purpose of enabling the construction work to be carried out, the contractor has authority to exclude from that area persons who are not attending in connection with the carrying out of the work and the work is not the maintenance of insulation on pipes, boilers or other parts of heating or water systems or its removal from them
   (b) the installation, maintenance or repair of any gas system, or any work in relation to a gas fitting

   (c) the installation, maintenance or repair of electricity systems
   (d) work with ionising radiations except work in one or more of the categories set out in Schedule 3 to the Ionising Radiations Regulations 1985.
5. The use of ionising radiations for medical exposure (within the meaning of regulation 2(1) of the Ionising Radiations Regulations 1985).
6. Any activity in premises occupied by a radiography undertaking in which there is carried on any work with ionising radiations.
7. Agricultural activities, and any activity at an agricultural show which involves the handling of livestock or working of agricultural equipment.
8. Any activity on board a seagoing ship.
9. Any activity in relation to a ski slope, ski lift, ski tow or cable car.
10. Fish, maggot and game breeding except in a zoo.

Where premises are multi-occupied, each part separately occupied is regarded as separate premises for the purpose of enforcement allocation.

2.49 The result is that HSE, through its various branches, is the enforcing authority for some 700,000 fixed sites, and an unknown number of transient sites. On the other hand, local authorities have the task of enforcing the law in respect of over 1,000,000 premises. In order to establish a certain amount of consistency of approach, HSE has established a Local Authority Unit, which prepares guidance for environmental health officers. This unit (LAU) provides the secretariat for HSE/LA Enforcement Liaison Committee (HELA) which acts as a forum for the exchange of information and informal discussions and also attempts to arrive at practical cooperation between HSE and local authorities. Additionally, each HSE area office has a liaison officer, whose task it is to maintain links with local authorities and provide advice and assistance, with particular reference to the provision of training and the dissemination of information.

Self inspection

2.50 On the principle that there shall be no self inspection, HSE will inspect the premises of the local authorities, and the local authorities will inspect those belonging to HSE (even though it is a Crown body). Although it might be expected that local authorities should be regarded as good employers and aware of their responsibilities, there have been several cases where they have been prosecuted by HSE and convicted of offences under HSWA. Clearly, this is an indication of human weaknesses within the organisation, rather than a wilful or neglectful disregard of the standards on health and safety.

Transfer of authority

2.51 Regulation 5 of the 1989 regulations enables the responsibility for enforcement to be transferred in a particular case from HSE to a local authority, or from a local authority to HSE. This may be done by HSC or by agreement between the enforcing authority which has current responsibility and the authority to which it is proposed to transfer. The new enforcing authority will then give notice of the transfer to persons affected by it. If the transfer has been made by HSC, notice will be given to both enforcing authorities.

2.52 In cases of uncertainty, in respect of any premises, part of premises or any activity, responsibility may be assigned to the local authority or HSE as appropriate by the other enforcement authority. Alternatively either authority may apply to HSC, and if it thinks that uncertainty exists it will take into account the views expressed, inform each party of the views expressed by the other (*R v Health & Safety Commission, ex parte Spelthorne Borough Council*) and assign accordingly, giving notice to the authorities and persons affected by it. Any proposal to transfer the responsibility for premises occupied or controlled by the Crown can only be done with the combined agreement of HSE, the local authority, and the Government department concerned.

2.53 However, if there is a change in the main activity being carried on at the premises, there is an automatic transfer of responsibility from one enforcing authority to the other. It is not necessary to go through the formal procedure for effecting a transfer, because this would result in there being a period of time when there would be no one charged with the task of enforcement (*Hadley v Hancox*).

2.54 It will be recalled that responsibility for enforcing legislation relating to air pollution (including s.5 of HSWA) will be transferred to HM Inspectorate of Pollution, which is under the control of the Department of the Environment, or local authorities, as appropriate, see para 2.5).

Employment Medical Advisory Service (EMAS)

2.55 There has been a medical branch of the Factory Inspectorate since 1898, but the new streamlined medical service was created by the Employment Medical Advisory Service Act 1972, and it commenced operations in 1973. Its existence was continued by virtue of Part II of HSWA, and the Service is now an integral part of HSE.

2.56 The functions of EMAS are laid down in s.55 of HSWA, and are as follows:

(a) securing that the Secretary of State, HSC, employers' organisations, trade unions, and occupational health practitioners can be kept informed and adequately advised on matters of which they ought to take notice, concerning the safeguarding and improvement of the health of persons who are employed or who are seeking employment or training for employment

(b) giving to employed persons and persons seeking employment or training for employment, information and advice on health in relation to such employment or training

(c) other purposes of the functions of the Secretary of State relating to employment.

2.57 EMAS is headed by a Director of Medical Services, with Senior Employment Medical Advisers to be found throughout the various regions of the country. There is also a Chief Employment Nursing Adviser, and specialist advisers in toxicology, respiratory diseases, pathology research, and the medical aspects of rehabilitation. From its head office, EMAS controls a force of about 140 Employment Medical Advisers (EMAs) who are qualified registered medical practitioners and Employment Nursing Advisers (ENAs) who are also qualified in occupational health.

2.58 In order to exercise its statutory functions, EMAS has responsibility for:

(a) advising the inspectorate on the occupational health aspects of regulations and Approved Codes of Practice
(b) regular examinations of persons employed on known hazardous operations;
(c) other medical examinations, investigations and surveys
(d) giving advice to HSE, employers, trade unions and others about the occupational health aspects of poisonous substances, immunological disorders, physical hazards (noise, vibrations, etc), dust, and mental stress, including the laying down of standards of exposure to processes or substances which may harm health
(e) research into occupational health
(f) advice on the provision of occupational medical, nursing and first aid services
(g) advice on the medical aspects of rehabilitation and training for and placement in employment.

Powers of EMAS

2.59 An Employment Medical Adviser has the same power of entry and investigation as inspectors have under s.20 (above) by virtue of an appointment as such. He can examine workers in those employments which regulations require that they shall be examined at regular intervals (eg Control of Lead at Work Regulations 1980) but he cannot force a person to be examined against his will. Nor will he prescribe any treatment, but will refer workers to their own family general practitioner.

2.60 Advice is also given on the medical aspects of employing young persons (ie below the age of eighteen). Employers are obliged to notify the local careers office whenever a young person is taken into employment, and this enables a check to be kept on those young persons who have a medical problem and ensures that there is a continuous watch being kept on those who may need further medical supervision.

2.61 ENAs are an integral part of the service and will visit premises on request or as a result of a visit by an inspector, and give advice and assistance to employers, trade unions, safety officers, safety representatives, etc. They will also give advice to the

Disablement Resettlement Officers and others about the advisability of employing someone who has a health problem, enforce the First Aid Regulations and undertake biological monitoring.

2.62 Thus information about suspected health hazards will reach EMAS from a number of sources, enabling an investigation to take place, and advice given on how hazards can be reduced or eliminated. EMAS is frequently used as an advisory service and is constantly engaged in research into health problems, in collaboration with HSE.

Safety representatives

2.63 One of the more important innovations to be found in HSWA is contained in s.2(4), which enabled the Secretary of State by regulations to provide for the appointment by recognised independent trade unions of safety representatives from among the employees, who will represent them in consultation with the employers and have other prescribed functions. It will then be the duty of every employer to consult with such representatives with a view to the making and maintenance of arrangements which will enable him and his employees to cooperate effectively in promoting and developing measures to ensure the health and safety at work of the employees, and in checking the effectiveness of such measures (s.2(6)).

2.64 The relevant regulations have been made (Safety Representatives and Safety Committees Regulations 1977) together with an Approved Code of Practice and non-statutory Guidance Notes. In addition, there is an Approved Code of Practice on Time Off for the Training of Safety Representatives. These are all published in one document.

Appointment of safety representatives (s.2(4))

2.65 A safety representative may be appointed by an independent trade union which is recognised by the employer for the purposes of collective bargaining. To be a trade union, it must be on the list of trade unions maintained by the Certification Officer under s.2 of the Trade Union and Labour Relations (Consolidation) Act 1992. It will be an independent trade union if it has applied for and received a Certificate of Independence from the Certification Officer (issued if it can show that it is not under the domination or control of the employer, whether by way of the provision of financial benefits or otherwise) under s.6 of the same Act. It will be a recognised trade union if the employer recognises it for the purpose of negotiations relating to or connected with one or more of the matters specified in s.244 of the 1992 Act. There is no need to have a formal agreement concerning recognition; it is a question of fact, to be determined by the circumstances of each case as to whether or not the employer does recognise the trade union concerned (*NUTGW v Charles Ingram & Co. Ltd*).

2.66 Only an independent trade union which is recognised for the purposes of collective bargaining is legally entitled to appoint safety representatives. In *Cleveland County Council v Springett*, union representatives, who were members of the Association of Polytechnic Teachers, claimed that they had been denied time off work with pay in accordance with the regulations. The union was not formally recognised by the local authority which ran the polytechnic, although it was represented on the national Burnham Committee, a body which made recommendations on teachers' pay. It was held that this did not constitute recognition by the employer. Further, the fact that the union had had previous dealings with the employer when representing an individual employee of the polytechnic did not constitute recognition for the purpose of collective bargaining.

2.67 If an employer refuses to consult with the appointed safety representatives on the ground that he does not recognise the trade union concerned, it is likely that HSE will invoke the aid of the Advisory Conciliation and Arbitration Service (ACAS) to provide advice, but since the provisions of the Employment Protection Act 1975, ss.11–16 (which provided for a machinery whereby a trade union could obtain a formal declaration of recognition rights from ACAS) have been repealed (Employment Act 1980, s.19), there is no way this matter can be resolved without instituting proceedings in the magistrates' court for a breach of s.2(6).

2.68 The system whereby the legal right to appoint safety representatives is confined to trade unions has been the subject of some criticism. It is argued that it tends to perpetuate the divisions in industry between "us" and "them". Safety, after all, should be the concern of all, be they employers, managers, employees, union officials, and so on, and it is wrong that safety representatives are to be seen against the backcloth of the battleground of industrial relations. Against this, it is argued that the disputes which may arise over the functions and rights of a safety representative can more readily be resolved within the existing framework of collective bargaining machinery, and that to place the safety representative outside that machinery is to leave no avenue available for the resolution of disputes.

2.69 It should further be noted that in a non-unionised situation, there is nothing to stop an employer from creating his own system of safety representation, and although persons appointed will lack the statutory backing of HSWA and the regulations, they can operate on a voluntary basis on the same lines as those who are union sponsored.

2.70 Although a safety representative is appointed by the recognised trade union, he need not be a member of the trade union. The only requirements are that he shall, so far as is reasonably practicable, have been employed by his employer throughout the preceding two years or have had at least two years' experience in similar employment (Safety Representatives, etc Regulations, regulation 2). Again, this raises some argument in practice. Some trade unions will appoint shop stewards to be the safety representatives, on the ground that they are better trained, will not be overawed by management, and can handle the appropriate dispute procedures. On the other hand, this can cause some problems, for, as a shop steward, he may be subject to the processes of re-election, or there may be a conflict arising out of his functions as a shop steward and those he exercises as a safety representative. For example, if there are disciplinary proceedings being taken against an employee (see chapter 9) who has acted in breach of safety rules, the shop steward who has to represent his member will have to reconcile his actions with his belief that the safety rules must be upheld. To avoid such conflict, some trade unions will refuse to appoint shop stewards and look to other members to carry out this important work. This has the added advantage of spreading the workload and training opportunities, and involving more members in the activities of the union. Clearly, no single pattern will meet all the circumstances, and the matter must be regarded from a pragmatic viewpoint.

2.71 Neither the regulations nor the Approved Code of Practice specify how many safety representatives should be appointed by the trade union concerned, and certain difficulties may well exist in multi-union situations. The Guidance Notes attached to the regulations suggest that the appropriate criteria should be based on:

(a) the total number of employees in the workplace
(b) the variety of different occupations
(c) the size of the workplace and the variety of workplace locations
(d) the operation of shift systems
(e) the type of work activity and the degree and character of inherent dangers.

2.72 A person who has been appointed safety representative shall cease to be such when:

(a) the trade union which appointed him notifies the employer in writing that the appointment has been terminated; or
(b) he ceases to be employed at the workplace. However, if he was appointed to represent employees at more than one workplace he shall not cease to be a safety representative so long as he continues to be employed at any one of them
(c) he resigns.

Consultations with safety representatives

2.73 Once an employer has been notified in writing by or on behalf of a trade union that a person has been appointed as a safety representative, and of the group of employees he is to represent, the safety representative shall have the right to be consulted by the employer with a view to the making and maintaining of arrangements which will enable the employer and his employees to cooperative effectively in promoting and developing measures to ensure the health and safety at work of the employees, and to check the effectiveness of those measures (HSWA, s.2(6)). The Management of Health and Safety at Work Regulations 1992 have introduced new consultation provisions to the Safety Representative, etc Regulations which require the employer to consult with the safety representatives in good time with regard to:

(a) the introduction at the workplace of any measure which may substantially affect the health and safety of the employees who are represented by the safety representative
(b) his arrangements for appointing or nominating his safety assistant/adviser and person responsible for evacuation procedures
(c) any health and safety information required to be provided by the employer to employees the safety representative concerned represents
(d) the planning and organisation of any health and safety training required to be provided by the employer to the employees the safety representative represents, and
(e) the health and safety consequences of the introduction of new technologies into the workplace.

2.74 The employer shall also provide such facilities and assistance as safety representatives may reasonably require for the purpose of carrying out their statutory functions.

Functions of safety representatives

2.75 Regulation 4 of the Safety Representatives and Safety Committees Regulations lays down a number of functions which a safety representative shall be entitled to perform. These are:

(a) to investigate potential hazards and dangerous occurrences at the workplace (whether or not they are drawn to his attention by the employees he represents) and to examine the causes of accidents at the workplace. This right is not confined to having time off work (with pay) to make the investigation inside the workplace, for there may be circumstances when it is necessary to go outside in order to investigate (eg to interview an injured employee at home, see *Dowsett v Ford Motor Co.* para 2.93)
(b) to investigate complaints by any employee he represents relating to that employee's health, safety or welfare at work
(c) to make representations to the employer on the above matters
(d) to make representations to the employer on general matters affecting the health, safety or welfare at work of the employees at the workplace
(e) to carry out inspections (see below)
(f) to represent employees in consultations at the workplace with inspectors of HSE or any other enforcing authority
(g) to receive information from inspectors (see para 2.39)
(h) to attend meetings of the safety committee where he attends in his capacity as safety representative in connection with any of the above functions.

2.76 As an employee, the safety representative is subject to the general requirements imposed by ss.7–8 of HSWA (see chapter 3) but no function conferred on him as noted above shall impose any duty on him. This means that he cannot be prosecuted for a failure to perform his duty as a safety representative, or for performing his duties badly. Nor can he be sued civilly for a failure to perform his statutory duty, although he is subject to the ordinary law of negligence in the usual way (see chapter 8).

2.77 A safety representative is expected to act responsibly, and, in particular, he should not ignore established internal procedures. In *O'Connell v Tetrosyl Ltd*, a safety representative was dismissed because he made direct calls to the Factory Inspectorate concerning alleged breaches of safety regulations. The employers considered his actions to be misconduct, because he should have drawn management's attention to the matters before going to an outside body. By a majority, an industrial tribunal had found his dismissal to be fair and an appeal against that decision was rejected by the Employment Appeal Tribunal. The employers had reasonable grounds for believing that he had bypassed internal procedures by going to the outside body, and this conduct did constitute a fair reason for dismissal.

2.78 Following the enactment of the Trade Union Reform and Employment Rights Act 1993 safety assistants, safety representatives, members of safety committees, and employees generally, have protection against being subjected to a detriment or being dismissed, when taking certain actions connected with their functions as such, or health and safety generally (see para 9.39).

Inspection of the workplace

2.79 Safety representatives are entitled to inspect the workplace or any part of it on three occasions.

2.80 First, if they have not inspected it within the previous three months. They must give reasonable notice to the employer in writing of their intention to do so. More frequent inspections may be carried out with the agreement of the employer.

2.81 Second, where there has been a substantial change in the conditions of work (whether by way of the introduction of new machinery or otherwise), or where new information has been published by HSC or HSE relevant to the hazard since the last inspection. Then, after consulting with the employer, a further inspection may be carried out notwithstanding that less than three months have elapsed since the last inspection.

2.82 Third, where there has been a notifiable accident or dangerous occurrence (see chapter 6) or a notifiable illness has been contracted there, and:

(a) it is safe for an inspection to be carried out, and
(b) the interests of the group of employees represented by the safety representatives might be involved.

2.83 In these circumstances, the safety representatives may carry out an inspection of the part of the workplace concerned (and so far as is necessary to determine the cause, they may inspect any other parts of the workplace). Where it is reasonably practicable for them to do so, they shall notify the employer of their intention to carry out the inspection.

2.84 The employer shall provide such facilities and assistance as the safety representatives may reasonably require, including facilities for independent investigation by them and private discussions with employees, but the employer or his representative is entitled to be present in the workplace during the inspection.

Inspection of documents

2.85 For the performance of their duties, safety representatives are entitled, on giving reasonable notice to the employer, to inspect and take copies of any document relevant to the workplace or to employees they represent which the employer is required to keep by virtue of any relevant statutory provision. Thus, they can inspect and take copies out of the general register, reports of the examination of hoists, lifts, cranes, steam boilers, etc. However, they are not entitled to see a copy of the fire certificate issued under the Fire Precautions Act 1971 as this is not one of the relevant statutory provisions. Nor are they entitled to inspect or take copies of any document consisting of or relating to any health record of an identifiable individual.

Disclosure of information to safety representatives

2.86 Safety representatives will be entitled to receive information from two main sources. First, regulation 7(2) requires the employer to make available information within his knowledge which is necessary to enable the safety representatives to perform their functions. However, the employer need not disclose:

(a) information the disclosure of which would be against the interests of national security
(b) any information which he could not disclose without contravening a prohibition imposed by or under an enactment
(c) any information relating specifically to an individual, unless that individual has consented to it being disclosed
(d) any information, the disclosure of which would, for reasons other than its effect on health, safety or welfare at work, cause substantial injury to the employer's undertaking, or, where the information was supplied to the employer by some other person, to the undertaking of that other person
(e) any information obtained by the employer for the purpose of bringing, prosecuting or defending any legal proceedings.

2.87 Nor do the regulations require the employer to disclose any document or to allow the inspection of it if it does not relate to health, safety or welfare at work.

2.88 The restriction concerning the discovery of documents used for the purpose of legal proceedings was an issue before the House of Lords in *Waugh v British Railways Board* (see chapter 8) where it was held that for a document to be privileged, the dominant purpose in preparing it must have been for its use in possible litigation. Thus, if an accident report is prepared as a matter of routine practice in order to establish the cause, and is subsequently required for the purpose of litigation, the safety representative will be entitled to see it, for the dominant purpose in preparing it was not for the purpose of litigation.

2.89 The Approved Code of Practice makes a number of recommendations concerning the nature of the information which should be disclosed to safety representatives. These include:

(a) information about the plans and performance of the undertaking and any changes proposed in so far as they affect the health and safety at work of employees
(b) information of a technical nature about the hazards of health and the precautions deemed necessary to eliminate or minimise them, in respect of plant, machinery, equipment, processes, systems of work, and substances in use at work, including any relevant information provided by consultants and designers, or the manufacturer, importer or supplier of any article or substance used at work
(c) information which the employer keeps relating to the occurrence of any accident, dangerous occurrence or notifiable disease, and any statistical records relating to those matters
(d) any other information specifically relating to matters affecting health and safety at work, including the results of any measurements taken by the employer (or person acting on his behalf) in the course of checking the effectiveness of his health and safety arrangements
(e) information on articles or substances which an employer issues to his homeworkers.

2.90 The second source of information for safety representatives may come from the inspector, who, by virtue of s.28(8) of HSWA may give information to employees or their representatives to ensure that they are adequately informed about matters affecting their health, safety or welfare (see above, para 2.39). This may be factual information relating to the premises or anything therein, or information regarding any action taken or proposed to be taken by the inspector (eg the issuing of a prohibition or improvement notice). The inspector must give the like information to the employer.

Time off work for safety representatives

2.91 A safety representative is entitled to have time off work, with pay, during his working hours, for the purpose:

(a) of performing his functions as a safety representative

(b) to undergo training in aspects of those functions as may be reasonable having regard to the Approved Code of Practice issued by HSC.

2.92 If his pay does not vary with the amount of work done, then he shall be paid as if he had worked throughout the whole of the time. If his pay varies with the amount of work done, then he shall be entitled to be paid his average hourly earnings for his work, or, if no fair estimate of his earnings can be made, the average hourly earnings for work of that description of persons in comparable employment, or, if there are no such persons, then the average hourly earnings which are reasonable in the circumstances.

2.93 The right to investigate potential hazards and dangerous occurrences is not confined to having time off (with pay) to make an investigation inside the workplace. In *Dowsett v Ford Motor Co.* an employee was injured in an accident. The applicant, who was the safety representative, investigated the incident, and concluded that no further action was necessary. Five weeks later, he attended a meeting of the works safety committee where the safety engineer gave a report on the incident. The applicant wanted to have time off work with pay to visit the employee at home in order to make further enquiries, but this was refused, so he made an application to the industrial tribunal. It was held that the regulations were sufficiently wide to enable the safety representative to go outside the workplace if it was necessary to perform his functions. However, this was a question of fact and degree. In this case, he had not done anything for five weeks, and would not have acted had he not heard the report at the safety committee. Consequently, it was not necessary to make any further enquiries. In principle, however, the industrial tribunal made it quite clear that there could be circumstances where it would be necessary to interview the injured person (or others) and to perform this function satisfactorily it may be necessary to go outside the workplace.

Training of safety representatives

2.94 The Approved Code of Practice on "Time off Work for the Training of Safety Representatives" states that as soon as possible after they have been appointed they should be permitted to have time off work to attend basic training facilities approved by the TUC or their own trade union. Further training, similarly approved, should be undertaken when they have special responsibilities, or when this is necessary because of changed circumstances or new legislation. The trade union should inform management of the course it has approved and supply a copy of the syllabus if the employer asks for it. The trade union should give a few weeks' notice, and the number of safety representatives attending at one time from the same employer should be that which is reasonable in the circumstances, bearing in mind the availability of the relevant courses and the operational requirements of the employer. Unions and management should endeavour to reach agreement on the appropriate numbers and arrangements, and refer any problems to agreed procedures.

2.95 It will be recalled that the status of the code of practice is not of a rule of law; it is guidance to good practice. Thus there is no absolute rule that training should be only on a union approved course. In *White v Pressed Steel Fisher Ltd* the applicant was appointed safety representative by the T & GWU. The union wanted him to go on a union-sponsored training course, but management wanted to provide an in-company course and refused to permit him to have time off work with pay to attend the union course. It was held by the EAT that the employers were not acting unreasonably in refusing him time off work to go on the union course. The provisions in regulation 4(2) were for such training as may be reasonable in all the circumstances. It was therefore necessary to consider all the circumstances, including the Code of Practice. The approval of a course by the trade union was a factor to be taken into account, but (unlike s.168 of the Trade Union and Labour Relations (Consolidation) Act 1992 which relates to time off work for training in trade union duties) the Safety Representative and Safety Committee Regulations do not require that the course must be approved by the TUC or by the trade union. If the course provided by the employer was adequate, and contained all the necessary material, including the trade union aspects of safety, then it could be perfectly proper for the employer to insist that the safety representative went on the in-house course.

2.96 Whether it is reasonable for a safety representative to have time off work for training depends on whether, looked at overall, it is reasonable for him to attend for training. It does not depend on management's view of what is reasonable. In *Gallagher v Drum Engineering Co. Ltd*, two management members of a safety committee were sent on a training course dealing with the impending introduction of the COSHH Regulations and a third manager was due to go on another course. The union wanted to send three of its members who were on the safety committee to a course run by the TUC, but the company refused to permit this, although they were prepared to allow one union member to go. The applicant, one of those refused permission, applied to an industrial tribunal alleging a breach of the Safety Representatives and Safety Committees Regulations, and his claim was upheld. There was no unreasonable expense involved, no operational problems arose out of allowing three union representatives to attend the course and the union members had a large part to play in applying the regulations. In all the circumstances, the industrial tribunal thought that it was reasonable to allow the applicant time off work with pay to attend the TUC sponsored course.

2.97 In determining whether it is reasonable in the circumstances to have time off work with pay, the employer's decision is to be judged by standards of reasonableness which are similar to those used in unfair dismissal cases. For example, in *Scarth v East Hertfordshire District Council*, a safety representative applied for time off work, with pay, to attend a training course specifically designed for local government representatives. The request was refused, because the manager who made the decision thought it was not suitable, even though he had not seen the syllabus. Three days later he saw the syllabus, and granted the applicant three days' leave with pay. An industrial tribunal held that at the date he made his decision, the manager had not acted reasonably because he had not seen the syllabus for the course. Further, the figure of three days' pay had been "plucked out of the air" without any particular reason. Thus it was held that the applicant had been unreasonably refused time off work, and her claim for a further three days' pay was upheld.

2.98 The Code of Practice also gives guidance on the contents of a safety training syllabus. Basic training should provide for an understanding of the role of a safety representative, of safety committees, and of trade union policies and practices in relation to:

(a) the legal requirements relating to health and safety at work
(b) the nature and extent of workplace hazards, and of the measures necessary to eliminate or minimise them
(c) the health and safety policy of the employer, and the organisations and arrangements necessary to fulfil these policies.

2.99 In addition, they will need to develop new skills, including how to carry out a safety inspection, how to make use of basic sources of legal and official information, etc.

2.100 A safety representative is entitled to go on a specialised training course in order to become familiar with potential hazards. In *Howard v Volex Accessories Division*, the applicant, who was a safety representative, found that the work involved coming into contact with lead and various chemicals. She applied for time off work to attend a TUC course on chemical hazards. Management refused the request because they took the view that they were doing everything that could be done by way of investigating and checking hazards. She decided to use two of her holiday days to go on the course, and then made a claim to an industrial tribunal under regulation 4(2). The industrial tribunal thought that she was entitled to learn more about the chemical and other hazards at work and that the TUC course would help her to acquire that knowledge. It was held that she was entitled to be paid for attending the course and she was also awarded £50 compensation for the loss of her two days' holiday.

2.101 However, it may be inappropriate for a newly appointed safety representative to seek to go on a specialist training course before he has had his initial basic training (*Knight v Shell UK Ltd*).

2.102 If there are more safety representatives in the organisation than are warranted by the genuine safety needs of the firm, then the employer may well be justified in refusing time off work with pay in particular circumstances, because such time off will not be "necessary for the purpose of . . ." the performance of their functions as safety representatives (*Howard & Peet v Volex plc*).

Non-employees as safety representatives

2.103 The regulations specify that if the safety representatives have been appointed by the British Actors' Equity Association or the Musicians' Union, it is not necessary that they shall be employees of the employers concerned. This is because such people are performers in theatres, etc which are not owned by their employer, and are generally itinerant workers.

Safety committees

2.104 The Safety Representatives and Safety Committee Regulations lay down (regulation 9) that the employer must establish a safety committee if requested to do so in writing by two safety representatives. In order to do this, he must consult with safety representatives who made the request and with the representatives of any recognised trade union whose members work in the workplace in respect of which he proposes to establish the committee. The duty is one of consultation, not negotiation or agreement, so that actual composition of the committee is a matter for the employer to determine. However, he must establish the committee within three months of the request. He must also post a notice stating the composition of the committee and the workplace covered by it, and the notice shall be posted in a place where it may easily be read by the employees.

2.105 Section 2(7) of HSWA states that the function of the safety committee shall be to keep under review the measures taken to ensure the health and safety at work of employees and such other functions as may be prescribed. Apart from this vague generalisation, neither the regulations nor the Code of Practice give any further indication as to its functions. However, the Guidance Notes give some very helpful information. HSC believe that the detailed arrangements necessary will evolve from discussions and negotiations between the parties, who are best able to determine the needs of the particular workplace. Since the circumstances of each case will vary a great deal, no single pattern is possible.

2.106 Certain guides may be followed. The safety committee should have its own separate identity and not have any other function or tasks assigned to it. It should relate to a single establishment although group committees can play an additional role. Finally, its functions should be clearly defined. A suggested brief for the committee might go along the following lines:

- (a) a study of the trends of accidents, dangerous occurrences and notifiable diseases, so that recommendations may be made to management for corrective action to be taken
- (b) the examination of safety audit reports, to note areas where improvements can be made
- (c) consideration of reports and factual information from the enforcing authority
- (d) the consideration of reports made by the safety representatives
- (e) assisting in the development of safety rules and safe systems of work
- (f) an evaluation of the effectiveness of the safety content of employee training
- (g) monitoring of the adequacy of health and safety communication and publicity
- (h) acting as a link between the company and the enforcing authority

(i) evaluating the safety policy and making recommendations for its revision.

Safety committees are not specifically empowered to deal with welfare matters, though there is nothing to prevent this happening should the parties so decide.

Membership of the committee

2.107 The aim should be to keep the membership reasonably compact, with adequate representation from all interested parties. Management representatives should include persons involved in health and safety matters, eg works engineers, works doctor, safety officer, etc and there should be seen to exist some form of mechanism for the consideration and implementation of the recommendations by senior management. The committee must contain sufficient expertise to evaluate problems and come up with solutions. Outside specialists may be made ex officio members. There is no requirement that safety representatives should be members of the committee but it would clearly be desirable to have some representation, depending on the numbers involved. There is no provision for time off work to be paid for attendance at the meetings of the committee, but this should be obvious. It is also desirable that a senior member of the company attends the meetings and plays a leading role, eg the company chairman or a board director.

Meetings

2.108 The safety committee should meet on a regular basis, as frequently as necessary, depending on the volume of business. The date of the meetings should be notified well in advance, and provision should be made for urgent meetings. An agenda should be drawn up, minutes kept, with action taken noted. Probably the most important function of the committee will be to monitor action taken on any recommendations made.

Safety committees in non-unionised workplaces

2.109 HSC has issued some guidance on safety committees in those premises where there is no recognised independent trade union. Since there is no formal trade union machinery, and no legal requirement to set up a committee, the initiative will presumably come from management. Again, there should be adequate representation of appropriate management skills, and the employee representatives should be chosen by their fellow employees. In cases of difficulty, HSE will give further guidance.

Enforcement of the regulations

2.110 A safety representative may present a complaint to an industrial tribunal that:

(a) the employer has failed to permit him to take time off for the purpose of performing his functions as a safety representative, or to permit him to go on a training course, or

(b) the employer has failed to pay him for his time off.

2.111 The complaint must be presented within three months from the date when the failure occurred or, if it was not reasonably practicable to do so within that time, within such further period of time as the industrial tribunal considers to be reasonable. If the industrial tribunal upholds the complaint that the employer has failed to permit him to have time off, a declaration to that effect shall be made. Additionally, the industrial tribunal may make an award of compensation to be paid by the employer to the employee, which shall be of such amount as the tribunal considers to be just and equitable in all the circumstances, having regard to the employer's default in failing to permit the employee to have the time off, and to any loss suffered by the employee as a result of that failure. The compensation awarded would normally be a modest amount, for it will be rare that an employee actually suffers any loss. In *Owens v Bradford Health Authority* a trade union appointed as a safety representative a man who was within a year of retirement. He applied to go on a training course, but the employers refused, as they did not think it was reasonable for a safety representative so near to retirement to go on a training course. The industrial tribunal upheld the employee's complaint, and awarded him £50 compensation. It is the prerogative of the trade union to make the appointment and a refusal to send someone on a training course because he was near to retirement was not justified.

2.112 If the complaint is that of a failure to pay for the time off work, and it is upheld by the industrial tribunal, an award of the amount due to be paid will be made.

2.113 The enforcement of the other duties in the Act and the regulations is the responsibility of the appropriate enforcing authority. Thus if the employer fails to consult with the safety representatives, as required by s.2(4), or fails to set up a safety committee as required by s.2(7), or fails to provide the necessary information as required by regulation 7, he will be in breach of the law and thus commits a criminal offence. HSC has issued Guidance Notes on how HSE should attempt to deal with the enforcement of these matters. In three cases, they will not go to immediate enforcement, but will try other means. These are:

(a) HSE must be satisfied that all voluntary means have been explored, including the taking of advice from or using the services provided by the Advisory, Conciliation and Arbitration Service (ACAS)

(b) if there is some doubt as to whether or not the trade union has made a valid appointment as a safety representative. For example, the employer may allege that the trade union is not recognised by him. This problem might be resolved by using the services of ACAS

(c) if the problem relates to time off work, or a failure to pay, the specified remedy of using the machinery of the industrial tribunal should first be explored.

2.114 Enforcement by HSE might be appropriate in other cases, for example:

(a) if the trade union or safety representative complain that the employer is not carrying out his obligations after full use has been made of any consultative machinery or disputes procedure
(b) where the employer is refusing to acknowledge the existence of the safety representative who has been validly appointed
(c) where the employer refuses to make particular information available, or refuses to provide particular facilities to enable the safety representative to perform his functions
(d) where the employer has refused or failed to set up a safety committee after being requested to do so under regulation 9.

2.115 Since the employer will be in breach, and is "contravening one or more of the relevant statutory provisions" it is possible that instead of prosecuting for such breaches, the inspector may issue an improvement notice under s.21. To date, this tactic does not appear to have been necessary. Indeed, it is a credit to all concerned that the implementation of the provisions relating to safety representatives has, despite original fears, proceeded with great smoothness.

Safety officers

2.116 Under the Management of Health and Safety at Work Regulations 1992 (see chapter 4) every employer shall appoint one or more competent persons to assist him in undertaking the protective and preventative measures which have been identified in consequence of an assessment as to the measures he needs to take in order to comply with the relevant statutory provisions. There is also a requirement to appoint safety supervisors or competent persons to ensure compliance with statutory requirements under certain regulations, eg Clay Works Regulations 1948, Construction (General Provisions) Regulations 1961, Ship Building and Shiprepairing Regulations 1960, Diving Operations at Work Regulations 1981 and Ionising Radiations Regulations 1985, etc. No formal standards of training are laid down, the obligation is merely to ensure that he has sufficient time to discharge his duties efficiently, has the experience and expertise necessary to carry out those duties, and the authority to perform his duties.

2.117 There are also a number of statutory provisions which require an employee to be "qualified" or "trained", and other provisions require that certain things may only be done by or under the supervision of a "competent person" (see para 1.100). These phrases are usually left undefined, and it may well be that the burden is on the employer to show in any given case that the person who performed the task in question was qualified, trained or competent, as the case may be. The possession of some formal certificate or qualification would no doubt assist in discharging this burden, but it may also be shown that the person concerned has pursued some approved course of training or instruction, as well as possessing practical experience of the work.

2.118 The existence of a safety officer, with details of his functions and powers, would be one of the things an employer would refer to in the written statement of his general policy on health and safety at work, as required by s.2(3) of HSWA, being part of the organisation and arrangements in force for the carrying into effect of that policy.

2.119 The relevant professional organisation for safety officers is the Institute of Occupational Safety and Health (IOSH), which was formed in 1953, and has about 7,000 members. The Institute's examining body is the National Examination Board in Occupational Safety and Health (NEBOSH). Two qualifications may be awarded:

(a) Certificate. This examination comprises of two written papers (Identifying and Controlling Hazards, and Management of Safety) and a practical test. This course is suitable for those who have a part-time involvement in occupational health and safety.
(b) Diploma. This course comprises of five papers (Risk Management, Health and Safety Law, Occupational Health and Hygiene, Safety Technology and Case Study).

2.120 A person who has passed the Diploma and has had three years' professional experience can become a member of IOSH, and may apply to become a Fellow after five years.

2.121 There are about 50 educational and training establishments throughout the country which offer Certificate or Diploma courses.

2.122 HSE has produced a useful discussion document on the role and functions of safety officers which is available on request.

Occupational health services

2.123 The Management of Health and Safety at Work Regulations 1992 (see chapter 4) require an employer to provide employees with such health surveillance as is appropriate having regard to the risks to their health and safety identified by the risk assessment which has been carried out, but this does not give rise to a general legal obligation to provide medical services at the place of work (but see Health and Safety (First Aid) Regulations 1981, chapter 6). Many employers engage trained medical personnel to ensure the immediate treatment of injuries or illnesses which may occur during the employment, carry out pre-employment screening, investigate existing or potential medical hazards, or generally to provide a health care service for the benefit of employees. Occupational health services, by their very nature, are usually found in large firms, although there is a recent trend for smaller firms to pool together their resources and run a joint scheme. Sometimes the impetus comes from the need to reduce the incidence of accidents or ill health and consequently reduce the number of days lost through absenteeism. In other cases, the service may be part of the company's philosophy to provide additional welfare services on the premises for the use of all employees. Whatever the motive, occupational health services are on the increase.

2.124 Doctors who practice in industry may obtain a Diploma in occupational health or an MSc degree in occupational medicine. State Registered Nurses may obtain the Occupational Health Nursing Certificate.

2.125 The relationship between works doctors (or nurses), management, trade unions, the individual and his own family doctor is a complex one, for problems of confidentiality and conflicting interests may arise. The Royal College of Physicians has issued a booklet *Guidance on Ethics for Occupational Physicians*, and the Royal College of Nursing has issued a list of duties which may be expected to be performed by an occupational nurse.

Other institutions

Royal Society for the Prevention of Accidents

2.126 RoSPA is the largest independent safety organisation in Europe. A major part of its activities is concerned with occupational health and safety and it publishes three journals on the subject: (1) *Occupational Safety and Health*, (2) *RoSPA Bulletin*, (3) *Safety Representative*. RoSPA also organises conferences and training courses, and gives advice and assistance to members. Its address is Cannon House, The Priory, Queensway, Birmingham B4 6BS.

British Safety Council

2.127 A non-profit making independent body, financed entirely by subscriptions from its members, the BSC provides information and training on all aspects of health and safety, will undertake loss control surveys, issues posters and booklets, runs a National Safety Award scheme, and issues a Diploma in Safety Management. BSC also publishes a magazine *Safety Management* and a newsletter *Health and Safety at Work Act*. The address is 62/64 Chancellor's Road, Hammersmith, London W6 9RS.

British Standards Institute

2.128 The BSI was incorporated by Royal Charter in 1929, and has as its objectives:

(a) to coordinate the efforts of producers and users for the improvement, standardisation and simplification of engineering and industrial materials so as to simplify production and distribution and eliminate national waste of time and material in the production of unnecessary varieties of patterns and sizes of articles used for one and the same purpose
(b) to set up standards of quality and dimensions, prepare and promote the adoption of BSI specifications and schedules, revise, alter and amend these from time to time as experience and circumstances may require
(c) to register, in the name of the Institute, marks of all descriptions, and to approve, affix, and license the affixing of such marks
(d) to take any other action as may be necessary or desirable to promote the objects of the Institute.

2.129 The Institute is governed by an executive board consisting of 35 members, who appoint a director general. Over 1,000 technical committees perform the day-to-day work of developing appropriate standards. When these are agreed, the final standard can be adopted. The Institute is financed from Government funds, sales revenue and individual subscriptions.

2.130 Manufacturers who adopt the approved standards are entitled to use the BSI Kite Mark, but must agree to supervision and sample testing.

2.131 The Institute increasingly works closely with the International Organisation for Standardisation and other European organisations which have objects similar to its own. BSI is a member of the European Committee for Standardisation (CEN) and the Committee for Electrotechnical Standardisation (CENELEC), see para 10.26.

Industrial Safety Protective Equipment Manufacturers' Association

2.132 ISPEMA is a trade association which represents the views and activities of manufacturers of protective equipment. It provides technical information to the BSI and represents the industry at international level. It also provides training and educational programmes for industry relating to hazard analysis and the proper selection and usage of personal and environmental protective equipment.

2.133 An associated organisation is the Safety Equipment Distributors Association (SEDA) which comprises distributors of products of ISPEMA members. SEDA feed back information from the user, thus helping in the improvement in the design, comfort, and wearability of the product.

3

Health and Safety at Work etc Act 1974

The scope of the Act

3.1 The Health and Safety at Work etc Act 1974 (HSWA) is based on principles and details which are fundamentally different from other health and safety legislation. These differences are designed to bring about a greater awareness of the problems which surround health and safety matters, a greater involvement of those who are, or who should be, concerned with improvements in occupational health and safety and a positive movement away from the apathy and indifference which tended to surround the whole subject.

3.2 In the first place, the Act applies to people, not to premises. It covers all employees in all employment situations. We will not be concerned with problems of interpretation as to whether or not certain premises are, or are not, a factory, a shop, an office, etc. The nature or location of the work is irrelevant. At one stroke, the Act brought within the ambit of protective legislation some 7–8,000,000 people (the "new entrants") who were hitherto not covered by the various statutes in force, eg Factories Act 1961. Subject only to the exception in respect of domestic employees (see below) every employer needs to know and to carry out duties required under the Act. Further, the Act requires all employers to take account of the fact that persons who are not in their employment may be affected by work activities, and there are additional duties in this regard. Obligations are placed on those who manufacture, design, import or supply articles or substances for use at work to ensure that these can be used in safety and are without risks to health.

3.3 Next, the Act is basically a criminal statute, and does not give rise to any civil liability (but see para 3.14). No tort action in respect of a breach of statutory duty can be brought, for prevention and punishment (rather than compensation) is the key-note. However, to assist the courts when interpreting the Act, regard may be had to legal precedents which have arisen from civil as well as criminal proceedings, provided, of course, that it is appropriate to do so in the context. Additionally the inspectorates are given new powers of enforcement in order to eliminate or minimise an actual or potential hazard before an incident occurs, rather than take action afterwards.

3.4 Finally, there are some provisions which are designed to bring about a greater personal involvement and individual responsibility so as to actively encourage and promote health and safety, being part of the greater self-regulatory system which the Robens Committee thought to be desirable. Safety policies, safety representatives and safety committees should increase the awareness that the main responsibility for the elimination of accidents and ill-health in employment lies with those who create the dangers.

3.5 The new requirements that employers should carry out assessments (see para 6.150) will focus minds on key problem areas, health surveillance and monitoring should assist in dealing with certain illnesses at an early stage, and also act as a warning sign of possible deficiences in health and safety practices. Employers are required to give information, training, etc, not only to their own employees, but sometimes to non-employees. In other words, health and safety is now high on the agenda.

3.6 How successful the Act has been, or will be in the future, is something we may never know. It is impossible to state how many accidents did not happen as a result of this legislation. Statistics may illustrate trends, and perhaps even lead to some satisfaction, but these are notoriously inconclusive. New machinery, new processes, new designs, new substances, etc may decrease hazards irrespective of legislative arrangements. If nothing else, the Act should play a positive role in ensuring that technological change does not increase the exposure to risks at work. On the other hand, the increasing consciousness of the problems, the growing acceptance that health and safety is the concern of all—from the most senior person in the organisation to the most junior—the vast increase in training opportunities and the general streamlining of legal rules should all have a considerable effect in reducing the annual accident figures progressively each year. There must be a limit, however, to the power of the law to influence human conduct, for a majority of accidents occur in situations where there is no actual breach of a legislative provision, but are regarded as common occurrences or human failings (slipping, tripping, falling, etc), which legal control can only prevent if it can induce a state of mind. A knowledge of the legal framework may make a positive contribution to this.

3.7 The Act is sometimes referred to as an "enabling Act". This is merely descriptive of the role envisaged by the Robens Committee, ie that all the old law should be progressively swept away, and replaced by a single statute, supplemented by regulations and Codes of Practice. Since 1974, this pattern has been adopted, so that by the turn of the century the major legislative provisions which were pre-1974 will have considerably reduced significance or relevance.

3.8 The Act is divided into four parts. Part I will be the subject of this chapter; Part II provides for the continuation of the Employment Medical Advisory Service (see chapter 2); Part III (now repealed) made amendments to the Building Regulations (and was the main reason for the curious addition of the word "etc" in the title of the Act) and Part IV contains some miscellaneous provisions. There are also ten schedules to the Act.

Application of the Act

3.9 The Act applies to all employment in Great Britain (ie England, Wales and Scotland) but not to Northern Ireland. However, by the Health and Safety at Work (Northern Ireland) Order 1978 the provisions of the Act have been repeated so far as Northern Ireland is concerned, with some modifications. The Act does not apply to the Isle of Man or to the Channel Islands, but does apply to the Isles of Scilly.

3.10 By the Health and Safety at Work (Application outside Great Britain) Order 1989 the provisions of the Act have been extended to cover persons working on offshore installations and pipeline work within British territorial waters or the UK sector of the continental shelf, as well as to certain diving and construction work carried on within territorial waters. These provisions are in addition to the Mineral Workings (Offshore Installations) Act 1971 and the Regulations made thereunder, the Petroleum and Submarine Pipelines Act 1975, and the Offshore Safety Act 1992.

Application to the Crown

3.11 The provisions of Part I apply to the Crown with the exception of ss.21–25 and 33–42. This means that it is not possible to issue improvement or prohibition notices against the Crown or in respect of Crown premises. However, HSE has taken to issuing Crown Notices (see para 3.103) which have a moral effect. Also, it is not possible to prosecute the Crown for any offence committed (based on the theory that the Queen cannot be prosecuted in her own courts), but s.48(2) provides that ss.33–42 (ie the criminal sanctions sections) shall apply to persons in the service of the Crown as they apply to other persons. This means that an individual Crown employee who commits an offence (eg under ss.7, 8, 37, etc) can be prosecuted if necessary. By the National Health Service and Community Care Act 1990, s.60, the National Health Service is not to be regarded as part of the Crown for the purpose of health and safety legislation. Thus prosecutions may be carried out and enforcement notices issued against the NHS.

Trainees

3.12 By the Health and Safety (Training for Employment) Regulations 1990 a person is to be treated as being at work for the purpose of HSWA if he is being provided with relevant training, which is defined as being work experience provided pursuant to a training course or programme, or training for employment, except training provided on a course run by an educational establishment, or training given under a contract of employment. In other words, for the purposes of HSWA, persons on all training for employment schemes (as opposed to training in employment) are to be regarded as employees at work, even though technically they are not employees. The employer, for the purpose of the regulations, is the person whose undertaking is providing the training.

Domestic employees

3.13 Section 51 provides that none of the statutory provisions shall apply in relation to a person by reason only that he employs another, or is himself employed, as a domestic servant in a private household.

Civil liability (Section 47)

3.14 As we have already noted, HSWA is essentially a criminal statute enforced by criminal sanctions. Section 47 specifically provided that nothing in Part I (which contains the relevant provisions so far as this book is concerned) shall be construed as conferring any right of action in any civil proceedings in respect of a failure to comply with any duty imposed by ss.2–7 or a contravention of s.8. Thus no civil action under HSWA can be brought for a breach of statutory duty (compare, for example, the situation with regard to the Factories Act, etc, see chapter 5) as a result of an accident. However, if a prosecution is brought under the Act and is successful, it would appear, under the provisions of s.11 of the Civil Evidence Act 1968, that the fact of that prosecution may be raised and pleaded in an action for damages caused by negligence, leaving the defendant with the burden of proving that he was not negligent. Additionally, s.47(2) provides that any breach of duty imposed by health and safety regulations shall be actionable in a civil claim except in so far as the regulations provide otherwise. HSWA does not alter the present rights at common law (see chapter 8), but does not add to them except as stated.

The general purposes

3.15 The provisions of the Act shall have effect with a view to:

(a) securing the health, safety and welfare of persons at work
(b) protecting persons other than persons at work against risks to health or safety arising out of or in connection with the activities of persons at work
(c) controlling the keeping and use of explosives or highly flammable or otherwise dangerous substances, and generally preventing the unlawful acquisition, possession and use of such substances
(d) controlling the emission into the atmosphere of noxious or offensive substances from premises.

3.16 The general purposes of the Health and Safety at Work Act have been extended to include the following:

(a) securing the safety, health and welfare at work of persons on offshore installations or engaged on pipeline works

(b) securing the safety of such installations and preventing accidents on or near them
(c) securing the proper construction and safe operation of pipelines and preventing damage to them, and
(d) securing the safe dismantling, removal and disposal of offshore installations and pipelines (see Offshore Safety Act 1992, s.1, which has the effect of transferring responsibility for all aspects of offshore safety from the Department of Energy to HSE).

3.17 The general purposes of the Health and Safety at Work Act shall also include safety matters relating to on-shore pipelines, in particular:

(a) securing the proper construction and safe operation of pipelines and preventing damage to them
(b) ensuring that, in the event of an accidental escape or ignition of anything in a pipeline, immediate notice of the event will be given to persons who will or may have to discharge duties or take steps in consequence of the happening of the event, and
(c) protecting the public from personal injury, fire, explosions and other dangers arising from the transmission, distribution, supply or use of gas (including liquid gas) (see Offshore Safety Act 1992, s.2(1), repealing, *inter alia*, s.18(1) of the Gas Act 1986).

3.18 The general scheme of things is to progressively replace all the enactments specified in Schedule 1 of the Act (and regulations, etc made thereunder) by a system of regulations and Approved Codes of Practice which are designed to maintain and improve standards of health, safety and welfare. Since 1974, this policy has been steadily followed. Parts of the Factories Act have already been repealed in addition to other enactments, regulations have been introduced, and Codes of Practice have been approved. It is therefore essential for all concerned to keep up-to-date with the latest developments with a field of law which is constantly changing.

The general duties (s.2(1))

It shall be the duty of every employer to ensure, so far as is reasonably practicable, the health, safety and welfare at work of all his employees

3.19 This is the prime duty under the Act, in respect of which all the other subsequent duties imposed by s.2 are more detailed. As we have seen (see chapter 1), what is reasonably practicable is a question of fact and evidence in each case.

3.20 The duty extends to employees while they are in the course of their employment, but is not confined to the times when the employee is actually working. It is broken if the employer makes available unsafe plant or an unsafe system of work, etc, even though these have not yet been put into operation or use. In *Bolton*

Metropolitan Borough Council v Malrod Insulations Ltd, contractors were engaged to strip asbestos insulation, for which task a special decontamination unit was to be used. Before the work had commenced, an Environmental Health Officer inspected the decontamination unit, and discovered several defects, which could have given rise to electric shocks. The contractors were prosecuted for a breach of s.2(1) and 2(2) of the Act. In their defence, it was argued that no offence could be committed until the employees were "at work" using the decontamination unit. The argument was upheld in the Crown Court, but the decision was reversed by the Divisional Court. The employer's duty under s.2(2) was "to provide" safe plant and safe systems of work, and thus the duty arose in respect of employees who *will be* at work, as well as those who *are* at work. To hold otherwise would mean that an inspector who came on to the premises at the end of a working day and discovered breaches of the law would be powerless to take any action because the employees were not actually at work at the time of the inspection, a conclusion which is not consistent with the statutory health and safety provisions. Further, the duty under s.2(1) of the Act applies to the employer's duty to all his employees, not just to those employees who are engaged on a specific process. An employee can be exposed to a risk of injury from unsafe plant even though he is not engaged on the process or work being carried on.

3.21 The phrase "health, safety and welfare" is not defined. Clearly, health includes mental as well as physical health and safety refers to the absence of any foreseeable injury. Welfare, on the other hand, is a somewhat elusive concept. Schedule 3 of HSWA provides that regulations may be made for "Securing the provision of specified welfare facilities for persons at work, including, in particular, such things as adequate water supply, sanitary conveniences, washing and bathing facilities, ambulance and first aid arrangements, cloakroom accommodation, sitting facilities and refreshment facilities." It is clear that this list is not an exhaustive definition of welfare, and indeed, some of them may well be regarded as health matters. Social clubs may be generally regarded as being part of a firm's welfare facilities, but since employees do not use them in the course of their employment, they are not within the scope of the Act. There is no obligation on an employer to concern himself with health, safety or welfare matters which arise outside the employment, although this is being done increasingly as part of advanced personnel policies.

Particular duties (s.2(2))

3.22 The above general duty is particularised by five specific duties which are placed on the employer, which spell out the general duty in detail. These duties, which as we have noted are essentially criminal in nature, are very similar to the duties of care which an employer owes to his employees at common law and which are frequently raised in civil actions (see chapter 8). They must all be fulfilled "as far as is reasonably practicable". Thus meanings which have been given to certain words and phrases in civil actions may be used as an aid in interpreting the words used in the Act, for although the issues in criminal and civil proceedings are different, the canons of statutory interpretations (see para 1.80) generally apply to both types of proceedings.

3.23 It must further be borne in mind that the particular duties which follow are spelt out in even greater detail by the new regulations outlined in chapter 4, ie Management of Health and Safety at Work, Provision and Use of Work Equipment, Workplace (Health, Safety and Welfare), Personal Protective Equipment at Work, Manual Handling Operations and Health and Safety (Display Screen Equipment). Thus, s.2 of HSWA must be read in conjunction with these regulations.

To provide and maintain plant and systems of work that are safe and without risks to health (s.2(2)(a))

3.24 An employer "provides" when the plant, etc is in a place where it can be easily come by, or when he gives clear directions as to where it can be obtained (*Norris v Syndic Manufacturing Co.*). Thus, in *Woods v Durable Suites* the employee was working with a synthetic glue, which could cause dermatitis unless certain precautions were taken. The employers instructed the employee in the proper procedure to be followed and provided washing facilities and a barrier cream, but the employee did not take the necessary precautions and contracted dermatitis. It was held that the employers had fulfilled their common law duty of care, for they had provided the necessary precautions. They were under no duty to compel the employee to use the barrier cream or to stand over him to ensure that he used the washing facilities.

3.25 The duty to provide may be observed even though the employee does not use that which is provided. In certain cases, however, it has been held that the employers' common law duty may be something more than the passive one of providing and includes the more active duty of encouraging, persuading and even insisting on the use of the precautions (see chapter 8). On the other occasions the law may well go further and place an obligation on the employee *to use* the precautions supplied, eg under the Personal Protective Equipment at Work Regulations 1992, see chapter 4. But if the employer fails to provide the necessary equipment, or provides defective equipment, he will be in breach of his duty. In *Lovett v Blundells and Crompton & Co.* the employee erected a makeshift staging in order to do his work. This collapsed and he was injured. It was held that the employer had not provided adequate equipment for the work to be done in safety.

3.26 Once having provided the necessary plant, etc the employer must ensure that it is maintained and in a condition which makes it fit for use. Plant and systems of work are "maintained" safe when they are kept in efficient working order at all times. Thus if there is a single failure of a component, this will normally be sufficient evidence that the equipment has not been properly maintained. Under the absolute provisions of the Factories Act 1961 it would not be a defence for an employer to argue that he could not have discovered the defect before an accident occurred, (*Galashields Gas Co. v O'Donnell*) but under s.2(2)(a) the burden on the employer is to fulfil his obligation so far as is reasonably practicable. Maintenance is a matter of forethought and foresight. There must be a proper system of regular inspection with the reporting of defects to a responsible person. In *Barkway v South Wales Transport*

Co. a coach crashed owing to a burst tyre and the plaintiff's husband was killed. Although the defendants could show a system of testing and inspecting tyres, they did not require their drivers to report incidents which could produce impact fractures and were thus held liable for negligence.

3.27 Maintenance also requires the rectification of known defects, either by repairs or replacement, as necessary. In *Taylor v Rover Car Co.* the employee was injured when a splinter of steel flew from the top of a chisel he was using. The chisel had previously been used by a leading hand on the production line, who had himself been injured when a splinter had flown off, but this incident was not reported. It was held that the employers were liable, for they should have had a system whereby defective tools were reported and withdrawn from circulation and replaced by ones which were not defective.

3.28 Routine maintenance, as well as revealing defects, can prolong the life of the plant or machinery, etc, thus creating a cost benefit for the employer as well as making it safe for the user. It is further suggested that manufacturers of articles for use at work should include maintenance schedules along with the articles they sell, as being part of "the conditions necessary to ensure that when put to use it will be safe and without risks to health" (see s.6, below).

3.29 Section 53(1) states that the term "plant" includes any machinery, equipment or appliance. In accordance with the *ejusdem generis* rule of interpretation, it is unlikely that the word includes "buildings" of any kind (contrary to the popular use of the word) as these would be covered by s.4 of the Act (see para 3.59). But the definition is not exhaustive, and there is no indication of what else may be included. At common law, a van was held to be "plant" (see *Bradford v Robinson Rentals*, para 8.31).

3.30 Systems of work was defined by Lord Greene in *Speed v Thomas Swift & Co. Ltd*, who said, "It may be the physical layout of the job—the setting of the stage, so to speak—the sequence in which the work is to be carried out, the provision in proper cases of warnings and notices, and the issue of special instructions". To this we may add the provision of safety equipment and the taking of adequate safety precautions. Whatever system of work is adopted, the employer must ensure, so far as is reasonably practicable, that it is a safe one.

To ensure the safety and the absence of risks to health in connection with the use, handling, storage and transport of articles and substances (s.2(2)(b))

3.31 Thus in appropriate cases, protective clothing, proper equipment and tools, etc must be provided in relation to use. The handling must be organised in a safe manner, eg excessive weights should be considered, contamination should be guarded against, dangerous parts should be covered, etc. Storage facilities must be adequate and safe, eg proper racks provided, fork-lift truck drivers must be instructed in proper stacking techniques. The transportation must be done in a safe manner: loads must be properly tied down, with an even distribution of weight, goods must be packed properly so as to be safe when being transported.

To provide such information, instruction, training and supervision as is necessary to ensure the health and safety at work of all employees (s.2(2)(c))

3.32 Thus, information must be given to employees about the hazards involved in the work, and the precautions to be taken to avoid them. Since the employer will, in most cases, be in a better position to know of those hazards, he must provide the information, not wait for the employees to request it. In addition to the general requirement of s.2(2), there are a number of specific statutory provisions which require an employer to provide detailed information to employees in particular circumstances (see chapter 4).

3.33 The information which is provided must be accurate and meaningful. In *Vacwell Engineering Ltd v BDH Chemicals Ltd* the plaintiff purchased a quantity of boron tribromide from the defendant. The chemical was delivered in ampoules which were labelled "Harmful vapour". The chemical was poured on to some water, and an explosion resulted, causing damage to the plaintiff's premises. It was held that the defendants were liable for negligently labelling a dangerous substance. The information given was misleading and did not accurately describe the hazard.

3.34 Proper and clear instructions must be given as to what is to be done, and what must not be done, for workers performing routine tasks are frequently heedless of their own safety. Greater care must be taken when dealing with employees whose command of English is weak so that they understand clearly the nature of the dangers and the precautions to be taken. Young and inexperienced workers must be given clear instructions.

3.35 The employer's duty to provide information and instruction to ensure the health and safety of his own employees includes a duty to provide such information and instruction to the employees of a subcontractor where this is necessary to ensure the health and safety of the employees. In *R v Swan Hunter Shipbuilders Ltd*, the employers distributed a booklet to their employees giving practical rules for the safety of users of oxygen equipment, in particular warning of the dangers of oxygen enrichment in confined spaces. The booklet was not distributed to employees of a subcontractor except on request. A fire broke out on a ship which the appellants were building and because an employee of a subcontractor left an oxygen hose in the deck, the fire became intense because that part of the ship, which was badly ventilated, became oxygen enriched. As a result, eight workmen were killed. The appellants were prosecuted on indictment for a breach of s.2(2)(a) (failure to provide a safe system of work), s.2(2)(c) (failure to provide information and instruction) and s.3(1) (duty to non-employees, see below). The appellants were convicted in the Crown Court, and an appeal was dismissed by the Court of Appeal. If the provision of a safe system of work for the benefit of an employer's own employees involved the provision of information and instruction as to potential dangers to persons other than his own employees, then the employer was under a duty to provide such information and instruction. In the circumstances, it was reasonably practicable to do so.

3.36 Training in safe working practices should be undertaken on a regular basis; where special courses are available, employees should be required, not merely encouraged, to go on them (eg for fork-lift truck drivers, or when handling heavy weights). Where appropriate, "in-house" training can be given. The employee is under a legal duty to cooperate with the employer (s.7(b), below), and hence a refusal to go on an appropriate training course, as well as being a possible offence under the Act, may well be grounds for fair dismissal (see chapter 9). Sometimes regulations will specify the actual training to be given (eg Abrasive Wheels Regulations 1970), including the syllabus, but otherwise the training may be carried out by the employer or an independent body. As long as it is adequate, the requirements of HSWA will be met.

3.37 A failure to provide training for employees could lead to an improvement notice being issued. In *Sunner v Radford*, a local authority inspector while inspecting a supermarket noticed that a fork-lift truck was not being operated correctly. He also discovered that the two employees who drove the truck had never received any formal training. He served an improvement notice requiring the employer to send the men on a course of training for fork-lift truck drivers, and, on appeal, an industrial tribunal upheld the notice. The employer had failed to provide such training as was reasonably practicable to ensure the safety of employees at work.

3.38 A suitable and satisfactory system of supervision must be provided with properly trained and competent supervisors who have authority to ensure that safety precautions are implemented, safety equipment used, and safe systems followed. Young and inexperienced employees in particular must be properly supervised.

To ensure the maintenance of any place of work under the employer's control in a condition that is safe and without risks to health, and the provision and maintenance of means of access and exit that are safe and without such risks (s.2(2)(d))

3.39 Thus premises must be safe and maintained safe. Obstacles must be removed, dangerous wiring replaced, defective floors and stairs repaired, roads, pavements, pathways, doors, etc must all be safe.

The provision and maintenance of a working environment that is safe, without risks to health, and adequate as regards facilities and arrangements for the welfare of employees at work (s.2(2)(e))

3.40 Thus the employer must pay proper regard for systems of noise control, eliminate noxious fumes and dust, lighting must not be excessive or inadequate. Welfare arrangements and facilities must be adequate, eg toilet accommodation, washing facilities, cloakroom arrangements, etc. Ergonomic factors, such as seating, posture, reaching, etc may also need to be considered.

3.41 It will be recognised that the above statutory duties bear a strong resemblance to those duties owed by an employer to an employee at common law (see chapter 8) spelt out in greater detail. Under s.2 of HSWA these duties may only be enforced by criminal sanctions or by the use of an enforcement notice (see para 3.103).

Safety policies (s.2(3))

3.42 Every employer shall prepare (and as often as may be appropriate revise) a written statement of his general policy with respect to:

(a) the health and safety at work of his employees; and
(b) the organisation and arrangements in force for the time being for carrying out that policy,

and bring the statement and any revision of it to the notice of all his employees.

3.43 However, this duty does not apply to any employer who carries on an undertaking in which for the time being he employs less than five employees (Employers' Health and Safety Policy Statements (Exception) Regulations 1975). In *Osborne v Bill Taylor of Huyton Ltd* the employer owned and controlled 31 betting shops. Each shop employed three people, but two of them were entitled to have a day off work each week during which time replacement relief staff were employed. An improvement notice was served on the employer requiring him to prepare a written safety policy and when he failed to do so he was prosecuted for contravening the notice. The Divisional Court held that the words "for the time being" meant "at any one time" and thus the relief staff were to be excluded when determining the number of employees employed for the purpose of the Exception Regulations. However, the further question to be asked was whether the employer was carrying on 31 separate businesses or one business in 31 different places. In the latter case the employer would not be excluded from the duty to prepare a written safety policy. It was held that there was one business with more than five employees employed at any one time, and therefore the prosecution could succeed. To determine whether there is a single business run through a number of outlets, or whether a person has set up a series of separate businesses (albeit that each of those businesses are of the same nature) it is necessary to look at the manner in which the activities are run. If there is a series of separate legal bodies running each enterprise, almost certainly each will be a separate undertaking. Close control from the centre is a strong indication that there is a single undertaking.

3.44 The drawing up of the safety policy is the beginning of the commitment of the employer to safety and health at work. There is no standard policy, no precedent which can be adopted. Each employer must work it out for himself, bearing in mind the nature of the hazards involved and the precautions and protections needed. General advice on the drawing up of safety policies may be sought from a number of sources (employers' associations, safety organisations, etc) but the responsibility is placed fairly and squarely on the shoulders of each employer. Studies have revealed that whilst some policy statements lay down a general commitment, they lack details of "the organisation and arrangements in force" for the carrying out of the policy. Moreover, there is a need to constantly revise the policy statement when appropriate.

3.45 The Act requires the statement to be brought to the notice of all employees. This is not done merely by affixing a policy statement to a notice board. Some employers issue the statement as a paper communication which conforms with the law but is not necessarily good practice, for sheets of paper are frequently lost or destroyed. Perhaps the best method is by introducing the policy statement on an induction course and publishing it together with the works rules or information handbook which is given to employees. Particular attention should be paid to those employees whose command of English is limited and steps must be taken to draw attention to the policy in a language they understand.

3.46 A safety policy can be drawn up in the following manner.

General statement

3.47 This will specify the commitment of the employer to a standard at least as high as that required by law. It should make clear that management considers it to be a binding commitment and that safety will rank as a prominent and permanent feature of all activities. The objectives should be spelt out, eg to reduce and eliminate accidents, to achieve a safe and healthy working environment, and so forth.

Organisation

3.48 The distribution of responsibility should be detailed, starting with the management board, through the different levels of management, supervision, safety officer and safety representatives, medical personnel and ending with the responsibilities of employees. Where there are a number of sites or departments, responsibilities should be fixed as appropriate. It is probably good practice to identify the person responsible in each case, either by name or by position. The lines of communication for dealing with grievances, complaints or suggestions about health and safety matters should be stated.

Arrangements in force

3.49 The existence of the arrangements must be stated in relation to the objectives to be achieved in each case. For example, on health, state details of the first aid facilities, fire precautions, medical arrangements, etc. On safety, specify training, supervision, safety equipment, safety precautions, safety rules, maintenance practices, etc. On welfare, specify washing facilities provided, requirements relating to ventilation, heating, lighting, etc. Stress the need for all employees to be involved in good housekeeping, to cooperate with management and to report any defects or potential hazards.

Review

3.50 Safety policies should be reviewed (and revised if necessary) when there are changes in the law, new processes introduced, new hazards revealed, or when health and safety problems are revealed.

3.51 Safety policies cannot be adequately reviewed unless there is periodic monitoring. This may well be one of the functions of the safety committee but the prime responsibility must always rest with senior management. The statement should be dated and signed by the senior person in the organisation so that employees will recognise that it is an authoritative document and will note the ongoing commitment.

3.52 Safety policies should be seen to work. They should not be a mere formality to satisfy the curiosity of visiting inspectors.

General duties owed to others (s.3)

3.53 Every employer is under a duty to conduct his undertaking in such a way as to ensure, so far as is reasonably practicable, that persons not in his employment who may be affected thereby are not exposed to risks to their health and safety. A similar duty is imposed on self-employed persons, in respect of themselves and other persons not being their employees (s.3(2)). The Genetic Manipulation Regulations 1989 provide that the reference to a self-employed person shall include a reference to any person who is not an employer or employee in relation to any activity involving genetic manipulation. This would include, for example, a research student.

3.54 Section 3 is designed to give protection to the general public to ensure that they are not at risk from industrial hazards, etc. Thus, it would be an offence under the Act (irrespective of any other heading of legal liability) if a construction firm were to permit an explosion to take place which causes windows to break in nearby houses, or for a firm to permit the seepage of a poisonous chemical into a private water supply. Visitors who come on to the employer's premises, subcontractors who come to work there, students who are on a university campus, etc are all within the class of persons who may be affected by the way the undertaking is being carried on. Whether such people have a right of civil action is irrelevant to the criminal liability of the employer in respect of a breach of the duty.

Further, "the risks" to which non-employees should not be exposed to include the possibility of danger or injury, and s.3(1) is not confined to actual accidents or instances of ill health. In *R v Board of Trustees of the Science Museum*, it was alleged that an air-conditioning system at the Science Museum exposed members of the public to risks to their health from Legionella Pneumophilia (LP), because there was a failure to institute a system of regular cleaning and disinfection, etc. For the Museum it was argued that the prosecution had to show that members of the public actually inhaled the bacterium, but this argument was rejected by the Court of Appeal. The term "risk" conveys the notion of possible danger, not actual danger. This is in accordance with the purposive construction which the courts give to the Act so as to promote the preventative aims.

3.55 The duty imposed by s.3(1) is wide enough to include the duty to provide information and instruction to persons who are not in the employer's employment (*R v Swan Hunter Shipbuilders Ltd* (see para 3.35)).

3.56 The words "conduct his undertaking" do not appear to apply to the effects which a deleterious product may have on an ultimate consumer, where the ordinary law of negligence (as in *Donoghue v Stevenson*) or the provisions of the Consumer Protection Act 1987) will apply.

3.57 However, a person may be "conducting his undertaking" even though his "business" is closed. In *R v Mara*, the accused was a director of a small cleaning company which had a contract to clean the premises of a supermarket each weekday morning. It was also agreed that the cleaning machines used by the company would be left on the supermarket's premises to be used by the latter's employees. The accused knew that an electric cable on a cleaning machine was defective. An employee of the supermarket used the cleaning machine and—because of the defect—was electrocuted. The accused was charged with consenting to and conniving with (see s.37, *post*) a breach of the Health and Safety at Work Act s.3(1), in that the company had failed to conduct its undertaking in such a way as to ensure that persons not in its employment were not exposed to risks to their health and safety. For the accused it was argued that at the time of the accident the company was not carrying on its undertaking because it was closed and the only undertaking being carried on was that of the supermarket. This contention was rejected by the Court of Appeal. It was the business of the company to provide cleaning services. To do this it cleaned the premises on weekday mornings and left the cleaning machines for the use of employees of the supermarket. Those employees were clearly persons who may be affected by the way the company carried on its undertaking and the conviction was upheld.

3.58 In such cases as may be prescribed, and in the circumstances and prescribed manner, it shall be the duty of every employer and every self-employed person to give to persons who are not his employees, but who may be affected by the way he conducts his undertaking, the prescribed information about such aspects of the way he conducts his undertaking as might affect their health or safety (s.3(3)). This subsection is clearly designed to ensure that persons living near to some hazardous operation have some form of advance notification of what they may expect if something goes wrong and the necessary action they should take. To date, no regulations requiring the disclosure of any such information have been made.

However, under the Control of Industrial Major Accident Hazards Regulations 1984 (CIMAH), as amended (see para 6.99) employers who control installations carrying out certain dangerous activities must prepare a site emergency plan for dealing with any major accident.

General duties of controllers of premises (s.4)

3.59 This section imposes duties on people who have the control over non-domestic premises, or of the means of access thereto or exit therefrom, or of any plant or substances therein, which are used by persons (who are not employees) as a place of work or as a place where they may use plant or substances provided there for their use. The duty is to take such measures as it is reasonable for a person in his position to take to ensure, so far as is reasonably practicable, that the premises, the means of access and exit, and any plant or substance in or provided for use there, is or are safe and without risks to health.

3.60 Residential premises are clearly domestic premises, but the common parts of those premises, ie those parts which are not exclusively used for domestic purposes, are non-domestic. In *Westminster City Council v Select Managements Ltd*, the defendants owned and managed a block of flats. An improvement notice was served on them relating to the lifts and electrical installations which serviced the common parts of the flats. They appealed against the notice, arguing that the lifts, etc were "domestic premises" within the meaning of s.4 of the Act. The validity of the notice was upheld by the Court of Appeal. The common parts of the block of flats (eg the hallway, lift, stairs, landing, etc) were non-domestic premises. These common parts were available to persons who were not in the employment of the flat owners as a place of work or as a place where they may use plant (eg the lifts). Thus an improvement notice could properly be served.

3.61 It would appear from this decision that premises will be regarded as being non-domestic if they are not in the exclusive occupation of the occupants of a private dwelling.

3.62 Section 4 is the criminal counterpart of the civil liability contained in the Occupiers' Liability Act 1957 (and the Occupiers' Liability (Scotland) Act 1960) (see para 8.83) and would apply in those cases where an employee is using premises which are not controlled by the employer, eg a visiting window cleaner. However, the effect of the section is somewhat wider than that. Thus a coin-operated launderette would be covered, even though no one was employed there, for a customer would be using plant or substances provided for use. Universities would have a duty under this section to ensure that their premises (libraries, etc) are safe; schools have duties towards their pupils using laboratories, etc.

3.63 Further, a person who, by virtue of any contract or tenancy, has an obligation to maintain or repair any premises used by others as a place of work or as a place where they may use plant or substances, or to maintain the means of access or exit, or to ensure the safety or absence of risks to health arising from the use of such plant or substances, will be the person upon whom the above duty will lie, s.4(3). For example, a maintenance contractor who is responsible for the maintenance of plant, or a specialist adviser who has to deal with the control of a dangerous substance, will have those duties imposed by this section to persons other than his employees.

3.64 When a person makes available premises for the use of another person, the reasonableness of the measures taken to ensure the safety of those premises must be determined in the light of the controller's knowledge of the anticipated use of those premises and of his knowledge of the actual use. In *Austin Rover Group Ltd v Inspector of Factories*, an employee of a firm of subcontractors was killed while working on the premises of Austin Rover. On the facts of the case, Austin Rover had given clear instructions, and the accident was caused by employees of the subcontractor acting contrary to those instructions. The prosecution of Austin Rover was dismissed. If premises are not a reasonably foreseeable cause of injury to anyone acting in a way in which a human being may reasonably be expected to act in circumstances which may reasonably be expected to occur, then it would not be reasonable to take further measures to prevent the occurrence of unknown and unexpected events.

3.65 For the purpose of s.4, the premises in question must be used by the person in control by way of a trade, business or other undertaking (whether for profit or not). The question may well arise as to whether the word "undertaking" is to be construed *ejusdem generis* with "trade or business", as implying some form of commercial activity.

Duty to prevent pollution (s.5)

3.66 Every person having control of any premises of a class prescribed shall use the best practicable means for preventing the emissions into the atmosphere from the premises of noxious or offensive substances, and for rendering harmless and inoffensive such substances as may be emitted. The "means" to be used include a reference to the manner in which the plant is used, the supervision of any operation involving the emission of the noxious or offensive substances, as well as any device used to prevent them entering the atmosphere or for rendering them harmless.

3.67 The Health and Safety (Emissions into the Atmosphere) Regulations 1983, as amended, contains the list of prescribed premises (see Schedule 1) and then goes on to list the substances which are deemed to be noxious or offensive (see Schedule 2).

3.68 The standard of "best practicable means" is the highest standard short of absolute liability. A comparison may be made with the Environmental Protection Act 1990, which requires that for all prescribed processes, the Best Available Technique Not Entailing Excessive Cost (BATNEEC) must be used to control pollution.

3.69 Additionally, we may note the new requirements of pollution control laid down in the Environmental Protection Act 1990, which introduced a new, two-tiered system of control. Processes covered by the Act are listed in the Environmental Protection (Prescribed Processes and Substances) Regulations 1991. Those classified as "Part A" processes are subject to a new regime of Integrated Pollution Control, administered by HM Inspectorate of Pollution, whereas "Part B" processes remain the responsibility of local authorities, who are only concerned with air pollution. This new system will run parallel with s.5 of HSWA until all the prescribed processes have been brought under the Environmental Protection Act regime, which is likely to occur in 1997.

3.70 It should further be noted that by the Control of Industrial Air Pollution (Transfer of Powers of Enforcement) Regulations 1987, the responsibility for the enforcement of s.5 of HSWA has been transferred away from HSC to the Secretary of State for the Environment.

General duties of designers, manufacturers, importers and suppliers (s.6)

3.71 Section 6 lays down duties on any person who designs, manufactures, imports or supplies any article for use at work, and on any person who manufactures, imports or supplies any substance for use at work. The basic objective is to introduce safety measures at source, rather than leave this to the ultimate user. Before we consider the nature of these duties, we must first ascertain the scope of the above words.

3.72 "An article for use at work" is defined as being "any plant designed for use or operation (whether exclusively or not) by persons at work and any article designed for use as a component in any such plant". The word "plant" includes "any machinery, equipment or appliance". A "substance" is "any natural or artificial substance (including micro-organisms) whether in solid or liquid form, or in the form of gas or vapour" (s.53). "Work" in this connection means at work as an employee or as a self-employed person. Thus a sale to a "do-it-yourself" enthusiast is not within s.6, for although he may be working, he is not at work. Consumer sales are not included within the Act, but since s.53 states that the article need not be exclusively designed for use at work, an item which is capable of being used at work is within the scope of the section even though it is also capable of being a consumer item. It may be that a test will emerge which asks if it was reasonably foreseeable that an employer would purchase the item for use at work.

3.73 The article or substance must be "for use". Thus if it is part of the stock-in-trade, or is purchased for resale purposes, the section does not apply. Nor does it apply to goods which are manufactured, etc for export, for the Act does not apply extra-territorially.

3.74 "Supply" in this connection means the supply of an article or substances by way of sale, lease, hire or hire purchase, whether as a principal or as an agent for another. However, s.6(9) recognises the commercial nature of hire-purchase agreements, conditional sales agreements, and credit-sales agreements, and draws a distinction between the ostensible supplier and the effective supplier. The ostensible supplier is in reality merely financing the transaction even though in the course of the transaction he may become the legal owner of the goods in question. The liability under s.6 is on the effective supplier, ie the manufacturer, etc, who sells to the finance company, who then sells to the customer. A similar provision is to be found in the Health and Safety (Leasing Arrangements) Regulations 1992, whereby if the ostensible supplier is merely acting as a financier for a leasing arrangement made between the effective supplier and the customer, then, subject to certain conditions, the effective supplier and not the ostensible supplier will have the duties of s.6 imposed on him.

3.75 It will be noted that in respect of articles the designer has certain duties, as well as manufacturers, importers and suppliers. It is not clear whether this means the person who actually designs the product or the employer of the designer. It is likely that HSE policy will be to leave the employee to be prosecuted under s.7, and take action against the employer of the designer under s.6. This is because subsection (7) of s.6 reminds us that the duties only apply "to things done in the course of a trade, business or undertaking carried on by him" and presumably it is the employer of the designer who is carrying on the trade, business or undertaking. If the employer had no reason to suspect that the designer was incompetent, or had made a faulty design, presumably he could rely on the defence that he took all steps which were reasonably practicable.

3.76 Section 6 of HSWA was amended by the Consumer Protection Act 1987 (Schedule 3). It is clear that there is a close connection between occupational safety and consumer safety generally, and indeed it will frequently occur that goods are manufactured, etc for consumers as well as for persons at work. It was recognised that it is strongly desirable to introduce enforcement at the earlier point of supply and the ultimate use for which the goods are intended should not be particularly relevant. In other words, safety has to be built into the design and manufacture of the product, rather than at the user end. Thus more extensive obligations were placed on those who put goods into circulation. A new subsection (6(1)A) was added relating to articles of fairground equipment, although this is more for the protection of the general public than for persons at work. Again, however, the obligations relating to safety were placed at the earlier point in time, ie with the manufacturer, etc.

3.77 Section 6 lays down six duties in respect of articles, and five duties in respect of substances.

Articles

3.78 (1) It shall be the duty of any person who designs, manufactures, imports or supplies any article for use at work to ensure, so far as is reasonably practicable, that the article is so designed and constructed that it will be safe and without risks to health at all times when it is being set, used, cleaned or maintained by a person at work. However, s.6(10) goes on to state that the absence of safety, or, a risk to health shall be disregarded in so far as it is shown to be an occurrence which could not reasonably be foreseen. Further, in determining whether the duty has been performed, regard shall be paid to any relevant information or advice which has been provided by the designer, manufacturer, importer or supplier.

3.79 (2) Designers, manufacturers, importers and suppliers must carry out (or arrange for the carrying out) of such testing and examination as may be necessary for the performance of the above duty, but there is no need to repeat any testing or examination which has previously been carried out, in so far as it is reasonable for him to rely on the results thereof.

3.80 (3) Designers, manufacturers, importers and suppliers must take such steps as are necessary to ensure that the person supplied by him with the article is provided with adequate information about the use for which it has been designed or tested, and about any condition necessary to ensure that it will be safe and without risks to health when it is being set, used, cleaned or maintained.

3.81 (4) Designers, manufacturers, importers and suppliers must take such steps as are necessary to secure, so far as is reasonably practicable, that persons who have been provided with information are also provided with any revisions of the information as are necessary by reason of it becoming known that there is a serious risk to health or safety.

3.82 (5) It is the duty of designers and manufacturers (but not importers or suppliers) to carry out (or arrange for the carrying out of) any necessary research with a view to the discovery and elimination or minimisation of any risks to health or safety to which the design or article may give rise. Again there is no need to repeat any research which has already been done insofar as it is reasonable to rely on the results thereof.

3.83 (6) It shall be the duty of any person who erects or installs any article for use at work in any premises where the article is to be used by persons at work, to ensure, so far as is reasonably practicable, that nothing about the way the article is erected or installed makes it unsafe or a risk to health when it is being set, used, cleaned or maintained by a person at work.

Substances

3.84 (1) It shall be the duty of any person who manufactures, imports or supplies any substance to ensure, so far as is reasonably practicable, that the substance will be safe and without risks to health at all times when it is being used, handled, processed, stored or transported by a person at work or in premises to which s.4 of the Act (see para 3.59) applies. Again, the absence of risks to health or safety may be disregarded insofar as the occurrence was one which could not be reasonably foreseen, and regard shall also be had to any relevant information or advice provided by the person by whom the substance was manufactured, imported or supplied.

3.85 (2) To carry out or arrange for the carrying out of such testing and examination as may be necessary to perform the above mentioned duty. However, it is not necessary to repeat any testing or examination which may have been previously carried out insofar as it is reasonable for him to rely on the results thereof.

3.86 (3) To take such steps as are necessary to secure that persons supplied by him with the substance are provided with adequate information about any risks to health or safety to which the inherent properties of the substance may give rise, about the results of any relevant tests carried out and about any conditions necessary to ensure that the substance will be safe and without risks to health at all times when it is being used, handled, processed, stored, transported and disposed of.

3.87 (4) To take such steps as are necessary to secure, so far as is reasonably practicable, that persons supplied with the information are provided with all revisions of the information as are necessary by reason of it becoming known that there is a serious risk to health or safety.

3.88 (5) A manufacturer of a substance is under a duty to carry out (or arrange to carry out) any necessary research with a view to discovering and, so far as is reasonably practicable, the elimination or minimisation of any risks to health or safety to which the substance may give rise at all times when it is being used, handled, processed, stored or transported. Again, there is no need to repeat any research which has been carried out previously insofar as it is reasonable to rely on the results thereof.

3.89 The above duties only extend to a person in respect of things done in the course of a trade, business or other undertaking carried on by him (whether for profit or not) and to matters within his control, s.6(7). This appears to exclude employees from the scope of s.6 (though not, of course, from s.7). Whether the matters are within the control of a person is a question of fact. If he has the right of control, but fails or refuses to exercise it, the matters are still within his control.

Indemnity clauses (s.6(8))

3.90 Where a person designs, manufactures, imports or supplies an article to or for another person on the basis of a written undertaking by that other person to take specific steps sufficient to ensure, so far as is reasonably practicable, that the article will be safe and without risks to health when it is being set, used, cleaned or maintained, the undertaking will have the effect of relieving the first-mentioned person from the duty of ensuring that it is designed and constructed so as to be safe, to such an extent as is reasonable having regard to the terms of the undertaking. Thus if a person supplies secondhand machinery to another on the basis of that other's assurance that he will ensure that it is properly serviced and examined before being put to use, or where a manufacturer supplies machinery made specifically to certain specifications or to a certain design, the supplier or manufacturer may be relieved from legal responsibility under s.6(1)(a). However, there must be a written assurance, which implies a specific commitment in the instant case, not a general standard commitment. Further, the exclusion is only from the liability under s.6(1)(a), not from the liability imposed by ss.6(1)(b) or 6(1)(c) or 6(2). In other words, the obligations to test, provide information and carry out research, remain. Further, the terms of the undertaking may be looked at to discover the extent to which the designer, etc is to be absolved. HSE appear to take the view that this may lead to a partial relief, depending on the terms of the undertaking, but this may be misleading. A breach of s.6 is a criminal offence; either an offence has been committed or it has not. There is no such thing as "partially guilty". Mitigating circumstances can only arise if an offence has been committed, and the extent of the mitigation will be for the court to determine.

Further liability of importers

3.91 Nothing in s.6(7) or (8) shall relieve an importer of any article or substance from any of his duties under the Act as regards anything done or not done which was within the control of a foreign designer or foreign manufacturer of an article or substance. Thus importers of unsafe products may be liable for the acts or omissions of foreign designers or manufacturers even though they have no control over their activities (s.6(8A)).

The effect of section 6

3.92 The exact scope and meaning of s.6 has still to receive authoritative judicial interpretation, for although there have been some prosecutions, there appears to be a marked reluctance on either side to challenge these findings in the High Court. The purpose is to try to ensure that acceptable levels of health and safety are built into articles and substances at the design and manufacturing stage, whether by way of compliance with recognised standards (eg BSI) or HSE Guidance Notes or other acceptable tests. But the fact that the manufacturer, etc may be in breach of his duty under s.6 is irrelevant to the employer's liability under the general law to take reasonable care to ensure the health and safety of his employees, or the absolute duty to fence dangerous machinery (s.14 of FA and regulation 11 of the Provision and Use of Work Equipment Regulations 1992). A modern practice is for purchasers of products for use at work to make the contract conditional upon compliance by the supplier with s.6 of HSWA, thus leaving it open for the purchaser to reject the product. It will be recalled that nothing in HSWA gives rise to any civil liability, but it would be an interesting argument if the purchaser rejected a product on the grounds that a failure to comply with the requirements of s.6 rendered the product not of merchantable quality as required by the Sale of Goods Act 1979.

General duties of employees (s.7)

3.93 Two main duties are placed on an employee.

(1) *To take reasonable care for the health and safety of himself and of others who may be affected by his acts or omissions at work*

3.94 Thus an employee who refuses to wear safety equipment or use safety precautions is liable to be prosecuted under this section. Further, if through his carelessness or negligence someone else is injured, he could again be prosecuted. Thus an employee who is prone to horseplay or skylarking, with the result that he or another is injured, commits an offence. A supervisor who encourages an employee to take an unsafe short cut or to remove effective guards may equally be guilty under this section.

(2) *As regards any duty or requirement imposed on his employer or other person by or under any of the relevant statutory provisions, to cooperate with him insofar as is necessary to enable that duty or requirement to be performed or complied with*

3.95 This duty to cooperate is potentially very wide. An employee who announces that he intends to refuse to wear a safety belt or refuses to use a safety precaution provided by his employer in pursuance of the latter's duty under s.2 is failing to cooperate with the employer and thus a prosecution may again succeed.

3.96 In addition, the Management of Health and Safety at Work Regulations 1992 impose further duties on employees to report dangerous situations and shortcomings in the employer's protection arrangements (see para 4.46).

Interference or misuse (s.8)

No person shall intentionally or recklessly interfere with or misuse anything provided in the interests of health, safety or welfare in pursuance of any of the relevant statutory provisions.

3.97 This obligation is again wider than the corresponding provision in the Factories Act which referred to wilful conduct in the sense of being deliberate or perverse. Intentional or reckless conduct does not need to be perverse.

3.98 It should be noted that s.8 is not restricted to employees, and could, for example, apply to visitors, burglars, etc.

Duty not to charge (s.9)

No employer shall levy or permit to be levied on any employee of his any charge in respect of anything done or provided in pursuance of any specific requirement of the relevant statutory provisions.

3.99 This provision originally applied only to the specific requirements of relevant statutory provisions, but most of these have now been repealed by virtue of the Personal Protective Equipment at Work Regulations (see para 4.154). Section 9 now applies to all personal protective equipment deemed necessary by those regulations.

Enforcement of the Act

3.100 A breach of the Act or of health and safety regulations can be dealt with in two ways. First, there are the powers given to the inspectors to issue enforcement notices or to seize and destroy. Second, a prosecution may take place in respect of the commission of a criminal offence.

Enforcement notices (ss.21–24)

3.101 There are two types of enforcement notices which may be issued. These are (1) improvement notice and (2) prohibition notice (which may be immediate or deferred). In addition, the inspectorate have taken to issuing Crown Notices in respect of premises belonging to the Crown, but although there is no legal basis for such notices (it will be recalled that ss.21–24 do not bind the Crown) they have a moral and persuasive effect. A failure to comply with a Crown Notice would lead to an approach by HSE to the Government department concerned, and the Government has announced that in such circumstances the necessary action would be taken to ensure compliance. Moreover, a copy of the Crown Notice will be given to the representatives of the employees, thus drawing attention to the hazard.

3.102 Enforcement notices may be issued by HSE inspectors and Environmental Health Officers of a local authority, all of whom must act within the powers contained in the instrument of their appointment. However, it must be shown that the premises concerned are within the scope of the relevant legislation. In *Dicker & Sons v Hilton* a notice was served requiring the appellant to comply with s.36 of the Factories Act which lays down that air receivers shall be cleaned and examined by a competent person every 26 months (see chapter 4). The notice was cancelled on appeal when the industrial tribunal learned that the appellant ran a one-man business. Since his premises were not a factory (which is defined as being premises where persons are employed) the relevant statutory provision did not apply.

Improvement notice (s.21)

3.103 If an inspector is of the opinion that a person:

(a) is contravening a relevant statutory provision, or
(b) has contravened one or more provisions in circumstances that make it likely that the contravention will continue or be repeated.

then he may serve an improvement notice, which must state:

(a) that he is of that opinion
(b) the provisions in question
(c) particulars of the reasons for his opinion.

and requiring that person to remedy the contravention or matters occasioning the contravention within such period as the notice may specify, but not earlier than 21 days after the notice has been served (which is the period in which the person affected may lodge an appeal against the notice).

3.104 In other words, if there is a statutory requirement that a certain thing shall be done (or not done) an inspector may serve a notice requiring the thing be done (or not done) any time after 21 days. But the fact that a period of grace is permitted does not absolve the person concerned from any criminal or civil liability in respect of anything which may happen prior to the notice taking effect.

3.105 An inspector may (but is not bound to) attach a schedule of the remedial steps to be taken (s.23). If he does, and it is unclear or vague, this will not affect the validity of the notice (*Chrysler (UK) Ltd v McCarthy*) but the industrial tribunal may clarify or alter the schedule.

3.106 If the requirement of the statutory provision is absolute, then there can be no defence in the case of a breach (*Ranson v John Baird*). If the statutory requirement is to do that which is reasonably practicable, the industrial tribunal may exercise its own judgment in accordance with the circumstances of the case when hearing an appeal. Thus in *Roadline (UK) Ltd v Mainwaring*, an improvement notice required an employer to provide heating in a transit shed. The industrial tribunal thought that the cost of doing so was excessive in relation to the marginal improvement which would result.

3.107 Section 3(2) of the Act requires every self-employed person to conduct his undertaking so as to ensure, so far as is reasonably practicable, that he and other persons who may be affected thereby are not exposed to risks to their health and safety. In *Jones v Fishwick* an environmental health officer served an improvement notice on a butcher requiring him to use a chainmail apron whilst boning meat. Applying the "cost/risk" analysis (see para 1.90) the industrial tribunal noted that there had been a number of serious accidents in that industry during boning out procedures, and the cost of acquiring a chainmail apron was £32.40. Thus it was reasonably practicable to take the necessary precautions and the improvement notice was confirmed.

Prohibition notice (s.22)

3.108 If an inspector is of the opinion that activities are being carried on or are likely to be carried on in relation to which any of the relevant statutory provisions apply, and which involve or will involve a risk of serious personal injury, he may serve a prohibition notice. This will:

(a) state that the inspector is of such an opinion
(b) specify the matter which in his opinion is giving or will give rise to the risk of serious personal injury
(c) if the matter also involves a contravention of a relevant statutory provision, he will state the statutory provision, and give particulars of the reason as to why he is of that opinion; and
(d) direct that the activities to which the notice relates shall not be carried on by or under the control of the person on whom the notice has been served unless the matters specified in the notice (and any associated contraventions of statutory provisions) have been remedied.

3.109 The prohibition notice will take effect immediately (if it so declares) or at the end of the period specified in the notice. Again, the inspector may but is not bound to, attach a schedule of the remedial steps to be taken. It will be noted that to issue a prohibition notice, the inspector need only be satisfied that the activities complained of give rise to a risk of serious personal injury and there is no need for there to be a breach of a relevant statutory provision (*Roberts v Day*). However, if he has little information on which to form such an opinion, the notice may be cancelled by the industrial tribunal (*Bressingham Steam Preservation Co. Ltd v Sincock*).

Supplementary provisions (s.23)

3.110 As already noted, an improvement and prohibition notice may (but need not) include directions as to the measures to be taken to remedy any contravention, for the inclusion of details of the precise nature of the breach, and the remedial matters which will have to be taken to remedy it, is an option, not an obligation (*MB Gas Ltd v Veitch*). The measures to be taken may be framed by reference to any Approved Code of Practice or may give a choice as to different ways of taking remedial action. However, if the improvement notice refers to a building, or a matter connected with a building, the notice may not direct that measures shall be taken which are more onerous than the requirements of any building regulations which are applied in respect of new buildings. If the notice refers to the taking of measures affecting the means of escape in the case of fire, the inspector must first consult the fire authority.

3.111 In the case of an improvement notice or a deferred prohibition notice, these may be withdrawn at any time by the inspector before the date on which they are to take effect, and also the period for compliance may be extended by him provided an appeal is not pending.

3.112 Once the matter which has been the subject of an improvement or prohibition notice has been attended to, or the person to whom it is addressed has complied with any requirement contained therein, the activity may be carried on without any further need to contact the inspector, although prudence may well advise such a course in order to ensure that he is satisfied with the rectification. This is particularly important in view of the fact that a failure to comply with the requirements of an enforcement notice exposes the offender to potentially severe punishment. However, the prohibition notice does not lapse on compliance. It continues in force so long as the activities in question are being carried on, for there is no procedure to remove it.

Appeals against enforcement notices (s.24)

3.113 A person on whom a prohibition or improvement notice has been served may appeal to an industrial tribunal within 21 days of its receipt, and the tribunal may confirm or cancel the notice. If it is confirmed, this may be done in its original form, or with such modifications as the industrial tribunal thinks fit. An appeal may be made on a point of law or of fact.

Procedure for appeals

3.114 The Industrial Tribunals (Improvement and Prohibition Notices Appeals) Regulations 1974 lay down the procedure to be followed for the making of an appeal against the decision of an inspector to issue a notice. The appellant shall send a Notice of Appeal to the Central Office of Industrial Tribunal (in Bury St. Edmunds or Glasgow, as appropriate):

(a) stating his name and address for service of documents
(b) the date of the notice appealed against
(c) the address of the premises concerned
(d) the name and address of the respondent (ie the inspector)
(e) particulars of the requirements or directions appealed against, and
(f) the grounds for the appeal.

3.115 The appeal must be lodged within 21 days from the date of the service of the notice on the appellant, although the industrial tribunal may extend the time limit on application if it is satisfied that it was not reasonably practicable to bring the appeal earlier. The 21 day time limit runs from the date of the receipt of the notice (*DH Tools Co. v Myers*).

3.116 If the appeal is against the imposition of an improvement notice the lodging of the appeal will automatically suspend the operation of the notice until the appeal is disposed of. If the appeal is against the imposition of a prohibition notice the appellant may apply for it to be lifted pending the hearing of the appeal, although the notice will continue to take effect despite the fact that an appeal is pending. Since a prohibition notice which takes immediate effect can have serious repercussions on the employer's business, appeals against them are often heard as a matter of urgency, if necessary the very next day (*Hoover Ltd v Mallon*).

3.117 Industrial tribunals have wide powers to deal with preliminary matters prior to the appeal. They can require further and better particulars of the application, grant discovery of documents, issue attendance orders compelling witnesses to attend and so on. As a rule, at least fourteen days' notice of the date of the hearing is given, unless a speedier hearing can be arranged by agreement between the parties. The hearing will normally be in public, unless a party applies for it to be heard in private on grounds of national security or if there may be evidence the disclosure of which would be seriously prejudicial to the interests of the appellants undertaking other than its effect on collective bargaining. Either side may be represented by a solicitor, barrister, or by any other person whom he desires to represent him, including a trade union official or the representative of an employers' association. If written submissions are made, these must be sent to the industrial tribunal seven days prior to the hearing and a copy must be sent at the same time to the other party.

3.118 Each side is entitled to make an opening statement, give evidence on oath, call witnesses, cross-examine witnesses from the other side, introduce documentary or other evidence and make a closing submission. The tribunals do not appear (to date) to have found it necessary to appoint assessors to assist them, but they can, and do, visit the premises in order to make their own informed judgment (eg *Wilkinson v Fronks*).

3.119 The tribunal will then make its decision, which may be a unanimous one or by a majority. If the tribunal consists only of two members, the chairman has a casting vote. The decision may be given orally, or in writing after consideration, but it will always be promulgated in writing and a copy sent to each side.

Grounds for appeal

3.120 An appeal may be lodged on the ground that the inspector lacked the legal power to impose an enforcement notice. This may be because the premises are not covered by the relevant statutory provisions (*Dicker & Sons v Hilton*, above) or because the inspector has misinterpreted the statutory provision in question. But the fact that the employer has complied with the requirements previously laid down by some official authority is not by itself sufficient objection to a subsequent requirement made on grounds of health or safety. In *Hixon v Whitehead*, the appellant had received permission from the district Environmental Health Officer to store 4,000kg of liquified petroleum gas on the premises. As a result of complaints from local residents, another inspector issued a notice limiting the holding to 500kg. The notice was affirmed by the industrial tribunal. There was no question of estoppel arising against the local authority for the tribunal had to consider the avoidance of serious injuries to employees and to other persons who may be affected. Similarly, in *Williamson Cliff Ltd v Tarlington* the company installed a tank containing 29,000 gallons of butane. Planning permission had been given for this after a fire hydrant had been installed. Subsequently another inspector insisted that a spray system be installed. Although the industrial tribunal expressed sympathy with the company which had installed the correct system initially, only to find that they were now required to add another one even though there was no new knowledge in relation to safety, the improvement notice was confirmed. The overriding consideration was the safety of employees and other persons who were likely to be affected should an explosion occur.

Appeals against improvement notices

3.121 An improvement notice may be issued if there is a breach of a relevant statutory provision. This may be HSWA or any other appropriate legislation or regulations. The provision in question may be an absolute one, or prefaced by the requirement that something shall be done "so far as is reasonably practicable". In either case, the issues will be determined largely by the evidence which can be adduced.

3.122 Thus in *Murray v Gadbury* a farmer and his labourer used a rotary grass cutter for 26 years without incident. An inspector issued an improvement notice requiring the farmer to have the cutter guarded in accordance with the Agriculture Machinery Regulations 1962. It was argued that since the machine had been used for such a long time without accident, the notice was unnecessary. The industrial tribunal rejected the appeal and confirmed the notice. The farmer appealed to the Divisional Court, claiming that the law only required him to do that which was reasonably practicable. Again, the appeal was dismissed. The provisions of the regulations were quite clear and were mandatory. On the other hand, in *Associated Dairies v Hartley*, the appellants, who used roller trucks, provided safety footwear for employees at cost price. One day the wheel of a truck ran over the foot of an employee who was not wearing protective footwear, causing a fracture. An inspector issued an improvement notice requiring the employers to provide suitable safety footwear free of charge. An appeal against this notice was allowed. There was no statutory requirement that such footwear should be provided and the obligation under s.2 of HSWA to make arrangements for securing safety at work is subject to the limitation "so far as is reasonably practicable". In determining whether or not a requirement was reasonably practicable, it was proper to take into account the time, trouble and expense of the requirement and to see if it was disproportionate to the risks involved. In this case, it would cost £20,000 in the first year to provide the boots, and £10,000 each year thereafter. On the other hand, the likelihood of such an accident occurring was fairly remote and there was no evidence that employees would use the boots if they were provided free. The tribunal concluded that the present arrangement whereby the employers made safety footwear available was satisfactory.

3.123 The fact that employees are content with existing arrangements is also irrelevant. In *File Tile Distributors v Mitchell* the firm had a cold water supply, with a gas ring and kettle on which they could heat water. Employees used this method without complaint, but an improvement notice requiring the firm to provide running hot water was upheld. The statutory requirements are designed to improve facilities for employees and their acquiescence in lower standards must be discounted.

3.124 Nor is it relevant that there has not been a previous accident or dangerous occurrence. In *Sutton & Co. Ltd v Davies* the inspector issued an improvement notice requiring a machine to be fenced. The company produced evidence that there had not been an accident arising from this particular machine in 27 years. Nonetheless, the notice was affirmed. The requirements of the statute were absolute. One need not wait for an accident to happen before condemning a system as being dangerous or unsafe.

3.125 The fact that it is financially and physically possible to comply with an improvement notice does not mean that it is reasonably practicable to do so. In *West Bromwich Building Society v Townsend* an inspector served an improvement notice on a branch of a building society requiring them to erect anti-bandit screens for the protection of employees. The society appealed to an industrial tribunal and the inspector sought to treat the appeal as a test case for all building societies in the area. The industrial tribunal held that the risks were more than minimal, and that the measures required were financially and physically possible. Thus the notice was confirmed. On a further appeal, the Divisional Court reversed the decision. The industrial tribunal had concentrated on the general desirability of having anti-bandit screens, whereas they should have decided whether screens were needed for this particular office. Further, they had decided that it was physically and financially possible to erect the screens, instead of whether it was reasonably practicable to do so.

3.126 The statutory requirements are not met by providing substitutes, unless some other equally efficacious method is permitted by the legislation. In *Belhaven Brewery v McLean* the inspector issued an improvement notice requiring the company to securely fence transmission machinery by the use of an interlocking device attached to the doors or gates. This would switch off the power when the doors were opened. The company argued that this would be very expensive and they wanted to deal with the problem by erecting safety screens. They would also put up a notice warning employees of the danger. Since the employees were of sufficient intelligence to see that the gates were in position while the plant was working, and since there was a high level of supervision, they wanted the notice cancelled or modified. The notice was confirmed without modification. The requirements of s.13 of the Factories Act could not be met by erecting a screen. Moreover, under s.2(1) of HSWA it was reasonably practicable to fit the interlocking device. The sacrifice in terms of cost was not disproportionate to the risk and dangers.

3.127 Industrial tribunals are more willing to allow appeals to the extent that the appellant requires more time to comply with the requirements of the notice. In *Campion v Hughes* an improvement notice was issued requiring the employer to make changes to the means of escape in the event of fire. It was held that the appeal would be allowed only for the purpose of extending the time for compliance. One of the requirements was that the fire escape be made on land which belonged to the local authority, and consent for doing the work had not been given. An extension of time for a further three months was given in order to enable the employer to obtain the appropriate consent.

3.128 Similarly, in *Porthole Ltd v Brown* a firm enlarged its kitchen on the ground floor and this took away the stairway which led to the first floor lavatory used by employees. An outside stairway was erected to provide the necessary access to the lavatory, and an inspector issued an improvement notice requiring this to be covered. The operation of the notice was suspended to permit the firm to obtain the consent of the landlord and planning permission from the local authority.

3.129 An unusual extension of time arose in the case of *Cheston Woodware Ltd v Coppell*, where an improvement notice was issued requiring the appellant to fit an exhaust appliance to a planning machine used for thicknessing. The firm pointed out that if the machine was being used for thicknessing and surfacing, no such exhaust appliance would be required by the Woodworking Machine Regulations 1974. The tribunal agreed that this was somewhat odd, and postponed the operation of the notice to enable the appellant to apply for an exemption certificate.

3.130 As a general rule, an appeal cannot succeed merely because the employer is unable financially to comply with the requirements. In *Harrison (Newcastle-under-Lyme) Ltd v Ramsey* an improvement notice was issued requiring the company to clean and paint its walls in accordance with s.1(3) of the Factories Act. The company appealed on the ground that it could not afford to spend the money on the work, in view of its grave financial position. The notice was confirmed by the tribunal. To hold otherwise would enable an employer to ignore the statutory requirements because of expense and undercut his competitors who were so complying.

3.131 However, the industrial tribunals are not totally unsympathetic with the financial plight of firms, and will take into account the record of compliance in the past. In particular, they are more likely to postpone (as opposed to cancel) the operation of an improvement notice where the matter concerns a "health" rather than a "safety" aspect (*R A Dyson & Co. Ltd v Bentley*).

3.132 An improvement notice may be successfully challenged on the ground that the employer is in fact complying with the statutory requirements. In *Davis & Sons v Leeds City Council* the tenancy of a flat above a small bakery shop was subject to a condition that employees at the shop could use the toilet facilities at all times. An improvement notice was issued requiring the shop occupiers to provide readily accessible sanitary facilities instead of this arrangement, in order to comply with s.9(1) of OSRPA. The industrial tribunal allowed an appeal against the notice. Section 9(5) of the Act recognised that facilities might have to be shared with others, and in a circular addressed to local authorities the (then) Ministry of Labour had stated that the effect of s.9(5) would be that "workers in a lock-up shop might have to use the conveniences and facilities in adjacent premises". The tribunal, having visited the premises, concluded that the toilet facilities in the flat were conveniently accessible, and cancelled the notice.

3.133 A similar result was reached in *Alfred Preedy & Sons Ltd v Owens*, where an improvement notice was served alleging that a stone stairway leading to a storage room was in a dangerous condition. The tribunal cancelled the notice after hearing evidence from a witness with a long experience in property management and maintenance that the defects were minimal and of no practical significance.

3.134 A notice may be successfully challenged on the ground that the inspector has misunderstood the application of the statutory provision. In *NAAFI v Portsmouth City Council* an improvement notice was served requiring the appellants to maintain a constant temperature of 55 degrees, so as to conform with s.6(1) of OSRPA. The appellants argued that as the premises were used for the storage of fresh food, a temperature of between 41 and 50 degrees was adequate. The tribunal noted that s.6(3)(b) of the Act provides for an exception where it is a room in which the maintenance of a reasonable temperature would cause the deterioration of goods, provided employees had conveniently accessible means of keeping themselves warm. Since a warm room was provided, together with suitable clothing, the notice was cancelled.

3.135 Nor may an inspector impose a non-statutory requirement. In *Chethams v Westminster Council* a notice was issued because the appellants were allegedly in breach of regulation 7(1) of the OSRPA (Hoists and Lifts) Regulations. The notice required that the latest British Standards for lifts be adopted. This requirement was struck out, because British Standards are merely a guide for new work and are not a statutory provision.

3.136 The fact that the breach in question is a trivial one is irrelevant. In *South Surbiton Co-operative Society v Wilcox* an improvement notice required the employers to replace a wash basin which was cracked. On appeal, the notice was confirmed.

The surface of the basin was not "impervious" as required by the Washing Facilities Regulations 1964, and consequently it was not "properly maintained" in accordance with s.10(2) of OSRPA. That the infringement was trivial was irrelevant to the validity of the notice.

3.137 Nor does the validity of the notice depend on the instructions for remedying the defect being precise. In *Chrysler (UK) Ltd v McCarthy* two improvement notices were issued following a fire at the company's premises. Appeals were lodged on the ground that one of the notices was imprecise. On a preliminary point of law, the tribunal dismissed the appeal, and this was confirmed by the Queen's Bench Divisional Court. It was pointed out that industrial tribunals have wide powers under s.24 of HSWA to modify the requirements of the notice as they think fit in the circumstances. However, when the matter was returned to the tribunal, it felt that they lacked sufficient information on which to make such a modification, and the notice was suspended to permit the parties to agree between themselves what requirements should be laid down.

3.138 When modifying the notice, an industrial tribunal may add to the inspector's requirements as well as vary them (*Tesco Stores Ltd v Edwards*). If the requirements of the inspector are vague or imprecise, the industrial tribunal may exercise its power to amend them (*Chrysler (UK) Ltd v McCarthy*), but there is no power which enables the industrial tribunal to amend a notice so as to include further allegations that an employer is in breach of other provisions of the Act (*British Airways Board v Henderson*).

Appeals against prohibition notices

3.139 A prohibition notice may be issued if the inspector considers that there is a risk of serious personal injury, irrespective of whether or not there is a breach of any relevant statutory provision. Consequently, a certain amount of subjectivity is involved in the formation of such opinion and accordingly this assessment can be challenged. In *Nico Manufacturing Co. Ltd v Hendry* a power press operated by the company was examined and tested by a competent person who found certain defects. In accordance with the Power Presses Regulations 1965 he made a report to the company and to the inspector of factories. A few weeks later a director of the company operated the press, and when this came to the attention of the inspector, he issued a prohibition notice. An appeal was lodged on the ground that the worn state of the press did not constitute a likely source of danger to the employees and that the deprivation of the use of the machine would cause a serious loss of production and endanger the jobs of other employees. It was held that the notice would be confirmed. The industrial tribunal preferred the evidence of the expert witness called on behalf of the inspector in so far as his evidence as to the danger was in conflict with that of the company's technical director. Although there was a small likelihood that the press would break up, there was a danger that parts would fracture which would constitute a serious danger to operatives.

3.140 Thus if a defect could lead to a catastrophic failure, or there was a substantial risk of a serious injury, the industrial tribunal is unlikely to be impressed by arguments of financial hardship or loss of profits. In *Grovehurst Energy Ltd v Strawson*, a prohibition notice was served on the company preventing it from using a receiver, which had been declared unsuitable for further use by a qualified engineer who had carried out a statutory inspection on the firm's boilers and receivers. The company was finding some difficulty in obtaining a replacement receiver and so it applied for the prohibition notice to be suspended. The managing director of the company (who was a qualified engineer) was confident that a replacement receiver would be available in a few weeks, and offered to take extra precautions until it arrived. If he were unable to use the existing receiver, he would suffer a considerable loss of profit. Nonetheless, the industrial tribunal affirmed the notice. The consequences of a catastrophic failure would have been very serious, and the receiver was a substantial risk of injury to anyone who happened to be passing at the time of a failure and to others who worked nearby.

3.141 However, if a machine or process has been in use for a long time without any history of accident or injury, it may be easier to challenge the inspector's view that the activities will involve a risk of serious personal injury. In *Brewer & Sons v Dunston* an inspector issued a prohibition notice on a hand-operated guillotine. The company had used the machine for eighteen years without incident, and also had nine other similar machines. The tribunal, having visited the premises and seen the machine in operation, were satisfied that there was no risk of serious personal injury, and cancelled the notice.

3.142 The industrial tribunals take a similar attitude to appeals based on expense or a request for an extension of time as they do with improvement notices. Thus in *Otterburn Mill Ltd v Bulman* the company operated four machines with no guards. After making a number of visits to the premises, the factory inspector insisted that the appropriate guards be fitted, and when this was not done, he issued deferred prohibition notices requiring the guards to be fitted within three months. The company appealed against the time limit imposed, and requested that they should be allowed to fence one machine every six months, as they did not have the necessary finance to make the improvements. This argument was rejected by the tribunal. It would not be right to insist that a prosperous company should do the work in a short time, while a struggling company should be given a much longer period. However, since it was a deferred notice, in that the risk was not imminent, the time taken to put the matter right was always a factor to be taken into account. As the last (and only) accident recorded at the factory was about nine years ago, the tribunal was prepared to grant an extension of time in respect of one machine, in order to avoid serious embarrassment to the company.

3.143 The number of enforcement notices issued will, of course, vary from year to year, but there is little doubt that they are, and will continue to be, used increasingly by the enforcement authorities.

3.144 Currently, HSE are issuing some 12,000 enforcement notices each year, and a similar number are issued by local authorities.

3.145 Additionally, HSE issue about 50 Crown Notices each year.

Application for review

3.146 An application may be made within fourteen days after the promulgation of the decision to an industrial tribunal to review its decision, on the grounds that:

(a) the decision was wrongly made as a result of an error on the part of the tribunal staff
(b) a party did not receive notice of the proceedings
(c) the decision was made in the absence of a party
(d) new evidence has come to light since the making of the decision, the existence of which was not previously known or foreseen
(e) the interests of justice require a review.

3.147 It must be remembered that an application for review is not an appeal against the decision of the industrial tribunal, and thus it must fall strictly within one of the above five grounds. The application may be refused by a chairman of tribunals sitting on his own if he thinks that it stands no reasonable prospect of success. In making the application, the appellant should state the facts or evidence upon which he seeks to base his case. If the tribunal decides to hear the application, it may vary or revoke the original decision and order a rehearing, or dismiss the application.

Costs

3.148 Unlike other proceedings before industrial tribunals, costs are normally awarded against the loser to the party who wins the case. The amount awarded may be a specific sum, or, in default of agreement between the parties, the amount may be taxed in accordance with the County Court scales, as directed. However, the award of costs is always a matter for the discretion of the tribunal. Thus in *South Surbiton Co-operative Society v Wilcox* (see para 3.136) an improvement notice was confirmed on appeal, but because the breach in question was a trivial one, the industrial tribunal refused to make an order for costs.

Further appeals

3.149 An appeal from a decision of an industrial tribunal which relates to an enforcement notice can only be made to the Queen's Bench Divisional Court on a point of law.

Failure to comply

3.150 A failure to comply with the requirements of a prohibition notice or an improvement notice is a criminal offence under s.33(1)(g) of the Act. The offence is an absolute one, and it is no defence to argue that the accused had done that which was reasonably practicable in the circumstances. The question of reasonably practicable and allied matters must be raised on appeal to an industrial tribunal, not as a defence in the magistrates' or Crown Court (*Deary v Mansion Hide Ltd*).

Power to deal with imminent danger (s.25)

3.151 Where an inspector finds any article or substance in any premises which he has power to enter, and has reasonable cause to believe that, in the circumstances in which he finds it, the article or substance is a cause of imminent danger of serious personal injury, he may seize it and cause it to be rendered harmless (whether by destruction or otherwise). Before doing so, if it is reasonably practicable to do so, he must take a sample and give it to a responsible person at the premises where it was found, marked in a manner sufficient to identify it. After the article or substance has been seized and rendered harmless, the inspector will prepare and sign a written report giving particulars of the circumstances in which the article or substance was seized and dealt with by him, and shall:

(a) give a signed copy to a responsible person at the premises where it was found, and
(b) unless that person is the owner, give a copy to the owner. If the inspector cannot ascertain the name or address of the owner, the copy will be given to the responsible person in question.

3.152 Additionally, for the purpose of facilitating the exercise of any power by an enforcing authority, a customs official may seize any imported article or substance, and detain it for not more than two working days (s.25A).

Prosecutions for criminal offences (ss.33–42)

3.153 Historically, the various branches of the inspectorate have always sought to ensure compliance with health and safety legislation by giving advice and using persuasion, rather than compulsion. Prosecutions for offences are generally used as the weapon of last resort, and a decision to prosecute will frequently be influenced by such factors as the previous record of the person, the number of visits made by an inspector to secure compliance, the gravity of the incident (if one has occurred) the public interest in prosecuting for the offence, and so on. In England and Wales, a prosecution in respect of an offence under any of the relevant statutory provisions may only be instituted by an inspector, or by or with the consent of the Director of Public Prosecutions (s.38), and an inspector, if authorised by the enforcing authority, may conduct the prosecution before a magistrates' court even though he is not a solicitor or a barrister (s.39). In Scotland prosecutions are undertaken by the Procurator Fiscal.

3.154 Sentencing powers have recently been altered by the Criminal Justice Act 1991 and the Offshore Safety Act 1992.

3.155 Prosecutions under HSWA may be brought in respect of the following offences:

Offence	*Summary conviction*	*On indictment*
1. Failure to discharge a duty under ss.2–6	£20,000	Fine
2. Contravening ss.7–9	£5,000	Fine
3. Contravening Health and Safety Regulations	£5,000	Fine
4. Contravening any requirement made by regulations relating to investigations or enquiries made by the Commission, etc under s.14, or obstructing anyone exercising his powers	£5,000	
5. Contravening any requirement under s.20 (powers of inspectors)	£5,000	
6. Contravening any requirement under s.25 (power of the inspector to seize and render harmless articles or substances likely to cause imminent danger)	£5,000	Fine
7. Preventing a person from appearing before an inspector or from answering questions under s.20(2)(j) (examinations and investigations)	£5,000	
8. Contravening a requirement or prohibition imposed by an improvement notice	£20,000 and/or 6 months' imprisonment	Fine and/or 2 years' imprisonment
9. Contravening a requirement or prohibition imposed by a prohibition notice	£20,000 and/or 6 months' imprisonment	Fine and/or 2 years' imprisonment
10. Intentionally obstructing an inspector	£5,000	
11. Contravening a notice served by the Commission under s.27(1) requiring information	£5,000	Fine

Offence	*Summary conviction*	*On indictment*
12. Using or disclosing information in contravention of s.27(4) (disclosure by the Crown or certain Government agencies of information to the Commission or Executive)	£5,000	Fine and/or 2 years' imprisonment
13. Disclosure of information obtained under s.27(1) or pursuant to any statutory provision, not within the exceptions of s.28	£5,000	Fine
14. Making a false or reckless statement in purported compliance with a statutory provision, or for the purpose of obtaining the issuance of a document under any statutory provision	£5,000	Fine
15. Intentionally making a false entry in any register, book, or other document required to be kept, or to making use of such entry, knowing it to be false	£5,000	Fine
16. Forging a document, or, with intent to deceive, using a forged document	£5,000	Fine
17. Pretending to be an inspector	£5,000	
18. Failing to comply with an order of the court under s.42 (order to remedy)	£20,000 and/or 6 months' imprisonment	Fine and/or 2 years' imprisonment
19. Acting without a licence which is necessary under a relevant statutory provision	£5,000	Fine and/or 2 years' imprisonment
20. Contravening the terms of such licence	£5,000	Fine and/or 2 years' imprisonment
21. Acquiring, using or possessing explosives contrary to the relevant statutory provisions	£5,000	Fine and/or 2 years' imprisonment
22. Breach of regulations made for the purpose of s.1(1) of the Offshore Safety Act 1992	£20,000	Fine and/or 2 years' imprisonment

3.156 HSE prosecute about 2,000 cases each year, and a similar number are brought by local authorities. The conviction rate is about 90%. Average fines appear to be on the increase, and are currently around the £900 mark. The highest recorded fine was £750,000 on an oil company in respect of two offences arising out of an accident when several people were killed. To date, no one has actually served a prison sentence, although there have been several cases when a suspended prison sentence has been imposed.

Burden of proof (s.40)

3.157 As a general rule, it is for the prosecution to prove its case beyond reasonable doubt. However, s.40 provides that if the offence consists of a failure to comply with a duty or requirement to do something "so far as is practicable" or "so far as is reasonably practicable" or to "use the best practicable means", it shall be for the accused to prove that it was not practicable or not reasonably practicable to do more than was in fact done or that there was no better practicable means than was in fact used to satisfy the duty or requirement. However, when this burden is placed on the accused, he need only satisfy the court on the balance of probabilities that what he has to prove has been done (*R v Carr-Briant*).

Offences due to the fault of another person (s.36)

3.158 Where the commission of an offence by any person is due to the act or default of some other person, that other person shall be guilty of an offence and may be charged and convicted whether or not proceedings are taken against the first-mentioned person (s.36(1)). If an offence is committed by the Crown, but the Crown cannot be prosecuted (see para 3.11) and the offence is due to the act or default of a person other than the Crown, that person shall be guilty of the offence and may be charged and convicted accordingly (s.36(2)). Thus employees of the Crown may be convicted, even though the Crown itself is immune.

Offences by directors, managers, secretaries, etc (s.37)

3.159 Where an offence committed by a body corporate is proved to have been committed with the consent or connivance of, or attributable to any neglect on the part of, any director, manager, secretary or other similar officer of the body corporate, or a person who was purporting to act in such capacity, then he, as well as the body corporate shall be guilty of that offence and shall be liable to be proceeded against (s.37(1)). This section was considered in *Armour v Skeen*, where the Strathclyde Regional Council and its Director of Roads were both prosecuted for a breach of safety regulations, lack of a safe system of work and failing to notify an inspector that certain work was being undertaken. As a result of these failures, an employee of the council was killed. The alleged neglect on the part of the Director of Roads was a failure to have a sound safety policy for his department, failing to provide information to his subordinates and a failure to provide training and instructions in safe working practices. He was convicted of the offences and the conviction was upheld on appeal. The fact that s.2 of HSWA imposes a duty on the employers to provide a safe system of work did not mean that there was no duty on his part to carry out that duty. Section 37(1) refers to "any neglect", not to the neglect of a duty imposed. The offences were committed by the body corporate, but were due to his neglect. Further, although his title as "Director of Roads" did not mean he was a "director" within the meaning of s.37(1), he was within the ambit of the words "manager . . . or similar officer".

3.160 Persons who purport to act as directors, managers, secretaries or similar officers are equally liable. Thus if a person acts as a director even though he has been disqualified from doing so under the Companies Act, he is purporting to act as such. Nor do the words "purporting to act" imply that there is a fraudulent or false intention in so acting. Anyone who acts in a managerial capacity may be held liable under s.37(1) whatever title he may have. If the affairs of the body corporate are being managed by its members (eg a workers' cooperative), then the acts of a member which are in connection with his managerial functions are within the meaning of this section (s.37(2)).

3.161 For a person to be convicted under this section, it must be shown that he has some responsibility for the making of management decisions, and be in a position of responsibility. In *R v Boal*, the accused was the assistant general manager of Foyle's bookshop. He had been given no management training, and in particular, none in health and safety matters, or fire precautions. He was, however, in charge of the shop while the general manager was away on a week's holiday. During this period, the premises were visited by officers from the local fire authority, who discovered that there were serious breaches of the fire certificate which had been issued.

Foyle's and the accused were charged with a number of offences under the Fire Precautions Act 1971—Foyle's as the "body corporate" and the accused because the 1971 Act provides that ". . . where an offence committed by a body corporate is proved . . . to be attributable to any neglect on the part of any director, manager, secretary or other similar officer of the body corporate . . . he as well as the body corporate shall be guilty of that offence . . .".

3.162 Foyle's were convicted on eleven counts, and were fined. The accused pleaded guilty to three counts, and was found guilty of seven others. He was sentenced to three months' imprisonment, suspended for twelve months. He then appealed against the conviction on the ground that he was not a ". . . manager or other similar officer . . ." within the meaning of the Act.

3.163 The Court of Appeal (Criminal Division) allowed his appeal. A person was "a manager" if he had power of ". . . the management of the whole of the affairs of the company . . ." or was ". . . intrusted with power to transact the whole of the affairs of the company . . ." or was ". . . managing in a governing role the affairs of the company itself . . .". The Court further thought that the intended scope of s.23 of the Fire Precautions Act was "... to fix with criminal liability only those who are in a position of real authority, the decision makers within the company who have both the power and responsibility to decide corporate policy and strategy. It is to catch those responsible for putting proper procedures in place; it is not meant to strike at underlings."

Additional powers of the court (s.42)

3.164 If a person is convicted of an offence under any of the relevant statutory provisions in respect of any matter which appears to the court to be something which is in his power to remedy, the court may (in addition to, or instead of, any other punishment) order him, within such time as may be fixed, to take specified steps to remedy the matter. An application may be made to the court for an extension of time within which to comply with the order.

3.165 If a person is convicted of an offence under s.34(4)(c) (acquiring, possessing or using an explosive article or substance in contravention of a relevant statutory provision), the court may order the article or substance to be forfeited or destroyed or dealt with in such other manner as the court may order. Before making a forfeiture order the court must give an opportunity to the owner (or any other person with an interest in the article or substance) an opportunity to show cause why the order should not be made.

3.166 A failure to comply with an order under s.42 (eg if a person fails to take the necessary remedial action) is punishable by a fine of up to £20,000, and/or six months' imprisonment on summary conviction, and an unlimited fine and/or two years' imprisonment if convicted in the Crown Court.

Disqualification of directors

3.167 Under the Company Directors Disqualification Act 1982, s.2, the court may disqualify a person from being a director of a company if he is convicted on an indictable offence, whether on indictment or summarily, if the offence was in connection with the management of the company. A magistrates' court may impose a disqualification for up to five years, whilst the higher court may disqualify for up to fifteen years. One such disqualification has been made against a company director for an offence under s.37 of HSWA for breach of a prohibition notice. The disqualification can be in addition to any other penalty imposed.

Time limits for prosecutions

3.168 By virtue of s.127 of the Magistrates' Courts Act 1980 a prosecution for a summary offence must be commenced by the laying of an information (ie issuing a summons) within six months from the date of the commission of the offence.

However, s.34 of HSWA specifies that in certain cases an extension of the time limit may be possible. These are:

(a) where there has been a special report made by a person holding an investigation under s.14(2)(a) (see para 2.9)
(b) where a report is made by a person holding an enquiry under s.14(2)(b) (see para 2.10)
(c) a coroner's inquest is held touching the death of a person which may have been caused by an accident happening at work, or a disease contracted at work
(d) a public enquiry is held into a death so caused under Scottish legislation

and it appears from the report, inquest or inquiry that a relevant statutory provision was contravened, then summary proceedings may be commenced at any time within three months from the making of the report, or the conclusion of the inquest or inquiry (s.34(1)).

3.169 If an offence is committed by a designer, manufacturer, importer or supplier (ie s.6 offences) then summary proceedings may be commenced at any time within six months from the date when the enforcing authority had sufficient evidence, in its opinion, to justify a prosecution (or, in Scotland, to justify the making of a report to the Lord Advocate). A certificate of an enforcing authority stating that such evidence came to its knowledge on a specified date shall be conclusive evidence of that fact (ss.34(3), (4), (5)). However, this provision appears to be otiose since the passing of the Criminal Law Act 1977 (see *Kemp v Leibherr (GB) Ltd*) because s.6 offences are hybrid offences (ie triable either summarily or on indictment).

3.170 When an offence is committed by reason of a failure to do something within a fixed time, the offence shall be deemed to continue until that thing be done and time will not run until then (s.34(2)).

Indictable offences

3.171 Because of the maxim "Time does not run against the Crown" a prosecution in respect of an indictable offence is never barred by time limits. Since most of the offences under HSWA are triable either way (ie potentially indictable), the six months' time limit has limited effect and applies to those offences which are summary only. Hybrid offences are deemed to be indictable offences so far as time limits for prosecution are concerned (*Kemp v Leibherr (GB) Ltd*).

4

Health and safety at work—the new law

4.1 In 1989 the Council of Ministers of the European Community adopted the health and safety "Framework Directive" (89/391/EEC) which deals with the general principles to be applied throughout the Community on health and safety in all work activities (except domestic service). The primary duty for ensuring health and safety at work was placed upon employers, although self-employed persons and employees were also embraced. Five additional "daughter" Directives were subsequently adopted dealing with more specific proposals, ie (a) Workplace Directive (89/654/EEC), (b) Use of Work Equipment Directive (89/655/EEC), (c) Personal Protective Equipment Directive (89/656/EEC), (d) Manual Handling of Loads Directive (90/269/EEC) and (e) Display Screen Equipment Directive (90/270/EEC). Further Directives have been adopted on Carcinogens, Biological Agents, Temporary Workers, Asbestos Workers Protection, Physical Agents, Construction Sites, Safety Signs, and Pregnant Workers. A number of other Directives with health and safety implications are currently being discussed with a view to adoption (see chapter 10).

4.2 Following the adoption of the Framework and first five daughter Directives, HSC issued six Consultative Documents, with proposals for new regulations to implement the Directives, together with Approved Codes of Practice or Guidance Notes. After extensive consultation, six new regulations were approved by Parliament, and except for specified transitional periods, came into force as from 1 January 1993.

4.3 HSC took the view that whilst in general the Health and Safety at Work etc Act 1974 was adequate as a means of achieving the appropriate standards, the Directives were more prescriptive and detailed, and thus it was necessary to extend the law in order to meet the new standards required by the Directives. It was hoped to achieve the desired results by avoiding any disruption with the basic framework laid down in HSWA, and at the same time to continue with the process of modernising the law and repealing out-of-date legislation. Thus the new regulations, together with the Approved Codes of Practice and Guidance Notes should meet the EC standards, and UK law has been adapted accordingly within the existing framework.

4.4 It will be recalled that, as a general principle, health and safety regulations may give rise to civil as well as criminal liability. Thus where certain familiar statutory provisions, which have hitherto been a prolific source of civil litigation, have been repealed, civil proceedings may in general be brought under the new regulations in due course. But attention must be paid to the individual regulations in order to determine whether civil claims may be brought. All the regulations impose criminal liabilities. This chapter will be devoted to a discussion of the new law.

Management of Health and Safety at Work Regulations 1992

4.5 These regulations implement the provisions of the Framework Directive (89/391/EEC) and also the Temporary Workers Directive (91/383/EEC) and came into force on 1 January 1993. They apply to all work activities to which HSWA applies, including off-shore activities and trainees, but not to merchant shipping. The Secretary of State for Defence may, in the interests of national security, exempt the armed forces and visiting armed forces.

4.6 Generally, the regulations impose duties on employers, although in certain circumstances self-employed persons and employees have duties with which they must comply. The regulations are accompanied by an Approved Code of Practice.

4.7 *It should be noted that these regulations do not give rise to any claim for civil liability, and are thus only enforceable by criminal sanctions.* The reason appears to be that they should be regarded as an extension of the duties laid down in ss.2–8 of HSWA, which itself is solely a criminal statute. Regulation 15 specifically excludes a right of action in civil proceedings. The main provisions of the regulations are discussed below.

Risk assessment (regulation 3)

4.8 Every employer shall make a suitable and sufficient assessment:

(a) of the risks to the health and safety of his employees to which they are exposed whilst at work, and
(b) of the risks to the health and safety of persons not in his employment arising out of, or in connection with, the conduct by him of his undertaking,

for the purpose of identifying the measures he needs to take to comply with the relevant statutory provisions.

4.9 A similar duty is placed on every self-employed person in respect of his own safety and persons not in his employment.

4.10 Once the assessment has been made, it shall be reviewed by the employer (or self-employed person) if he has reason to suspect that it is no longer valid, or if there are significant changes in the matters to which it relates. If, as a result of the review, changes in the assessment are required, these shall be made.

4.11 The ACOP suggests that a risk assessment involves an identification of the hazards and an estimation of the risks, taking account of the existing precautions available and used, and a consideration of what else need to be done. The employer (or self-employed person) should be able to decide what measures need to be taken in order to comply with his duties under the relevant statutory provisions.

4.12 A risk assessment will be "suitable and sufficient" if:

(a) it identifies the significant risks arising from the work
(b) it enables the employer (or self-employed person) to identify and prioritise the measures which need to be taken to comply with the relevant statutory provisions, and
(c) it is appropriate to the nature of the work and remains valid for a reasonable period of time.

4.13 Risk assessments should be reviewed at regular intervals, but in particular when the nature of the work changes or there has been further appreciation of hazards and risks. The monitoring of the health and safety arrangements required by regulation 4 may reveal further hazards which can be dealt with by a revised assessment.

4.14 There are no fixed rules about how a risk assessment should be carried out, for this will depend on the nature of the undertaking and the type of hazards and risks present. For small undertakings it can be a simple process based on judgment, and will require no specialist skills or complicated techniques. At the other extreme, it may be the basis for a complete safety case. In intermediate cases, specialist advice may be necessary in respect of unfamiliar risks. Separate assessment exercises may be necessary in particular operations or groups of hazards. A structured approach should always be adopted.

4.15 In particular, the ACOP suggests that a risk assessment should adopt the following approach:

(a) ensure that all the relevant risks or hazards are addressed
(b) look at what actually happens in the workplace or during work activities
(c) ensure that all groups of employees (and others who might be affected) are considered
(d) identify those groups of workers who might be particularly at risk
(e) take account of existing preventative and precautionary measures.

4.16 Where an assessment is required to be made under some other regulation (eg COSHH, etc, see para 6.150), that will cover in part the obligation to make assessments under the Management Regulations, and need not be repeated as long as it remains valid. On the other hand, an assessment under the Management Regulations may reveal that a further assessment is needed under the other regulations.

4.17 Employers who employ five or more employees must record the significant findings of the assessment and any group of his employees identified as being especially at risk. Normally this would be in writing but it could be recorded by other means (eg electronically) as long as it is retrievable for use or examination.

4.18 Once the assessment has been made, it should be possible to take action on the necessary preventative and protective measures which will be needed. The ACOP suggests the following principles should be adopted:

(a) where possible, the risk should be avoided, eg by not using a particular substance which is dangerous, if it is not essential to the business
(b) the risk should be combatted at source, rather than by using palliative methods
(c) when considering the design of the workplace, the choice of work equipment and the choice of working methods, these should be adapted to the individual. Where possible, monotonous work should be avoided, so as to reduce possible adverse effects on health and safety
(d) advantage should be taken of modern technology, which is generally safer
(e) if risks cannot be prevented or avoided, risk prevention measures should progressively reduce them
(f) priority should be given to those measures which protect the workforce as a whole, thus yielding the greatest benefit
(g) all workers need to understand what they are required to do
(h) avoidance, prevention and reduction of risks should be an accepted part of the philosophy at all levels of the organisation, in respect of all its activities.

Health and safety arrangements (regulation 4)

4.19 Every employer shall make and give effect to such arrangements as are appropriate, having regard to the nature of his activities and the size of his undertaking, for the effective planning, organisation, control, monitoring and review of the preventive and protective meaasures. Where the employer employs five or more workers, these arrangements shall be recorded.

4.20 The ACOP suggests that there should be a systematic approach which identifies priorities and sets objectives. The organisational structure should be set up to ensure a progressive improvement in health and safety performance. Control mechanisms should ensure that decisions for promoting health and safety are being implemented as planned, and monitoring and review are required to achieve progressive improvements. The record of these arrangements (which should also identify the competent persons appointed under regulation 6, see below) together with the risk assessment made under regulation 3 (above) could form part of the same document which contains the safety policy statement required by s.2(3) of HSWA.

Health surveillance (regulation 5)

4.21 Every employer shall ensure that his employees are provided with such health surveillance as is appropriate having regard to the risks to their health and safet which are identified by the assessment.

4.22 The ACOP states that once the risk assessment has been done, it should b possible to identify the circumstances when health surveillance is required by specific health and safety regulations (eg COSHH, Asbestos Regulation, etc). Health surveillance should also be introduced when:

(a) there is an identifiable work-related disease or adverse health condition
(b) valid detection techniques are available
(c) there is a reasonable likelihood that the disease or condition may occur under the particular working conditions, and
(d) surveillance is likely to further the protection of the employees to be covered.

4.23 The object of surveillance is to detect adverse health effects at an early stage, thus preventing further harm. Additionally the effectiveness of control measures can be checked, as well as the accuracy of the risk assessment. If health surveillance is appropriate, individual health records can be kept. Health surveillance procedures will depend, for their suitability, on the circumstances.

Health and safety assistance (regulation 6)

4.24 Every employer shall appoint one or more competent persons to assist him in undertaking the measures he needs to take to comply with the requirements and prohibitions imposed on him by the relevant statutory provisions. This does not apply to a self-employed person (who is not in partnership with another person) where he has sufficient knowledge or training and experience and other qualities to do this himself. Nor does regulation 6 apply to a partnership which employs persons where at least one of the partners has sufficient training and experience or knowledge and other qualities to carry out the measures needed to comply with the relevant statutory requirements and prohibitions, and can properly assist the partnership in carrying out those measures.

4.25 If the employer appoints more than one person, he shall make arrangements to ensure adequate cooperation between them. The number of persons appointed and the time and means made available to them to fulfil their functions shall b adequate having regard to the size of his undertaking, the risks to which th employees are exposed, and the distribution of those risks throughout th undertaking.

4.26 The person designated to provide health and safety assistance need not be a employee of the employer. However, if an outside consultant is appointed, th employer must inform him of all the factors known to the employer which ma affect the health and safety of any person who may be affected by the conduct of th undertaking. The employer must also give the outside consultant access to th information referred to in regulation 8 (below).

4.27 For the purpose of this regulation, a person shall be regarded as being competent where he has sufficient training and experience or knowledge and other qualities to enable him properly to assist in carrying out the measures which the employer needs to take in order to comply with the relevant statutory provisions.

4.28 The ACOP suggests that the appointment of a competent person should be included among the health and safety arrangements recorded under regulation 4 (above). The person appointed may be an employee, or an external specialist, but in the latter case he will usually only have an advisory role. The appointment of a safety assistant does not in any way detract from the overall responsibility of the employer and/or departmental managers acting within their own spheres. The employer must satisfy himself as to the adviser's competence, the complexities of the work situation being matched to the skills required.

Procedures for serious and imminent danger and for danger areas (regulation 7)

4.29 Every employer shall establish, and give effect to, appropriate procedures to be followed in the event of serious and imminent dangers to persons at work in his undertaking. Competent persons shall be nominated to implement evacuation procedures. The procedures shall, so far as is practicable, require any persons at work who are exposed to serious and imminent danger to be informed of the nature of the hazard, and of the steps to be taken to protect them from it. They should be able to stop work and immediately proceed to a place of safety and, save in exceptional cases specified in the procedures (eg emergency services) require the persons concerned to be prevented from resuming work while there is still a danger.

4.30 The employer shall also ensure that none of his employees have access to any area occupied by him to which it is necessary to restrict access on grounds of health and safety unless the employee concerned has received adequate health and safety instruction.

4.31 The ACOP suggests that the risk assessment will usually identify the events which are likely to give rise to serious and imminent danger. In most cases, this is likely to be the risk of fire (and possibly bomb alerts). But some workplaces will pose their own additional risks (eg the release of toxic gases), and these must also be catered for. Some employees will be allocated specific tasks to be performed in emergencies, others will need training so as to bring the event under control. Emergency events can develop rapidly, and employees should be required to act without waiting for further guidance.

4.32 Emergency procedures should be written down, under regulation 4 (above), and be made known to safety assistants under regulation 6 (above), to employees under regulation 8 (below) and to non-employees under regulation 10 (below). They should also form part of any induction course (regulation 11, below). Test exercises should be carried out.

4.33 Work should not be resumed after an emergency if a serious danger remains. After the emergency has passed, consideration can be given to a review of the risk assessment.

Information for employees (regulation 8)

4.34 Every employer shall provide his employees with comprehensible and relevant information on:

(a) the risks to their health and safety identified by the assessment
(b) the preventative and protective measures
(c) the procedures for dealing with serious and imminent dangers
(d) the identity of persons nominated to oversee evacuation procedures, and
(e) the risks which have been notified to him by another employer with whom the workplace is shared.

4.35 The ACOP states that the information should be capable of being understood by the employees concerned, and will thus take account of their level of training, knowledge and experience. Special attention should be given to persons with language difficulties or physical disabilities which may affect their receipt of information (eg blind persons). Persons who are on fixed-term contracts are required to have additional information (see regulation 13 below).

Cooperation and coordination (regulation 9)

4.36 Where two or more employers (or self-employed persons) share a workplace (whether on a temporary or permanent basis), each employer shall:

(a) cooperate with the other employers concerned so far as is necessary to enable them to comply with their statutory duties
(b) take all reasonable steps to coordinate health and safety measures, and
(c) take all reasonable steps to inform the other employers concerned of the risks to their employees' health and safety arising out of the conduct by him of his undertaking.

4.37 The ACOP points out that where the worksite is under the control of a main employer, other employers (or self-employed persons) on the site should assist in assessing shared risks and coordinating any necessary measures. Equally, the controlling employer will have to establish site-wide arrangements, and this information should be passed on, as appropriate. If there is no employer in control, joint arrangements should be agreed, and consideration should be given to the appointment of a health and safety coordinator.

Visiting workers (regulation 10)

4.38 Every employer shall ensure that the employer of any visiting worker is provided with comprehensible information on:

(a) the risks to the employees' health and safety, and
(b) the measures taken to ensure compliance with the statutory requirements insofar as they relate to the visiting workers.

4.39 The employer shall then ensure that every visiting worker is provided with appropriate instructions and comprehensible information regarding any risks to that person's health and safety which arise out of the conduct of the employers' undertaking. Employers must also ensure that the employer of any visiting worker, as well as the visiting workers, are provided with sufficient information to identify the person responsible for evacuation procedures.

4.40 This regulation also applies to self-employed persons.

4.41 The ACOP points out that whereas regulation 9 deals with shared workplaces, regulation 10 is concerned with visiting workers, eg persons coming to carry out cleaning, repairs or maintenance work, etc as well as temporary employees who come from an employment business.

Capabilities and training (regulation 11)

4.42 When entrusting tasks to his employees, every employer shall take account of their capabilities as regards health and safety. The employer shall also ensure that his employees are provided with adequate health and safety training:

(a) when they are recruited
(b) when they are being exposed to new or increased risks because of being transferred, or given changed responsibilities, or when new work equipment, new technology or new systems of work are introduced.

4.43 The training should be repeated periodically where appropriate, and adapted to take account of new or changed risks. Training should take place in working hours.

4.44 The ACOP suggests that training needs are likely to be greatest on recruitment. Basic training should include arrangements for first aid, fire and evacuation, as well as general health and safety matters. Refresher training may be needed if particular skills are used infrequently. If it is necessary to arrange training outside working hours, this should be treated as an extension of time at work.

Duties of employees (regulation 12)

4.45 Every employee shall use any machinery, equipment, dangerous substances, transport equipment or safety device provided to him in accordance with any training received by him and any instructions provided to him by his employer.

4.46 Every employee shall inform his employer (or the employee responsible for health and safety matters):

(a) of any work situation which a person with his training and instruction would reasonably consider to represent a serious and immediate danger to health and safety, and
(b) of any matter which a person with his training and instruction would reasonably consider represented a shortcoming in the employer's protection arrangements for health and safety.

4.47 However, this duty only arises insofar as the situation affects the employee's own health or safety, or arises out of his own activities at work. Also, the matter must be one which has not previously been reported to the employer or safety adviser.

4.48 The ACOP points out that employees have certain duties under s.7 of HSWA, but this regulation clearly goes much further. The employee must use the various things provided for him, in accordance with the training and instructions provided. He must also report to the employer any work situation which might be a serious and imminent danger to himself, or to others if it flows from his work activity. Further he should report shortcomings in the employer's arrangements even when no danger exists, so that the employer can take remedial action.

Temporary workers (regulation 13)

4.49 If an employer engages an employee on a fixed-term contract, or engages a person employed by an employment business, the employer must provide that person with comprehensible information on:

(a) any special occupational qualifications or skills required to be held by that employee if he is to carry out his work safely, and
(b) any health surveillance required to be provided to that employee.

4.50 This information is to be provided before the employee concerned commences his duties.

4.51 Where an employer is seeking to have work done by persons who will be provided by an employment business, he must provide the person carrying on that business with comprehensible information on:

(a) any special occupational qualifications or skills required to be held by the employees if they are to carry out their work safely, and
(b) the specific features of the jobs to be filled by those employees insofar as those features are likely to affect their health and safety.

4.52 The person carrying on the employment business will pass on the information to the employees concerned.

4.53 The ACOP points out that both the user employer and the person carrying on the employment business have duties to provide information to the employees concerned. There is considerable overlap and interchange with regulations 8, 10 and 13, which needs to be carefully followed.

Exemption certificates (regulation 14)

4.54 As already noted, the Secretary of State for Defence may, in the interests of national security, issue a certificate exempting the armed forces and visiting armed forces from the requirements of the regulations.

Exclusion of civil liability (regulation 15)

4.55 A breach of duty imposed by these regulations shall not confer a right of action in any civil proceedings.

4.56 Thus a breach of the regulations will not support a civil claim based on a breach of statutory duty (see para 8.9), although proof of a criminal conviction under the regulations may be used as evidence in a civil case (see para 3.14).

4.57 The regulations also amend the Safety Representatives and Safety Committee Regulations 1977 by including a duty for employers to consult with, and provide facilities and assistance for, safety representatives.

Workplace (Health, Safety and Welfare) Regulations 1992

4.58 The object of these regulations is to implement most of the requirements of the EC Directive 89/654/EEC, while the remaining requirements will be dealt with by other legislative provisions (eg on fire precautions, etc). It is also thought that some requirements of the Directive are adequately dealt with by existing British law, and no changes are proposed in these areas (eg first aid). However, other existing legislation, though adequate, is not comprehensive enough, because it only applies to certain defined premises (eg factories, offices, shops and railway premises, etc). Thus most of these provisions will eventually be repealed or revoked, to be replaced by the new comprehensive provisions which will apply to all workplaces. The regulations are accompanied by an Approved Code of Practice with guidance.

4.59 The regulations will take effect in two stages. With regard to workplaces (including any modifications, extensions or conversions) which are used for the first time on or after 1 January 1993, these must comply with the regulations as soon as they are in use. With regard to existing workplaces (ie in use prior to 1 January 1993), the regulations will take effect from 1 January 1996, giving employers a three year lead-in period within which to ensure compliance. Until then, the "old" law remains applicable, though it will cease to have effect from 1 January 1996.

4.60 The regulations apply to all workplaces, ie any premises (which are not domestic premises) which are made available to any person as a place of work, including any place within the premises to which a person working has access while at work, and any room, lobby, corridor, staircase, road or other place used as a means of access to or egress from the workplace, or where facilities are provided for use in connection with the workplace, other than a public road. The regulations only apply immediately to those new premises and to modifications, extensions or conversions which are occupied after 31 December 1992 (whether on existing, or new workplaces) and these will only form part of the workplace when completed.

4.61 The application of the regulation is, therefore, very wide. They will apply not only to the traditional factories, offices and shops, but also to schools, hospitals, theatres, common parts of shared buildings, private roads on industrial estates, hotels, nursing homes, etc; in fact almost anywhere where people work other than domestic premises (homeworkers are thus not covered by the regulations).

4.62 There are, however, certain statutory exceptions, where the regulations will not apply, or where only limited compliance is required. These are as follows:

- (a) means of transport, including ships, aircraft, trains and road vehicles, although regulation 13 (below) will apply when these places are stationary inside a workplace or when a vehicle is not on a public road
- (b) mines, quarries and other sites where minerals are being explored or extracted, including offshore sites and installations (these workplaces have their own separate legislation)
- (c) sites where building operations or works of engineering construction are being carried out. If construction work is being carried on within a workplace, the site will be excluded if it is fenced off, otherwise the Construction Regulations and the Workplace Regulations will both apply
- (d) so far as temporary sites are concerned, the welfare provisions of the Regulations (regulations 20–25, below) will apply "so far as is reasonably practicable". A temporary site is one used for a short period or infrequently, eg a fairground
- (e) so far as agriculture and forestry work is concerned, regulations 20–22 (below) apply so far as is reasonably practicable.

4.63 In general, the regulations place duties on employers in respect of workplaces under their control and where their employees work. In addition, duties are placed on controllers of premises in respect of matters within their control. For example, the owner of a multi-occupancy building will be responsible for the common provision of services and facilities (toilets, ventilation plant, etc), thus extending the legal obligations set out in s.4 of HSWA (see para 3.59).

Maintenance of workplace, and of equipment, devices and systems (regulation 5)

4.64 This regulation applies to equipment, devices and systems, a fault in which is liable to result in a failure, to comply with other regulations. Examples of equipment, devices and systems include mechanical ventilation systems, emergency lighting, fencing, fixed equipment used for cleaning windows, powered doors, escalators and moving walkways, etc. The workplace, and all such equipment, devices and systems shall be maintained in an efficient state, in efficient order, in good repair, and cleaned as appropriate.

4.65 The ACOP points out that regular maintenance shall be carried out at suitable intervals, dangerous defects remedied, and a suitable record kept.

Ventilation (regulation 6)

4.66 Effective and suitable provision shall be made to ensure that every enclosed workplace is ventilated by a sufficient quantity of fresh or purified air. Any plant used shall include an efficient device which gives a visible or audible warning of any failure. Certain enclosed workplaces are excluded from the regulation (see regulation 6(3)).

4.67 Additional information on compliance with this Regulation is given in the ACOP and guidance.

Temperature in indoor workplaces (regulation 7)

4.68 During working hours, the temperature in all workplaces inside buildings shall be reasonable. A method of heating shall not be used which results in the escape into the workplace of fumes, gas or vapour which may be injurious or offensive. A sufficient number of thermometers shall be provided.

4.69 The ACOP suggests that the temperature should provide reasonable comfort without the need for special clothing. It should be at least 16°C unless the work involves severe physical effort, when it should be at least 13°C. These temperatures do not apply to workplaces where lower maximum room temperatures are required by law (eg Fresh Meat Export (Hygiene and Inspection) Regulations 1987).

Lighting (regulation 8)

4.70 Every workplace shall have suitable and sufficient lighting, which, so far as is reasonably practicable, shall be by natural light. Sufficient emergency lighting shall be provided in any room where persons are exposed to danger if artificial lighting fails.

4.71 The ACOP points out that lighting should also be placed at places of particular risk, eg pedestrian crossing points on traffic routes, dazzling lights and glare should be avoided, and light fittings should not cause a hazard. Lights should not be permitted to become obscured, they should be replaced, repaired or cleaned as necessary.

Cleanliness and waste materials (regulation 9)

4.72 Every workplace, and the furniture, furnishings and fittings therein shall be kept sufficiently clean. Surfaces of floors, walls and ceilings shall be capable of being kept sufficiently clean. So far as is reasonably practicable, waste materials shall not be allowed to accumulate except in suitable receptacles.

4.73 The ACOP states that floors and indoor traffic routes should be cleaned at least once each week. If dirt or refuse is not in suitable receptacles, it should be removed daily.

Room dimensions and space (regulation 10)

4.74 Every room where persons work shall have sufficient floor area, height and unoccupied space for purposes of health, safety and welfare. It will be sufficient compliance in a workplace which is not a new workplace, conversion or extension, and which, immediately before 1 January 1993, was subject to the provisions of the Factories Act 1961, if the workplace complies with the provisions which were contained in s.2 of the Factories Act, ie $11m^3$ per person (ignoring space more than 4.2m from the floor, see Schedule 1, Part 1 to the regulations).

4.75 The ACOP adopts the standard of $11m^3$ per person, although it suggests ignoring space which is more than 3m high when making this calculation. There are exceptions in certain employment where space is limited, eg retail sales kiosks, attendant's shelters, etc. The number of persons who may work in a room at any particular point in time will also depend on the space taken up by furniture, equipment, etc.

Workstations and seating (regulation 11)

4.76 Every workstation shall be so arranged that it is suitable for the person at work and for any work likely to be done there. A workstation which is out of doors shall be so arranged that:

(a) so far as is reasonably practicable, it provides protection from adverse weather
(b) it enables any person at the workstation to leave it swiftly or be assisted in the event of an emergency
(c) it ensures that any person at the workplace is not likely to slip or fall.

4.77 If a substantial part of the work can be done while the person at work is seated, then a suitable seat shall be provided. The seat must be suitable for the person and for the operations to be performed. A suitable footrest shall be provided where necessary.

4.78 The ACOP states that workstations should be so arranged that each task can be carried out safely and comfortably. The worker should have adequate freedom of movement, spells of work carried out in cramped conditions should be limited, seating should provide adequate support for the lower back, and so on.

Condition of floors and traffic routes (regulation 12)

4.79 Workplace floors and surface traffic routes shall be so constructed that they are suitable for the purposes. The floor or surface shall not have a hole or slope, or be uneven or slippery so as to expose a person to a risk to his health or safety and shall have effective means of drainage as appropriate. Suitable and sufficient handrails and guards shall be provided on all traffic routes which are staircases.

4.80 The ACOP gives some practical advice on the construction of floors, stairs, etc, and pays particular attention to hazards from spillages and contamination by liquids. Appropriate control measures should be taken.

Falls or falling objects (regulation 13)

4.81 So far as is reasonably practicable, suitable and effective measures shall be taken to prevent any person falling a distance likely to cause personal injury, and any person being struck by a falling object likely to cause personal injury. If there is an area where there is a risk of these events happening, this shall be indicated where appropriate. Every tank, pit or structure which contains a dangerous substance shall be securely fenced or covered if there is a risk of a person falling in.

4.82 The ACOP recommends that secure fencing should be provided wherever possible at any place where a person might fall 2m or more, although this standard is lowered if there are factors which might increase the risk of serious injury. Fixed ladders should not be provided if it would be practicable to install a staircase. Further advice is given on roof work, tanks, pits, etc which contain dangerous substances, stacking and racking, loading and unloading vehicles, scaffolding, etc.

Windows, and transparent or translucent doors, gates and walls (regulation 14)

4.83 Every window, transparent or translucent surface in a wall, partition, door or gate shall, where necessary for reasons of health or safety, be of safety material or protected against breakage. It shall also be appropriately marked.

Windows, skylights and ventilators (regulation 15)

4.84 Windows, skylights or ventilators shall not be opened, closed or adjusted in a manner which exposes any person performing such an operation to a risk to his health or safety. Nor must they pose a risk to health and safety when open.

Ability to clean windows, etc safely (regulation 16)

4.85 All windows and skylights in a workplace shall be of a design or so constructed that they may be cleaned safely.

Organisation, etc of traffic routes (regulation 17)

4.86 Every workplace shall be organised in such a way that pedestrians and vehicles can circulate in a safe manner. [Traffic routes shall be suitable for the persons or vehicles using them, sufficient in number, in suitable positions and of sufficient size.] Suitable measures shall be taken to ensure that pedestrians or vehicles may use traffic routes without causing danger to persons at work nearby, and there is sufficient separation between vehicles and pedestrians. Traffic routes shall be suitably indicated.
Note: The requirement in brackets is to the standard of "so far as is reasonably practicable" for existing workplaces.

4.87 The ACOP gives considerable advice on how safe traffic routes may be achieved. A safe circulation of movement of persons and vehicles requires a suitable combination of the physical layout and safe system of use.

Doors and gates (regulation 18)

4.88 Doors and gates shall be suitably constructed, and fitted with any necessary safety devices. Sliding doors or gates shall have a device to prevent them from coming off tracks during use, an upward opening door or gate shall have a device to prevent it falling back, a powered door or gate shall have a suitable and effective feature to prevent it causing injury by trapping any person, and shall be capable of being operated manually (unless it opens automatically if the power fails), and a door or gate which is capable of being pushed from either side shall provide, when closed, a clear view of the space close to both sides.

Escalators and moving walkways (regulation 19)

4.89 Escalators and moving walkways shall function safely, be equipped with any necessary safety device, and fitted with one or more emergency stop controls which is easily identifiable and readily accessible.

Sanitary conveniences (regulation 20)

4.90 Suitable and sufficient sanitary conveniences shall be provided at readily accessible places. They shall be adequately ventilated and lit, kept in a clean and orderly condition, and separate rooms containing conveniences shall be provided for men and women, except where each convenience is in a separate room the door of which is capable of being secured from the inside.

4.91 So far as workplaces which were in use prior to 1 January 1993 are concerned, and which were subject to the provisions of the Factories Act 1961, it is sufficient compliance if the sanitary conveniences consist of at least one water closet for use by females only for every 25 females, and one for every 25 males (see Schedule 1, Part 2 of the regulations).

Washing facilities (regulation 2)

4.92 Suitable and sufficient washing facilities, including showers if required by the nature of the work for health reasons, shall be provided at readily accessible places. These shall be provided in the immediate vicinity of sanitary conveniences (whether or not provided elsewhere) and include a supply of clean hot and cold or warm running water. Soap or other means of cleaning and towels or other suitable means of drying shall be provided. The rooms shall be sufficiently ventilated and lit, kept clean and orderly, and have separate facilities for men and women, except where they are provided in a room which is capable of being secured from inside.

4.93 The ACOP specifies the minimum number of sanitary conveniences and washing stations which should be provided, and deals with, in particular, remote workplaces and temporary work sites.

Drinking water (regulation 22)

4.94 An adequate supply of wholesome drinking water shall be provided for all persons at work in the workplace. This shall be at readily accessible places and be conspicuously marked by an appropriate sign. A sufficient number of suitable cups or other drinking vessels shall be provided, unless the supply is from a jet from which persons can drink easily.

Accommodation for clothing (regulation 23)

4.95 Suitable and sufficient accommodation for clothing shall be provided for clothing not worn during working hours, and for special clothing worn at work which is not taken home. The accommodation must be in a suitable location, and where facilities to change clothing are required by regulation 24 (below) suitable security must be provided. There must be separate accommodation for clothing worn at work where necessary to avoid risks to health (or damage to the clothing), and, so far as is reasonably practicable, the accommodation must allow or include facilities for drying clothing.

Facilities for changing clothing (regulation 24)

4.96 Suitable and sufficient facilities shall be provided for any person at work in the workplace to change clothing where the person has to wear special clothing for the purpose of work, and he cannot, for reasons of health or propriety, be expected to change in another room. Separate facilities for men and women shall be provided where necessary for reasons of propriety.

Facilities for rest and to eat meals (regulation 25)

4.97 Suitable and sufficient rest facilities shall be provided at readily accessible places. In the case of new workplaces, extensions or conversions, where necessary for reasons of health or safety, one or more rest rooms shall be provided. In other cases, a rest room or rest areas may be provided. Where food is eaten in a workplace which would otherwise become contaminated, suitable facilities for eating meals shall be provided.

4.98 Rest rooms and rest areas shall include suitable arrangements to protect non-smokers from discomfort caused by tobacco smoke. Suitable facilities shall be provided for any person at work who is a pregnant woman or nursing mother to rest.

4.99 Suitable and sufficient facilities shall be provided for persons at work to eat meals, where meals are eaten regularly in the workplace.

4.100 The ACOP suggests that suitable seats should be provided as appropriate, eating facilities should be kept clean to a suitable hygiene standard, and general advice is further given on compliance with this regulation.

Exemption certificates (regulation 26)

4.101 The Secretary of State for Defence may, in the interests of national security, exempt the armed forces and visiting armed forces from the requirements of the regulations, subject to conditions and a time limit.

Repeals and revocations (regulation 27 and Schedule 2)

4.102 The following statutory provisions are repealed in respect of new premises (see para 4.59), as from 1 January 1993:

- (a) Factories Act 1961, ss.1–7, 18, 29, 57–60, 69
- (b) Offices, Shops and Railway Premises Act 1963, ss.4–16
- (c) Agriculture (Safety, Health and Welfare Provisions) Act 1956, ss.3, 5, 25(3)(6).

4.103 Some 36 regulations and Orders, dating from 1906 onward, have also been revoked, either in whole or in part, from the same date, in respect of new premises.

4.104 In respect of existing premises (see para 4.59) the above repeals and revocations will take effect from 1 January 1996.

Provision and Use of Work Equipment Regulations 1992

4.105 These regulations are designed to implement EC Directive 89/655/EEC on the minimum health and safety requirements for use of work equipment at the workplace. They are accompanied by Guidance Notes.

4.106 To some extent there is an overlap between the Work Equipment Regulations and the provisions of the Machinery Directive (89/392/EEC as amended), which are implemented by the Supply and Machinery (Safety) Regulations 1992. The "Supply" Regulations impose obligations on manufacturers and suppliers of work equipment to meet essential health and safety requirements (in line with the provisions of s.6 of HSWA, see para 3.71), and work equipment which is able to satisfy the requirements of the Machinery Directive ("Supply" Regulations) will be exempt from some of the specific requirements of the Work Equipment Regulations, contained in regulations 11–24.

4.107 There is a further overlap between the Work Equipment Regulations and a number of other legislative provisions. The general rule to be adopted is that compliance with specific legal requirements will be sufficient to comply with more general requirements. For example regulation 19 of the Work Equipment Regulations requires isolation from sources of energy, but, so far as electrical power is concerned, regulation 12 of the Electricity at Work Regulations would be the more appropriate legal rule to follow.

4.108 HSC took the view that some of the requirements of the Work Equipment Directive were already met by existing UK legislation, and thus no further changes were sought. However, in general the new regulations tend to make explicit that which was thought to be implicit in HSWA, although an opportunity was taken to extend the legal requirements in certain areas.

4.109 One significant result of the new regulations will be the eventual repeal of some familiar sections of the Factories Act (ss.12–16, 17, and 19, see para 5.35), s.17 of OSRPA, and the revocation of some 17 sets of regulations (in whole or in part). This is a consequence of the process of modernisation of the law and its extension into areas of employment not previously covered.

4.110 However, it is important to bear in mind that the regulations will come into effect in two stages.

4.111 The general requirements of regulations 5–10 will apply from 1 January 1993. The more specific requirements of regulations 11–24, and Schedule 2 (which repeals and revokes old legislation) will come into effect:

(a) in respect of work equipment *first provided for use* on or after 1 January 1993, from 1 January 1993
(b) in respect of work equipment *first provided for use* before 1 January 1993, from 1 January 1997.

4.112 Thus the legislation which is scheduled for repeal will continue in force until 1 January 1997 in respect of work equipment provided for use prior to 1 January 1993, so that industry will have a four year period in which to replace or modernise existing work equipment. The test to be applied is the date on which the work equipment was first provided for use in the work premises. This is not necessarily the date when the equipment was first brought into use. Thus equipment which was delivered prior to 1 January 1993 (and not used before that date, eg because it was in the stores) will not be required to comply with the relevant provisions of the regulations until 1 January 1997. If secondhand work equipment is purchased after 1 January 1993, then it is regarded as being new equipment, and must comply with the regulations. This is also true of equipment which has been hired or leased. But if work equipment is purchased before 1 January 1993 and is then moved to another part of the work premises belonging to the same undertaking, it will be regarded as existing equipment, and compliance will not be necessary until January 1997.

Application of the Regulations

4.113 The regulations apply to all employers (except to the employer of the master and crew of seagoing ships), to self-employed persons in respect of work equipment they use at work, to those who control non-domestic premises in respect of work equipment used in such premises (see s.4 of HSWA, para 3.59), to off-shore installations, and to the occupiers of factories.

4.114 The phrase "work equipment" is defined widely, as being "any machinery, appliance, apparatus or tool, and any assembly of components which, in order to achieve a common end, are arranged and controlled so that they can function as a whole." Vehicles which are not privately owned are also included in the definition (see *British Railways Board v Liptrot*, para 5.42). Excluded would be substances, livestock and buildings.

4.115 Work equipment is in "use" when it is involved in any activity, including starting, stopping, programming, setting, transporting, repairing, modifying, maintaining, servicing and cleaning.

4.116 The following provisions (regulations 5–9) apply to all work equipment, whether provided for use before or after 1 January 1993.

Suitability of work equipment (regulation 5)

4.117 Every employer shall ensure that work equipment is so constructed or adapted as to be suitable for the purpose for which it is used or provided. In selecting work equipment, every employer shall have regard to the working conditions and the risks to the health and safety of persons which exist in the premises in which it is to be used, and any additional risk posed by the use of the work equipment. The operations for which, and the conditions under which, work equipment is to be used must be suitable in any respect which it is reasonably foreseeable will affect the health or safety of any person.

4.118 The Guidance Notes point out that the risk assessment to be carried out under the Management of Health and Safety at Work Regulations (see para 4.8) will help employers to select work equipment and assess its suitability for particular tasks. The location where work equipment is to be used must also be assessed, to take account of risks which may arise in the particular circumstances, as well as the particular process.

Maintainance (regulation 6)

4.119 Every employer shall ensure that work equipment is maintained in an efficient state, in efficient working order and in good repair. If a maintenance log is used, it shall be kept up to date.

4.120 This regulation refers to the condition of work equipment as it affects health and safety, and is not concerned with its productivity, although the two concepts are clearly associated. The Guidance Notes state that maintenance work should be carried out by persons who have received adequate information, instruction and training. Routine maintenance includes periodic lubrication, inspection and testing, taking into account the manufacturer's recommendations as well as legal requirements. Planned preventative maintenance should be designed to prevent failures when the equipment is in use.

Specific risks (regulation 7)

4.121 Where the use of work equipment is likely to involve a specific risk to health or safety, every employer shall ensure that the use of that equipment is restricted to those persons who have been given the task of using it, and that repairs, modifications, maintenance and servicing is restricted to those persons who have been specifically designated to perform operations of that description, and that they have been given adequate training to do this type of work.

Information and instructions (regulation 8)

4.122 Every employer shall ensure that all persons who use work equipment have available to them adequate health and safety information and, where appropriate, written instructions about the use of work equipment. This also applies to persons who supervise or manage the use of work equipment. The information and/or written instructions shall include:

(a) the conditions in which and the methods by which work equipment may be used
(b) foreseeable abnormal situations, and the action to be taken should these occur, and
(c) any conclusions drawn from experience in using the work equipment.

4.123 The information and instructions shall be readily comprehensible to those concerned.

4.124 The Guidance Notes point out that it is for the employer to decide whether it is appropriate to give the information in writing or verbally. The individual circumstances should be taken into account, including the degree of skill of the employees involved, their experience and training, the degree of supervision and the complexity and length of the job. Information provided by manufacturers should be referred to, and all the information and instructions should be available to supervisors and managers. The information and instructions should be presented in clear English or other languages where necessary. Special arrangements may be needed for those with reading difficulties.

Training (regulation 9)

4.125 Every employer shall ensure that all persons who use work equipment have received adequate training for purposes of health and safety, including methods which may be adopted when using work equipment, any risks which such use may entail, and precautions to be taken. An identical provision applies to supervisors and managers.

4.126 The Guidance Notes point out that where specific legislation requires detailed training, that will continue to apply. Special attention should be given to the needs of young persons.

Conformity with Community requirements (regulation 10)

4.127 With respect to work equipment first provided for use for the first time after 31 December 1992, every employer shall ensure that it complies with any enactment which implements in Great Britain any relevant EC Directive listed in Schedule 1 to the regulations. If it does so comply, the requirements of regulations 11–24 (below) are disapplied.

4.128 The Guidance Notes point out that in future, employers should ensure that work equipment purchased complies with any legislation which implements the relevant EC Directive, if necessary checking that there is a CE mark and requesting a copy of the EC Declaration of Conformity. The relevant regulations implementing the EC Directives will be drawn up by the Department of Trade and Industry in due course. However, EC Product Directives do not operate retrospectively, and therefore secondhand equipment introduced for the first time will have to comply with regulations 11–24.

4.129 The "new approach" Directives (passed under Article 100A of the Treaty of Rome) lay down essential safety requirements which must be met before any products may be sold anywhere within the Community. Manufacturers will be able to fix a common "CE Mark" which will indicate compliance with harmonised standards. Directives which are relevant to safety at work include the Machinery Directive (implemented by the Supply of Machinery (Safety) Regulations 1992), the Personal Protective Equipment Directive (implemented by the Personal Protective Equipment (EC Directive) Regulations 1992) and the Simple Pressure Vessels

Directive (implemented by the Simple Pressure Vessels (Safety) Regulations 1991). Others will doubtless follow in due course.

4.130 The following provisions (regulations 11–24 and Schedule 2 (which contains the repeals and revocations) come into force:

(a) with regard to work equipment first provided for use after 31 December 1992, from 1 January 1993
(b) with regard to work equipment first provided for use before 1 January 1993, from 1 January 1997. Thus the Acts and regulations which are scheduled for repeal will continue in force in respect of such work equipment until that date, thus giving a four year period in which to ensure compliance.

Dangerous parts of machinery (regulation 11)

4.131 The purpose of this regulation is to require the employer to take measures which are effective to:

(a) prevent access to any dangerous part of machinery or to any rotating stock bar, or
(b) stop the movement of any dangerous part of machinery or rotating stock bar before any part of a person enters a danger zone.

4.132 The measures to be taken are:

(a) the provision of fixed guards enclosing every dangerous part or rotating stock bar where and to the extent that it is practicable to do so. However, if this is not practicable, then
(b) the provision of other guards or other protection devices where and to the extent that it is practicable to do so. However, if this is not practicable, then
(c) the provision of jigs, holders, push-sticks or similar protection appliances used in connection with the machinery where and to the extent that it is practicable to do so. However, if this is not practicable, then
(d) the provision of information, instruction, training and supervision.

4.133 All guards and protection devices and protection appliances shall:

(a) be suitable for the purpose for which they are provided
(b) be of good construction, sound material and adequate strength
(c) be maintained in an efficient state, in efficient working order and in good repair
(d) not give rise to any increased risk to health or safety
(e) not be easily bypassed or disabled (this does not apply to protection appliances)
(f) be situated at sufficient distance from the danger zone (this does not apply to protection appliances)

(g) not unduly restrict the view of the operating cycle of the machinery, where such a view is necessary
(h) be so constructed or adapted that they allow operations necessary to fit or replace parts, allow maintenance work, and restrict access so that this is allowed only to the area where the work is to be carried out—if possible without having to dismantle the guard or protection device (this does not apply to protection appliances).

4.134 A "danger zone" is defined as "any zone in or around machinery in which a person is exposed to a risk to health or safety from contact with a dangerous part of machinery or a rotating stock bar".

4.135 The Guidance Notes indicate that if a hazard could present a reasonably foreseeable risk to a person's health or safety, then the part of machinery which generates that hazard is a "dangerous part". The regulation lays down a hierarchy of measures, to be followed sequentially, ie (a) fixed enclosing guards, (b) other guards or protection devices, (c) protection appliances, and (d) provision of information, etc. The risk assessment carried out under the Management of Health and Safety at Work Regulations will no doubt identify the hazards and indicate the appropriate action to be taken. Attached to the Guidance Notes is Appendix 3, giving further information on action to be taken with respect to dangerous parts of machinery in order to ensure compliance with regulation 11.

Protection against specific hazards (regulation 12)

4.136 Every employer shall ensure that exposure of any person using work equipment to certain specified hazards is prevented or (where that is not reasonably practicable), adequately controlled. The hazards specified are:

(a) any article or substance falling or being ejected from work equipment
(b) rupture or disintegration of parts of work equipment
(c) work equipment catching fire or overheating
(d) the unintended or premature discharge of any article, or of any gas, dust, liquid, vapour or other substance which is produced, used or stored in the work equipment
(e) the unintended or premature explosion of the work equipment or any article or substance produced, used or stored in it.

4.137 The measures to be taken to comply with this regulation are:

(a) measures other than the provision of personal protective equipment, or of information, instruction, training and supervision, so far as is reasonably practicable, and

(b) measures to minimise the effects of the hazard as well as reducing the likelihood of the hazard occurring.

4.138 However, this regulation does not apply in those circumstances already covered by existing regulations, ie:

(a) Control of Lead at Work Regulations
(b) Ionising Radiation Regulations
(c) Control of Asbestos at Work Regulations
(d) Control of Substances Hazardous to Health Regulations
(e) Noise at Work Regulations
(f) Construction (Head Protection) Regulations.

4.139 Again, the Guidance Notes point out that the risk assessment will identify the hazards and the measures which need to be taken to ensure compliance with the regulation.

High or very low temperature (regulation 13)

4.140 Every employer shall ensure that work equipment (including parts) and any article or substance produced, used or stored in work equipment which is at a high or very low temperature shall have protection where appropriate so as to prevent injury to any person by burn, scald or sear.

4.141 The Guidance Notes point out that although engineering methods should be considered first, other forms of protection may be necessary, eg personal protective equipment, warning signals and alarms, etc.

Controls for starting or changing operating conditions (regulation 14)

4.142 Every employer shall ensure that, where appropriate, work equipment is provided with one or more controls for the purpose of starting the work equipment, or controlling the speed or pressure of work equipment. It should not be possible to perform either function except by a deliberate action on a control other than restarting or changing operating conditions as a result of the normal operating cycle of an automatic device.

Stop controls (regulation 15)

4.143 Every employer shall ensure that, where appropriate, work equipment is provided with one or more readily accessible controls, the operation of which will bring the work equipment to a safe condition in a safe manner. These controls shall bring the work equipment to a complete stop where necessary for reasons of health or safety. The controls will switch off all sources of energy after stopping the functioning of the work equipment. Stop controls shall operate in priority to any control which starts or changes the operating conditions.

Emergency stop controls (regulation 16)

4.144 Every employer shall ensure that work equipment is provided with an accessible emergency stop control, unless this is not necessary by reason of the nature of the hazard and the time taken for the work equipment to come to a complete stop after using other stop controls. Emergency stop controls shall operate in priority to other controls.

Controls (regulation 17)

4.145 Every employer shall ensure that all controls are clearly visible and identifiable, including by appropriate marking where necessary and should not be in a position where any person operating them is exposed to a risk to his health or safety. The operator should be able to ensure that no person is in a place where he would be exposed to any risk to his health or safety as a result of the operation of the control, but, if this is not reasonably practicable, systems of work should be effective to ensure that when the work equipment is about to start no person is in a place where he would be exposed to a risk to his health or safety. Finally, if neither of these is reasonably practicable, then an audible, visual or other suitable warning shall be given whenever the work equipment is about to start. Appropriate measures shall also be taken to ensure that persons who are in a place where they would be exposed to a risk as a result of the starting or stopping of work equipment have sufficient time and sufficient means to avoid the risk.

Control systems (regulation 18)

4.146 Every employer shall ensure that, so far as is reasonably practicable, all control systems of work equipment are safe. A control system shall not be safe unless its operation does not create any increased risk to health or safety, it ensures, so far as is reasonably practicable, that any fault or damage or loss of energy supply cannot result in additional or increased risk to health or safety, and it does not impede the operation of any stop controls or emergency controls.

Isolation from sources of energy (regulation 19)

4.147 Every employer shall ensure that where appropriate work equipment is provided with suitable means to isolate it from all its sources of energy. Such means shall be clearly identifiable and readily accessible. Reconnection of an energy source must not expose any person using the work equipment to any risk to his health or safety.

Stability (regulation 20)

4.148 Every employer shall ensure that work equipment is stabilised by clamping or otherwise where necessary for the purposes of health or safety.

Lighting (regulation 21)

4.149 Every employer shall ensure that suitable and sufficient lighting is provided, taking account of the operations to be carried out.

Maintenance operations (regulation 22)

4.150 Every employer shall take appropriate measures to ensure that work equipment is so constructed or adapted that, so far as is reasonably practicable, maintenance operations which involve a risk to health or safety can be carried out while the work equipment is shut down. In other cases, maintenance operations must be able to be carried out without exposing the person doing them to a risk to his health or safety, or appropriate protection measures are taken.

Markings (regulation 23)

4.151 Every employer shall ensure that work equipment is marked in a clearly visible manner with any marking appropriate for reasons of health or safety.

Warnings (regulation 24)

4.152 Every employer shall ensure that work equipment incorporates any warnings or warning devices which are appropriate for reasons of health or safety. Such warnings shall be unambiguous, easily perceived and easily understood.

Exemption certificates (regulation 25)

4.153 The Secretary of State for Defence may, in the interests of national security, exempt the armed forces and visiting armed forces from any of the requirements of these regulations, subject to time limits and/or conditions.

Personal Protective Equipment at Work Regulations 1992

4.154 These regulations are designed to implement EC Directive 89/656/EEC on the Minimum Health and Safety Requirements for the Use of Personal Protective Equipment at the Workplace. They came into force on 1 January 1993. They should be considered along with the Personal Protective Equipment at Work Regulations 1992 which implement the Personal Protective Equipment Product Directive (89/686/EEC) dealing with the quality and marking of personal protective equipment.

4.155 There are in existence a number of health and safety regulations made under HSWA relating to personal protective equipment (PPE), ie Control of Lead at Work Regulations 1980, Ionising Radiation Regulations 1985, Control of Substances

Hazardous to Health Regulations 1987, Noise at Work Regulations 1989, Construction (Head Protection) Regulations 1989, and Control of Asbestos at Work Regulations 1987. These regulations will continue in force, although they have been modified slightly so as to conform with the new regulations, so that the latter will not apply to the extent the former require the provision of personal protective equipment.

4.156 On the other hand, there are a large number of pre-HSWA regulations which deal with personal protective equipment, and most of these have been revoked (including the familiar Protection of Eyes Regulations) as they are no longer necessary. Certain legislative provisions which deal with specialised subjects (eg docks, electricity, construction and off-shore installations) are retained, and are complemented by the new regulations. Also, the new regulations do not apply to the master or crew of a seagoing ship, to ordinary clothes or uniforms which do not specifically protect the health and safety of the wearer, portable devices for detecting risks and nuisances, ppe used for protection while travelling on a road, equipment used during the playing of competitive sports or an offensive weapon used for self-defence or deterrence.

4.157 Personal protective equipment is defined as being all equipment (including clothing affording protection against the weather) which is intended to be worn or held by a person at work and which protects him against one or more risks to his health or safety. The Guidance Notes suggest that ppe includes protective clothing (aprons, waterproof clothes, gloves, safety footwear, safety helmets, high visibility waistcoats, etc), and protective equipment (eye protectors, life-jackets, respirators, underwater breathing apparatus and safety harnesses). Ordinary working clothes and protective clothing used for the purpose of hygiene would not be included.

4.158 The Personal Protective Equipment at Work Regulations 1992 implement the EC Product Directive, and, where appropriate, ppe will have to bear the CE mark. However, ppe obtained before this Regulation came into force may continue to be used as long as it remains suitable for the purpose.

Provision of Personal Protective Equipment (regulation 4)

4.159 Every employer shall ensure that suitable personal protective equipment is provided to his employees who may be exposed to a risk to their health or safety while at work, except where and to the extent that such risk has been adequately controlled by other means which are equally or more effective. A similar obligation is imposed on self-employed persons in respect of their own activities.

4.160 Personal protective equipment shall not be suitable, unless:

(a) it is appropriate for the risk involved and the conditions at the place where exposure to the risk may occur
(b) it takes account of the ergonomic requirements and the state of health of the wearer

(c) it is capable of fitting the wearer correctly (if necessary after adjustment)
(d) so far as is practicable, it is effective to prevent or adequately control the risks involved without increasing overall risk
(e) it complies with any enactment which implements relevant EC Directives applicable to that item of personal protective equipment.

4.161 The Guidance Notes suggest that personal protective equipment should be regarded as a "last resort". Engineering controls and safe systems of work should first be considered, so that risks are controlled or prevented at source. PPE should be readily available, and generally supplied to employees on an individual basis, although there may be circumstances where it can be shared (eg if only required for a limited period).

4.162 No charge may be made for the provision of ppe (see HSWA s.9, see para 3.99), even if the employer permits the use by the employee outside working hours.

4.163 When considering the provision of personal protective equipment, it is important to bear in mind the need to avoid "overkill". For example, if there is a noise hazard, the protection must match the volume of noise which is hazardous, but not eliminate harmless (or even useful) noise, for this could result in a greater hazard being created. An employee who wears every single item of protective clothing provided by his employer would probably resemble someone from outer space, and is likely to be a positive menace to himself and to others.

4.164 Personal protective equipment must be suitable for each employee to use or wear, for the legal duty is owed to them as individuals, not collectively (*Paris v Stepney Borough Council*).

4.165 The legal problems involved in enforcing the use of personal protective equipment will be examined in Chapter 9.

Compatibility of Personal Protective Equipment (regulation 5)

4.166 Every employer shall ensure that where the presence of more than one risk makes it necessary for his employee to wear or use simultaneously more than one item of personal protective equipment, such equipment is compatible and continues to be effective against the risks in question. A similar obligation is placed on self-employed persons.

Assessment of personal protective equipment (regulation 6)

4.167 Before choosing personal protective equipment, employers (and self-employed persons) shall ensure that an assessment is made in order to determine whether the personal protective equipment he intends to provide is suitable. The assessment shall include:

(a) risks which have not been avoided by other means
(b) the definition of the characteristics which the personal protective equipment must have in order to be effective
(c) a comparison of the characteristics of the personal protective equipment available with those needed to avoid the risk.

4.168 Employers (and self-employed persons) shall review any such assessment if they have reason to believe that it is no longer valid, or if there has been a significant change in the matters to which it relates. If any changes are required as a result of the review, these shall be made.

4.169 The Guidance Notes (Appendix 1) give a specimen risk survey table which may be used to determine whether or not personal protective equipment is required. There is also considerable advice given on the selection, use and maintenance of ppe in widely different circumstances.

Maintenance and replacement of personal protective equipment (regulation 7)

4.170 Every employer shall ensure that any personal protective equipment provided to his employees is maintained in an efficient state, in efficient order, in good repair and is replaced or cleaned as appropriate. A similar obligation is placed on self-employed persons.

4.171 The Guidance Notes suggest that ppe should be examined when issued, before it is used or worn, and it should not be used or worn if found to be defective or unclean. A sufficient stock of spare parts should be available, and maintenance programmes should include, where appropriate, cleaning, disinfection, examination, repair, testing and record keeping. Manufacturers' maintenance schedules and instructions should normally be followed.

Accommodation for personal protective equipment (regulation 8)

4.172 Every employer shall ensure that appropriate accommodation is provided for personal protective equipment when it is not being used.

4.173 The Guidance Notes point out that accommodation may be simple, as long as it is appropriate. It should protect ppe from contamination, loss or damage.

Information, instruction and training (regulation 9)

4.174 Where personal protective equipment is provided, employers shall ensure that the employee is provided with such information, instruction and training as is adequate and appropriate to enable the employee to know:

(a) the risks which the personal protective equipment will avoid or limit

(b) the purpose for which, and the manner in which the personal protective equipment is to be used, and
(c) any action to be taken by the employee to ensure that it remains in an efficient state, in efficient working order and in good repair.

4.175 The information and instructions given will not be adequate and appropriate unless it is comprehensible to the persons to whom it is provided.

4.176 The Guidance Notes point out that the extent of the training will vary with the complexity of the equipment. Training should be both theoretical and practical, and its duration and frequency will depend on the individual circumstances. Refresher training should be considered if necessary.

Use of personal protective equipment (regulation 10)

4.177 Every employer shall take all reasonable steps to ensure that any personal protective equipment provided to his employees is properly used.

4.178 Every employee shall use personal protective equipment provided to him in accordance with the training given to him and the instructions respecting its use. Self-employed persons shall also make full and proper use of personal protective equipment. Employees and self-employed persons shall take all reasonable steps to ensure that personal protective equipment provided is returned to the accommodation provided for it after use.

Reporting loss or defect (regulation 11)

4.179 Every employee who has been provided with personal protective equipment shall forthwith report to his employer any loss or obvious defect.

Exemption certificates (regulation 12)

4.180 The Secretary of State for Defence may exempt the armed forces and visiting armed forces from the regulations, subject to conditions and/or limitations of time.

Extension outside Great Britain (regulation 13)

4.181 The regulations apply to off-shore installations, pipelines within territorial waters and areas designated under the Continental Shelf Act 1964 (see para 1.108).

Repeals, revocations and modifications (regulation 14)

4.182 The regulations revoke some twenty old regulations dealing with personal protective equipment, repeal s.65 of the Factories Act 1961, and modify six regulations (see para 4.155) so that they harmonise with the new law.

Manual Handling Operations Regulations 1992

4.183 These regulations are designed to implement EC Directive 90/269/EEC of the minimum health and safety requirements for the manual handling of loads. They are accompanied by Guidance Notes, and came into force on 1 January 1993.

4.184 Accidents caused by manual handling of loads account for some 25% of all reportable accidents. The cost to industry in terms of lost time, compensation payments, etc and the cost to the State by way of medical attention, social security benefits, etc is huge. Accidents of this nature occur in all types of employment and to all categories of workers. Previous legislation had a somewhat limited application, and was usually framed in a general manner. Some specific industries did have actual weight limits, but these were neither effective nor justifiable, because they failed to take into account individual capabilities.

4.185 Consequently, the new regulations have repealed a number of statutory provisions, including Factories Act 1961, s.72, Offices, Shops and Railway Premises Act 1963, s.23(1), and Agriculture (Safety, Health and Welfare Provisions) Act 1956, s.2. In addition, the Agriculture (Lifting of Heavy Weights) Regulations 1959 were revoked, as was regulation 55 of the Construction (General Provisions) Regulations 1961.

Application of the Regulations

4.186 The Regulations apply to all employers in respect of their employees at work, including offshore installations, pipelines, etc (see para 1.108). They also apply to self-employed persons in respect of their own activities. However, they do not apply to the master or crew of a seagoing ship.

4.187 The phrase "manual handling operations" is defined as any transporting or supporting of a load (including the lifting, putting down, pushing, pulling, carrying or moving) by hand or by bodily force. A "load" includes any person or animal. However, an injury does not include any contact with a corrosive or toxic substance.

4.188 A breach of the regulations may give rise to civil and/or criminal liability.

Duties of employers (regulation 4)

4.189 Every employer shall, so far as is reasonably practicable, avoid the need for his employees to undertake any manual handling operations which involve the risk of their being injured.

4.190 Where this is not reasonably practicable, the employer shall make a suitable and sufficient assessment of all such manual handling operations, taking into account the factors which are specified in Schedule 1 to the regulations, and considering the associated questions.

4.191 The factors and the questions are as follows:

Factors	Questions
1. The Tasks	Do they involve: – holding or manipulating loads at distance from the trunk? – unsatisfactory bodily movement or posture, especially: twisting the trunk? stooping? reaching upwards? – excessive movement of loads, especially: (a) excessive lifting or lowering distances (b) excessive carrying distances? – excessive pushing or pulling of loads? – risk of sudden movement of loads? – frequent or prolonged physical effort? – insufficient rest or recovery periods? – a rate of work imposed by a process?
2. The Loads	Are they: – heavy? – bulky or unwieldy? – difficult to grasp? – unstable, or with contents likely to shift? – sharp, hot or otherwise potentially damaging?
3. The Working Environment	Are there: – space constraints preventing good posture? – uneven, slippery or unstable floors? – variations in level of floors or work surfaces? – extremes of temperature or humidity? – conditions causing ventilation problems or gusts of wind? – poor lighting conditions?
4. Individual Capability	Does the job: – require unusual strength, height, etc? – create a hazard to those who might reasonably be considered to be pregnant or to have a health problem? – require special information or training for its safe performance?
5. Other Factors	Is movement or posture hindered by personal protective equipment or by clothing?

Thus, having regard to those factors, and the answers to the questions posed, the employer shall take appropriate steps to reduce the risk of injury to those employees to the lowest level reasonably practicable.

4.192 The employer shall also provide general indications and precise information (where it is reasonably practicable to do so) on the weight of the load, and the heaviest side of any load whose centre of gravity is not positioned centrally. The assessment which has been carried out shall be reviewed if there is reason to believe that there has been a significant change in the operations, and such revisions made as are appropriate in the circumstances.

4.193 The Guidance Notes which accompany the regulations are extremely informative, and will repay detailed study. It is pointed out that the aim of the regulations is to prevent injury to any part of the body, and thus account must be taken of the external properties of the load (eg slipperiness, sharp edges, etc) as well as its weight, size, bulk, etc. Hazards from the contents of the load (eg corrosive substances) are not generally covered, although this should be considered under other appropriate legislation (eg COSHH Regulations, etc). The load may be animate or inanimate, but generally will not be a tool or instrument.

4.194 The first task of the employer is to avoid manual handling where possible and where this is not possible the next task is to make an assessment, taking into account the matters already mentioned. Proper records should be kept, and any evidence which reveals an indication of a relationship between manual handling and ill-health (eg absenteeism due to some form of back injury) should be noted. Employees and safety representatives should be involved in redesigning the systems of work, loads should be reduced to manageable size or otherwise made risk free, and the capabilities of each employee assessed.

Duties of employees (regulation 5)

4.195 Each employee while at work shall make full and proper use of any system of work provided for his use by his employer in compliance with the latter's duty to take appropriate steps to reduce the risk of injury.

4.196 This duty should be read together with the employee's duty under s.7 of HSWA. Also of relevance is regulation 12 of the Management of Health and Safety at Work Regulations (see para 4.45), which requires employees to use appropriate equipment provided.

Exemption certificates (regulation 6)

4.197 The Secretary of State for Defence may, in the interests of national security, exempt the armed forces and visiting armed forces from the requirements of certain parts of the regulations, subject to conditions and/or time limits.

Health and Safety (Display Screen Equipment) Regulations 1992

4.198 These regulations are designed to implement EC Directive 90/270/EEC on the minimum health and safety requirements for work with display screen equipment. They are accompanied by Guidance Notes.

4.199 Currently, there are no other legislative provisions on this topic, other than the general duties laid down by HSWA. However, the advent of modern technology in this field has brought in its wake a number of health and safety problems, including musculo-skeletal injuries, visual fatigue and mental stress. Such illnesses are not an inevitable consequence of working with display screen equipment, but the introduction of sound ergonomic techniques can reduce the incidence.

Application of the Regulations (regulation 1)

4.200 The term "display screen equipment" refers to any alphanumeric or graphic display screen, regardless of the display process involved. The Guidance Notes state that this definition covers cathode ray tube and liquid crystal displays. As well as the typical office visual display terminals, non-electronic display systems such as microfiche are covered, but not screens used to show television or films, unless the main purpose is to display text, numbers and/or graphics.

4.201 The regulations are generally for the benefit of every person "who habitually uses display screen equipment as a significant part of his normal work". Clearly, the interpretation to be given to the words "habitually uses" and "significant part" is going to be crucial. The Guidance Notes suggest that a person will be covered by the regulations if most or all of the following criteria apply:

(a) whether the individual has to depend on the display screen equipment to do his job, because alternative means are not readily available for achieving the same results
(b) whether the individual has no discretion in using it
(c) whether the individual has had special training and/or particular skills in the use of the equipment
(d) whether the individual normally uses the equipment for continuous spells of an hour or more at a time on a more or less daily basis
(e) whether the fast transfer of information is an important requirement of the job
(f) whether the performance requirements of the system demands high level of attention and concentration.

4.202 The Guidance Notes give a list of examples of persons who are definitely users, eg word processing pool worker, data input operator, air traffic controller, and so on. Some possible users would be airline check-in clerks, customer support officers at a building society, depending on the circumstances. Persons who would not be users include receptionists who only use display screens occasionally.

4.203 Generally, the regulations are for the protection of two classes of persons, namely "users" and "operators". The former will be an employee, whether working at his employer's workstation, a workstation at home, or at another employer's workstation. The latter term is a self-employed person who habitually uses display screen equipment as a significant part of his normal work.

4.204 The regulations also cover "the workstation", which means the actual display screen equipment, optional accessories, peripheral equipment (disk drive, telephone, modem, printer, chair, desk, etc) and the immediate environment.

4.205 The regulations do not apply to:

(a) drivers' cabs or control cabs for vehicles or machinery
(b) display screen equipment on board a means of transport
(c) display screen equipment mainly intended for public use
(d) portable systems not in prolonged use
(e) calculators, cash registers or any equipment having a small data or measurement display
(f) window typewriters.

4.206 A breach of the regulations may give rise to civil and/or criminal liability.

Analysis of workstations (regulation 2)

4.207 Every employer shall perform a suitable and sufficient analysis of those workstations which:

(a) (regardless of who has provided them) are used for the purposes of his undertaking by users, or
(b) have been provided by him and are used for the purposes of his undertaking by operators,

for the purpose of assessing the health and safety risks to which those persons are exposed in consequence of that use. The assessment shall be reviewed if the employer has reason to believe it is no longer valid, and if revisions are required as a result, these shall be made. Risks which have been identified shall be reduced to the lowest extent reasonably practicable.

4.208 The Guidance Notes state that in simple and obvious cases, there is no need to record the assessment, ie if no significant risks are indicated. However, records are useful to ensure continuity and accuracy, and to check on risk reduction methods. The views of the individual users are an essential part of any assessment. Remedial action should be taken when risks are disclosed, especially postural problems, visual problems and fatigue and stress.

Requirements for workstations (regulation 3)

4.209 In respect of workstations first put into service on or after 1 January 1993, the employer shall ensure that the requirements which are laid down in the Schedule to the regulations are met. For workstations which were already being used on 31 December 1992, these requirements shall be met not later than 31 December 1996.

4.210 The Schedule requires that attention should be given to all the factors which might affect the health and safety of the user or operator, including:

(a) the display screen
(b) the keyboard
(c) the work desk or work surface
(d) environmental requirements, such as space, lighting, reflection and glare, noise, heat, radiation and humidity
(e) interface between the computer and operator or user, etc.

4.211 The Guidance Notes provide some useful advice on compliance with these requirements.

Daily work routine of users (regulation 4)

4.212 Every employer shall so plan the activities of users at work in his undertaking that their daily work on display screen equipment is periodically interrupted by such breaks or changes in activity as reduce their workload at that equipment.

4.213 The Guidance Notes suggest that spells of intensive screen work should be broken by activities which do not require broadly similar use of the arms or hands, or which are not equally visually demanding. Further guidance is given on the taking of rest breaks, which should be designed to prevent the onset of fatigue.

Eyes and eyesight (regulation 5)

4.214 This regulation is for the benefit of users (ie employees) and persons who are to become users in the undertaking in which they are employed. The employer shall ensure that such persons are provided (at their request) with an appropriate eye and eyesight test, to be carried out by a competent person. Such tests shall be carried out at regular intervals. Also, where a user experiences visual difficulties from using display screen equipment, the employer shall arrange such a test.

4.215 Further, every employer shall ensure that each user employed by him is provided with special corrective appliances appropriate for the display screen work being done by the user where:

(a) normal corrective appliances cannot be used, and
(b) the result of any eye and eyesight test the user has had under this regulation shows such provision to be necessary.

4.216 This is probably the most important provision in the regulations, but its limitations should be noted.

4.217 (1) The regulation only applies to employees who are users at the date when the regulations came into force, ie 1 January 1993, and (thereafter) to any employee who is a non-user and who is to become a user. There is no obligation to provide tests and/or appliances to prospective employees, although once they are employed as users, there would be an obligation if they experienced visual difficulties caused by the work (it is submitted that the legal interpretation given by the Guidance Notes on this regulation is not correct, and should therefore be treated with caution).

4.218 (2) The special corrective appliances need only be supplied where normal corrective appliances cannot be used. The Guidance Notes suggest that only a small minority of the working population would need the special appliances. Anti-glare screens, VDU spectacles, etc are not within this category. The employer's liability is to pay for the cost of a basic appliance necessary for the display screen work.

Provision of training (regulation 6)

4.219 Every employer shall ensure that each user (and a person about to become a user) shall receive adequate health and safety training in the use of the workstation on which he is required to work, and also when the workstation is substantially modified.

4.220 The Guidance Notes point out that the purpose of training in health and safety requirements is to minimise the risks of musculo-skeletal injuries, visual fatigue and mental stress. The aspects of training which should be covered are outlined.

Provision of information (regulation 7)

4.221 Every employer shall ensure that operators and users at work in his undertaking are provided with adequate information about:

(a) all aspects of health and safety relating to their workstations, and
(b) the measures taken by the employer to analyse the workstation (under regulation 2 above) and the measures taken to comply with the requirements of regulation 3 and the Schedule.

4.222 Further, every employer shall provide users (ie his employees) with adequate information about the measures he has taken to periodically interrupt the work activity (regulation 4), to provide eye and eyesight testing (regulation 5) and to provide training (regulation 6).

Exemption certificates (regulation 8)

4.223 The Secretary of State for Defence may, in the interests of national security, exempt home forces and visiting armed forces from the requirements of the regulations, subject to conditions and any limits of time.

5

Health, safety and welfare in existing premises

5.1 As noted in the previous chapter, the Work Equipment Regulations and the Workplace Regulations came into force on 1 January 1993 in respect of work equipment and work premises provided on or after that date. In respect of work equipment and work premises provided before that date, the "old law" will continue in force, until 31 December 1995, so far as work equipment is concerned, and until 31 December 1995 so far as work premises is concerned. The variation in these dates is permitted by the respective EC Directives, presumably on the ground that a three year lead in period would be sufficient to modify or adapt existing work premises to the required standards, whereas a four year period would be necessary to replace work equipment. After those dates, the relevant parts of the "old law" will cease to have effect.

5.2 Thus, of the Factories Act 1961, ss.12–16, 17(1), 19 and 20, and of the Offices, Shops and Railway Premises Act 1963, ss.17–18, will continue in force in respect of work equipment provided prior to 31 December 1992 until 31 December 1996, when they will cease to have effect. This is also true of the Mines and Quarries Act 1954, ss.81(1) and 82, and a number of existing regulations (either in whole or in part, see Schedule 2 of the Provision and Use of Work Equipment Regulations), which deal with different types of machinery.

5.3 So far as work premises which are provided prior to 31 December 1992 are concerned, of the Factories Act 1961, ss.1–7, 18, 24, 28 (except subsection 5, which relates to ladders), 29, and ss.57–60, will continue in force until 31 December 1995, when they will cease to have effect. This also applies to ss.4–16 of the Offices, Shops and Railway Premises Act 1963, and to ss.3–5 and s.25(3) and (6) of the Agriculture (Safety, Health and Welfare Provisions) Act 1956, and to the whole or part of a large number of regulations and Orders (see the Schedule to the Workplace Regulations).

5.4 The remnants of the above legislative provisions will remain in force beyond those dates, unless, of course, they are repealed in the normal course of events.

5.5 However, a consideration of the "old law" will still be necessary (a) because parts of that law will be in force until 31 December 1995 and 31 December 1996 as appropriate, (b) as a means of interpreting the new law on the basis of the doctrine of *in pari materia* (see para 1.84), and (c) because there will still be outstanding a number of legal actions for some considerable time arising from the "old law".

Health, safety and welfare in factories

5.6 It will be recalled (chapter 1) that the original purpose of factory legislation was to improve working conditions by means of the threat or application of criminal sanctions, although this receded into the background as civil claims increased which were based on a breach of a statutory duty. Some doubts have been expressed as to whether or not a civil claim will lie in respect of every provision of the Factories Act (particularly those which deal with welfare matters) but the point need not detain us here. Other legal problems which arise out of claims for injuries stemming from a breach of the Act and arising at common law are dealt with in chapter 8.

Application of the Act

5.7 The Factories Act will gradually be replaced. Until this process is completed, the Factories Act 1961 only applies to those premises which in law constitute factories. Hence, the duties are generally placed on the "occupier", rather than upon the employer, although in practice this will usually be the same person. An occupier is someone who runs the factory and who regulates and controls the work that is done there (*Ramsay v Mackie*). Some of the duties in the Act are placed on the owners of the premises, eg where separate parts of a building are let off to different tenants, and he will be responsible for those matters which are under his control, for example, the common parts of stairways and passages.

5.8 The Act is designed to protect all persons who work in a factory, whether or not they are employed by the owner, occupier or employer, or are employed by some other person, or are self-employed. For example, in *Wigley v British Vinegars Ltd* a window cleaner (who was an independent contractor) fell from a height of more than 10 feet, and was killed. His widow sued the factory owner for a breach of the Factories Act which required, in these circumstances (see para 5.109) a secure handhold or fencing. It was held that the defendants were liable. The relevant section of the Act was for the benefit of "any person", and whilst these words would not necessarily cover a trespasser, or a fireman who came to put out a fire, they did cover independent contractors. However, regulations under the Act may expressly or by implication only apply to a restricted class of person (*Canadian Pacific Steamship Ltd v Bryers*).

5.9 A number of regulations have been made under the Act (and its predecessors) which are still in force, and which may modify the Act to a material extent. In *Miller v William Boothman*, a worker was injured when using a circular saw which was fenced in accordance with the Woodworking Machinery Regulations 1922. He argued that he was entitled to rely on the provisions of s.14 of the Factories Act which are absolute in their requirement that dangerous parts of machinery must be securely fenced. It was held that he could not recover damages under s.14. The power was given to the Minister to modify the Act, and the regulations prevailed. Similar modifications of statutory provisions which apply to particular types of machinery can be found in the Abrasive Wheels Regulations 1970 (passed as a result of the decision in *Summers & Sons v Frost*) and the Power Presses Regulations. However, the fact that regulations exist do not absolve the occupier from taking proper steps in relation to those matters for which the regulations make no provision (*Automatic Woodturning Co. v Stringer*).

What is a factory?

5.10 Section 175(1) defines a factory as follows:

> any premises in which, or within the close or curtilage or precincts of which, persons are employed in manual labour in any process for or incidental to any of the following purposes, namely:
>
> (a) the making of any article or part of any article, or
> (b) the altering, repairing, ornamenting, finishing, cleaning or washing or the breaking up or demolition of any article, or
> (c) the adapting for sale of any article, or
> (d) the slaughtering of animals,
> (e) the confinement of such animals while awaiting slaughter (not being a cattle market),
>
> being premises in which the work is carried on by way of trade or for the purposes of gain and to or over which the employer of the persons employed therein has the right of access or control.

5.11 This somewhat extensive statutory definition requires further examination, for although it may be easy to describe a factory, it is not easy to define one and in practice many marginal situations occur. It is tempting to say that common sense should be applied in any particular situation, but the literal wording of the Act needs to be considered first.

5.12 There must be manual labour involved. This appears to mean "working with one's hands" although the degree of strength is irrelevant. Nor is the degree of skill significant as long as working with one's hands is the main or predominant activity. In *Joyce v Boots Cash Chemists* a porter carried parcels into a chemists shop. Although he was engaged in manual labour, the premises were not a factory, for his work was not "for or incidental to" the processes of a factory. In *Hoare v Robert Green Ltd* a girl who made wreaths, crosses and bouquets in a room behind a florist's shop was held to be working in manual labour and consequently the premises were a factory, for she was engaged in making an article, and the quantum of labour involved was irrelevant. In a leading case in which the authorities were examined, it was suggested that there are a large number of people who work with their hands (authors, painters, archaeologists, art restorers, etc), but who are really engaged in intellectual activities and the manual labour aspect is largely incidental. In this case (*J & F Stone Lighting and Radio Ltd v Haygarth*) a radio and television engineer diagnosed and repaired faults in radio and television sets in a room behind a shop, and it was held that he was working in manual labour, and the premises were a factory.

5.13 An "article" is anything corporeal, ie any commodity in bulk, whether solid, liquid or gaseous in form. Thus water is an article (*Longhurst v Guildford, Godalming and District Water Board*), as is coal gas (*Cox v Cutler & Sons Ltd*), but not a live animal (*Fatstock Marketing Corporation v Morgan*). Electricity stations are subject to their own special provisions in the Act (s.123).

5.14 The phrase "adapting for sale" is also a question of fact and degree. Thus packing sweets (*Fullers Ltd v Squire*), bottling beer (*Hoare v Truman, Hanbury Buxton & Co.*) and cutting timber up (*Smith v Supreme Wood Pulp Co Ltd*) have all been held to be activities which were adapting an article for sale. But the mere testing of an article is not adapting for sale, even though it is done prior to the sale. Something must be done to the article in some way which makes it different from what it was before (*Grove v Lloyds British Testing Co. Ltd*). Premises which are used for the pumping of water into peoples' homes are not a factory, as they are solely concerned with the distribution of the article, but a filtration plant is a factory as it is adapting water for sale (*Longhurst v Guildford, Godalming and District Water Board*).

5.15 The processes must be carried on by way of trade or for the purposes of gain. This results in the exclusion of activities carried out in the workroom of a prison (*Pullen v Prison Commissioners*), instruction classes carried out in an educational institution (*Weston v London County Council*), the kitchen of a State run hospital, etc. However, activities carried on by the Crown and municipal authorities are within the Act even though they may not be carried on by way of trade or for purposes of gain, in the sense that they are not profit-making (s.175(9)).

5.16 An open air site may constitute a factory, but there must be some geographical boundaries, even if these are not walls or fences (*Barry v Cleveland Bridge and Engineering Co. Ltd*).

5.17 The premises must be used for or incidental to the purposes of a factory. Thus, although a whole area may constitute a factory, it is possible that internal parts of premises within the curtilage of a factory are not part of the factory. In *Thomas v British Thomson-Houston Co. Ltd*, within a factory there was a restaurant which was used by the directors, while the rest of the workforce used a works canteen. A worker was injured while cleaning the windows of the restaurant and he brought a claim based on a failure to provide a safe means of access and a safe place at which to work (s.29, below). It was held that although the restaurant was within the curtilage of the factory, it was not used for, or incidental to, the purposes of the factory and the claim based on a breach of s.29 failed. However, in *Luttman v ICI Ltd*, an industrial canteen, used by the workforce, was held to be premises which were incidental to the purposes of a factory and was within the definition of s.175.

5.18 Section 175(2) goes on to specify a number of other premises which are to be regarded as factories, even though they do not come within the above definition. These include:

(a) any yard or dry dock in which ships are constructed, repaired, refitted, finished or broken up
(b) any premises in which the business of sorting any articles is carried on as a preliminary to work carried on in a factory
(c) any premises in which the business of washing or filling bottles or containers or packing articles is carried on incidentally to the purposes of the factory
(d) any premises in which the business of hooking, plaiting, lapping, making up or packing of yarn or cloth is carried on
(e) any laundry carried on as an ancillary to another business or incidentally to the purposes of any public institution
(f) any premises in which the construction, reconstruction, or repair of locomotives, vehicles or other plant for use for transport purposes is carried on as ancillary to a transport undertaking or other industrial or commercial undertaking
(g) any premises in which printing by letterpress, lithography, photogravure, or similar process, or bookbinding is carried on by way of trade or for purposes of gain or incidentally to another business carried on
(h) any premises in which the making, adaptation, or repair of dresses, scenery or properties is carried on incidentally to the production, exhibition or presentation by way of trade or for purposes of gain of cinematograph films or theatrical performances (not being a stage or dressing room of a theatre in which only occasional adaptations or repairs are made)
(i) any premises in which the business of making or mending nets is carried on incidentally to the fishing industry
(j) any premises in which mechanical power is used in connection with the making or repair of articles of metal or wood incidentally to any business carried on by way of trade or for purposes of gain
(k) any premises in which the production of cinematograph films is carried on by way of trade or for purposes of gain
(l) any premises in which articles are being made or prepared incidentally to the carrying on of building operations or works of engineering construction, not being premises in which such operations or works are being carried on
(m) any premises used for the storage of gas in a gasholder having a storage capacity of not less than 5,000 cubic feet.

Cleanliness (s.1)

5.19 Every factory shall be kept in a clean state, free from effluvia arising from any drain, sanitary convenience or nuisance. In particular, accumulations of dirt and refuse shall be removed daily by a suitable method from the floors and benches of workrooms, and from the stairs and passages, and the floor shall be cleaned at least once a week by washing or, if it is effective and suitable, by sweeping or other method. All inside walls and partitions, and ceilings which have a smooth impervious surface shall be washed at least once in every fourteen months with soap and hot water or other method approved by the inspector. If they are painted or varnished, they shall be repainted or revarnished at least every seven years and washed or cleaned every fourteen months or, in every other case, be whitewashed or colourwashed at least every fourteen months. The only exception arises when the factory does not use mechanical power and less than ten persons are employed there, unless the inspector requires otherwise. The Factories (Cleanliness of Walls and Ceilings) Order 1960 (as amended) lays down the standards for the repainting, revarnishing, whitewashing or colourwashing, and provides for exemptions in respect of certain types of premises.

5.20 Financial hardship cannot be pleaded successfully as an excuse for not conforming to the requirements of s.1. In *Harrison (Newcastle-under-Lyme) Ltd v Ramsey* an improvement notice was issued requiring the company to clean or paint its walls in accordance with s.1(3). The company had been in occupation of the premises for three years and appealed against the notice on the ground that it could not afford to do the work in view of its critical financial position. The industrial tribunal upheld the notice. The financial embarrassment of the factory occupier was irrelevant. To take this into account would mean that an employer could deliberately ignore health and safety provisions on the ground of expense and thus undercut his competitors who were complying with the statutory requirements.

Overcrowding (s.2)

5.21 A factory shall not be so overcrowded as to cause the risk of injury to persons employed in it. The maximum number to be employed shall be such that each person has 11m^3 (400 cubic feet) (unless an exemption applies) and space above 7.5cm (14 feet) from the floor is not to be taken into account for determining the cubic space available. A notice specifying the number of persons who may be employed in a workroom shall be displayed unless the inspector allows otherwise.

Temperature (s.3)

5.22 A reasonable temperature shall be provided and maintained. If a substantial proportion of the work is done sitting down and does not involve serious physical effort a temperature of less than 16°C (60°F) after the first hour shall not be deemed to be reasonable while the work is continuing. At least one thermometer shall be provided and maintained in a suitable position. A failure to provide an adequate temperature was held to be a breach of an implied term of the contract of employment in *Graham Oxley Tool Steels Ltd v Firth*, entitling the employee to resign and claim that she had been constructively dismissed (see chapter 9).

Ventilation (s.4)

5.23 Effective and suitable provision shall be made for securing and maintaining by the circulation of fresh air the adequate ventilation of the workroom. Section 63, which dealt with the removal of dust and fumes, was repealed by the 1988 COSHH Regulations (see para 6.135). However, s.30, which deals with working in confined spaces where fumes are present remains in force.

5.24 In *Nicholson v Atlas Steel Foundry and Engineering Co. Ltd* a factory process gave rise to a large amount of siliceous particles in the atmosphere. The only ventilation was provided by two doors. The employee contracted pneumoconiosis from which he died. It was held that the failure to ventilate the workroom must have exacerbated the hazard to which he was exposed and the dust in his lungs must have materially contributed towards his death. Consequently the employers were held liable. It should be noted that s.4 is only concerned with the circulation of fresh air, and does not, for example, require that masks or respirators should be provided (*Ebbs v James Whitson & Co. Ltd*).

5.25 The dust or fumes must have been caused by the work which is being carried on. If there is some other cause, the section will not apply. For example, in *Brophy v Bradfield & Co. Ltd* an employee had gone into a boiler room (into which he had no right to go), closed the door, and opened the furnace for warmth. He was overcome by carbon monoxide fumes and died. It was held that (a) the boiler room was not a workroom and (b) the fumes were not generated in the course of any process or work carried on in the factory, and the employers were thus not liable for a breach of statutory duty (for the claim based on common law negligence, see chapter 8).

Lighting (s.5)

5.26 Effective provision shall be made for securing and maintaining sufficient and suitable lighting, whether natural or artificial, in every part of the factory in which persons are working or passing. The Factory (Standards of Lighting) Regulations 1941 did lay down specific standards to be achieved, but these have been repealed, as it was thought that they were unnecessary. In *Thornton v Fisher and Ludlow Ltd* a cleaner employed by the defendants was walking along a factory road early in the morning. She tripped over a coil of wire and was injured. There were lights along the walls by the roadway, but these were not switched on. It was held that the defendants were liable for her injury, for by not ensuring that the lights were turned on they had failed to make effective provision for securing and maintaining sufficient lighting. However, if adequate lighting is provided, the fact that a shadow is cast over a piece of the work in progress thus reducing the amount of light within the area covered by the shadow does not constitute a breach of s.5 (*Lane v Gloucester Engineering Co. Ltd*).

5.27 The defendants were also liable for an injury in *Davies v Massey Ferguson Perkins Ltd*, where the plaintiff was descending a steel stairway. An illuminating light was not working, with the result that the bottom of the stairway was in shadow. The plaintiff missed his footing and injured his back. The learned judge thought that the obligation imposed by s.5 was absolute, and the duty would have been breached even though the light had been not functioning for only a short time.

5.28 All glazed windows and skylights used for lighting purposes must be cleaned on the inner and outer surfaces and kept free from obstruction, although these may be whitewashed or shaded in order to mitigate against glare or heat.

Drainage of floors (s.6)

5.29 If a process is carried on which renders the floor liable to be wet, and this is capable of being removed by drainage, effective means for doing this must be provided and maintained.

Sanitary conveniences (s.7)

5.30 Sufficient and suitable sanitary conveniences shall be provided, maintained and kept clean, with effective lighting. Where both sexes are employed, there must be separate accommodation for each sex. The Sanitary Accommodation Regulations 1938 lay down certain minimum standards to be observed. There must be one convenience for every 25 females and one for each 25 males (not merely suitable as a urinal), although if there are more than 100 males and there are sufficient urinals, it is only necessary to have four conveniences for the first 100 males and one for each forty thereafter. If there are more than 500 males, one convenience for every 60 males is sufficient.

5.31 It will be noted that the Act requires separate toilet facilities for men and women. The fact that there are no such separate facilities is not an excuse for refusing to employ a man or woman, as the case may be. The Sex Discrimination Act 1975, s.7 makes it permissible to discriminate against a person on grounds of sex where the sex of the person is a genuine occupational qualification for the job, and one of these arises where the employee is required to live in residential accommodation provided by the employer, and there is no separate sleeping and sanitary accommodation, and it is not reasonable to expect the employer to equip those premises with such facilities, or to provide other premises for the different sexes (s.7(2)(c)). If an employer wishes to rely on this genuine occupational qualification he must show that his needs are truly genuine. In *Hermolle v Government Communications HQ* a woman applied for a job on the Ascension Islands but was refused the post because, it was alleged, there was no separate sleeping accommodation or sanitary facilities. However, the cost of providing these was fairly modest, and the employers failed to discharge the burden of showing that it was unreasonable of them to make such separate facilities available. Thus, it is unlikely that such a defence would excuse an alleged discriminatory act by a factory occupier based on the absence of separate toilet facilities.

5.32 The conveniences shall be properly screened, conveniently accessible and the interior shall not be visible to persons of the opposite sex when the door is opened. The separate conveniences for each sex shall be indicated by a suitable notice.

Medical examinations (s.10A)

5.33 If an Employment Medical Adviser (EMA, see chapter 2) is of the opinion that a person's health has been or is being injured (or that it is possible that he is or will be injured) by reason of the work he is doing, the EMA may serve a notice on the factory occupier requiring the occupier to permit a medical examination of that person to take place. The notice will state the time, date and place of the examination, which must be at reasonable times during working hours. Every person to whom it relates shall be informed of its contents and of the fact that he is free to attend for that purpose. If the examination is to take place in the factory, suitable accommodation shall be provided.

Medical supervision (s.11)

5.34 If it appears to HSE that in a particular factory cases of illness have occurred due to the nature of the work or substances used, or young persons are employed in work which may cause risk of injury to their health, or there is a risk of injury to the health of other persons employed from any substance or materials or other conditions, HSE may, by order, require reasonable arrangements to be made for medical supervision of those persons. To date, the powers contained in this section do not appear to have been utilised.

General safety provisions (ss.12–16)

5.35 These sections have received more consideration in civil and criminal proceedings than any other sections of the Act. Clearly, this reflects the large number of accidents and potential injuries which are likely to result from the use of industrial machinery and a determination by the legislature to minimise those risks and to achieve the highest possible safety standards. The five sections form a single code, and may be interpreted as such (*Callow (Engineers) Ltd v Johnson*).

5.36 It must be stressed that so far as civil and criminal liability is concerned, the duties imposed by the Act are absolute, and the employer will be liable for failing to do that which the Act requires him to do. In civil cases, there is no need for the injured workman to prove negligence. However, there are rare occasions when, although the employer was in breach of his statutory duty, the conduct of the worker was so foolish as to disentitle him to damages altogether. There is no principle of law which prevents a court from finding that a worker contributed 100% to his own injuries (*Jayes v IMI (Kynock) Ltd*).

Prime movers (s.12)

5.37 Every flywheel connected to a prime mover and every moving part of a prime mover shall be securely fenced. A prime mover is any appliance which provides mechanical energy derived from fuel, steam, water or any other source (s.176(1)). Electric generators, motors and rotary converters and flywheels directly connected thereto shall be securely fenced unless they are in such a position or of such construction as to be as safe to every person employed or working on the premises as they would be if securely fenced.

Transmission machinery (s.13)

5.38 Every part of transmission machinery shall be securely fenced unless it is in such a position or of such construction as to be as safe to every person employed or working on the premises as it would be if securely fenced. Transmission machinery means every shaft, pulley, wheel, drum, coupling, clutch, driving belt or other device by which the motion of the prime mover is transmitted to or received by any engine or appliance. This includes machinery not driven by mechanical power (*Richard Thomas & Baldwins Ltd v Cummings*), but there must be some thing which moves or revolves. Thus a hydraulic accumulator is not transmission machinery (*Weir v Andrew Barclay & Co. Ltd*). An efficient device shall be provided and maintained in every room or place where work is being carried on, by which the power can be cut off from the transmission machinery in that room or place.

Other machinery (s.14)

5.39 Every dangerous part of any machinery (other than prime movers and transmission machinery) shall be securely fenced unless it is in such a position or of such construction as to be as safe to every person working or employed in the premises as it would be if securely fenced. Insofar as the dangerous part cannot be securely fenced by a fixed guard, the section will be complied with if there is an automatic device which prevents the operator from coming into contact with that dangerous part (s.14(2)). Stock bars which project beyond the head-stock of a lathe shall similarly be securely fenced unless their position makes them as safe to every person working or employed as they would be if they were securely fenced.

5.40 The following points arise out of the interpretation of these sections.

What is machinery?

5.41 The word "machinery" is a word with no specific meaning and it can embrace a wide range of objects. To give it a specific meaning within the context of the Factories Act, one must use a certain amount of common sense. Thus in *Mirza v Ford Motor Co. Ltd*, the plaintiff was operating an electrically controlled hoist crane, which was fitted with a special safety hook. He trapped his finger in the safety clip attached to the hook, injuring himself. He claimed that the employers were liable for a breach of statutory duty in that they had failed to ensure that a dangerous part of machinery had been securely fenced. His claim was dismissed, and the Court of Appeal upheld the decision. One member of the Court of Appeal thought that the safety hook was part of the machinery, but was not a dangerous part and therefore it did not need to be securely fenced. The two other judges concurring in the result thought that the safety hook was not part of the machinery. They went on to say that one way of considering the word "machinery" is to ask if the item in question could be fenced or given a fixed guard. If a reasonable person would not contemplate fencing or providing a fixed guard, it could well be that the item was not machinery within the meaning of the Act.

5.42 "Machinery" is a wider term than "machine". There is no requirement that the machinery must be driven by mechanical or electrical power, and it may include a large structure (*Quintas v National Smelting Co.*—a cable-way) or a small hand-tool (*Close v Steel Co of Wales*—an electric drill). Nor is machinery excluded from the Act because it is mobile, for the Act is designed to protect people from the dangerous parts, not from the movement of machinery. In *British Railways Board v Liptrot*, a mobile crane was mounted on a four-wheeled chassis with rubber wheels. The respondent was injured when he was caught between the revolving body of the crane and the wheels. It was held that the crane was "machinery" within the meaning of the Act. Mobility did not grant immunity and the fact that cranes and similar equipment are subject to detailed provisions in s.27 did not exclude the operation of s.14. If vehicles contain dangerous parts, these must be securely fenced.

Which machinery?

5.43 The machinery must be part of the equipment of the factory. Thus, if lorries, cars, etc come to visit the premises they are not part of the factory equipment and hence not within the scope of the Act. Equally, machinery which is being made in the factory is not covered (*Parvin v Morton Machine Co. Ltd*). But once machinery is installed in a factory, it is part of the equipment, even though it is only being tested for use (*Irwin v White Tomkins and Courage*). In *Thorogood v Van Den Burghs and Jurgens Ltd* an electric wall fan was taken from its position to an engineering workshop for repair. Since the latter premises were still part of the factory, it was held that the duty to fence the fan still applied.

What is a "dangerous part"?

5.44 Some limit must be placed on this phrase, and it cannot be applied to every object which causes injury, otherwise the most harmless physical things would have to be fenced (chairs, tables, etc) which could hardly be described as being "dangerous". The modern test has been restated in *Close v Steel Co. of Wales.* A part of machinery is dangerous if it is "a reasonably foreseeable cause of injury to anyone acting in a way in which human beings may reasonably be expected to act, in circumstances which may reasonably be expected to occur". In other words, a degree of foreseeability is required and this is largely (if not totally) a question of fact and degree. In *Mitchel v North British Rubber Co.*, Lord Cooper gave a further explanation which has subsequently been cited with approval by the House of Lords (*Summers Sons v Frost*):

> The question is not whether the occupiers of the factory knew that it was dangerous; nor whether the factory inspector had so reported; nor whether previous accidents had occurred; nor whether the victims of these accidents had, or had not, been contributorily

> negligent. The test is objective and impersonal. Is the part, in its character, and so circumstanced in its position, exposure, method of operation and the like, that in the ordinary course of human affairs danger may reasonably be anticipated from its use unfenced, not only to the prudent, alert and skilled operative intent upon his task, but also to the careless and inattentive worker whose inadvertent or indolent conduct may expose him to the risk of injury or death from the unguarded part.

Thus, the fact that there has never been a previous accident, or that the factory inspector has never prosecuted, may have some relevance in evidence, but cannot be conclusive.

5.45 It is reasonable to foresee that workers will disobey instructions not to put their hands into an unfenced part and that they will be careless in the way they operate the machine. In *Smith v Chesterfield and District Co-operative Society* the plaintiff worked on a machine the rollers of which were protected by a guard which came down to within three inches of the bed of the machine. Despite instructions to the contrary, she placed her fingers under the guard and was injured. It was held that there was a breach of s.14(1), for her conduct, though careless, was foreseeable. It is also possible to foresee that a worker will be indolent, disobedient, or simply tired. In *Woodley v Meason Freer* employees were specifically warned not to put their hands into a machine for the purpose of removing obstructions. When a worker acted in contravention to this instruction and was injured, it was held that the employers were guilty of an offence under the Act.

5.46 It is even possible to foresee that a workman will be stupid in his behaviour. In *Uddin v Associated Portland Cement Ltd* the plaintiff climbed a ladder in order to chase a pigeon which had flown into the roof of the factory. He slipped and caught his clothing on an unfenced part of machinery and was injured. The employers were held liable. The Act is designed to protect persons who are "employed or working" on the premises and the fact that the plaintiff had been guilty of an act of folly was only relevant in assessing the extent of his contributory negligence.

5.47 On the other hand, there comes a point where no amount of foreseeability can prevent an accident. In *Rushton v Turner Asbestos Ltd* the employee was specifically told that he must not attempt to put his hand into a machine. Nonetheless he did so and was injured. Although this failure to securely fence may have constituted a criminal offence which would have warranted prosecution, in the civil proceedings which ensued it was held that he was the sole author of his misfortune and the employers were not liable for breaking their statutory duty or for negligence. And in *Carr v Mercantile Produce Ltd* a girl forced her hand into a hole in a machine which was three inches in diameter. This act, of sheer perversity, was not foreseeable.

5.48 It is only possible to guard a machine against dangers which might reasonably be foreseen. It follows that if the situation is such that it can only be foreseen with the benefit of hindsight, it is not reasonably foreseeable. In *Burns v Joseph Terry Ltd* the plaintiff climbed some ladders in order to get some cocoa beans from a shelf. Just below the shelf were some cog wheels, which were part of the transmission machinery, and these were covered in front by a mesh guard. The ladder slipped and somehow the boy got his hand behind the guard and was injured. It was held that the incident was not reasonably foreseeable. The transmission machinery was guarded against such dangers as were foreseeable.

5.49 Foreseeability is relevant to the conduct of the worker, not to the operation of the machine. Thus if a worker is injured on an unfenced part of machinery and the injury would not have occurred if the part had been securely fenced, the employer will be liable even though the accident happened in an entirely unforeseen manner, eg if the machine makes an uncovenanted stroke (*Millard v Serck Tubes Ltd*).

Danger in juxtaposition

5.50 In several cases the problem has been posed as to whether or not a part of machinery is dangerous if the danger only arises because of a juxtaposition with the machine and materials used by the machine. The Act, after all, does not require the fencing of dangerous materials in the machine (*Bullock v John Power (Agencies) Ltd*). In *Eaves v Morris Motors* the plaintiff's hand was injured when it was caught on a sharp bolt being made on a moving machine tool, and it was held that the employers were not liable. However, in *Midland and Low Moor Iron and Steel Co. Ltd v Cross* the House of Lords held that whether a part of machinery was dangerous must be determined by considering what the machine was designed to do under normal circumstances. In this case, there was a power-driven machine for straightening metal bars by squeezing them between rollers. An employee fed the bars into the rollers, which were not fenced. His attention was distracted and his hand was nipped between the metal bar and the roller. The rollers themselves were not dangerous, as there was a sufficient gap between the moving lower and the stationary upper roller to escape any injury. The danger only arose because the bar was being inserted. It was held that the employers were in breach of the Act, for the danger arose from the normal operation of the machine.

5.51 Nor does a part of machinery cease to be dangerous merely because it is stationary, if the material being used is moving, and thus causes a potential danger (*Callow Engineers Ltd v Johnson*). In other words, if there is a juxtaposition of parts of a machine and a workpiece being used by the machine which causes a danger, it must be fenced. In *Wearing v Pirelli Ltd* the plaintiff was injured when his hand came into contact with a harmless rubber fabric which was attached to a dangerous revolving drum which was not fenced. The employers were held liable for the injury. But a tool being used on a machine does not constitute a dangerous part of machinery, and there is no requirement to fence a danger which arises from the use of the tool (*Sarwar v Simmons and Hawker Ltd*). Equally, the "workpiece" used or being made on the machine cannot be regarded as being a dangerous part of machinery (*Eaves v Morris Motors Ltd*).

5.52 There is no duty to fence against a danger arising from the juxtaposition of one piece of machinery and another, or a danger caused by the proximity of a moving part of machinery and some other extraneous object. In *Pearce v Stanley*

Bridges Ltd, the plaintiff injured his arm when it was caught between the rising platform of a lifting machine and a conveyor belt. It was held that the Act did not impose an obligation to fence a gap between two machines. Moreover, the alleged danger was not reasonably foreseeable, and for both these reasons the claim failed.

When is machinery "securely fenced"?

5.53 The obligation to securely fence is an absolute one, with the result that if the consequence of securely fencing the machine is to make it commercially impossible or impractical to use, the Act in effect prohibits its use, or the employer uses it at his peril (*John Summers & Sons Ltd v Frost*). The rigour of this rule may sometimes be militated by the Minister introducing special regulations modifying the Act in particular instances (eg Abrasive Wheels Regulations 1970).

5.54 A fence must not be a mere barrier (*Quintas v National Smelting Co.*), but sufficient to protect the worker adequately. On the other hand, it does not cease to be secure because its protection can be circumvented and rendered useless by some act of perverted and deliberate ingenuity (*Carr v Mercantile Produce*, above).

5.55 Since the obligation is to fence, a substitute for fencing clearly constitutes a breach of the Act. In *Chasteney v Nairn* the employers put up a notice which read "Do not put your hands in the machinery while it is in motion. Persons disregard this notice at their own risk." The court had no doubt that the machinery was not securely fenced.

The purpose of fencing

5.56 A fence must prevent the worker from coming into contact with the dangerous part of machinery. It is not intended that a fence should protect him from parts of the machine which may fly out. In *Close v Steel Co. of Wales*, the bit of a portable electric drill shattered and injured the plaintiff in his eye. Such shatterings were fairly common, but never before had a serious incident occurred. It was held that the employers were not liable for damages. Nor need the fence protect against flying parts of material being worked on the machine (*Nicholls v Austin (Leyton) Ltd*), though if an employer knows that parts of a machine or materials used by the machine are likely to fly out of the machine, this may give rise to liability for common law negligence, in that there may be a failure to ensure a safe system of working (see chapter 8) and an offence may have been committed under s.2 of HSWA.

5.57 If a worker is injured because a tool he is using is caught on a dangerous part of machinery, the employer will not be liable (*Sparrow v Fairey Aviation Ltd*), but in *Lovelidge v Anselm Odling Ltd* the plaintiff's tie was caught in a machine, as a result of which he was injured. It was held that the purpose of fencing was to guard against such contingencies, the clothing a worker wears is part of him for this purpose and employers were held liable.

5.58 Machinery which is being installed for the purpose of modification and development is required to be securely fenced, although it is possible that if it is in a separate building or set apart from the place where production was going on in the same building, it may be that s.14 does not apply (*TBA Ltd v Laine*).

Protection for whom?

5.59 In general, ss.12–16 are for the benefit of persons who are employed or working on the premises. This can mean employees, self-employed subcontractors, and so on. The fact that the employee is acting outside the scope of his employment is not relevant (*Westwood v Post Office*). For example, it was not part of the work of the plaintiff in *Uddin*'s case (above) to chase pigeons, but nonetheless he was able to recover damages for a breach of s.14(1). However, if the employee is neither employed nor working in the legal sense, but "doing a foreigner" in his spare time (even with the permission of the employer) the Act does not apply (*Napieralski v Curtis (Contractors) Ltd*).

5.60 It will be noted that s.14(2) (above) which permits the use of an automatic device instead of a secure fence is only expressed to be for the benefit of the operator.

5.61 The obligations in s.14 are absolute, and the fact that it is commercially impracticable or mechanically impossible to securely fence the machine (*Davies v Thomas Owen Ltd*), or to use the machine when securely fenced (*Summers & Sons Ltd v Frost*) is immaterial. Equally, it is relevant that the dangerous part was fenced by the best known methods (*Dennistoun v Charles Greenhill Ltd*), or that the machine has been used in that manner for thirty years without any accident or complaint from the factory inspector (*Sutherland v James Mills Ltd*), although such factors may be of evidential value as to whether or not the parts of machinery were dangerous, or whether they were securely fenced (*Carr v Mercantile Produce*).

5.62 The fact that the injured person does not know or cannot explain adequately how the accident occurred is irrelevant once a breach of the statute has been shown. In *Allen v Aeroplane and Motor Aluminium Castings Ltd* the plaintiff was injured on a machine which was not fenced. The judge did not believe his account of the incident, and gave judgment for the employers, but this was reversed on appeal. Once a breach has been shown, there is a presumption that the accident would not have happened but for the breach.

5.63 The obligations in this part of the Act are placed on the factory occupier. In *Biddle v Truvox Engineering Ltd* an employee was injured as the result of a failure to securely fence a machine, and he sued his employers. They in turn joined, as a third party to the action, the manufacturer from whom they bought the machine, but the claim against the latter was dismissed. The decision is not without its critics, but nowadays the manufacturer or seller would be criminally liable under s.6(8) of HSWA, and the injured person would have his remedy under the Employer's Liability (Defective Equipment) Act or at common law under the doctrine of *Donoghue v Stevenson* (see para 8.4).

Unfenced machinery (s.15)

5.64 If machinery is in the process of examination, lubrication or adjustment, it may well be that it is not in a safe position or of safe construction. In these circumstances, the provisions of ss.13–14 will not apply if the examination, lubrication or adjustment can only be carried out while the part of machinery is in motion. In the case of transmission machinery being used in any specified process where, owing to its continuous nature, the stopping of it would seriously interfere with that process, the lubrication or mounting or shipping of belts shall be carried out in such methods and in such circumstances as may be prescribed.

5.65 The Operations at Unfenced Machinery Regulations 1938 (as amended) lay down the conditions which must be complied with when examining, lubricating or adjusting unfenced machinery whilst in motion where dangerous parts are exposed. The factory occupier must appoint a person to carry out this operation, who must be over the age of 18, sufficiently trained for the purpose, and aware of the dangers involved. He must be given a copy of the precautionary leaflet issued by HSC and, except for the setting of a machine by a toolsetter, he must be provided with a single piece overall. Another person instructed in the steps to be taken in an emergency must be within sight or hearing distance, and steps must be taken to ensure that other persons are not in a position as to be exposed to any risk or injury. These provisions do not apply if the machinery is being moved by hand or by an inching button.

5.66 The regulations also deal with the lubrication, mounting, or shipping of belts in certain specified processes where this work cannot be deferred until the machinery is stopped (see the schedule to the regulations).

5.67 It will be noted that s.15 only provides a partial exemption from the stringent requirements of ss.13–14 when the work being carried on is that of examination, lubrication and adjustment, and even then only in the prescribed circumstances. Section 15 does not give any exemption in the case of the cleaning of a machine while it is in motion (see s.20 below).

Construction and maintenance of fencing (s.16)

5.68 All fencing or other safeguards shall be of substantial construction and constantly maintained, and kept in position while the parts required to be fenced or safeguarded are in motion or use, except when they are necessarily exposed for examination and for any adjustment or lubrication shown by such examination to be immediately necessary. "Maintained" means "kept in efficient working order at all times". Thus, if part of the machinery fails to work on a single occasion, this would constitute proof that it was not "constantly maintained" and it is therefore no defence to argue that the defect could not have been discovered by an examination. The requirement of the section is absolute (*Galashiels Gas Co Ltd v O'Donnell*). The phrase "in use" means "running as it was meant to run and doing the work it was meant to do" (*Richard Thomas and Baldwins Ltd v Cummings*). Thus if machinery is being repaired or being cleaned, it is not in use at the time. In *Knight v Leamington Spa Courier Ltd* a printing machine was being rotated slowly by an inching button. The object was to clean the machine during a slack period and it was held that it was not "in use" at the time. Acts which are preparatory to the machine being worked also do not make the machine in use (*Horne v Lee Refrigeration Ltd*) but in *Joy v News of the World*, paper was being threaded through the rollers of a printing machine which was running at its lowest speed, and it was held that the machine was in use at the time.

5.69 Even more difficult to understand is the phrase "in motion". Oddly enough, this does not mean "in movement"! It means "substantial movement of its normal workings, or . . . some movement reasonably comparable to its normal workings" (*Knight v Leamington Spa Courier Ltd*). Thus the slow, sporadic rotation or intermittent movement of machinery for the purpose of placing it in a more advantageous position in order to clean or repair it is not normal motion, whether this result is achieved by manpower or mechanical power. The distinction between motion and movement is one of fact and degree to be determined by the judge. It has also been held that regard had to be made to the character of the movement as well as to its purpose (*Mitchell v W S Westin Ltd*). Thus a machine which is revolving rapidly must be fenced whether the purpose of the movement is production, examination, demonstration, adjustment, repairing, testing or whatever. In *Stanbrook v Waterlow & Sons Ltd* the cylinder of a printing machine was made to revolve at a high speed for a fraction of a second, and it was held that the machine was in motion. There is clearly a distinction between being moved slowly and being in motion at a fast pace. If a machine is put into motion for its normal work, whether slowly or rapidly, it must be fenced. If the movement is slow, purposeful and deliberate, for the purpose of examination, lubrication or adjustment the fencing provisions do not apply, but if this work is done when the machine is put into motion at a rapid pace, the sections will apply.

5.70 If an operation can be performed with the guards being kept in position, then it cannot be said that the dangerous parts of machinery were "necessarily exposed" for any purpose and the exemptions of s.16 will not apply (*Nash v High Duty Alloys Ltd*).

Construction and sale of machinery (s.17)

5.71 Every set-screw, bolt or key on any revolving shaft, spindle, wheel or pinion shall be so sunk, encased or otherwise effectively guarded as to prevent danger, and all spur or other toothed friction gearing which does not require frequent adjustment while in motion shall be completely encased, unless it is so situated as to be as safe as it would be if completely encased.

5.72 Any person who sells or lets on hire (or acts as an agent of a seller or hirer) who causes or procures the sale or hire of any machine for use in a factory which is intended to be driven by mechanical power which does not comply with this section shall be guilty of an offence. It will be recalled that in *Biddle v Truvox Engineering Co. Ltd* the vendor of a machine was held not to be liable by virtue of this section to an injured workman as a joint tortfeaser along with the employer. However, if a machine has a defect which was negligently caused in the manufacture, an action for negligence would lie against the manufacturer at the instance of an injured person (*Hill v James Crowe Ltd*), and the actual employer of the injured person would be liable under the provisions of the Employers Liability (Defective Equipment) Act 1969 (see chapter 8). Additionally, the actual manufacturer, etc would be liable under s.6 of HSWA (see chapter 3).

Dangerous substances (s.18)

5.73 Every fixed vessel, structure, sump or pit which contains any scalding, corrosive or poisonous liquid, the edge of which is less than 920mm (3 feet) from the ground or platform from which a person might fall into it shall be securely covered or securely fenced to at least 920mm above that ground or platform. If it is not possible to do this by reason of the nature of the work, all practicable steps shall be taken to prevent any person from falling in. This protection is against the nature of the liquid, which must be dangerous when a person comes into contact with it; it is not protection against drowning *per se*. Further, no ladder, stair or gangway shall be placed above, across or inside the vessel, etc, which is not at least 460mm (18 inches) wide, securely fenced on both sides to a height of at least 920mm and securely fixed.

5.74 There are special regulations relating to the use of vats in dyeworks (Kiers Regulations 1938).

Self acting machines (s.19)

5.75 A "self acting" machine has a fixed part and a traversing part which moves backwards and forwards, and which may thus cause danger to someone trapped between these parts. Section 19 provides that if the traversing part (or any material carried on it) runs over a space over which any person is likely to pass, the traversing part, or materials on it, must not be allowed to go within 460mm (18 inches) of any fixed structure which is not part of the machine. If the person in charge of the machine *bone fide* believes that another person is clear of the machine, he does not allow that other to pass a traversing part (*Crabtree v Fern Spinning Co. Ltd*). (See further, Self-acting Mule Spinning Regulations 1905.)

Cleaning of machines (s.20)

5.76 A young person (ie below the age of 18) shall not clean any part of a prime mover or any transmission machinery while either is in motion, and shall not clean any part of any machine if the cleaning thereof would expose the young person to the risk of injury from any moving part of that machine or any adjacent machinery. In

Taylor v Mark Dawson Ltd a child was picking fluff from the rollers of a spinning machine which was in motion. The fluff had a resale value and was not therefore waste, and the purpose of his activities was to prevent the rollers from becoming clogged. It was held that he was engaged in cleaning the machine. Further, the meaning of "moving part" is not the same as "in motion" (see s.16 above). In *Denyer v Charles Skipper and East Ltd* a seventeen-year-old boy was allowed to clean rollers on a printing machine which involved rotating them with an inching button. It was held that there was a breach of s.20.

Training and supervision of young persons (s.21)

5.77 No young person shall work at any prescribed machine unless he has been fully instructed as to the dangers arising and the precautions to be observed, and:

(a) has received sufficient training in work at the machine, and
(b) is under adequate supervision by a person who has a thorough knowledge and experience of the machine.

5.78 The Dangerous Machines (Training of Young Persons) Order 1954 specifies the dangerous machines in question. These are:

(a) *machines worked with the aid of mechanical power*
- (1) Brick and tile presses
- (2) Opening or teasing machines in upholstery or bedding works
- (3) Carding machines in wool textile trades
- (4) Corner staying machines
- (5) Dough brakes
- (6) Dough mixers
- (7) Worm pressure extruding machines
- (8) Gill boxes in wool textile trades
- (9) The following machines used in laundries
  - (i) hydro-extractors
  - (ii) calenders
  - (iii) washing machines
  - (iv) garment presses
- (10) Meat mincing machines
- (11) Milling machines in use in metal trades
- (12) Pie and tart making machines
- (13) Power presses, including hydraulic and pneumatic presses
- (14) Loose knife punching machines
- (15) Wire stitching machines
- (16) Semi-automatic wood turning lathes

(b) *Machines whether or not worked with mechanical power*
- (17) Guillotine machines
- (18) Platen printing machines.

Hoists and lifts (s.22)

5.79 Every hoist or lift shall be of good mechanical construction, of sound material and adequate strength, and shall be properly maintained. They must be examined thoroughly by a competent person at least every six months, and a record containing the prescribed particulars (see Lifting Plant and Equipment (Records of Tests and Examination etc) Regulations 1992) available for inspection as if it forms part of the general register. If such examination reveals that certain repairs need to be carried out, a copy of the particulars contained in the record must be sent to the HSE inspector. There must be a substantial enclosure and outer gates so that when the gates are shut, it is not possible for any person to fall down the liftway or to come into contact with any moving part of the hoist or lift. There must be an efficient interlocking or other device to ensure that the gate cannot be opened except when the cage or platform is at a landing, and the cage or platform cannot move away from the landing until the gate is closed. The maximum load which can be safely carried shall be marked conspicuously, and it is an offence to carry a greater load. The provisions as to gates, etc do not apply to continuous lifts or hoists (ie paternosters) nor to ones which do not have mechanical power.

5.80 A fork-lift truck is not a hoist or lift within the meaning of s.22 (*Oldfield v Reed & Smith Ltd*). Such a vehicle is machinery within s.14 (*British Railways Board v Liptrot*), see para 5.42).

5.81 It will be noted that the section imposes an absolute duty. Good mechanical construction, sound materials, and adequate strength must exist not only at the time of purchase, but throughout the working life of the lift or hoist. "Sound materials" means materials which are sound, and not which appear to be sound (*Whitehead v James Stott & Co. Ltd*). "Maintained", according to s.176, means "maintained in an efficient state, in efficient working order, and in good repair".

Hoists and lifts for carrying persons (s.23)

5.82 Additional requirements are laid down when hoists and lifts are used for carrying persons, whether with goods or otherwise. Efficient and automatic devices shall be provided and maintained to prevent the cage or platform from overrunning, every point of access shall have a gate with an efficient device to ensure that the cage cannot be raised or lowered unless the gate is closed, and the cage will come to rest when the gate is open.

Teagle openings (s.24)

5.83 Every teagle opening or similar doorway used for hoisting or lowering goods or materials shall be securely fenced and shall be provided with a handrail on each side. The fencing shall be properly maintained and, except when the hoisting or lowering of goods or materials is being carried on, shall be kept in position.

Exceptions (s.25)

5.84 A lifting machine is not to be regarded as being a hoist or lift within the meaning of the above sections unless it has a platform or cage the direction of movement of which is restricted by a guide or guides. Thus a fork-lift truck is not a hoist or lift (*Oldfield v Reed and Smith Ltd*). The power of the Secretary of State to grant exemptions from the requirements of ss.22–25 has been repealed, but the Hoists Exemptions Order 1962 (which is still in force) sets out a list of classes or descriptions of hoists and hoistways which come within the exemption order, specifying the requirements of the Act which do not apply, subject to the conditions laid down in the order.

Chains, ropes and lifting tackle (s.26)

5.85 No chain, rope or lifting tackle used for the purpose of raising or lowering persons, goods or materials shall be used unless it is of good construction, sound materials, adequate strength and free from patent defect. A defect is "patent" when it is visible, even though no one notices it (*Sanderson v National Coal Board*). Further, the words "patent defect" are not qualifying words, and do not weaken the statutory obligation so far as latent defects are concerned. In other words, they impose an additional requirement, not a lowering of standards. A table showing the safe working loads shall be posted in the stores where they are kept and in a prominent position on the premises. Chains, ropes or lifting tackle must not be used in excess of the safe working load as shown on the table, they must be examined by a competent person at least every six months, and (except for fibre rope or fibre rope slings) must not be used in a factory for the first time unless they have been thoroughly examined and tested by a competent person, and a record of that test and examination, and the results, containing the particulars required by the Lifting Plant and Equipment (Records of Test and Examination etc) Regulations 1992, has been obtained. The particulars in that record must be kept for inspection.

5.86 The purpose of s.26 is to prevent persons from being injured, either from a fall whilst they are being lifted, or from some object falling from broken lifting tackle, which must have physical propensities adequate for the job. The section does not lay down any requirement that the tackle shall be suitable for the purpose. Thus in *Beadsley v United Steel Companies Ltd* an accident resulted because the wrong type of lifting tackle was selected. The tackle was sound and of good construction, but was unsuitable for the task in hand. It was held that there was no breach of s.26. However, a civil claim based on negligence would probably succeed in such circumstances (*Dawson v Murex Ltd*).

Cranes and other lifting machines (s.27)

5.87 A lifting machine is any crane, crab, winch, teagle, pulley, block, gin wheel, transporter or runway. It has been held that a fork-lift truck is a lifting machine (*McKendrick v Mitchell Swire*). All parts and working gear, whether fixed or moveable, including the anchoring and fixing appliances, of every lifting machine shall be of good construction, sound material, adequate strength, free from patent defect, and shall be properly maintained. Again, "patent defect" is an additional requirement, for latent defects are clearly within the scope of the section (*McNeil v Dickson* and Mann Ltd). It has been held that an electrical operating and control button is within the meaning of "parts and working gear", so a workman who injured his finger while pressing a stiff button was entitled to bring a successful claim under the Act (*Evans v Sanderson Bros and Newbould Ltd*), though the decision must be a marginal one.

5.88 All parts and gear shall be thoroughly examined by a competent person at least once in every period of fourteen months, and the particulars prescribed by the Lifting Plant and Equipment (Records of Test and Examination etc) Regulations 1992 shall be kept in the prescribed register (F88). If the examination shows that the lifting machine cannot be used safely without certain repairs being carried out, a copy of a report to that effect shall be sent to the HSE inspector. All rails, tracks, etc shall be of proper size and adequate strength and have an even running surface. They shall be properly laid, adequately supported or suspended and properly maintained.

5.89 Every lifting machine shall be marked with its safe working load, except a jib crane with a variable working load which depends on the raising or lowering of the jib, in which case there must be an automatic indicator of safe working loads, or a table indicating the safe working load at the corresponding inclination of the jib or corresponding radii of the load. A lifting machine shall not be used for the first time in a factory unless it has been tested and thoroughly examined by a competent person and a certificate specifying the safe working load has been signed by him and kept available for inspection. Thereafter, no lifting machine shall be loaded beyond the safe working load except for the purpose of a test.

5.90 If any person is employed or working on or near the wheel track of an overhead travelling crane in any place where he would be liable to be struck by the crane, effective measures shall be taken by warning the driver of the crane to ensure that the crane does not approach within 6m (20 feet) of that place. "Any place" does not mean a fixed spot, but a broad area (*Holmes v Hadfields Ltd*). The measures taken must be effective; thus, if an accident occurs, the measures can hardly be said to be effective. In *Lotinga v North Eastern Marine Engineering Co. (1938) Ltd*, a workman was killed whilst working near the wheel track of an overhead crane. A notice was affixed to the crane stating that it must not be allowed to approach within 20 feet of men working. This was held not to be effective measures.

5.91 If a person is working above floor level, where he would be liable to be struck by an overhead travelling crane, or by a load carried by such crane, effective warnings must be given, unless his work is so connected with or dependent on the movement of the crane as to make a warning unnecessary.

Floors, passages and stairs (s.28(1))

5.92 All floors, steps, stairs, passages and gangways shall be of sound construction, properly maintained, and shall, so far as is reasonably practicable, be kept free from any obstruction and from any substance likely to cause persons to slip.

5.93 The opening words of the section must be interpreted in accordance with a certain amount of common sense. Thus a roadway (*Thornton v Fisher and Ludlow*

Ltd) or "mother earth" (*Newberry v Westwood & Co.*) or planks laid in an irregular manner over a gantry (*Tate v Swan Hunter and Wigham Richardson Ltd*) do not constitute "floors", but planks across a duct may be a "gangway" (*Hosking v De Havilland Aircraft Co. Ltd*).

5.94 The floors must be of sound construction, which means fit for the work which it is anticipated is to be done on it (*Mayne v Johnstone and Cumbers Ltd*). Thus if a heavy machine or object falls on to the floor, causing it to give way, it may be that the floor is still sound for normal purposes, as long as it can withstand such further stress as may reasonably be expected to occur (*Mayne v Johnstone and Cumbers Ltd*). Sound construction means well made, not well designed, but if the floor becomes worn through normal use, it may well be that it has not been properly maintained (*Fisher v Port of London Authority*).

5.95 An obstruction is something which should not be there. Thus if bales, packages, etc are being stored on the floor, these do not constitute obstructions (*Pengelley v Bell Punch Co. Ltd*). A trolley being used in the ordinary course of work is not an obstruction (*Marshall v Ericson Telephones*) but it may be so if it was left unused for an unnecessary period of time.

5.96 Whether a substance is likely to cause someone to slip is probably a question of foreseeability. Thus water (*Taylor v Gestetner Ltd*), oil (*Latimer v AEC Ltd*) and grease (*Williams v Painter Bros Ltd*) are obvious examples. In *Dorman Long (Steel) Ltd v Bell*, metal plates left temporarily on the floor became slippery when slag dust collected on them and it was held that it was irrelevant that the slippery substance was not actually in contact with the floor.

5.97 It will be noted that as far as the requirements which relate to obstructions and slippery substances are concerned, they are qualified by the words "so far as is reasonably practicable". This again must be a question of fact; in some circumstances it may not be possible to remove the offending items immediately (*Jenkins v Allied Ironfounders Ltd*) or the employers may be able to point to a regular system of cleaning up the floors or removing obstructions (*Braham v J Lyons & Co.*). As we have noted, the burden of proof is on the defendants to show that it was not reasonably practicable to do more than was done. In *Bennett v Rylands Whitecross Ltd* the plaintiff tripped over a piece of wire and was injured. There was no explanation as to how the wire got there and it was held that the fact that the obstruction might have been created unwittingly or in a highly improbable manner did not absolve the defendants from liability unless they could show that it was not reasonably practicable for them to have prevented or removed the obstruction.

Staircases, rails (s.28(2), (3))

5.98 Every staircase in a building or forming the means of exit shall have a substantial handrail provided and maintained, and if there is an open side, it shall be on that side. If there are two open sides, there must be a handrail on each side. To be substantial, the handrail must act as a guardrail, as well as for holding purposes (*Corn v Weir's Glass (Hanley) Ltd*). The Act refers to a staircase, not to stairs *per se*. In *Kimpton v Steel Co. of Wales Ltd* it was held that three steps leading to a machine did not constitute a staircase. Any open side of a staircase must also have a lower rail or other effective guard (s.28(3)).

Openings in floors (s.28(4))

5.99 All openings in floors shall be securely fenced, except when the nature of the work renders such fencing impracticable. In *Barrington v Kent Rivers Catchment Board* the plaintiff fell into an open inspection pit at a garage. At the time, no work was being carried on and thus the employers could not successfully argue that the nature of the work rendered it impracticable to fence. The fact that it may be inconvenient to fence does not make it impracticable to do so (*Street v British Electricity Authority*).

5.100 An opening in the floor does not need to be of such a size as to warrant a fence surround; it is still an opening even if a simple cover could be placed over it. In *Saunders v F H Lloyd & Co. Ltd*, the plaintiff sprained his ankle when he placed his foot into a small pit, which was 30 inches long, 8 inches deep and 17 inches wide. It was held that this was an opening within the meaning of s.28, that it could have been securely fenced by placing a cover over it and that as the defendants had not shown that it was impracticable to do so, they were liable for the injury.

Ladders (s.28(5))

5.101 All ladders shall be soundly constructed and properly maintained. Again, the duty is an absolute one, and it is no excuse that the employer took all reasonable steps to ensure that ladders were of sound construction (*Cole v Blackstone & Co. Ltd*).

Safe means of access (s.29(1))

5.102 So far as is reasonably practicable, there shall be provided and maintained a safe means of access to every place where any person has to work. The means of access must be safe wherever they lead to. In *Lavender v Diamints Ltd* a window cleaner climbed over a roof made from asbestos sheeting in order to reach some windows. He fell through the roof and was injured. It was held that the occupiers were liable. The subsection was not confined to the means of access to the inside of a factory, but to any place where a person had to work. For example, if a person has to climb a ladder to get to his place of work, a failure to foot it at the bottom or to secure it at the top may mean that the means of access are not safe (*Geddes v United Wires Ltd*). But the access must be to a place of work, not, for example, to a canteen (*Davies v De Havilland Aircraft Co. Ltd*) or to a lavatory (*Rose v Colvilles Ltd*).

5.103 The means of access may be unsafe because of some structural defect, or obstructions or defect in the floors, etc. Since the subsection contains the words "so far as is reasonably practicable", there is no guarantee of safety, especially if there is a misuse of the means of access by others which cause the injury. For example, in *Higgins v Lyons & Co. Ltd* the plaintiff was injured by a lorry which was being driven in a yard leading to the place of work and the employers were held not liable. It has been suggested that the obligation is to provide and maintain a means of access which is structurally sound, and that this does not impose obligations to eliminate transient and temporary conditions (*Levesley v Thomas Firth and John Brown Ltd*). Thus if the means of access becomes hazardous because of snow or ice, it may not be reasonably practicable to take immediate steps to do something about it, and a temporary delay may be expected (*Latimer v AEC Ltd*). However, there must be some reasonable attempts to deal with the problem (*Thomas v Bristol Aeroplane Co. Ltd*).

5.104 The duty to provide a safe means of access appears to include not only the physical propensities of that access but also the environmental conditions. Thus, if the means of access are unsafe because of excessive noise or heat or insufficient lighting, etc there will be a breach of the section (*Carragher v Singer Manufacturing Ltd*). It also encompasses the risk of falling from heights (*Nimmo v Alexander Cowan Ltd*). However, the duty on the occupier is to provide safe means of access; if he does this, but workmen choose another route and are injured, the occupier may well escape liability (*Street v British Electricity Authority*). It should be noted that the duty of the occupier is to any person working on the premises, including an independent contractor and his employees (*Lavender v Diamints Ltd*).

5.105 If the employer provides a means of access which is safe, but the employee uses another means of access not provided, then unless it can be shown that the employer has approved, adopted or permitted that means of access, the employer will not be liable for failing to provide a safe means of access (*Smith v British Aerospace*).

Safe place of employment (s.29(1))

5.106 So far as is reasonably practicable, every place of work shall be made and kept safe for any person working there. This refers to the actual working place, as opposed to the access to that place.

5.107 However, whereas under the first part of s.29(1), the "means of access" must be "provided and maintained safe", under the second part of s.29(1), the "actual place of work" must be "made and kept safe". This means that there can be a breach of the employer's duty under the second part of s.29(1) even though the danger is temporary or transient. In *Cox v HCB Angus Ltd*, an electrician was working inside the cab of a fire engine. He slipped on a loose piece of piping and fell from the cab to the ground, injuring himself. It was held that the cab was a place of work, the occupier was under a duty to keep that place of work safe, and that it was reasonably practicable for this to be done. The plaintiff was entitled to recover damages.

5.108 Again, the duty is owed to every person who is working there, including an independent contractor, and it therefore exists irrespective of whether the independent contractor is under a separate duty, eg under the Construction Regulations (*Whincup v Woodhead & Sons Ltd*). It follows that if an independent contractor is carrying on work within a factory, the occupier must take some steps to familiarise himself with the situation and take reasonably practicable steps to deal with any potential hazard which may arise (*Taylor v Coalite Oils and Chemicals Ltd*).

If an employer wishes to defend a claim brought under s.29(1) it is necessary both to plead and to prove that it was not reasonably practicable to make and keep the place of work safe. It is not incumbent on the plaintiff to prove that the danger was reasonably foreseeable, for this is a test which may be applied at common law in an action for negligence, but is not used in actions for breach of statutory duty (*Larner v British Steel plc*).

Working at heights (s.29(2))

5.109 Where any person has to work at a place from which he will be liable to fall a distance of more than 2m (6½ feet) then, unless the place is one which affords a secure foothold (and, where necessary, a secure handhold), means shall be provided, so far as is reasonably practicable, by fencing or otherwise, for ensuring his safety. A handhold is something which a person can hold onto from time to time, eg the upright of a ladder (*Wigley v British Vinegars Ltd*). A foothold does not cease to be secure because in abnormal circumstances (such as an explosion) a person is thrown off (*Tinto v Stewarts and Lloyds Ltd*). The burden of proof is on the plaintiff to show that the absence of a secure foothold or handhold was responsible for the accident.

5.110 If the occupier is unable to provide a secure foothold or handhold, other safety precautions must be provided. This can be fencing, the provision of safety belts (*McWilliams v Sir William Arrol & Co. Ltd*) or other suitable means.

Confined spaces (s.30)

5.111 If work has to be done in any chamber, tank, vat, pit, pipe, flue or similar confined space in which dangerous fumes are likely to be present to such an extent as to involve a risk of persons being overcome by them, certain precautions must be observed. Unless there is some other adequate means of exit, there must be a manhole not less than 460 × 410mm (18 × 16 inches) (or, if circular, 460mm (18 inches) in diameter) or, in the case of tank wagons or other mobile plant, 410 × 360mm (16 × 14 inches) (or 410 mm (16 inches) in diameter if circular). No person shall enter or remain therein unless he is wearing suitable breathing apparatus, has been authorised to enter by a responsible person, and, where practicable, is wearing a belt with a rope securely attached. There must be a person keeping watch outside and capable of hauling him out by holding the free end of the rope. Breathing apparatus need not be used if the confined space has been certified to be free from fumes for a specified period by a responsible person, as long as the person entering the confined space has been warned when the safe period will expire. A sufficient supply of approved breathing apparatus, of belts and ropes, and of reviving apparatus and oxygen, shall be provided and kept readily available, and shall be thoroughly examined at least once a month, with a report, signed by a competent person, kept available for inspection (see the Breathing Apparatus, Etc (Report on Examination) Order 1961). A sufficient number of persons shall be trained and have adequate practice in the use of the apparatus and in the methods of restoring respiration.

5.112 No person shall enter or remain in any confined space in which the oxygen in the air is liable to have been substantially reduced unless he is wearing breathing apparatus or the space has been tested and certified as being safe for entry with such apparatus. No work shall be permitted in any boiler, furnace or boiler flue until it has been sufficiently cooled so as to make it safe.

Explosive or inflammable substances (s.31)

5.113 Where, in connection with any grinding, sieving or other process giving rise to dust which may cause an explosion on ignition, all practicable steps shall be taken to prevent such explosion by enclosure of the plant, by removal or prevention of accumulation of dust, and by the exclusion or effective enclosure of possible sources of ignition. This section is designed to deal with the dangers inherent in the grinding of coal or other carbonaceous material and other dust likely to explode if ignited. Unless the plant is so constructed as to withstand the pressure likely to be produced from any such explosion, all practicable steps shall be taken to restrict the spread and effects by the provision of chokes, baffles, vents or other equally effective appliances. Special provisions must be taken in connection with the grinding of magnesium (Magnesium (Grinding of Castings and Other Articles) Special Regulations 1946).

5.114 Before any part of a plant which contains explosive or flammable gas or vapour under pressure is opened, the flow shall be effectively stopped by a stop valve or otherwise, and before the fastening is removed, the gas or pressure must be reduced to atmospheric pressure.

5.115 Any tank plant or vessel which has contained any explosive or flammable substance shall not be subjected to any welding, brazing or soldering operation, or any cutting operation, which involves the application of heat for the purpose of taking it apart unless all practicable steps have been taken to remove the substance, or to render it non-explosive or non-flammable. Once such operation has been carried out, no explosive or inflammable substance shall be allowed to get into the relevant container until the metal has cooled sufficiently to prevent the risk of ignition taking place. HSE has power to make certain exemptions from these latter provisions.

Steam boilers (ss.32–34)

5.116 Every part of every steam boiler shall be of good construction, sound material and adequate strength, and free from patent defect. Attached to steam boilers shall be a suitable safety valve, stop valve, correct steam pressure gauge, at least one water gauge, sufficient means for attaching a pressure gauge, and, unless externally fired, shall be provided with a suitable fusible plug or an efficient low water alarm device. There are a number of exemption certificates in force in respect of particular types of steam boilers and those manufactured by certain firms.

5.117 Every steam boiler and all its fittings and attachments shall be properly maintained. It shall not be used in a factory unless it has been examined in accordance with the Examination of Steam Boiler Regulations 1964. A report of every such examination shall be entered into or attached to the general register signed by the person making the examination. A new steam boiler shall not be used unless the manufacturer has issued a certificate specifying the maximum permissible working pressure (s.33, and see the Examination of Steam Boilers Reports (No. 1) Order 1964). Again, a number of exemption certificates are in force.

5.118 No person shall enter into any steam boiler which is one of a range of two or more unless all inlets through which steam or hot water might enter have been disconnected, or all valves controlling the entry of steam or hot water are closed and securely locked.

Steam receivers and steam containers (s.35)

5.119 Every part of every steam receiver shall be of good construction, sound material, adequate strength and free from patent defect. Steam receivers shall be properly maintained, and thoroughly examined by a competent person at least once in every 26 months. A report containing the prescribed particulars shall be entered into or attached to the general register. Again, a number of exemption certificates are in force.

5.120 Every steam receiver which is not constructed so as to withstand with safety the maximum pressure which can be obtained from any other source of supply shall be fitted with:

(a) a suitable reducing valve or other automatic device to prevent the safe working pressure being exceeded
(b) a suitable safety valve so adjusted as to permit the steam to escape as soon as the safe working pressure is exceeded
(c) a correct steam pressure gauge
(d) a suitable stop valve
(e) a plate bearing a distinctive number which is easily visible (except when only one steam receiver is in use).

Air receivers (s.36)

5.121 Every air receiver and its fittings shall be of sound construction and properly maintained. They shall have marked on them the safe working pressure, and if connected to an air compressor plant, shall be able to withstand the maximum pressure or be fitted with a suitable reducing valve. A suitable safety valve shall be fitted, so adjusted as to permit air to escape as soon as the safe working pressure is exceeded, and shall be fitted with a correct pressure gauge, a draining appliance, means whereby the interior can be cleaned, and, if more than one is in use in the factory, a distinguishing mark which is easily visible. Every air receiver shall be thoroughly cleaned and examined at least once in every 26 months except in the case of a receiver of solid drawn construction which can be examined within four years from the previous examination. The examination and test shall be carried out by a competent person, and a report, containing the prescribed particulars shall be attached to or entered in the general register. Again, a number of exemption certificates are in force.

5.122 It should be noted that the provisions relating to steam boilers and air receivers are specifically stated to apply to building operations and to works of engineering construction undertaken by way of trade or business, or for the purpose of any industrial or commercial undertaking (see s.127). However, ss.32–34 (above) do not apply to boilers belonging to or exclusively used by the Crown, or belonging to and used by the UK Atomic Energy Authority, or belonging to and used by ships or railway companies.

5.123 It should be noted that ss.32, 33, 35 and 36 will be repealed as from 1 July 1994 (see Pressure Systems and Transportable Gas Containers Regulations 1989, Schedule 6).

Water sealed gasholders (s.39)

5.124 Every gasholder which has a storage capacity of at least $140m^3$/5,000 cubic feet shall be of sound construction and properly maintained. They must be examined externally by a competent person at least every two years, and a record containing the prescribed particulars entered into or attached to the general register (see the Gasholders (Record of Examinations) Order 1938).

General welfare provisions

5.125 Part III of the Act is designed to ensure that certain minimum standards of welfare are observed. The fact that the employees are contented with existing facilities, or have not complained, is irrelevant (*File Tile Distributors Ltd v Mitchell*, see chapter 2). At one time it was suggested that no civil action can be based on a breach of these provisions, although claims succeeded in those cases where the point does not appear to have been taken, and it is now believed that the weight of authority is in favour of such claims. It will be noted that the provisions are for the benefit of persons employed.

Supply of drinking water (s.57)

5.126 An adequate supply of wholesome drinking water shall be provided and maintained at suitable points conveniently accessible to all persons employed. If the supply is not laid on, it shall be contained in suitable vessels, renewed daily, and all practicable steps shall be taken to preserve the water and the vessels from contamination. Except where there is an upward jet, one or more suitable cups shall be provided at each point of supply.

Washing facilities (s.58)

5.127 There shall also be provided and maintained for use of employed persons adequate and suitable facilities for washing, including a supply of clean running hot and cold water, soap and clean towels or other suitable means for drying, and these facilities shall be conveniently accessible and shall be kept clean and in orderly condition. In *Reid v Westfield Paper Co. Ltd* it was held that an employee who suffered dermatitis as a result of employer's failure to provide adequate washing facilities could recover damages for that breach. An HSE inspector may issue an exemption certificate in certain cases (see Washing Facilities (Running Water) Exemption Regulations 1960).

Accommodation for clothing (s.59)

5.128 There shall be provided and maintained for the use of employed persons adequate and suitable accommodation for clothing not worn during working hours and such arrangements as are reasonably practicable for drying such clothing. In *McCarthy v Daily Mirror* it was held that in determining whether or not the accommodation provided was suitable, regard must be had to the possibility of the clothing being stolen, so that if it is unsuitable by this standard, an employee may be able to bring a successful claim against the employer.

Sitting facilities (s.60)

5.129 Where it is possible for employees to have reasonable opportunities to sit in the course of their work, suitable and sufficient facilities shall be provided and maintained. Where a substantial proportion of the work can be done seated, there shall be provided a seat of a design, construction and dimensions suitable for the employee and for the work, together with a footrest, and the seat shall be properly supported while in use for that purpose.

First aid (s.61)

5.130 This section (and regulations made thereunder) has been repealed by the Health and Safety (First Aid) Regulations 1981, which came into force in July 1982. An approved Code of Practice with Guidance Notes has also been issued (see para 6.74).

Removal of dust or fumes (s.63)

5.131 This section has been repealed by the COSHH Regulations 1988 (see para 6.135).

Meals in dangerous trades (s.64)

5.132 This section has also been repealed by the COSHH Regulations.

Protection of eyes (s.65)

5.133 This section permitted the Secretary of State to make regulations requiring the provision of screens or suitable goggles in certain processes. However, the Protection of Eyes Regulations 1974 have been repealed by the Personal Protective Equipment at Work Regulations, as from 1 January 1993, and it is to the new regulations that one must now look (see Chapter 4).

Miscellaneous premises (ss.68–69)

5.134 These sections deal with humid factories and underground rooms respectively.

Lifting of heavy weights (s.72)

5.135 This section has been repealed from 1 January 1993 by the Manual Handling Operations Regulations 1992 (see Chapter 4).

Women and young persons in certain lead processes (ss.74, 131)

5.136 Women and young persons shall not be employed in certain lead processes being carried on in a factory and may not be employed in painting any part of a building with lead paint, other than as apprentices or doing certain decorative work. Other restrictions on women and young persons working with lead are now to be found in the Control of Lead at Work Regulations 1980. Action taken to comply with these sections does not contravene the Sex Discrimination Act 1975 (see para 6.20).

Certificate of fitness (s.119)

5.137 If an inspector is of the opinion that the employment of a young person in a factory or a particular process is prejudicial to his health or to the health of other persons, he may serve a written notice to this effect on the occupier. The latter will not be able to continue to employ that young person in that place or on that process until the employment medical adviser has examined him and certified that he is fit to work in the factory or on the process.

Notice of employment of young persons (s.119A)

5.138 When a factory occupier takes a young person into employment, he shall, within seven days, send specified particulars to the local careers office. This section is due to be repealed from a date specified by the Secretary of State.

Special applications (ss.121–127)

5.139 These sections make special provisions for applying the requirements of the

Act (with appropriate modifications) to parts of buildings let off as a separate factory, electrical stations, charitable or reformatory institutions, docks, wharves, warehouses, ships, building operations and works of engineering construction.

Homeworkers (s.133)

5.140 In certain prescribed cases, the factory occupier (or contractor employed by him) shall keep a list of the names and addresses of all outworkers directly employed by him, and send a copy to the inspector and the local council. Further details can be found in the Factories Home work Order 1911 as amended.

Notices and returns (s.137)

5.141 Every person who occupies premises as a factory must, one month prior to going into occupation, send to the inspector a notice stating the name or title of the occupier, the postal address of the factory, the nature of the work, stating whether or not mechanical power is being used, the name of the local authority and other prescribed particulars.

General Register (s.140)

5.142 Every factory shall have a General Register (Form F31 is available for this purpose, obtainable from HMSO). The following information is still currently required to be recorded in the Register (see Factories Act General Register Order 1973):

Pt. 1 name and address of occupier, nature of work carried on
Certificate as to means of escape in case of fire
Particulars of persons appointed as machinery attendants for purposes of Operations at Unfenced Machinery Regulations
Pt. 2 Particulars of young persons employed
Pt. 5 Particulars of washing, painting, whitewashing, etc
Pt. 6 Testing or examination of fire warning systems.

There are separate registers for docks wharves, quays and warehouses, and building operations and works of engineering construction.

5.143 Attached to the General Register shall be kept all other matters which are required to so be, eg reports on the examination of hoists and lifts (ss.22–25), steam boilers, steam receivers and air receivers (ss.32–38) and other matters specified in the appropriate regulations.

5.144 The General Register shall be kept for inspection by an inspector or employment medical advisers for at least two years after the date of the last entry.

Enforcement of the Act (s.155)

5.145 The main liability for criminal penalties is placed on the occupier of the factory, or, in certain cases, the owner. If a person contravenes the provisions of a regulation or order made under the Act which expressly imposes a duty on him, then that person shall be guilty of an offence, and the owner or occupier shall not be guilty of an offence unless it is proved that he failed to take all reasonable steps to prevent the contravention (s.155(2)). The onus is on the prosecution to prove that the occupier or owner failed to take all reasonable steps to prevent the contravention (*Wright v Ford Motor Co. Ltd*).

Penalties

5.146 The Factories Act is one of the existing statutory provisions for the purpose of s.33(3) of HSWA (see Schedule 1), and therefore offences are punishable by a fine of up to £5,000 on summary conviction and an unlimited fine in respect of a conviction on indictment.

Application to the Crown

5.147 The Act applies to factories belonging to or in the occupation of the Crown and to building operations or works of engineering construction undertaken by or on behalf of the Crown (s.173).

Offices, Shops and Railway Premises Act 1963

5.148 This Act applies to office premises, shop premises, and railway premises, being premises wherein persons are employed under a contract of employment (or apprenticeship) for an aggregate of at least 21 hours. Thus if only voluntary labour is working on the premises or if casual workers are employed for less than 21 hours in total, the Act does not apply.

5.149 Also excluded are the following:

(a) any premises wherein the only person employed is the husband, wife, parent, grandparent, son, daughter, grandchild, brother or sister of the person by whom they are employed (s.2(1))
(b) premises of homeworkers (s.2(2))
(c) premises which form part of a factory for the purpose the Factories Act, or which are below the ground and constitute a mine for the purpose of the Mines and Quarries Act (s.85). However, it is possible that part of the premises may be a factory and part a shop. In *Hoare v Green* (see chapter 4) a workroom behind a florist's shop was held to be a factory, and thus covered by the provisions of the Factories Act, whereas the shop part of the premises where the flowers were sold would presumably come under the scope of OSRPA
(d) premises to which exemption orders apply.

5.150 The Act does not confer on any member of certain visiting forces a right to sue his government (or another member of those forces) in tort in respect of anything done or omitted to be done in the course of his duty. This applies to those governments which are so specified under the Visiting Forces Act 1952 as well as organisations designated under the International Headquarters and Defence Organisations Act 1964 (s.84).

5.151 It is also a defence in any civil proceedings brought to recover damages for a breach of statutory duty (see chapter 8), or in any criminal proceedings based on a contravention of the Act, to prove that at the time of the breach or contravention the premises were being used for a temporary or transitional purpose of not more than six weeks in the case of a fixed structure or six months in the case of a moveable structure (s.86). If the premises are to be used on a temporary basis, it is still necessary to notify the appropriate authority under s.49(1) (see para 5.204), although if a prosecution was brought in respect of a failure to do so, it would be a defence to show that the persons in question were employed in premises to be used only for temporary occupation (s.86(2)).

5.152 It will be recalled that the various statutory provisions only apply to those premises which fall within their respective scope, apart from HSWA, which is ubiquitous in nature and applies to all employment scenes. But OSRPA applies only to those premises which fall exactly within the statutory definitions, and while there are many marginal situations other exclusions are quite clear. Thus doctors' surgeries, night clubs, schools, dance halls, universities, etc may all come under HSWA, but not other legislation unless there is a specific provision which applies.

5.153 Many of the provisions of OSRPA follow closely the pattern and wording which can be found in the Factories Act, and it is generally accepted that both statutes can be interpreted *in pari materia* (see para 1.84). For obvious reasons, more cases fall to be decided under the latter Act than the former.

Office premises (s.1(2))

5.154 These are defined as being a building or part of a building, the sole or principal use of which is an office or for office purposes. This latter phrase includes the purposes of administration, clerical work, handling money and telephone and telegraph operating. Clerical work includes writing, bookkeeping, sorting papers, filing, typing, duplicating, machine calculating, drawing, and the editorial preparation of matter for publication. The term "building" implies a permanent structure of some sort, and would therefore include a hut or shed, etc if used for office purposes. Any part of the premises which is ancillary to the main purpose of an office is also covered by the Act, eg canteens, dining rooms, storerooms, washrooms, lavatories (s.1(5)) although in respect of some of these rooms there are specific legal requirements.

Shop premises (s.1(3))

5.155 This phrase is slightly more complicated and is defined as follows.

5.156 (a) A shop. Although this term was given a somewhat wide meaning in the Shops Act 1950 ("any premises from which retail trade or business is carried on") no such definition appears in OSRPA and it would not therefore be correct to assume that the two Acts should be construed together. Redgrave, *Health and Safety* (p. 647) takes the view that "shop" is a genus of "shop premises" and therefore nothing can be a shop unless it also consists of premises. On this view, a mobile shop would be excluded from the Act. The point does not appear to have been authoritatively decided, but since mobility does not mean immunity (*British Railways Board v Liptrot*, see para 5.42), a shop does not necessarily cease to be one because it is mobile. Further, the word "shop" has many colloquial uses. Workers in factories frequently refer to their place of work as being a "shop"; there is a "closed shop", which is a union membership agreement; one talks about a betting shop, shopfloor, workshop, and even a knocking shop! However, it would appear that the prime characteristic of a shop is the carrying on of retail trade. On this basis, a hairdressing salon which sold goods incidentally to its main business would not be a shop, but a salon in a large departmental store would be.

5.157 (b) A building or part of a building which is not a shop but of which the sole or principal use is the carrying on there of a retail trade or business. The fact that there is a requirement for the business to be "carried on" implies some degree of permanence, but retail trade means supplying customers for their own use and would exclude premises used for wholesale purposes (but see para 5.159 below). Retail trade also suggests a dealing in goods, not services. On this interpretation, dry cleaning premises would not be included, though they would be within the meaning of para 5.160 below.

5.158 Retail trade is defined as including off licences, take away food shops, cafes, restaurants, public houses, retail auctions and private lending libraries (s.1(3)(b)). A building includes a structure (s.90(1)) and thus a permanent market stall (indoor or covered outdoor) would be within the definition, but not a stall erected for temporary purposes, eg a fair or garden fête.

5.159 (c) A building occupied by a wholesale dealer where goods are kept for sale wholesale. Thus a wholesale warehouse or market or display premises fall within the Act.

5.160 (d) A building or part of a building to which members of the public are invited to resort for the purpose of delivering there goods for repair or other treatment, or of themselves carrying out repairs to or treatment of goods. Thus a watch repair shop or a coin-operated laundrette are within the definition.

5.161 (e) Fuel storage premises which sell solid fuel (coal, coke, etc) but not dock storage or colliery storage premises.

Railway premises (s.1(4))

5.162 This phrase means a building occupied by railway undertakers (ie persons authorised by or under a statute to construct, work or carry on a railway) for the purpose of the railway undertaking carried on by them, but this does not include office or shop premises, premises used for the provision of living accommodation for persons employed in the undertaking, hotels or electrical stations (for which see Factories Act, s.123).

Canteen or restaurant facilities (s.1(5))

5.163 Any premises which are used in conjunction with office, shop or railway premises for the sale or supply of food or drink to persons employed in the premises shall be treated as being premises of the class in respect of which they are so used. Thus, a canteen which serves office workers shall be treated as being an office, etc.

Cleanliness (s.4)

5.164 All premises and all furniture, furnishings and fittings shall be kept in a clean state. Dirt or refuse must not be allowed to accumulate and all floors and stairs shall be cleaned not less than once a week by washing or, if it is effective and suitable, sweeping or other method (this does not apply to fuel storage premises which are wholly in the open).

Overcrowding (s.5)

5.165 Rooms shall not be so overcrowded, while work is going on, as to cause a risk of injury to the health of persons working therein. In determining whether or not a room is overcrowded, regard shall be had not only to the number of persons who may be expected to be working in the room at any one time, but also to the space occupied by furniture, fittings, machinery, plant, equipment, appliances and other things.

5.166 The number of persons employed at any time to work in a room shall be such that there is a minimum of 3.7m^2 of floor space per person, or 11m^3 per person. To make this calculation, it is permissible to ignore the presence of furniture, equipment, etc, ie desks and chairs but not walls and walls of filing cabinets, etc. However, if the room is one to which the public are invited to resort (eg a shop) the numerical space standards do not apply, but the general requirement not to permit overcrowding remains.

Temperature (s.6)

5.167 Effective provision shall be made for securing and maintaining a reasonable temperature in every room where persons are employed to work otherwise than for a short period, but no method shall be used which results in the escape into the air of any fume of such a character and to such an extent as to be likely to be injurious or offensive to persons working therein. Where the work does not involve physical effort, a temperature of below 16°C (60.8°F) after the first hour shall not be deemed to be reasonable. However, this does not apply to a room which is office premises where members of the public are invited to resort and in which the maintenance of a reasonable temperature is not reasonably practicable. Nor does it apply to a room which is a shop or railway premises where the maintenance of a reasonable temperature is not reasonably practicable or would cause the deterioration of goods. However, in both these cases there must be a conveniently accessible and effective means of enabling persons employed to work there to warm themselves, and a reasonable opportunity to use such facilities must be given. For example, in *NAAFI v Porstmouth City Council* the appellants appealed against an Improvement Notice served on them because the temperature in their premises was unreasonably low. It was pointed out that the premises were being used for the storage of fresh food and a temperature of between 41°F and 50°F was necessary. A warm room and suitable warm clothing were provided for employees, and it was held that the notice should be cancelled.

5.168 On each floor where there is a room to which the Act applies there must be a thermometer in a conspicuous place and in a position where it can be easily seen and used by persons employed there.

5.169 The Act does not specify a maximum temperature, but this too must be reasonable (see HSWA s.2(2)(e)). Thus if there is an exceptional heatwave, a reasonable temperature must still be observed.

Ventilation (s.7)

5.170 Effective and suitable provision shall be made for securing and maintaining, by the circulation of adequate supplies of fresh air or artificially purified air, the ventilation of every room in which persons are employed.

Lighting (s.8)

5.171 Effective provision shall be made for securing and maintaining sufficient and suitable lighting (whether natural or artificial) in every part of the premises in which persons are working or passing. All glazed windows used for lighting purposes shall, so far as is reasonably practicable, be kept clean on both sides and free from obstruction, except when the windows have been whitewashed or shaded for the purpose of mitigating heat or reducing glare. Artificial lighting shall be properly maintained.

Sanitary conveniences (s.9)

5.172 Suitable and sufficient sanitary conveniences shall be provided at places conveniently accessible to persons employed. These shall be kept clean and properly maintained, with effective provision made for lighting and ventilation. Section 9(5) acknowledges that arrangements may be made for employees to use facilities which are provided for the use of others and as long as they are conveniently accessible the Act will have been complied with. In *Davis & Sons v Leeds City Council*, the tenancy of a flat above a shop was subject to the condition that employees at the shop could use the lavatory facilities at any time. An improvement notice was issued by an inspector requiring the occupier of the shop to provide accessible sanitary conveniences instead of this arrangement. The industrial tribunal allowed an appeal against the notice. Evidence was given by a shop assistant that she had not been inconvenienced by this arrangement during her fifteen years' employment, and a circular from the Ministry of Labour addressed to local authorities was admitted into evidence which stated that "workers in a lock-up shop might have the use of conveniences and facilities in adjacent premises". After having visited the premises the industrial tribunal concluded that the lavatory facilities in the flat were conveniently accessible and cancelled the notice. However, in *Moorhouse v Effer*, the shared toilet facilities were in a shop which was some distance away and across a busy road and the industrial tribunal held that these were not conveniently accessible.

5.173 The Schedule to the Sanitary Conveniences Regulations 1964 lays down certain minimum standards as to the numbers of water closets and urinals which must be provided depending on the number of persons employed, and arrangements are not suitable unless they are at least in accordance with the scales laid down. Public conveniences are not to be taken into account. Lavatories shall not be situated in any room where any person has to work (other than an attendant) and there are further provisions relating to the siting of conveniences, providing effective ventilation, protection from the weather, ensuring privacy, marking for separate sexes and the disposal of sanitary dressings.

Washing facilities (s.10)

5.174 Suitable and sufficient washing facilities shall be provided at places which are conveniently accessible, including a supply of clean, running hot water and cold or warm water, together with soap and clean towels or other suitable means of cleaning or drying. The place where these facilities are provided shall be kept clean and in an orderly condition, and washing or drying apparatus shall be kept clean and properly maintained. There shall also be effective means for lighting.

5.175 The provisions of this section are complied with if there is suitable shared accommodation on the lines relating to the provision of sanitary conveniences (above).

5.176 The Washing Facilities Regulations 1964 lay down certain minimum standards as to the numbers of washbasins (or troughs or washing fountains) which must be provided, depending on the number of persons employed. All washing facilities shall be covered and enclosed to ensure sufficient protection from the weather and effective provision must be made, as far as is reasonably practicable, for ventilation. If there is separate accommodation for each sex, this shall be clearly marked.

5.177 Washbasins, troughs and washing fountains are defined in the regulations. They must have a smooth impervious surface and waste pipes. In *South Surbiton Co-operative Society v Wilcox* an inspector issued an improvement notice which required the occupiers to replace a cracked washbasin. This action was confirmed by the industrial tribunal. The surface was not impervious as required by the regulations and it was not properly maintained as required by s.10(2). The fact that the company had a previous good record or that the breach was a trivial one was irrelevant.

Supply of drinking water (s.11)

5.178 An adequate supply of wholesome drinking water must be provided and maintained at suitable places conveniently accessible to persons employed to work in the premises. If it is not piped, it must be contained in suitable vessels and renewed at least daily. All practicable steps must be taken to preserve it and the vessels from contamination. If the water is not supplied from a jet there shall also be provided (and renewed as often as is required) a supply of drinking vessels of a kind to be discarded after use, or other drinking vessels together with facilities for rinsing them in clean water. Again, it is permissible to use shared facilities which are conveniently accessible.

Accommodation for clothing (s.12)

5.179 At suitable places there shall be suitable and sufficient provision made for enabling persons employed to hang clothing not worn by them during working hours and such arrangements as are reasonably practicable to enable clothing to be dried. If special clothing is worn at work and is not taken home, similar arrangements must be made. It would appear that the possibility of there being a theft of clothing is a factor to be taken into account in determining whether or not the accommodation is suitable (*McCarthy v Daily Mirror Newspapers Ltd*).

Sitting facilities (s.13)

5.180 Where persons have, in the course of their work, a reasonable opportunity to sit down without detriment to their work, there shall be provided at suitable places, which are conveniently accessible, suitable facilities sufficient to enable them to take advantage of those opportunities. If persons are employed in shop premises in a room where the public are invited to resort and have a reasonable opportunity for sitting in the course of their work, the facilities provided shall not be deemed to be sufficient unless there is a ratio of one seat for every three employees. It is an offence if an employer fails to allow his employees to use the seating facilities whenever such use does not interfere with the employee's work.

Types of seats (s.14)

5.181 If the work (or a substantial part of it) can be done sitting down, the seats provided must be of a suitable design, construction and dimension, together with a footrest on which the employee can readily and comfortably support his feet (if he cannot do so without one). The seat and footrest must be adequately and properly supported while in use for the purpose for which it was provided. In *Tesco Stores v Edwards*, the seating provided for assistants at the check-out of a supermarket had no footrests, were not adjustable, had no backrest, could not swivel and were generally uncomfortable. An improvement notice was confirmed requiring the employers to provide suitable chairs.

Eating facilities (s.15)

5.182 Where persons employed in shop premises eat meals there, suitable and sufficient facilities for eating meals shall be provided.

Floors, passages and stairs (s.16)

5.183 All floors, stairs, steps, passages and gangways shall be of sound construction and properly maintained and shall so far as is reasonably practicable be kept free from obstruction and from any substance likely to cause persons to slip. Every staircase must have a substantial handrail which, if there is an open side, must be on that side. In *Haverson & Sons Ltd v Winger* the employer provided a heavy duty rope as a handrail alongside a staircase. An inspector served an improvement notice requiring that a rigid handrail be installed in order to comply with s.16, but this was cancelled after an appeal to an industrial tribunal. The Act does not require the handrail to be fixed or rigid, only that it should be substantial, and in the circumstances a rope handrail was adequate.

5.184 If the staircase has two open sides, or if it is specially liable to cause accidents because of the nature of its construction, or because of the condition of the surface of the steps, or other special circumstances, then the handrail must be provided and maintained on both sides. Any open side of a staircase shall be guarded by the provision and maintenance of efficient means of preventing any person from accidentally falling through the space.

5.185 All openings in the floor shall be securely fenced except insofar as the nature of the work renders such fencing impracticable.

5.186 Section 16 does not apply to fuel storage premises, but in respect of these, the ground surface shall be of good repair, all steps and platforms shall be of sound construction and properly maintained and all openings in platforms shall be securely fenced except insofar as the nature of the work makes this impracticable.

Fencing (s.17)

5.187 Every dangerous part of any machinery used as, or forming part of, the equipment of the premises shall be securely fenced unless it is in such a position or of such construction as to be as safe to every person working in the premises as it would be if securely fenced. It will be noted that there is no provision in OSRPA corresponding to ss.12 and 13 of the Factories Act relating to prime movers and transmission machinery and such items must therefore be considered under s.17 of OSRPA. Also, the machinery in question must form part of, or be used as, the equipment of the premises, which is the interpretation placed on s.14 of the Factories Act (*British Railways Board v Liptrot*).

5.188 If a fixed guard cannot be provided, the fencing requirements will be complied with if a device is provided which automatically prevents the operator from coming into contact with the dangerous part.

5.189 Fencing shall be of substantial construction, be properly maintained and kept in position while the parts are in motion or use.

5.190 It is of interest to note that parts of s.17 have been repealed (Employment Act 1989, Schedule 7). The reason is that the provisions of the Act were only relevant if regulations were in force (comparable to the Operation of Unfenced Machinery Regulations 1938, see para 5.65). However, no regulations have been made and there are no plans to do so. Consequently, the repealed parts of s.17 were no longer necessary.

Young persons cleaning machines (s.18)

5.191 No person under the age of eighteen shall clean any machinery used as, or forming part of the equipment of the premises if by doing so he is exposed to the risk of injury from a moving part of that machinery or any adjacent machinery. In *Dewhurst Ltd v Coventry Corporation*, a sixteen-year-old boy was cleaning a hand-operated bacon slicer. The cutting edge was partially protected by a guard which had to be removed when the edge was being cleaned. The slicer had no locking device. The boy was instructed to clean one half of the blade and then rotate it to expose the other half for cleaning. In breach of this instruction he pressed a pad against the cutting edge and rotated the blade, which resulted in him cutting off the top of his finger. It was held that the employers were guilty of an offence under s.18. Although the blade should not have been moved while cleaning, the cutting edge was still a moving part, and the prohibition in the section was absolute. The employers also failed to establish a defence under s.67 (below) that they had used all due diligence to secure compliance with the section.

Training and supervision (s.19)

5.192 No person shall work on any prescribed machines unless he has been fully instructed as to the dangers arising and the precautions to be observed and (a) has received sufficient training and (b) is under adequate supervision by a person who has a thorough knowledge and experience of the machine.

5.193 The Prescribed Dangerous Machines Order 1964 specifies the type of machines in question, which are, generally speaking, mincing, chopping and slicing machines, ie:

5.194 (a) *Machines worked by mechanical power*; worm type mincing machines, rotary knife bowl type chopping machines, dough brakes, dough mixers, food mixing machines when used with attachments for mincing, chipping or any other cutting operation or for crumbling, pie and tart making machines, vegetable slicing machines, wrapping and packing machines, garment presses, opening or teasing machines used for upholstery or bedding work, corner staying machines, loose knife punching machines, wire stitching machines, machines with circular saw blades, band or strip saws, planing machines, verticle spindle moulding machines and routing machines used for cutting wood, wood products, fibre board plastic or similar material.

5.195 (b) *Machines whether or not worked by mechanical power*; circular knife slicing machines used for cutting bacon and other foods (whether similar to bacon or not), potato chipping machines, platen printing machines, including when used for cutting and creasing and guillotine machines.

Hoists and lifts

5.196 The Offices, Shops and Railway Premises (Hoists and Lifts) Regulations 1968 apply to lifts and liftways which are situated in office premises, shop premises and railway premises to which the Act applies. The obligations under these regulations fall upon the owner or owners of the building in respect of matters within that person's control or within the control of his servants or agents. Otherwise, the duty to comply with the regulations falls upon the occupier of the premises.

5.197 Every lift shall be of good mechanical construction, sound material and adequate strength and properly maintained. They shall be examined by a competent person every six months and a record containing the prescribed particulars sent to the owner (see Lifting Plant and Equipment (Records of Tests and Examination etc) Regulations 1992). This report shall be kept for two years and kept readily available for inspection by an inspector. If the examination reveals that the lift cannot continue to be used with safety unless certain repairs are carried out immediately or within a specified time, the person making the report shall also send a copy to the enforcing authority (ie the local authority or HSE).

5.198 Every liftway shall be efficiently protected by a substantial enclosure fitted with gates, and every gate shall be fitted with an interlocking device to ensure that it cannot be opened except when the lift is at a landing and the lift cannot be moved until the gate is closed.

5.199 Every lift shall be marked conspicuously with the maximum working load and no greater load shall be carried. Additionally, if the lift is used for carrying persons (as well as goods) efficient automatic devices shall be provided and maintained to prevent the cage overrunning and each side from which access is reached from the landing shall be fitted with a gate and an efficient device to ensure that the cage cannot be raised or lowered unless the gate is closed, and will come to rest when the gate is open.

Prohibition of heavy work (s.23)

5.200 This section has been repealed as from 1 January 1993 by the Manual Handling Operations Regulations 1992 (see Chapter 4).

First aid (s.24)

5.201 This section has been repealed and replaced by the provisions of the Health and Safety (First Aid) Regulations 1981, which came into force as from July 1982 (para 6.74).

Multi-occupancy buildings (s.42)

5.202 A building which is under the ownership of one person but parts of which are leased or licensed to another must have clean common parts, and all furniture, furnishings and fittings in such common parts shall be kept in a clean state. Effective provision shall be made for securing and maintaining in common parts suitable and sufficient lighting (whether natural or artificial), and all glazed windows and skylights shall, so far as is reasonably practicable, be kept clean on both sides and free from obstruction (except when whitewashed or shaded for the purpose of reducing heat of glare). Floors, stairs, steps, passages and gangways shall be of sound construction and properly maintained, and shall, so far as is reasonably practicable, be kept free from any substance likely to cause any person to slip. Staircases shall be provided with a substantial handrail or handhold, and any open stairway shall be guarded by the provision and maintenance of efficient means of preventing any person from accidentally falling through the space.

5.203 In the event of a contravention of this section, the owner of the building will be guilty of an offence. He will also be liable for a contravention of ss.9 and 10 (see above) where the sanitary conveniences or washing facilities are used in common.

Notification of employment (s.49)

5.204 Before a person begins to employ persons in any office, shop or railway premises, he shall serve on the appropriate authority (ie the enforcement authority) two copies of a notice containing the necessary information. The Schedule to the

Notifications of Employment of Persons Order 1964 contains the notice in a prescribed form for use for the purpose of this section. A failure to comply may lead to a fine on summary conviction.

Offences (s.63)

5.205 Since most of the obligations imposed by the Act are placed on the occupier of the premises, it is he who will be primarily liable. If the Act provides that some other person shall be held responsible as well as the occupier, then both shall be liable. The owner is liable in certain multi-occupancy situations (see above).

Defences (s.67)

5.206 It shall be a defence for a person charged with an offence under the Act or a regulation to prove that he used all due diligence to secure compliance with that provision (see para 1.78). This defence is, of course, applicable to criminal proceedings, not to civil liability, although in the latter case a plea of "no negligence" may equally succeed. "Due diligence" and "reasonable care" are similar concepts. It will be recalled that in *J H Dewhurst Ltd v Coventry Corporation* (see para 5.191) the defence of due diligence failed, for although the defendants had given the boy instructions, put up notices, and had received regular visits from the inspectors without adverse comment, the court considered that in view of the statutory prohibition, there was a special obligation to provide the necessary supervision. However, the defence succeeded in *Tesco Ltd v Natrass* (see para 1.78).

Power to modify agreements (s.73)

5.207 If a person is prevented from doing any structural or other alteration to the premises necessary to comply with a provision of the Act because of the terms of a lease or agreement, he may apply to the local county court, which may make an order modifying or setting aside the terms of that lease or agreement as the court thinks just and equitable. If such alterations do become necessary, the court may also apportion the expense of doing so between the parties having an interest in the premises.

Application of the Act (s.83)

5.208 Insofar as the Act imposes duties which may give rise to civil liability (based on an action in tort) the Act is binding on the Crown (except in respect of the Armed Forces). So far as enforcement is concerned, although HSE can inspect Crown premises it is not possible to prosecute the Crown in the criminal courts.

6

Other health and safety legislation

Employers' liability insurance

6.1 By the Employers' Liability (Compulsory Insurance) Act 1969 every employer (subject to certain exceptions, see below) must take out and maintain an insurance policy with an authorised insurer against liability for bodily injury and disease sustained by his employees and arising out of and in the course of their employment. The policy must provide cover of at least £2,000,000 arising out of any one occurrence. A contract of insurance is one of *uberrimae fidei*, ie of the utmost good faith, and the proposer must disclose all the information which would affect the mind of a prudent insurer. If, therefore, the employer fails to make such disclosure, the policy may be void, and as well as being without the necessary cover to meet a claim the employer will be liable for a criminal offence. It must be stressed that the Act applies to every employer carrying on a trade or business, including sports and social clubs, as long as a person is an employee within the legal definition. It is not necessary to take out an insurance policy if the employer engages persons as independent contractors, domestic servants (who are not employed for the purposes of a business), close relatives and persons who are not normally resident in Great Britain and who are working here for fewer than fourteen consecutive days.

6.2 The following employers are exempt from the Act:

(a) nationalised industries, local authorities and nuclear power installation operators
(b) shipowners covered by mutual insurance
(c) police authorities
(d) any joint board or committee whose members include representatives of a local authority
(e) certain other bodies financed out of public funds (see Employers' Liability (Compulsory Insurance) Exemption Regulations 1971).

6.3 A certificate of insurance will be issued by the insurance company and this must be displayed at each place of business for the information of employees. An inspector can request to see the certificate and also the policy itself (on reasonable notice being given). The policy, which must be an approved one (see Employers' Liability (Compulsory Insurance) General Regulations 1971) may be subject to the condition that the insurer may be able to reclaim from the insured any compensation paid to the injured employee from the employer, in specified circumstances, but may not make the employers' liability conditional upon the employer exercising reasonable care, or performing his statutory duty.

6.4 Any employer who is not insured in accordance with the Act shall be guilty of an offence punishable by a fine of £1,000 for each day when he is in default and if the offence is committed with the consent, connivance, or facilitated by the neglect of any director, manager, secretary or other officer, then he, as well as the employer (if a body corporate) shall be guilty of an offence and punishable accordingly.

6.5 It is also an offence, punishable by a fine of £400:

(a) to fail to display the certificate or a copy of the insurance certificate
(b) to fail to send the certificate or a copy to the inspector when so required
(c) to fail to produce the certificate or a copy on demand by an inspector
(d) to refuse to allow the inspector to inspect the actual policy document.

6.6 The fact that the employer has a valid policy in force does not confer any automatic right to compensation for an injured employee, as this must be determined by reference to the legal rights of the parties (see chapter 8). However, it does mean that if an employee succeeds in his claim, there will be funds available with which to satisfy the judgment.

6.7 For further information, see *Short Guide to the Employers' Liability (Compulsory Insurance) Act 1969*, available from HSE or Department of Employment.

Fire certificates and fire precautions

6.8 The law relating to fire certificates and general fire safety is contained in the Fire Precautions Act 1971, as amended by HSWA, the Fire Safety and Safety of Places of Sport Act 1987 and the Fire Precautions (Factories, Offices, Shops and Railway Premises) Order 1989.

6.9 The following places of work must have a fire certificate, ie offices, shops, railway premises and factories where:

(a) more than 20 persons are employed at any one time
(b) more than 10 persons are employed to work at any one time elsewhere than on the ground floor, or
(c) the premises is part of a larger building which meets the conditions in (a) or (b) above, or
(d) explosive or highly flammable materials are stored or used.

6.10 In respect of certain special premises (see Fire Certificate (Special Premises) Regulations 1976), HSE will issue the fire certificate. Otherwise it will be issued by the local fire authority who can, however, grant an exemption on the ground that the fire risk to occupants is not sufficiently serious as to warrant the issue of a certificate. If exemption is not granted, the authority will inspect the premises and must be satisfied that the means of escape, the method of escape, the means of fighting fire and the fire warning systems are adequate. If they are, a fire certificate will be issued. If not, the fire authority will issue a notice stating the necessary steps which must be taken before a certificate can be issued.

6.11 The Fire Precautions (Factories, Offices, Shops and Railway Premises) Order 1989 provides that certain premises may be exempt from the need to have a fire certificate. The exemption applies to offices, shops, factories and railway premises in which:

(a) not more than 20 persons work at any one time, and
(b) not more than 10 people work at any one time elsewhere than on the ground floor.

6.12 This exemption will not arise if the premises form part of a larger building where the total number working there exceeds twenty (or exceeds ten working elsewhere than on the ground floor), or the premises is a factory where explosive or highly flammable materials are stored or used in sufficient quantities as to constitute a fire risk.

6.13 However, even though the premises may be exempt, the employer must still provide adequate means of escape and adequate means of fighting fire.

6.14 Under the provisions of the proposed Fire Precautions (Places of Work) Regulations (which are designed to implement the fire safety requirements of the Framework Directive and the Workplace Directive) employers must make an assessment of the fire risk at the place of work, prepare an evacuation plan, train their staff in fire precautions, and keep appropriate records.

Protection of the environment

6.15 Basically, health and safety legislation is concerned with the protection of workers and those affected by work activity. There is an obvious link between these objectives and the need for general environmental protection, and in many cases there is an overlap. As governments became more aware of the need to prevent pollution of the environment, both on a national and international level, new strategies have been developed, and complex legislative provisions enacted.

6.16 The Environmental Protection Act 1990 (EPA), together with other relevant legislation (Water Resources Act 1991, the unrepealed parts of the Control of Pollution Act 1974, etc) provide the basic framework of pollution control legislation. The 1990 Act established a system of Integrated Pollution Control, administered by HM Inspectorate of Pollution (HMIP) in England and Wales, HM Industrial Pollution Inspectorate in Scotland and local authority air pollution control (LAAPC) throughout the country. These authorities are responsible for all aspects of pollution control carried on by polluting industrial processes. Certain prescribed processes require prior authorisation before they may be operated and such permission will not be granted unless various conditions are met, including ensuring that the Best Available Techniques Not Entailing Excessive Cost (BATNEEC) are used for preventing the release of substances prescribed into any environmental medium and for rendering harmless any other substance which might cause harm if so released. The Department of the Environment has issued a guidance document giving its interpretation of BATNEEC. "Best" means the best technology available anywhere in the world; patented processes are "available" if they are available under licence; "techniques" include operational factors (numbers and qualifications of staff, training, supervision, etc) as well as the design, construction, lay out and maintenance of buildings; to determine whether the technique entails "excessive cost" one considers whether the additional costs are justified by the corresponding reduction in emissions. To enable the enforcing authorities to apply consistent standards when applying BATNEEC, process Guidance Notes have been prepared, to which they may have regard.

6.17 It is a criminal offence to break a condition to which an authorised process is subject. Additionally, in criminal proceedings, it shall be for the operator to show that there was no better technique available not entailing excessive cost than the one used. Enforcing authorities have power to issue prohibition notices, they may vary authorisations already granted and revoke them. There is a right of appeal to the Secretary of State.

6.18 Integrated pollution control inspectors have very wide powers under the Act. They may enter, inspect and examine premises, take measurements, photographs, samples, etc, require persons to give information and produce documents, and so forth, very much on the lines of HSE inspectors (see para 2.35). Public registers will be kept of applications for authorisations and other information, with certain safeguards for the necessity for withholding information on the grounds of national security or commercial confidentiality.

Food safety

6.19 The provisions of the Food Safety Act 1990 are peripheral to health and safety at work legislation, but are mentioned here in brief for the sake of completeness. Generally speaking, local authorities are to be the "food authorities" and they will appoint "authorised officers" to act in matters arising under the legislation. It is an offence to render food so as to be injurious to health (eg by adding or abstracting anything), or to sell food not complying with food safety requirements. An authorised officer may inspect and seize suspected food and may also serve improvement and/or prohibition notices. In many ways the Act is an enabling Act, and the precise measures to be taken in order to deal with its provisions will be found in regulations.

Working with lead

6.20 The Control of Lead at Work Regulations 1980 came into force in August 1981 and are designed to extend and rationalise the statutory provisions which deal with exposure to lead at the workplace. All existing statutory provisions dealing with lead (s.75 and ss.128–130 of Factories Act) and about twenty regulations made under the Act have thus been repealed in part or in whole, to be replaced by the new regulations and an Approved Code of Practice, which sets out acceptable methods of meeting the new requirements. The objective is to protect the health of workers who are exposed to lead dust, fume or vapour, by controlling and reducing the amount of absorption to an acceptable level, and to monitor the amount of lead absorbed by an individual so that he or she may be removed or temporarily suspended from work before health is adversely affected.

6.21 The original Code of Practice was amended in 1986 to take account of EC Directive 82/605, and a further revised Code was issued in 1990 (COP 41).

6.22 The code of practice lays down two standards.

(a) Lead in the air. This remains unchanged and is expressed to be 0.15 mgm^{-} of air expressed as an 8 hour time-weighted average concentration. A higher value 0.10 mgm^{-} is given to tetraethyl lead, which has greater toxicity.
(b) Lead in blood. This is now set at 70 μ/100 ml of blood. However, women of child-bearing age have greater vunerability to lead poisoning, and in their case the standard is reduced to 40 μ/100 ml of blood.

6.23 If the level of atmospheric lead exceeds half of the above standard, there will have to be regular monitoring; if the blood level content of lead exceeds 40 μ/100 ml tests must be taken on a regular basis. Thus once the danger levels have been identified, action can be taken.

Limitations

6.24 There is some work where the exposure to lead is regarded as being minimal and unlikely to cause any health problems. These include low temperature melting of lead, such as plumbing, soldering, linotype and monotype casting, painting with low solubility paints, work with material which does not contain more than one per cent lead, work with lead in emulsion or paste form so that lead dust or fume cannot be given off, the handling of clean solid metallic lead (ingots, pipes, sheets, etc) and lead from petrol driven vehicles. In these cases, the regulations will not apply, but reference should be made to the recommendations in the Code of Practice.

6.25 The regulations impose duties on the employer not only with regard to his employees, but also, so far as is reasonably practicable, in respect of any other person who is at work on the premises where work with lead is being carried on and who is consequently liable to be exposed to lead from that work.

Assessment

6.26 Where any work may expose any person to lead, the employer (or self-employed person) shall assess that work to determine the nature and degree of exposure. The assessment shall take place before the work commences and shall be revised whenever there is reason to suppose that the previous assessment is incorrect, or where there is a material change in the work, or when requested to do so by an inspector.

Information, instruction and training

6.27 Adequate information, instruction and training must be given by each employer to his employees who are liable to be exposed to lead, so that they are aware of the risks and precautions which must be observed. Similar information, instruction and training must be given to those employees who carry out assessment, cleaning, provide or maintain control measures, or carry out air monitoring (see below).

Control measures

6.28 Every employer shall, so far as is reasonably practicable, provide such control measures for materials, plant, processes as will adequately control the exposure of his employees to lead, otherwise than by the use of respiratory protective equipment or protective clothing by them.

Respiratory equipment

6.29 Every employer shall provide each employee who is likely to be exposed to airborne lead with such respiratory protective equipment as is approved by HSE, unless the control methods prove to be adequate.

Protective clothing

6.30 Every employer shall provide each employee who is liable to be exposed to lead with adequate protective clothing unless the exposure is not significant.

Washing and changing facilities

6.31 Every employer shall provide:

(a) adequate washing facilities
(b) where protective clothing is provided, adequate changing facilities and facilities for the storage of protective clothing and personal clothing not worn during working hours.

Eating, drinking and smoking

6.32 Employers shall take adequate steps to ensure that:

(a) so far as is reasonably practicable, his employees do not eat, drink or smoke in any place which is liable to be contaminated by lead
(b) suitable arrangements are made for employees to eat, drink or smoke in a place which is not liable to be contaminated by lead.

6.33 An employee also commits an offence if he eats, drinks or smokes in any place which he has reason to believe to be contaminated by lead.

Cleaning

6.34 Adequate steps shall be taken to secure the cleanliness of workplaces, premises, plant, respiratory protective equipment and protective clothing.

Avoiding contamination

6.35 Every employer, his employees, and every self-employed person shall, so far as is reasonably practicable, prevent the spread of contamination by lead from the place where work is being carried out.

Use of control measures

6.36 Employers who provide control measures, respiratory protective equipment, protective clothing or other thing or facility shall ensure, so far as is reasonably practicable, that they are properly used or applied.

6.37 Every employee shall make full and proper use of any control measure and other thing provided and if he discovers any defect he shall report it forthwith to his employer.

Maintenance of control measures

6.38 All control measures provided by the employer shall, so far as is reasonably practicable, be maintained in an efficient state, in efficient working order and in good repair.

Air monitoring

6.39 Every employer shall have adequate monitoring procedures to measure the concentrations of lead in air to which his employees are exposed, unless the exposure is not significant, and he shall also measure the concentration of lead in air in accordance with those procedures.

Medical surveillance and biological tests

6.40 If an employee is employed on work which exposes him to lead, he must be under medical surveillance by an employment medical adviser or appointed doctor if the exposure to lead is significant or if the adviser or doctor certifies that he should be under such surveillance. The certificate may state that the employee should not be employed on work which exposes the employee to lead or that he should only be employed subject to certain conditions. Every employee shall present himself for a medical examination or biological tests during working hours when required to do so by his employer.

Records

6.41 Every employer shall ensure that adequate records are kept of the assessment, maintenance, air monitoring, medical surveillance and biological tests and make these available for inspection by his employees. This does not enable a person to see the health record of an identifiable individual. Entries in these records shall be kept for two years.

6.42 Under the regulations (and at common law) the employer may owe a duty of care not only to the employee, but also to members of the employee's family who may be exposed to significant risks of lead poisoning consequent on the employee's own exposure (see *Hewett v Alf Brown's Transport Ltd*, para 8.56).

Safety notices

6.43 There are a number of legislative provisions which require the display of notices relating to issues of safety and/or health. These include:

(a) Coal and Other Mines (Managers and Officials) Order 1956, which requires a danger sign around dangerous areas.
(b) Stratified Ironstone, Shale and Fireclay Mines (Explosives) Regulations 1956 which require warning notices when shot firing is being carried on.
(c) Miscellaneous Mines (Explosives) Regulations 1959, which require notices warning that shotfiring is about to commence.
(d) Gravel and Sand Quarries (Overhanging) (Exemption) Regulations 1958, which require warning notices where there is danger from falls.
(e) Ionising Radiations Regulations 1985 require the designation and demarcation of controlled areas.
(f) Factories (Testing of Aircraft Engines) Special Regulations 1952 require notices prohibiting smoking in test areas.
(g) Shipbuilding and Ship Repairing Regulations 1960 require warning notices when persons are working or passing underneath any place from which articles may fall, and notices prohibiting smoking or the use of naked lights near acetylene generating plants.
(h) Highly Flammable Liquids and Liquified Petroleum Gases Regulations 1972 require various notices warning persons of the presence of flammable liquids, and prohibiting smoking near such liquids.
(i) Control of Substances Hazardous to Health Regulations 1988 require notices to be affixed to premises when certain fumigation is to be carried out, and removed when the premises are safe to enter.

Safety Signs Regulations 1980

6.44 These regulations came into force on 1 January 1981, following an EC Directive designed to standardise safety signs throughout the Community. They were only in force in respect of new signs; because of the high cost of changing existing signs a five year period was allowed for during which all existing signs were required to be progressively changed to the new format. The regulations did not require signs to be erected; they only require that if signs are erected, they must be in the new form. The new symbols will apply to all places of employment except for coal mines, although internal works road signs (including those relating to pedestrians) must conform to Road Traffic Act signs. Signs which are placed near roads or railways must not be put where they can be confused with signs for the control of the traffic. Safety signs must comply with British Standard 5378.

6.45 The regulations do not cover certain matters for which there are as yet no internationally agreed symbol, eg emergency exits, fire-fighting equipment, etc and any existing legal requirements should continue to be observed. There is a 1990 British Standard on Fire Safety signs, notices & graphic symbols (BS 5499).

6.46 A revised EC Safety Signs Directive has been adopted, and is due to be implemented by mid-1994 (see para 10.20).

6.47 There are four categories of signs, each with its own distinctive shape and colour.

Prohibition signs

6.48 These will be circular with a red border and crossbar over a black symbol on a white background. It is meant to indicate a hazard which must not be ignored, eg "No Smoking".

Warning signs

6.49 These will be triangular in shape with a black border and symbol on a yellow background. It will denote a hazard which could be fatal if overlooked, eg "Caution".

Mandatory signs

6.50 These will be circular on a blue background with symbols in white. These will indicate specific instructions that must be obeyed, where there is an obligation to use safety equipment, eg "Hearing protection must be worn".

Safe conditions

6.51 These will be square or oblong (depending on the size of the text or symbol) and will consist of a green background with white symbols. These will denote some safety consideration, eg "First Aid post".

Examples of safety signs and their meanings

No Smoking

Smoking and naked lights prohibited

No Pedestrians

Do not Extinguish with Water

Not Drinking Water

Warning signs: Triangular with a yellow background and a black border. The symbol, placed centrally, must be black. This sign warns of a particular hazard as follows:

Fire

Explosion

Toxic

Corrosive

Radiation

Overhead Load

Industrial Trucks

Electric Shock

Risk of Danger

Safety signs—*continued*

Laser beam

Mandatory signs: Round with a blue background and white symbol. This sign states what protective equipment must be worn as follows:

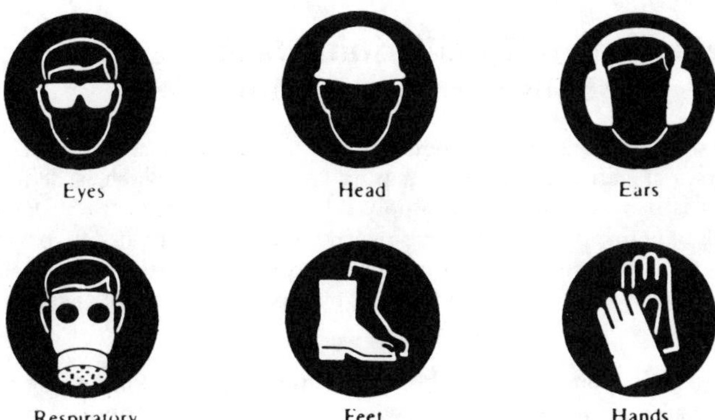

Emergency signs: Square or oblong with white symbols on green background. This sign indicates safe conditions such as first-aid posts or emergency routes.

First-Aid

Indication of Direction

Supplementary signs may be used for conveying further explanation.

Exceptions

Fire-fighting or rescue equipment and emergency exits are excluded from the Regulations as there is, as yet, no international agreement on the type of symbol which should be adopted. Any marking or label on a package or container is also excluded (but see 'DANGEROUS SUBSTANCES, PACKAGING AND LABELLING OF').

Furthermore, signs intended for use in the regulation of any form of transport are excluded. The Regulations require that road traffic signs must be used for road traffic inside a works (if not already covered by the Road Traffic Acts).

Dangerous Substances (Notification and Marking of Sites) Regulations 1990

6.52 These regulations require the notification and marking of sites where there is a total quantity of 25 tonnes or more of dangerous substances present at the site. A dangerous substance is any substance which is dangerous for conveyance within the meaning of the Classification, Packaging and Labelling of Dangerous Substances Regulations 1984 (see para 6.56). There must be notification to the fire authority and to the enforcing authority, with the specified information. Safety signs must be displayed which give adequate notice to firemen that a dangerous substance is present and access and location markings displayed.

Notification of Installations Handling Hazardous Substances Regulations 1982

6.53 These regulations require a person who stores, manufactures, processes, uses or transfers a specified minimum quantity of substance which is defined in the regulations as being hazardous to supply relevant information to HSE. This will enable HSE to define priorities in their inspection programme, notify local planning authorities so as to assist in development control, give necessary advice to emergency services and enable all persons concerned to be made aware of special hazards involved.

6.54 The notification must state the name of the person making it, the address of the site, the area of the site, the date when the activity will commence, a general description of the activity, the name of the local planning authority, and the name and the maximum quantity of each hazardous substance likely to be on the site. The information must be given at least three months before the commencement of the activity.

6.55 Regulations made under the Planning (Hazardous Substances) Act 1990 limit the quantity of hazardous substances which may be kept, until the appropriate authority has had an opportunity to assess the risks of an accident, and the consequences which are likely to flow for inhabitants of surrounding areas.

Dangerous substances

6.56 Under the provisions of the Classification, Packaging and Labelling of Dangerous Substances Regulations 1984 (CPL) (as amended) suppliers of certain specified industrial chemicals must put warning labels on containers to enable the user to speedily identify the main dangers and take the necessary precautions in handling and using. The chemicals must be in containers which are properly designed, constructed and secured in order to prevent accidental spillage in normal use. Similar provisions apply to the conveyance of dangerous substances.

6.57 The warning labels will consist of a pictorial symbol and key words. The symbol will be printed in black on an orange–yellow background so that it stands out and will thus identify the likely danger. The accompanying Authorised and Approved List to the regulations lists over 1,000 chemicals which are classified according to the main hazard, eg explosive, highly flammable, corrosive, toxic, irritant, harmful, oxidising and any combination of these hazards. Each label will carry risk phrases which spell out in detail the main dangers and will give advice on sensible safety precautions. The name of the chemical will be stated and also the name and address of the supplier or manufacturer who can assist in the event of an accident.

6.58 The substance must not be conveyed by road or otherwise supplied unless it is suitably packed and the receptacle designed, constructed, maintained and closed so as to prevent any of the contents escaping.

6.59 New regulations, Chemical (Hazard Information and Packaging) Regulations (CHIP), designed to consolidate all the existing law on the supply, labelling and packaging of dangerous substances and preparations, as well as implementing several EC Directives, are currently being discussed, and are likely to come into effect some time in mid-1993.

6.60 Other regulations control the transportation by road of dangerous chemicals, ie the Road Traffic (Carriage of Dangerous Substances in Packages etc.) Regulations 1992 as amended, the Road Traffic (Carriage of Dangerous Substances in Road Tankers and Tank Containers) Regulations 1992 as amended and the Road Traffic (Training of Drivers of Vehicles Carrying Dangerous Goods) Regulations 1992 as amended. These regulations deal with the design and construction, etc of vehicles, the duties of the operator to obtain, display and disseminate relevant information, the duties imposed on the drivers of vehicles, tanker markings, training and instruction of drivers, loading and unloading procedures, hazard warning panels, emergency action codes, etc.

6.61 There were a number of other specific statutory provisions which required the marking or labelling of articles and substances, but these have been repealed by the COSHH Regulations.

Reporting of accidents and occurrences

6.62 The Reporting of Injuries, Diseases and Dangerous Occurrences Regulations 1985 (RIDDOR) lay down a complete system for the notifying and reporting of injuries, dangerous occurrences and industrial diseases. A specified incident must be notified to the enforcing authority by the quickest practicable means (which will usually mean by telephone) and reported to the enforcing authority in writing within seven days (Form F 2508 revised is commonly used). The requirements relate not only to employees, but to persons on work training schemes, self-employed persons and non-employees who are affected by work activity.

6.63 The following events are specified when suffered as a result of an accident arising out of or in connection with work:

(a) the death of any person
(b) (i) fracture of the skull, spine or pelvis
(ii) fracture of any bone
(a) in the arm or wrist (but not a bone in the hand)
(b) in the leg or ankle (but not a bone in the foot)
(iii) amputation of a hand or foot, or a finger, thumb or toe (if the joint or bone is severed)
(iv) loss of the sight of an eye, a penetrating injury to the eye, or a chemical or hot metal burn to the eye
(v) either (a) injury (including burns) requiring immediate medical attention or
(b) loss of consciousness from an electric shock from any electric circuit or equipment
(vi) loss of consciousness resulting from a lack of oxygen
(vii) decompression sickness requiring immediate medical treatment (but not as the result of an operation to which the Diving Operations Act Work Regulations apply)
(viii) either (a) acute illness requiring treatment or
(b) loss of consciousness
from the absorption of any substance by inhalation, ingestion or through the skin
(ix) acute illness requiring medical treatment where there is reason to believe that this resulted from exposure to a pathogen or infected material
(x) any other injury which results in the person injured being admitted immediately into hospital for more than 24 hours
(xi) any dangerous occurrence of the type listed in Part 1 of Schedule 1 of RIDDOR.

6.64 The following incidents are also reportable:

(a) an injury whereby any person at work is incapacitated for his normal work for more than three days caused by an accident at work. The general view is if a person attends work after the accident, but, being unable to do his normal job, is given alternative (light?) work, the accident is still reportable
(b) the death of an employee which occurs some time after the reportable injury which led to the death, but not more than one year afterwards.

Reporting of diseases

6.65 Schedule 2 of RIDDOR contains a list of 28 reportable diseases, together with the work-related activity (if any). If a person does the specified type of work and suffers from the specified disease, this fact must be reported. The employer will generally learn of the disease from a written diagnosis received from a doctor, eg on a medical certificate. A disease does not have to be reported if the employee does not work in the listed job; conversely, the fact that the employee has contracted the disease does not mean that it was caused by the work.

6.66 The report should be on Form 2508A and sent to the local office of HSE or environmental health officer of the local authority.

Reporting gas incidents

6.67 Where (a) a supplier of flammable gas through a fixed pipe distribution system, or (b) a non-retail importer or supplier of a refillable container containing liquid petroleum gas, receives notification of a death, injury or disease of any person arising out of or in connection with the gas supplied, filled or imported, a report must be made to HSE, although the time limit is extended to 14 days.

6.68 Also, where a supplier of flammable gas has reason to suspect that a gas fitting or flue or ventilation is, as a result of its design, construction, installation, modification or servicing, likely to cause death or injury, because of accidental leakage of gas, or inadequate combustion of gas, or inadequate removal of fumes, he must report the fact within 14 days.

Obtaining further information

6.69 Once having received a report, HSE can, with the approval of the Commission, require further information about the reported incident. This may be further details about the circumstances which gave rise to the incident, details about the plant (including its design), details of safety systems, qualification experience and training of staff, protection arrangements, tests, levels of exposure, etc.

Exceptions to RIDDOR

6.70 There is no requirement to report a death or injury of a person when undergoing treatment in a hospital, or at a doctor's or dentist's surgery (including company surgeries and medical centres).

Keeping records

6.71 Employers are required to keep records of all events reported under the regulations. No specific design is required, and the records may be in the form of photocopies of accident report forms, or an accident book, or stored on a computer. All that is necessary is to comply with the requirements laid down in Schedule 3. In the case of a notifiable disease, the information must contain the occupation of the person affected, the name or nature of the disease, and the date of its diagnosis. In the case of a reportable accident or dangerous occurrence, the record must contain the date and time of the incident, the name, occupation and nature of any injury, the place where the injury or dangerous occurrence happened and a brief description of the circumstances.

Defences

6.72 If a person is prosecuted for an offence under the regulations, it will be a defence for him to show that he was not aware of the event which he was required to report or notify, and that he had taken all reasonable steps to have all such events brought to his notice.

Responsibility for reporting

6.73 The following persons are responsible for reporting the event under RIDDOR.

Reportable event	*Person affected*	*Person responsible for reporting*
Death, specified major injury or condition, or over three-day injury	an employee at work	the employer
	a person receiving training for employment	the person whose undertaking makes immediate provision of the training
	a self-employed person at work in premises under the control of someone else	the person for the time being having control of the premises in connection with the carrying on by him of any trade, business or undertaking
Specified major injury or condition, or over three-day injury	a self-employed person at work in premises under his control	the self-employed person (or someone acting on his behalf)

Reportable event	*Person affected*	*Person responsible for reporting*
Death or specified major injury or condition	A person who is not at work, but who is affected by work activities	the person having control of the premises in connection with the carrying on by him of any trade, etc at which, or in connection with the work at which, the accident happened
A dangerous occurrence (listed in Part 1, Schedule 1 of RIDDOR, eg collapse of lifts, hoists, cranes, certain fun-fair accidents, explosions of boilers, electrical fault causing fire, release of highly flammable liquid, explosions, etc and railway accidents)		the person for the time being having control of the premises in connection with the carrying on by him of any trade etc at which, or in connection with the work at which, the dangerous occurrence happened
A dangerous occurrence involving a pipeline		the owner of the pipeline
A dangerous occurrence involving a dangerous substance being conveyed by road		the operator of the vehicle

First aid

6.74 The Health and Safety (First-Aid) Regulations were made in June 1981 and came into force on 1 July 1982. Four statutory provisions were repealed (Factories Act, s.61; Mines and Quarries Act, s.115 (in part); OSRPA, s.24; and Agriculture (Safety, Health and Welfare Provisions) Act, s.6(1) and (4)). Additionally, some 42 regulations and orders were revoked, and thus the new regulations, supported by an Approved Code of Practice with guidance, are the main source of legal rules.

6.75 The regulations lay down two separate general requirements. First, an employer shall provide (or ensure that there is provided) such equipment and facilities as are adequate and appropriate in the circumstances for enabling first aid to be rendered to employees who are injured or become ill at work. Guidance on the phrase "equipment and facilities", and when these are "adequate and appropriate" can be found in the Approved Code of Practice.

6.76 Second, an employer shall provide (or ensure that there is provided) such number of suitable persons as is adequate and appropriate in the circumstances for rendering first aid to his employees if they are injured or become ill at work. A person shall not be regarded as being suitable for this purpose unless he has undergone:

(a) such training and has such qualifications as HSE may approve for the time being in respect of that case, and
(b) such additional training, if any, as may be appropriate in the circumstances of that case.

6.77 However, where such person is absent in temporary and exceptional circumstances it is sufficient compliance if another person is appointed to take charge of first aid during the period of absence. Further, where, having regard to the nature of the undertaking, the number of employees at work and the location of the establishment, it would be adequate and appropriate to appoint someone to be responsible for first aid (who may not necessarily be trained or qualified as above) the employer meets the legal obligations by making such appointment.

6.78 The employer must inform employees of the arrangements that have been made in connection with the provision of first aid, including the location of equipment, facilities, and personnel.

6.79 Self-employed persons shall provide (or ensure that there is provided) such equipment, if any, as is adequate and appropriate in the circumstances to enable them to render first aid to themselves while at work.

Approved Code of Practice

6.80 This Code deals with the need to provide the appropriate numbers and types of personnel to render first aid (or to ensure that it is rendered), and the equipment and facilities which will be needed. It then lays down the criteria which should be adopted to determine what each employer should do in the particular circumstances.

Personnel

6.81 The regulations require that "suitable persons" shall be appointed. These may be:

(a) *First-aider* This is a person who has been trained by an organisation approved by HSE, and who holds a current first-aid certificate.

(b) *Other persons* This category will include any other person who has undergone training and obtained qualifications approved by HSE.

6.82 Practising registered medical practitioners and practising registered nurses, ie whose names are entered in the appropriate part of the Single Professional Register, may also be regarded as first aiders for the purposes of the regulations.

6.83 The regulations also require that an appointed person shall be provided by the employer for the purpose of taking charge of the situation (eg to call an ambulance) if a serious injury or major illness occurs, and to be responsible for first-aid equipment if the first-aider is absent in exceptional or temporary circumstances. An appointed person is not an acceptable alternative to a first-aider. A first-aider should be provided at all times when employees are at work, although in very exceptional cases, where because of the low hazard nature of the undertaking or small number of employees, or location of the establishment, an appointed person may be considered "adequate and appropriate".

Equipment and facilities

6.84 The following should be provided as appropriate:

First-aid boxes and travelling first-aid kits

6.85 These should contain a sufficient quantity of suitable first-aid materials and nothing else. Detailed guidance as to the contents of boxes and kits is given in the Approved Code of Practice. The contents should be replenished as soon as possible after use, and items which deteriorate over a period of time should be replaced. Each self-contained working area should have its own first-aid box, which should be clearly identified and be in an accessible location. First-aid kits should be checked frequently to make sure that they are fully equipped and that all items are usable.

First-aid room

6.86 This would be needed in all establishments where there are unusual or special hazards, or whenever the employer considers it may be needed because there is dispersed working or because access to places of treatment is difficult. The number of employees on the premises must not be the only factor considered when deciding a first-aid room is necessary. A suitably qualified person should be responsible for the first-aid room and its contents and the room should not be used for any other purpose. It should contain suitable facilities and equipment (the ACOP provides advice on these), be clearly identified as such, have suitable waiting facilities provided and there should be effective means of communication between all work areas, the first-aid room and the first-aider on call.

Other equipment

6.87 Where an establishment either occupies a large area, or is divided into smaller separate/self-contained units it may be necessary to provide carrying equipment such as stretchers, carrying chairs, wheel chairs, etc to enable a sick or injured employee to be removed to a safer or more hygienic environment.

6.88 In determining what equipment and facilities an employer should provide, and what numbers and types of suitable persons should be appointed, regard should be had to the following matters.

The number of employees exposed to the risk

6.89 When considering the total number of first-aiders needed, account should be taken of the number of employees at work, the nature of the work undertaken at the establishment, whether the work is undertaken in scattered locations, whether or not there is shift work, and the distance from outside medical services. In establishments with a relatively low hazard, eg offices, shops, banks or libraries, etc it would be necessary to provide one first-aider for every 50 employees at work. If there is a greater degree of hazard, such as factories, dockyards, warehouses and farms, a minimum of not less than one first-aider should be appointed for every 50 persons employed, but consideration of the risks may require a greater number of first-aiders in order to provide adequate and appropriate cover in these high risk circumstances.

6.90 If the establishment has unusual or special hazards, the employer may again need to provide more than the numbers of first-aiders suggested above and the first-aiders may require additional specialised training in order to cope with the unusual hazards. If there is a shift working, sufficient first-aiders should be appointed to provide adequate coverage for each shift, taking into account the number of employees at work on the shift.

The nature of the undertaking

6.91 Some processes will involve special hazards and consequently different first-aid facilities will be needed. If there is a known danger or a recognised potentially harmful substance, the first-aider will need to be specially briefed and know how to take effective action immediately. If there is a special or unusual hazard, a first-aid room may be needed, and first-aiders given special instructions.

The size of the establishment and the distribution of employees

6.92 Every employee should have a reasonably rapid access to first aid. In a compact establishment, this might involve a central point, but in a large plant with staff dispersed over a wide area, first-aid equipment and personnel should be located in different parts. This may mean an increase in the numbers of suitable persons than the figures suggested above. If there is a large number of employees in self-contained working areas, the employer may need to provide centralised facilities (eg a first-aid room) and supplementary equipment and personnel in other locations.

The location of the establishment and locations of work

6.93 If access to emergency medical facilities (eg a hospital) is difficult because of distance or limited transport facilities, consideration should be given to the provision of a first-aid room even when the numbers of employees or nature of the hazards are such that this would not otherwise be justified. Additionally, one or more first-aiders may be provided even though there is a smaller number of employees working there than the numbers suggested above. If employees are working away from the employer's establishment, the employer must still ensure that adequate first-aid provision is made. Obviously, this would depend on all the circumstances, eg if they are working alone or in small groups, the nature of the hazards they are likely to encounter, and so on. For example, if employees work alone or in small groups in isolated locations, or a long way from medical services, or are using potentially dangerous tools or machinery, small travelling first-aid kits should be provided. If there is a large number of employees working in these circumstances, a first-aid box or even first-aid facilities and personnel should be considered, taking into account all the relevant factors. If employees are working with employees of another employer, the two employers may agree between themselves as to the provision of the necessary first-aid equipment, facilities and personnel (eg on the construction sites). The agreement should be in writing and each employer should keep a copy. The employer who is not making the necessary arrangements should ensure that the arrangements made by the other employer are adequate. Each employer should inform his own employees of the first-aid arrangements.

Control of asbestos

6.94 The Control of Asbestos at Work Regulations 1987, as amended by the Control of Asbestos at Work (Amendment) Regulations 1992 apply to premises whenever there is a likelihood of exposure to asbestos fibre. Thus, before any work commences, the employer must carry out an adequate assessment of the exposure (see para 6.155). Until the contrary is shown, the employer must assume that the material concerned is a more hazardous form of asbestos fibre, ie crocidolite or amosite and thus take more stringent precautions on occupational exposure limits. Employees must be informed about the risks, and instructed about the necessary precautions. If it is not reasonably practicable to control exposure below the level of control limits, respiratory protective equipment must be provided. Control measures must be maintained and kept in good repair, and, in particular, exhaust ventilation equipment must be regularly examined and tested and appropriate records kept. If a significant quantity of asbestos is likely to be deposited on an employee's clothing, adequate and suitable protective clothing must be provided.

Employers must prevent the spread of asbestos, and the places where asbestos was used must be kept clean and thoroughly cleaned when the work is completed. There must be facilities for washing, changing clothing and separate storage for personal and protective clothing and respiratory protective equipment must be provided.

6.95 The regulations lay down a new action level of exposure, above which it is necessary to notify HSE of the work being carried on, 28 days in advance of commencement. Records of air monitoring results must be kept for 40 years where the exposure is such that a health record is required under regulation 16 or for five years in any other situation, health records must be kept, and health surveillance should be carried out where appropriate (regulation 16). In addition, two Approved Codes of Practice associated with the regulations have been issued.

6.96 In addition to the 1987 regulations, asbestos is also controlled by several other statutory instruments. The Asbestos (Licensing) Regulations 1983 deal with the licensing of asbestos removal contractors who are concerned with asbestos insulation and asbestos coating. The holders of any such licence must ensure that their employees are medically examined. Employers who were not licenced (because they were using their own employees on their own premises) were under a duty to control exposure to the lowest level reasonably practicable. The Asbestos (Prohibition) Regulations 1992 prohibit the spraying of asbestos and certain other processes. The Asbestos Products (Safety) Regulations 1985 prescribe labelling requirements on the supply of products which contain asbestos, and prohibit the supply of products which contain crocidolite or amosite.

6.97 The Control of Asbestos in the Air Regulations 1990, together with the Health and Safety (Emissions into the Atmosphere) (Amendment) Regulations 1989 implement an EC Directive (87/217/EEC) on the prevention and reduction of environmental pollution by asbestos. There is a limit value for the discharge of asbestos into the air during the use of this substance, and regular measurements must be made from plants to which the regulations apply. There are controls on environmental pollution by asbestos resulting from the working of products or demolition of buildings, structures and installations containing asbestos.

Disaster planning

6.98 Growing public concern—in the UK, Europe and indeed throughout the world—following a number of industrial disasters have led to a more stringent control over planning for hazard contingencies. The major accidents which took place at Flixborough, Seveso, Mexico City, Bhopal, etc have drawn attention to the need to not only reduce the likelihood of such occurrences in the future, but to establish coordinated emergency plans in the event of such major accidents.

6.99 The Control of Industrial Major Accident Hazards Regulations 1984 (as amended) (CIMAH) follow the NIHHS Regulations (see para 6.53) which allowed major hazard installations to be identified. CIMAH deals with planning considerations, safety assessments and contingency plans.

6.100 The regulations basically apply to those installations carrying out an industrial activity referred to in Schedule 1, ie chemical and petro-chemical plants which have on their sites dangerous substances in quantities specified in Schedule 2. Excepted sites include nuclear installations, certain military installations and certain other premises which operate under licence. Regulation 4 requires that a manufacturer who has control of a relevant industrial activity must be able to demonstrate that he has identified the major accident hazards arising from the activities, and has also taken adequate steps to prevent such accidents, and to limit their consequences to persons and to the environment. In addition, persons working on the site must be provided with such information, training and equipment necessary to ensure their safety.

6.101 A major accident is defined as "An occurrence (including in particular, a major emission, fire or explosion) resulting from uncontrolled developments in the course of an industrial activity, leading to a serious danger to persons, whether immediate or delayed, inside or outside the installation, or to the environment, and involving one or more dangerous substance." If a major accident occurs, HSE must be notified immediately, and the following information must be provided:

(a) circumstances of the accident
(b) the dangerous substances involved
(c) the data available for assessing the effects of the accident on persons and the environment
(d) emergency measures to be taken.

This must then be followed with a statement of the steps envisaged to alleviate the medium or long-term effects of the accident (if any) and to prevent a recurrence of any such accident.

6.102 The manufacturer must also prepare an on-site emergency plan for dealing with major accidents. This must be drawn up in consultation with the local authorities and the emergency services. Off-site emergency planning is the responsibility of local authorities, but manufacturers must provide them with information to allow them to fulfil those responsibilities. Indeed, the manufacturer must endeavour to enter into an agreement with the local authority so that the latter can inform persons outside the site of the nature of the major accident hazard and of the safety measures and correct behaviour to be adopted in the event of a major accident. If no such agreement is reached, the manufacturer is responsible for making such information available to persons in the vicinity.

Radiation

6.103 The more dangerous type of ionising radiation comes from X-rays and other radioactive material, and non-ionising radiation can stem from laser beams, arc-welders, infra-red and ultra violet sources, microwave ovens, etc. The effect of radiation exposure will vary according to the dose and exposure time, but it is generally accepted that serious illnesses and even death can result, as well as damage being caused to a person's genetic structure, causing stillbirths and malformation in newly born children. The exposure limits at present adopted in this country are those recommended by the International Commission on Radiological Protection, and these limits vary with the area of the body exposed. However, there appears to be no valid proof that the thresholds recommended are in fact safe and any radiation exposure must therefore be regarded as being potentially damaging. Proper shielding is therefore essential (principally by the use of lead material), the equipment must be properly maintained so as to prevent leakage, radiation film badges should be worn at all times when there is a likelihood of exposure in order to measure the amount (or a dosimeter used), and whole body counts should be made when there is a danger that an affected person may have absorbed or ingested radiation. The National Radiological Protection Board has issued a guidance booklet *Protection against Ultra Violet Radiation in the Workplace* which should be consulted, and a number of other advisory publications can be obtained from HSE.

6.104 The current statutory requirements are laid down in the Ionising Radiation Regulations 1985, together with the Ionising Radiation (Protection of Persons Undergoing Medical Examination or Treatment) Regulations 1988. The current provisions are wider in scope than the 1968 and 1969 Regulations (which have been repealed) for the latter only applied to work in factories. The new law applies in all situations, including medical, hospital and dental work generally.

6.105 The primary duty is on every employer to take all necessary steps so as to restrict, so far as is reasonably practicable, the extent to which employees and others are exposed to ionising radiations. Schedule 1 specifies the dose limits of exposure to different parts of the body, ie the whole body, individual organs and tissues and eyes. There are lower limits for the abdomen of a woman of reproductive capacity and also for pregnant women.

6.106 The steps to be taken include the use of engineering controls and design features, such as shielding, ventilation, containment and the provision and use of safety features and warning devices. Suitable personal protective equipment (including respirators) shall be provided unless these would not further restrict exposure or they are not appropriate in the particular circumstances. Employers must ensure that employees are not exposed to the relevant dose limits, and employees must make full and proper use of the personal protective equipment provided by their employer. All personal protective equipment must be regularly examined and properly maintained. Monitoring equipment must be examined thoroughly and tested every 14 months and have performance checked before being taken into use for the first time.

6.107 Where a person is working in an area where he is likely to receive more than the specified dose, that area must be designated as a controlled or supervised area and entry must be restricted to specified persons and specified circumstances. Employees who are likely to receive more than the specified dose must be designated as classified persons. As such they must be assessed by a dosimetry service approved by HSE and records of the results kept for 50 years.

6.108 Employers must appoint radiation protection advisers and supervisors and make written rules for the conduct of work. The work must be properly supervised, and adequate information, instruction and training given to employees and others.

6.109 Radioactive substances should, so far as is reasonably practicable, be in a sealed source, and any container shall be suitably designed, constructed, maintained and tested. A radioactive substance in the form of a sealed source must not be held in the hand unless the instant dose is less than 75 $uSvh^{-}$. An unsealed substance must not be held by hand or manipulated by hand.

6.110 Before carrying out work with ionising radiations, the employer must make an assessment, identifying the nature and magnitude of the radiation hazards to employees and the general public. If this reveals that it is likely that the statutory dose will be exceeded, the employer must prepare a contingency plan to minimise exposure.

6.111 The regulations also impose duties on manufacturers, designers, importers and suppliers to ensure that any article for use at work with ionising radiation shall be so designed and constructed as to restrict the extent to which employees and others are likely to be exposed to ionising radiation.

6.112 Radiation which results from nuclear energy is controlled by the Nuclear Installations (Dangerous Occurrences) Regulations 1965, which are enforced by the Nuclear Inspectorate of HSE. Under the Radioactive Substances Act 1960, no person may keep or use any radioactive materials on premises used for the purpose of an undertaking carried on by him unless he is registered with the Department of the Environment or Scottish Office or is otherwise exempt.

6.113 Generally, the 1985 regulations conform to the EC Directive 80/836/ Euratom, as amended by 84/467/Euratom.

Working with electricity

6.114 The Electricity at Work Regulations 1989 replaced a range of inflexible and out-of-date legislation with a comprehensive and systematic set of main principles covering electrical safety in all work activities. They are supported by two Approved Codes of Practice relating to mines and quarries, and a Memorandum of Guidance. Some of the regulations contain absolute requirements, so that civil liability (based on the tort of breach of statutory duty) is retained, but so far as a criminal prosecution is concerned, it will be a defence for the accused to show that he used "due diligence".

6.115 In a number of ways, the new regulations differ from the approach taken by the previous law. There is no voltage threshold, no exemption for electrothermal operations, or for testing and research. The regulations apply in all circumstances where it is necessary to avoid danger, defined as meaning a risk of injury. This, in turn, means "death or personal injury from electrical causes, fire or explosion associated with the transmission, rectification, conversion, conduction, distribution, control, storage, measurement or use of electrical energy". Consequential or indirect injuries due to electrical malfunction are not generally included.

6.116 The regulations impose duties on employers and self-employed persons in relation to matters within their control. Further, employees are under a duty to comply with the provisions insofar as they relate to matters within their control, and they are also under a duty to cooperate with their employer so far as is necessary to enable the duties to be carried out. Persons who have control of non-domestic premises (see HSWA, s.4) come within the regulations because they will be either employers or self-employed persons.

6.117 Electrical systems must, so far as is reasonably practicable, be constructed and maintained so as to be safe, as must be the work activity and the adequacy of protective equipment. There is an absolute duty not to exceed the strength and capability of electric equipment so as to cause danger. If there are adverse or hazardous environmental circumstances, exposure is limited to that which is reasonably forseeable. There are provisions relating to insulation, protection, placing and earthing of conductors, and installing switches or other devices in neutral conductors. Excess current protection must be efficient and suitably located, and there must be provision for cutting off the supply and isolating it.

6.118 Probably the most significant feature of the regulations is the general prohibition on live working. This will only be permitted if all three of the following conditions are met:

(a) it is unreasonable in all the circumstances for the system to be dead
(b) it is reasonable in all the circumstances for the work to be carried out live and
(c) suitable precautions are taken to prevent injury.

6.119 There are no specific age restrictions on those who work with electricity, but those who do this type of work must have sufficient technical knowledge and experience to prevent danger and avoid injury, and if they do not have such expertise, they must be supervised as appropriate, having regard to the nature of the work.

Health and Safety (Information for Employees) Regulations 1989

6.120 These regulations dispense with the need to display abstracts of the Factories Act and Offices, Shops and Railway Premises Act, and instead require all employers to display a poster or distribute a leaflet entitled *Health and Safety Law – what you should know*, informing employees in general terms about the requirements of health and safety law. These can be obtained from HMSO. Employers must also inform employees of the local addresses of the enforcement authority (either HSE or the local authority) and the Employment Medical Advisory Service.

Noise at work

6.121 Although it has long been recognised that excessive noise levels at work could cause deafness (boiler-makers' deafness was well known in the 19th century) it is only in comparatively recent times that the law has began paying attention to the problem. It is now accepted that excessive exposure to noise levels in excess of 90 dB(A) will cause permanent damage to a person's hearing, as will exposure to louder impact noises (explosions, hammer guns, etc). However, not every deaf person can complain of the hazards of his occupation, for there are other causes of deafness, including presbyacusis, which is brought on by old age. Since noise is a common feature of everyday living, it cannot be assumed that occupational noise is the sole cause of deafness. Indeed, one wonders about the effect on the hearing of young people of the noise levels found in modern discos.

6.122 Occupational deafness was not given serious treatment by the authorities until the mid-1960s, when the various scientific evidence began to percolate through to industry. Several legislative provisions were enacted to deal with specific problems, eg Woodworking Machines Regulations 1974, Agriculture (Tractor Cabs) Regulations 1974, as amended, Offshore Installations (Construction and Survey) Regulations 1974, Offshore Installations (Operational Safety, Health and Welfare) Regulations 1976. The Department of Employment issued a Code of Practice in 1972, and it occasioned little surprise when the EC passed a Directive in 1986 (86/188/EEC). Following on this, the Noise at Work Regulations 1989 were enacted.

6.123 The regulations require action to be taken at three noise exposure levels, namely (a) 85dB(a), (b) 90dB(a) and (c) 200 Pascals (peak level for impact noise).

6.124 There is a general obligation on the employer to reduce the risk of hearing damage to the lowest level reasonably practicable. If the daily personal noise exposure is likely to be 85dB(A) or above, a noise assessment must be made by a competent person. Workers must be given adequate information, instruction and training about the risks to hearing, how the risk is to be minimised and personal ear protection must be provided on request. However, at this level, there is no obligation on the employer to ensure that they are used and no obligation on the worker to use them.

6.125 More stringent provisions apply if the noise levels are 90dB(a) or above. Ear protection zones should be marked with notices, ear protectors provided to those exposed to the noise and, so far as is reasonably practicable, exposure to noise shall be reduced by means other than ear protectors. Employees shall use such protectors (or other protective equipment) and report defects to the employer. Manufacturers and suppliers are required to supply adequate information on the generation of noise by the product. HSE may grant exemptions, particularly when the use of ear protectors may create a risk which outweighs the risk of hearing damage, or if the employer has adequate arrangements for ensuring that the average level over the whole working week will be below 90dB(a).

6.126 The chart below shows a summary of the legal requirements.

Action required where $L_{ED,d}$ is likely to be (1):	*below 85dB(A)*	*85dB(A) (first AL)*	*90dB(A) (second AL)*(2)
Employers' duties			
General duty to reduce risk			
Risk of hearing damage to be reduced to the lowest level reasonably practicable (reg. 6).	√	√	√
Assessment of noise exposure			
Noise assessments to be made by competent person (reg. 4)		√	√
Record of assessments to be kept until a new one is made (reg. 5).		√	√
Noise reduction			
Reduce exposure to noise so far as is reasonably practicable by means other than ear protectors (reg. 7).			√
Provision of information to workers			
Provide adequate information, instruction and training about risks to hearing, what employees should do to minimise risk, how they can obtain ear protectors if they are exposed between 85 and 90dB(A), and their obligations under the regulations (reg. 11).		√	√
Mark ear protection zones with notices, so far as is reasonably practicable (reg. 9).			√
Ear protectors			
Ensure so far as is practicable that protectors are:			
• provided to employees who ask for them (reg. 8(1)):		√	
• provided to all exposed (reg. 8(2)):			√
• maintained and repaired (reg. 10(1)(b)):		√	√
• used by all exposed (reg. 10(1)(a)):			√
Ensure so far as is reasonably practicable that all who go into a marked ear protection zone use ear protectors (reg. 9(1)(b)).			√
Maintenance and use of equipment			
Ensure so far as is practicable that:			
• all equipment provided under the regulation is used, except for the ear protectors provided between 85 and 90dB(a) (reg. 10(a)(a)):		√	√
• all equipment is maintained (reg. 10(1)(b)):		√	√

Action required where $L_{ED.d}$ is likely to be (1):	below 85dB(A)	85dB(A) (first AL)	90dB(A) (second AL)(2)
Employees' duties			
Use of equipment			
So far as is practicable:			
• use ear protectors (reg. 10(2)):			√
• use any other protective equipment (reg. 10(2)):		√	√
• report any defects discovered to the employer (reg. 10(2)).		√	√
Machine makers' and suppliers' duties			
Provision of information			
Provide information on the noise likely to be generated (reg. 12)		√	√

Notes: (1) The dB(A) action levels are values of daily personal exposure to noise ($L_{EP.d}$).
(2) All the actions indicated at 90dB(A) are also required where the peak sound pressure is at or above 200 Pa.
(3) This requirement applies to all who enter the zones, even if they do not stay long enough to receive an exposure of 90dB(A)$L_{EP.d}$.

6.127 The problem of noise at work can be tackled in four ways. First, by reducing the noise at its source. This involves new design techniques, new technology, new materials, etc. Consultations can take place with manufacturers (reminding them of their obligations under s.6 of HSWA). The level of 90dB(a) is a somewhat arbitrary level which it was thought could be afforded by industry, bearing in mind the cost of replacing existing machinery, but it is not a safe standard in absolute terms, and ideally, a level not exceeding 85dB(A) should be aimed at.

6.128 Second, noise reduction techniques can be implemented. This may involve isolating the source of the noise, so that work-people are unaffected by it, or blanketing walls and ceilings with noise absorbing materials which will have the effect of reducing noise levels, and so on.

6.129 Third, ear protection should be provided, appropriate to the dangers present. This can be achieved by ear plugs, ear muffs, helmets, etc but it is important that the correct protection is provided in each case, depending on the level of noise present. The object must be to reduce harmful sound, not sound itself, for it is essential to retain the latter (eg as a warning of danger, or to receive instructions, etc). Ear plugs should be fitted by a qualified person (occupational nurse, etc) otherwise the selection of a wrong size may render the protection ineffective. Ear muffs must be comfortable to wear, aesthetically acceptable to the wearer and must not interfere with the work or other protective equipment.

6.130 Fourth, exposure time to excessive noise can be reduced by allowing rest periods in rest rooms away from the noise, or operating a rota system.

6.131 The civil remedy in respect of occupational deafness is a claim for compensation based on common law negligence (see *Berry v Stone Manganese*). The existence of a duty of care is now well recognised, and while a failure to provide the necessary precautions will clearly amount to a breach of that duty, there is some room for argument as to the duty to compel, exhort or propagandise in order to ensure that they are used. An employee may not readily realise the insidious nature of the danger of working without the precautions or the fact that he may suffer permanent damage. Something more positive is required from the employer than the passive duty to provide ear muffs, plugs, etc. It also follows that if an employee fails to use the precautions after being instructed in their proper use, any compensation awarded can be reduced in respect of his contributory conduct. Compensation awards have been awarded in the region of £4,000–8,000, depending on the extent of the deafness (see *Smith v British Rail Engineering Ltd*). Any claim must be brought within three years from the damage (Limitations Act 1980), but since deafness is a process which takes place over the years, an affected person may not know in the early stages of the nature or extent of the damage caused.

6.132 The Social Security (Industrial Injuries) (Prescribed Diseases) Regulations 1975 (as amended) enable a worker to obtain industrial injuries disablement benefit (see para 8.104) if he suffers from occupational deafness. The worker must have been employed in the prescribed occupation for more than twenty years (and in at least one year before the claim), and he must suffer from an average hearing loss of at least 50 decibels in both ears. In at least one ear, the loss must be due to noise at work.

Pressure Systems and Transportable Gas Containers Regulations 1989

6.133 These regulations apply to plant containing compressed gas (at a pressure greater than 0.5 bar above atmospheric) with a pressure vessel in the system and to all steam systems with a pressure vessel used at work. The person in control of the system must establish the safe operating limits of the plant, and have a suitable written scheme drawn up or certified by a competent person for the examination at appropriate intervals of pressure vessels and safety devices as well as pipework which is potentially dangerous. The examinations must be carried out by a competent person. The plant must be properly maintained and adequate records kept of the most recent examination and any manufacturer's records supplied with new plant. Workers must be supplied with adequate operating instructions to ensure that the plant is being used within its safe operating limits and emergency instructions provided. The competent person who draws up the written scheme need not be the same person who undertakes the examinations. An organisation is competent to examine a pressure system if it employs staff who have adequate practical and theoretical knowledge to assess the condition of the plant and who can assess whether it will not cause danger when properly used up to the next examination. As well as using any instruction manual provided by the manufacturer, the person in control must provide on-the-job training and supervision.

6.134 The regulations will be fully in force by July 1994. However, the provisions relating to the supply of information for new plant, the proper installation of new plant and the establishment of safe operating limits on existing plant are already in force.

Control of Substances Hazardous to Health Regulations 1988 (COSHH)

6.135 These regulations are designed to protect workers against the risks of exposure to substances considered hazardous to health which arise out of or in connection with work under the control of their employer. The regulations, which must be read together with the accompanying Approved Codes of Practice, lay down a comprehensive system of legal rules applicable to all employers. In consequence, a number of statutory provisions and regulations have been repealed.

6.136 Apart from asbestos, lead, ionising radiations and mining activities, all of which have their own specific legislative provisions, COSHH applies to all other substances which may be hazardous to health. A substance is hazardous if it is a potential cause of harm; whether there is a risk from the substance will depend on the circumstances in which it is being used or controlled. Thus a substance which has a low hazard can be a substantial risk if poorly controlled. Equally, the most hazardous substance will have a lower risk if adequately controlled.

6.137 COSHH defines a substance as being hazardous to health if it is:

(a) a substance listed in Part 1A of the approved list as dangerous for supply within the meaning of the Classification, Packaging and Labelling of Dangerous Substances Regulations 1984 (see para 6.56), which is toxic, very toxic, harmful, corrosive or irritant; or
(b) a substance for which a maximum exposure limit is specified in Schedule 1 of the regulations, or for which HSC has approved an occupational exposure standard; or
(c) a micro-organism which creates a hazard to health; or
(d) dust of any kind, when present at a substantial concentration in the air; or
(e) a substance not mentioned above, which creates a hazard to the health of any person comparable to the hazards created by the above-mentioned substances.

6.138 Regulation 6 states that an employer shall not carry on any work which is liable to expose any employees to a substance hazardous to health unless he has made a suitable and sufficient assessment of the risks created by that work to the health of those employees and of the steps that need to be taken to eliminate or reduce those risks in accordance with the requirements of the regulations (see para 6.141).

6.139 Thus the first step is to make an assessment of the risk. This is done by identifying the hazardous substance, considering the circumstances in which it is being used, assessing the likelihood of exposure, contact, etc, identifying the harmful effects and so on. The assessment is essentially a practical exercise to ascertain what actually happens in the workplace in practice. This involves asking a great number of questions, ie from suppliers, manufacturers, trade and/or professional organisations, medical and other experts and so on. It means consultation with all levels in the workforce in order to ascertain what they are actually doing and what risks they are exposed to. It means looking at all substances which are used by the workforce, an assessment not only of the risks attendant on the work activity, but also those risks which can arise after the work activity ceases. It means checking on labels, information supplied, records of previous incidents, examination of trade data, HSE Guidance Notes and other published documentation. It means consideration of accidental leakage, spills or unexpected discharges. The length of exposure may be just as important as the amount of exposure.

6.140 It is submitted that all assessments should be done in writing, so that information gleaned can be followed through, omissions noted and dealt with, and comparisons made with past and future assessments.

6.141 Regulation 7 then provides that every employer shall ensure that exposure of employees to substances hazardous to health is either prevented or, if this is not reasonably practicable, adequately controlled. So far as is reasonably practicable, the prevention or control shall be secured by means other than the provision of personal protective equipment. However, if these measures do not prevent or adequately control exposure then, in addition the employer shall provide the employees with such suitable personal protective equipment as will adequately control their exposure. Measures must be taken to reduce the level of exposure to below the maximum exposure limit stated in Schedule 1 to the regulations, and if an occupational exposure standard has been approved it must not be exceeded. If respiratory protective equipment is provided, these shall be suitable and of a type or standard approved by HSE.

6.142 Thus control of the exposure to the hazard may be done in a number of ways. Primarily, the hazardous substance should be removed or replaced by a safer substance or the processes changed to avoid using the substance. In some circumstances, it may be possible to enclose the process, or use extraction equipment, or ventilation. Finally, safe working systems and handling procedures, including the provision of personal protective equipment, should be considered.

6.143 Regulation 8 requires employers to take all reasonable steps to ensure that control measures and personal protective equipment shall be properly used or applied. Employees are also under a duty to make full and proper use of them, and to report any defect to the employer. Control measures and personal protective equipment shall be maintained in an efficient state and in good repair. Local exhaust ventilation plant must be tested and thoroughly examined at least every fourteen months, and other controls at suitable intervals. Records of such tests and examinations shall be kept for five years.

6.144 Regulation 10 requires employers to monitor exposure to substances hazardous to health, and to keep suitable records. If these records are representative of the personal exposures of identifiable employees, they must be kept for 40 years, but in any other case, they need to be kept for 5 years. Regulation 11 provides that employees who are exposed to substances which are hazardous to health shall undergo health surveillance where appropriate (see Schedule 5). Health records shall be kept for at least 40 years.

6.145 Employers must provide employees with such information, instruction and training as is suitable for the employees to know the risks to health created by the exposure, and the precautions to be taken. In particular, the employee (or his representative) shall be informed forthwith if monitoring shows that the maximum exposure limit has been exceeded (Regulation 12).

6.146 In any criminal proceedings brought in respect of an alleged contravention of the regulations, it shall be a defence for any person to prove that he took all reasonable precautions and exercised all due diligence to avoid the commission of the offence.

6.147 There is little doubt that the COSHH Regulations are one of the most significant developments in UK law since the introduction of the Health and Safety at Work etc Act in 1974. They apply to all employers and require the introduction of pro-active safety policies. They are also in line with many of the likely changes which will be made in UK law following the adoption by the EC of a number of directives on health and safety (see chapter 10). HSE have published a number of documents which may be used for guidance.

Offshore Safety Act 1992

6.148 This Act makes existing offshore safety legislation "relevant statutory provisions" for the purpose of HSWA. The effect is to transfer responsibility for offshore safety from the Department of Energy to HSC/HSE, thus making HSE responsible for the enforcement of all safety legislation relating to offshore activities. Further, the reform of existing offshore legislation can now be achieved by means of health and safety regulations made under s.15 of HSWA.

6.149 Draft regulations have been produced requiring operators and owners of offshore installations to submit a "safety case" to HSE by a specified date in 1993, which must be accepted by a date in 1995 if they are to continue with their activities. The safety case will describe management systems and demonstrate that safety standards are adequate to avoid major accidents.

Risk assessments

6.150 There are a number of regulations which require an employer (or sometimes, also a self-employed person) to carry out a risk assessment. The nature of the duty and the obligations to be performed will vary in each case.

6.151 (1) *Control of Lead at Work Regulations 1980* (see para 6.20). Where any work exposes persons to lead, the employer (or self-employed person) shall assess the work to determine the nature and degree of such exposure. The assessment shall be carried out before the work is commenced. The assessment shall be revised where there is reason to suspect it is incorrect, or when there is a material change in the work, or when requested by an inspector.

6.152 Further, before choosing respiratory protective equipment or protective clothing, an employer shall make an assessment to determine whether it will satisfy the requirements of the regulations. The assessment shall comprise:

(a) the definition of the characteristics necessary to comply with the requirements of regulation 7 (provision of respiratory protective equipment) and regulation 8 (provision of protective clothing), and
(b) a comparison with the characteristics of the respiratory protective equipment or protective clothing available with the characteristics of the equipment or clothing needed in order to satisfy the requirements of regulations 7–8.

6.153 The assessment shall be revised if there is reason to suspect that it is no longer valid, or when there has been a significant change in the work to which it relates, and where changes are required, these shall be made.

6.154 An Approved Code of Practice gives further guidance on how the assessment is to be carried out, by whom, and the matters which should be considered, etc.

6.155 (2) *Control of Asbestos at Work Regulations 1987* (see para 6.94). An employer shall not carry out any work which exposes any of his employees to asbestos unless he has made an adequate assessment of that exposure, identifying the type of asbestos, determining the nature and degree of exposure, and setting out the steps to be taken to prevent or reduce this to the lowest level reasonably practicable. The assessment shall be reviewed regularly, and a new assessment substituted, when there is reason to suspect that the existing assessment is no longer valid, or where there is a significant change in the work to which the assessment relates.

6.156 An Approved Code of Practice accompanies the regulations, which spells out the tasks to be performed when making an assessment in greater detail.

6.157 (3) *Control of Substances Hazardous to Health Regulations 1988* (see para 6.135). An employer shall not carry on any work which is liable to expose any employees to any substance hazardous to health unless he has made a suitable and sufficient assessment of the risks created by that work to the health of those employees, and of the steps that need to be taken to meet the requirement of the regulations. The assessment shall be reviewed regularly or if there is reason to suspect that it is no longer valid or there has been a significant change in the work to which it relates, and changes shall be made in the assessment as required.

6.158 A number of Approved Codes of Practice have been issued, and HSE has produced a step by step guide to assessments.

6.159 (4) *Noise at Work Regulations 1989* (see para 6.121). Whenever any of his employees are exposed to a daily personal noise exposure of 85dB(A) or above (the first action level) or to a level of peak sound pressure of 200 pascals or above (the peak action level) every employer shall ensure that a competent person makes a noise assessment which is adequate for the purpose of identifying which of his employees are so exposed, and providing the employer with such information as will facilitate compliance with his duties under regulation 7 (reduction of noise exposure), regulation 8 (provision of ear protection) regulation 9 (designating ear protection zones) and regulation 11 (provision of information to employees).

6.160 HSE has published Guidance Notes to the regulations.

6.161 (5) *Management of Health and Safety at Work Regulations 1992* (see para 4.5). Every employer shall make a suitable and sufficient assessment of the risk to the health and safety of his employees to which they are exposed at work, and the risks to the health and safety of persons not in his employment arising out of the conduct by him of his undertaking, for the purpose of identifying the measures which the employer needs to take in order to comply with the requirements and prohibitions imposed on him by any relevant statutory provision. A similar assessment shall be made by every self-employed person. The assessment shall be reviewed by the employer (or self-employed person) if there is reason to suspect it is no longer valid, or there has been a significant change in the matters to which it relates. Where the employer employs five or more employees, he shall record the significant findings of the assessment, and identify any groups of his employees who are especially at risk.

6.162 The Approved Code of Practice attached to the regulations gives further guidance on the matters to be given attention to when carrying out the assessment, the general principles of risk assessment, and the follow-up with preventative and protective measures.

6.163 (6) *Manual Handling Operations Regulations 1992* (see para 4.183). Where it is not reasonably practicable to avoid the need for employees to undertake any manual handling operations which involve a risk of their being injured, every employer shall make a suitable and sufficient assessment of all such manual handling operations undertaken by the employees. Then, having regard to the questions specified in Schedule 1 to the Regulations (see para 4.191) the employer shall take appropriate steps to reduce the risk of injury to the lowest level reasonably practicable, and take appropriate steps to provide those employees with general indications and precise information on the weight of each load and the heaviest side of any load whose centre of gravity is not positioned centrally. The assessment shall be reviewed when the employer suspects it is no longer valid, or there has been a significant change in the manual handling operations to which it relates, and changes will be made to the assessment as are appropriate in the light of the review.

6.164 The regulations are accompanied by comprehensive Guidance Notes.

6.165 (7) *Personal Protective Equipment at Work Regulations 1992* (see para 4.154). Before choosing any personal protective equipment (PPE) required by regulation 4 (see para 4.159) an employer (or self-employed person) shall make an assessment to determine whether the PPE he intends to provide is suitable. The assessment shall consist of:

(a) risks which have not been avoided by other means
(b) the definition of the characteristics which the PPE must have in order to be effective against the above risks, and
(c) a comparison of the characteristics of the PPE with the characteristics of the PPE needed to be effective against those risks.

6.166 The assessment shall be reviewed forthwith if there is reason to suspect that any element of it is no longer valid, or there has been a significant change in the work to which the assessment relates. If, as a result of the review, changes in the assessment are required, these shall be made.

6.167 The regulations are accompanied by detailed Guidance Notes.

6.168 (8) *Health and Safety (Display Screen Equipment) Regulations 1992* (see para 4.198). Every employer shall analyse the workstations in his undertaking for the purpose of assessing the risks to the health and safety of any user which arise out of or in connection with a person's use of those workstations. Any risks identified by the assessment shall be reduced to the lowest extent reasonably practicable.

6.169 The regulations are accompanied by Guidance Notes which give further information on the form, method and purpose of the assessment.

6.170 (9) *Fire Precautions (Places of Work) Regulations 1990* (see para 6.14). When these regulations come into force, every employer will have to make an assessment of the fire risk at the place of work, prepare an evacuation plan, train their employees in fire precautions, and keep appropriate records.

Metrication

6.171 All unmetricated health and safety legislation (apart from certain offshore legislation) must now be expressed in metric units of measurement (see Health and Safety (Miscellaneous Provision) (Metrication etc) Regulations 1992, which implement EC Directive 80/181/EEC). However, special provision has been made for the measurement of temperature and humidity in humid textile factories, where use is made of wet and dry bulb temperatures. The regulations also harmonise the flashpoint test measures in the Petroleum (Consolidation) Act and supporting regulations with the Classification, Packaging and Labelling of Dangerous Substances Regulations 1984.

7

Particular health and safety problems

Employment of women

7.1 All restrictions on the hours of work which women may work have now been abolished, as well as most of the restrictions on the type of work they may perform (Employment Act 1989, ss.4–9 and Schedules 1 and 2). The remaining restrictions are as follows.

(1) A woman must not be employed in a factory within four weeks of childbirth (Factories Act 1961, 5th Schedule; Public Health Act 1936, s.205).
(2) Women are prohibited from working in certain processes and work activities involving lead products. These include:
   (a) the treatment and manufacture of lead, zinc, lead compounds, mixing or pasting in connection with the manufacture or repair of electric accumulators, or the cleaning of rooms where these processes are being carried out; Factories Act 1961, s.74 (the provisions also apply to premises which are not a factory (Factories Act 1961, s.128)
   (b) painting buildings with lead paint (Factories Act 1961, s.131)
   (c) manipulating lead colour (Paints and Colours Regulations 1907)
   (d) any lead process (Lead Smelting and Manufacture Regulations 1911)
   (e) mixing dry lead compound with indiarubber (Indiarubber Regulations 1922)
   (f) working in any room where raw lead oxide is manipulated or pasting is carried on (Electric Accumulators Regulations 1925)
   (g) specified processes in pottery manufacture involving lead (Pottery (Health and Welfare) Special Regulations 1950)
   (h) the Approved Code of Practice relating to the Control of Lead at Work Regulations 1980 sets a lower level of blood lead concentration for women of reproductive capacity than the level set for men.
(3) The Ionising Radiation Regulations 1985 (see para 6.103) set lower dose limits for exposure to ionising radiation for women who are still of reproductive capacity, and for pregnant women, than the limit set for men.
(4) There are restrictions on the employment of pregnant women as aircraft flight crew, air traffic controllers, and on merchant ships while at sea (Air Navigation Order 1985; Merchant Shipping (Medical Examination) Regulations 1983).

7.2 Indeed, it is lawful to discriminate against a woman insofar as it is necessary to comply with the above restrictions (Employment Act 1989, s.4).

7.3 As a general rule, it can be stated that the critical exposure of a pregnant woman to deleterious substances is not so much in terms of the quantity or amount, but in the timing of exposure. The first six weeks of pregnancy when the foetus is being formed (and when possibly the woman might not even know she is pregnant) might well be the most critical time of all, together with the last three months of pregnancy when the brain of the foetus is being formed. An American organisation—the National Institute of Occupational Safety and Health (NIOSH)—has issued guidelines which may usefully be followed when a woman is exposed to potentially harmful substances. These cover (a) when a pregnant woman may continue to work, (b) when she may continue to work but with environmental modifications to accommodate her working and (c) when she should not work at all. Similar guidance is available from the Society for Occupational Medicine.

7.4 The Employment Protection (Consolidation) Act 1978 (as amended by the Trade Union Reform and Employment Rights Act 1993) provides that a woman employee who is pregnant now has four rights.

First, s.33 gives her a general right to maternity leave of 14 weeks (or until the birth of her child, if later), during which time she is entitled to the benefit of her terms and conditions of employment (except remuneration). She must follow the statutory procedure for notifying her employer that she will be so absent (which cannot commence earlier than the 11th week prior to the expected week of childbirth).

7.5 Second, s.45 provides that she may be suspended from work on maternity grounds where, in consequence of:

(a) any requirement imposed by an enactment (or regulations made under an enactment), or
(b) any recommendation made by an Approved Code of Practice, she is suspended on the ground that she is pregnant, has recently given birth to a child, or is breastfeeding a child. Where she is so suspended, then if the employer has suitable alternative work, she has the right to be offered this. The work must be of a kind which is suitable in relation to her, and appropriate for her to do in the circumstances. The terms and conditions of employment must not be substantially less favourable to her than her previous terms and conditions.

She will have the statutory right to remuneration whilst suspended, but will not be so entitled if the employer has offered to provide her with suitable alternative work which she unreasonably refuses.

7.6 Third, s.60 of the Act provides that it will be unfair to dismiss an employee if the reason was:

(a) that she is pregnant, or any reason connected with her pregnancy, or
(b) her maternity leave period is ended by a dismissal and the reason for this was because she has given birth to a child, or
(c) she took maternity leave, or

(d) because before the end of her maternity leave period she produced a medical certificate stating that she would be incapable of work after the end of that period, and she was dismissed within four weeks from the end of her maternity leave period whilst her medical certificate was current, and the reason for the dismissal was that she had given birth to a child or was for any other reason connected with her having given birth to a child, or
(e) she was liable to be suspended from work on maternity grounds (above), or
(f) her maternity leave period ended for reason of redundancy, and she was not offered alternative employment where there was a suitable vacancy (see s.38).

7.7 To benefit from this right, it should be noted that it is no longer necessary for the woman to have two years' continuous employment.

7.8 Fourth, a woman who has been continuously employed for two years prior to the 11th week prior to the expected week of childbirth is entitled to return to work within 29 weeks from the actual week of confinement. The complex rules laid down in ss.39–44 of the Act must be followed.

7.9 It is generally accepted that English law would not provide a remedy for any injury suffered to a foetus while *en ventre sa mère*, there being no duty owed in tort and no statutory duty applicable. The thalidomide tragedy highlighted this problem, and the Congenital Disabilities (Civil Liability) Act 1976 was passed. It was intended to be a temporary measure, pending legislation consequent on the report of the Pearson Commission, but as the recommendations of the latter are unlikely to be the subject of Parliamentary action in the foreseeable future, the Act remains. It provides that a child who is born disabled as a result of any breach of duty (whether through negligence or breach of statutory duty) to either parent, will be able to bring a civil action against the person responsible. In practice this will mean that if something happens to a woman while she is pregnant which results in her child being born disabled, the child will have a separate right of action. Since the Limitation Act 1980 does not apply to a minor (ie one under the age of eighteen) he may be able to bring a claim any time within three years from attaining his majority, ie potentially 21 years after the event which caused the disability. There must be a breach of duty to the child's parent, but it is not necessary that the parent be injured. The disability may be something which happened to either parent which prevents the mother from having a normal child, or an injury to the mother while she is pregnant, or an injury to the foetus during pregnancy.

7.10 If the person responsible would have been liable to the parent, he is liable to the child. The child must be born alive, for there is no duty to the foetus as such. It is not relevant that the person responsible knew that the woman was pregnant, as long as a duty was owed to her. Thus if a woman is working with a chemical which causes her to have a disabled child as a result of ingesting minute particles, an action will lie against the employer by the child.

7.11 This can cause some concern among those employers who regularly use chemicals, for there are a number of substances which are suspect so far as pregnant women are concerned, eg vinyl chloride, benzene, mercury, anathetic fumes, lead, etc. Molecules of almost any substance can pass through the placenta, and therefore any woman may, by ingesting, inhaling, or through skin absorption, pass a deleterious ingredient into her body.

7.12 The Act poses problems for employers who have to balance delicately between the law against sex discrimination on the one hand and liability to unknown potential plaintiffs on the other.

Mental illness

7.13 This term encompasses a wide range of medical and psychological problems, but from the point of view of health and safety, an employer has to consider (a) whether to employ someone who has, or who has had, mental illness, (b) if he is employed, what steps should be taken to ensure that he is not a health or safety hazard to himself or to others, and (c) whether or not a past or present illness is sufficient ground for dismissal.

7.14 There are no relevant statutory provisions to give guidance, and it is not unlawful to refuse to employ someone who is suffering from, or who has suffered from, mental illness. The problem is one of medical evidence and recruitment should be done in consultation with such specialists as are available (eg company doctor, nurse, etc), so that a full and satisfactory assessment can be made of the illness and the risks involved in employing the applicant. Generally, mental illnesses are of two types, namely psychoneurosis and psychosis. The former is a species of "bad nerves", the latter is more serious and involves a lack of contact with reality. So far as psychoneurosis is concerned, recovery rate is good, and a person who has had a previous history of this sort of mental illness, but who is now fit and well, is no more likely to have a recurrence of the illness than a person who has no previous history is likely to have a mental breakdown. The prognosis for psychosis, however, is mixed, depending on the severity of the illness and the medical evidence which can be adduced.

7.15 Many companies, while they may be unwilling to take on persons with a history of mental illness, adopt a policy of social responsibility to existing employees and seek to provide suitable employment, rehabilitation units, and encourage the employee to obtain medical treatment. Satisfying work, of course, is a great therapy. The problem is one which requires sympathetic handling, involving the cooperation of all those who can contribute some expertise, as well as employees and management generally. Progress should be monitored, risks assessed, work planned and adequately supervised, and so on. Once the nature of the illness can be established, it may be possible to match it with employment where safety can be observed.

7.16 The fact that an employee "tells a lie" on a job application form and denies that he has ever had any history of mental illness is not, *per se* grounds for dismissal should the previous history come to light (*Johnson v Tesco Stores*), but if it can be shown that there is a good sound, functional reason why the person cannot be employed, it may be fair to dismiss him. In *O'Brien v Prudential Assurance Co.*, when the applicant was interviewed for a job he was given a medical examination and asked specific questions about his mental health. He made no mention of the fact that he had had a long history of mental illness, including psychosis, which necessitated the taking of drugs and a period of hospitalisation. When the truth came to light, the company consulted various medical experts and a decision was taken to dismiss him. He brought a claim for unfair dismissal, but it was held that the dismissal was fair for some other substantial reason. It was the company's policy not to appoint as district agents persons who had long histories of mental illnesses, as the job involved going into peoples' homes. Clearly, there was a risk that an unpleasant incident could occur which would seriously tarnish the company's image and thus the policy was not an unreasonable one. Had the company been aware of his long history of mental illness he would never have been appointed to the job.

7.17 The greater the risk of a serious incident occurring, the more management should consider dismissing the employee. In *Singh-Deu v Chloride Metals* the applicant was sent home from work after complaining that he felt unwell. His doctor diagnosed paranoid schizophrenia and when the company could not obtain a satisfactory assurance from a specialist that there would not be a recurrence, he was dismissed. This was held to be fair. If he had an attack of this illness during working hours, a catastrophic accident could have happened. There was no other suitable alternative employment for him, and the company could not be expected to wait until an accident occurred before taking some action (see *Spalding v Port of London Authority*).

Repetitive strain injury (RSI)

7.18 This is a generic term for a group of musculo-skeletal injuries which affect the muscles, tendons, joints and bones usually in the hand or arm, and is generally caused by repetitive work. A variety of illnesses can result, including tenosynovitis, tendinitis, carpal tunnel syndrome, epicondylitis bursitis, etc. From a legal point of view, an employee who suffers from this complaint may be able to sue for a breach of statutory duty and/or for common law negligence (see chapter 8). For example, in *McSherry v British Telecommunications plc* the plaintiff worked as a data processing officer. Her job was to key telephone meter readings into a computer controlled data system. She would be expected to reach a speed of some 13,000 key depressions per hour, and her work was regularly monitored to ensure that she maintained this speed. After doing this for about four years she began to feel pain in her hands, wrists, arms and shoulders, and her doctor diagnosed bilateral tenosynovitis (tennis elbow). It was established that these symptoms were attributable to the nature of the work, in that she was suffering from "repetitive strain injury". The main cause was poor postural positioning, due to unsuitable chairs and a modesty panel beneath her desk, which prevented her from stretching her legs. It was held that the employers were liable for a breach of statutory duty under the Offices, Shops and Railway Premises Act s.14 (failure to provide suitable seating together with a footrest, see para 5.180) and for common law negligence (failure to foresee that the sort of posture adopted by the plaintiff would, in the course of time, be likely to cause serious musculo-skeletal injury).

7.19 Once the problem of RSI is recognised, its incidence can be reduced or eliminated altogether by making an ergonomic assessment, and introducing proper seating, training in correct posture, introducing rest breaks or job sharing, and so forth.

7.20 Certain musculo-skeletal illnesses, such as cotton twister's cramp and chicken plucker's arm have been recognised as being industrial diseases since 1948, and currently cramp of the hand or forearm due to repetitive movements, brought about by prolonged periods of handwriting, typing or other repetitive movements of the fingers, hand or arm, is recognised under the Social Security (Industrial Injuries) (Prescribed Diseases) Regulations 1985 (see para 8.100).

7.21 **Note:** RSI is gradually being replaced by the term "work related upper limb disorders".

Working alone

7.22 There are some situations where there is a serious risk to a person if he is injured while working alone, because he is unable to summon help.

7.23 There are a number of legal provisions which specify systems of working which require more than one person. These include:

(1) Work in Compressed Air Special Regulations 1958
(2) Factories Act 1961, s.30
(3) Diving Operations Act Work Regulations 1981
(4) Construction (Working Places) Regulations 1966
(5) Control of Substances Hazardous to Health Regulations 1988
(6) Road Traffic (Carriage of Explosives) Regulations 1989
(7) Dangerous Substances (Conveyance by Road in Road Tankers and Tank Containers) Regulations 1981.

7.24 There are other provisions which require work to be done "under the immediate supervision of a competent person" or similar wording, which would suggest that the work, although carried out by one person, must be done in the presence of another.

7.25 HSE has produced a leaflet *Working alone in Safety* to which reference may be made. The CBI has also published a guidance document on the subject.

Working abroad

7.26 An employer may send an employee to another country to work, perhaps for a temporary period, and the question then arises as to the employer's duty to ensure the employee's health and safety. Since the duty is to take reasonable care, and does not involve an absolute guarantee, the circumstances of each case must be considered. In *Cook v Square D Ltd*, the plaintiff worked for the defendant company. Part of his duties took him to Saudi Arabia, where he worked on premises of a reputable oil company. Also working on the site was a reputable main contractor. The plaintiff was working in a computer control room, the floor of which consisted of large tiles. One of these tiles had been lifted by the main contractor, and the plaintiff tripped, and injured his knee. He claimed damages from his employers arguing that they had been negligent. A High Court Judge found in his favour, arguing that his employers had not taken proper steps to ensure his safety, but this decision was reversed by the Court of Appeal. It was noted that both the occupier of the premises and the main contractor were reputable companies, and it was not for the defendants to advise them of the need to take precautions against the type of hazard which caused the plaintiff's injury. Further, it was stated that "the suggestion that the home-based employer has any responsibility for the daily events of a site in Saudi Arabia has an air of unreality."

7.27 Nonetheless, it was suggested that if an employee is being sent to a foreign site to work there for a considerable period of time, an employer may be required to inspect the site and satisfy himself that the occupiers are conscious of their obligations concerning the health and safety of people working there.

7.28 Although an employer is required to take out compulsory insurance for the benefit of his employees (see para 6.1) there is no duty to do so in respect of employees who are working abroad. Nor need an employer advise an employee to take out his own insurance cover. In *Reid v Rush & Tompkins Group*, the plaintiff worked for the defendants in Ethiopia. He received severe injuries in a road accident which was the fault of the other driver, for whom the defendants had no responsibility. The plaintiff was unable to recover damages from the other driver, as there was no third party insurance in Ethiopia, and so he sued his employers in the UK. His statement of claim was struck out. The employer owed no duty to inform or advise on the potential danger of suffering economic loss in the form of uncompensated injuries.

Immigrant workers

7.29 There is no evidence to suggest that immigrant workers are more prone to accidents than any other group of employees, although since immigrants tend to be employed in those industries where there are greater dangers, obviously they may have a higher than average accident rate. The problem must be tackled by means of adequate training and language and cultural factors must be taken into account.

Safety instructions may have to be prepared in the language of the worker concerned and signs and posters which need little translation should be used to indicate the hazards and/or the precautions to be taken. In *James v Hepworth and Grandage Ltd* the employers put up a notice which stated that spats should be worn. Unknown to them, the plaintiff could not read English and he was injured through not wearing spats. His claim for compensation failed. He had observed other workmen wearing spats and his failure to make any enquiries about them led to the conclusion that he would not have worn them anyway. However, this case cannot be regarded as authority for the proposition that an employer fulfils his legal duty by merely drawing attention to a precaution (see chapter 8) and if there is a risk of a more serious injury, greater steps must be taken to ensure the use of protective clothing, etc. Further, in *Hawkins v Ian Ross (Castings) Ltd* an employee was injured partly because he was working alongside an immigrant who had a limited command of English and who misunderstood a warning shout. The court held that in such circumstances, a higher standard of care is required on the employers when considering the layout of the work and the steps to be taken to avoid accidents.

7.30 Language barriers may not be used as a device to exclude immigrants from employment and attempts to impose language tests have resulted in allegations of racial discrimination. The problem will no doubt be with us for many years, for although we tend to equate immigration with the influx from Asian or African countries, under article 48 of the Treaty of Rome the free movement of workers throughout the European Communities is guaranteed, and an influx of non-English speaking workers from Europe cannot be excluded. Training for safety officers may well include some form of instruction in foreign languages in the not-too-distant future.

Epileptics

7.31 Reconciling safety with social responsibility is one of the more difficult tasks of recruitment officers, and it is essential that judgments be made on the basis of informed opinion. This is particularly true of epilepsy, about which there is a great deal of ignorance. There is no reason in principle why an epileptic cannot be employed in most types of work, provided a full appraisal is made of the situation. Epilepsy does not conform to a single pattern; it varies in type, frequency, severity and timing. A candidate for a job who has all the necessary qualifications and experience should not be excluded from consideration on the ground of epilepsy without a full investigation, in which, of course, medical assessment would be invaluable.

7.32 A person who has a history of epilepsy cannot be permitted to drive a heavy goods vehicle or passenger vehicle (unless free from an attack for two years), or work as a specialist teacher of physical education. Other than these restrictions, objections to appointing an epileptic should be based on sound functional reasons. Once employed, safety considerations obviously become important, and if there is any risk to the employee or to his fellow employees, attempts must be made to find suitable employment where the risks are minimised. In the last resort, however, firmer action must be taken. For example, in *Harper v National Coal Board* the applicant had three epileptic fits in a period of two years. During these fits, quite unknowingly, he was violent to other workers. He was then medically examined, and it was recommended that he be retired on medical grounds, under a miner-workers pension scheme. He refused to accept retirement and was dismissed. This was held to be fair. The employers owed a duty to their other employees to ensure their safety as well. The applicant was working alongside other disabled employees and they were clearly at risk.

7.33 Advice on the employment of epileptics can be obtained from the British Epileptic Association and the Employment Medical Advisory Service may also be contacted when necessary.

Disabled employees

7.34 Under the Disabled Persons (Employment) Act 1958 every employer must employ at least three per cent registered disabled persons as part of his workforce. Certain occupations, such as car park and lift attendants are designated as being particularly suitable for disabled persons and a person who does not hold a "green card" may not be employed without giving first consideration to a disabled person. Unfortunately, many of the jobs which used to be suitable for disabled employees are beginning to disappear and it now appears that more than 60 per cent of all employers have failed to reach their quota. The problem arises partly because there are not enough registered disabled applicants who have the right qualifications for the vacant jobs and partly because many employers are reluctant to take on disabled applicants due to possible safety hazards. Although it is an offence not to employ the quota of disabled persons, a prosecution may only be brought with the consent of a special advisory committee, for the problem is one which must be solved by persuasion rather than by compulsion.

7.35 Under the Companies (Directors Reports) (Employment of Disabled Persons) Regulations 1980, every director's report made under the provisions of the Companies Act relating to a financial year shall contain a statement describing the policy of the company throughout that year for:

(a) giving full and fair consideration to applications for employment made by disabled persons, having regard to their particular aptitude and abilities
(b) continuing the employment of, and the arranging of appropriate training for, employees of the company who have become disabled persons during the period when they were employed by the company, and
(c) the training, career development and promotion of disabled persons employed by the company.

7.36 The regulations apply to every company which employs on average more than 250 employees throughout the year in question. It is hoped that the new legal requirements, by throwing a spotlight of publicity on the problem, will encourage more companies to provide job opportunities for disabled persons.

7.37 Once a disabled person has been taken into employment, he can of course be dismissed on health or safety grounds, but there is a high burden on the employer to show that he made a full appraisal of all the facts, and in particular that he searched around for suitable alternative employment before contemplating dismissal (see *Milk Marketing Board v Grimes* para 9.61). The employer must familiarise himself with the job, the disability and the hazard (*Littlewood v AEI Cables*), and extra efforts must be made to accommodate a disabled person. In *Cannon v Scandecor*, when the applicant, who was registered disabled, was employed it was recognised that her output would not be too high. She then had a series of illnesses and a car accident, and when she returned to work her daily output was that which she had previously achieved in an hour. She was dismissed, but this was held to be unfair. Much too short a period had elapsed between her return to work and her dismissal, and sufficient time had not been allowed in order to enable her to make a full recovery. She should have been given a reasonable trial period, and then, if her output had not reached her previous performance, her dismissal would have been fair.

7.38 It will thus be evident that employers who take on a disabled person have a special responsibility to do more than they would normally do to give him a period of time in which to reach acceptable standards. Some companies meet the problem by excluding disabled employees from departmental budgets, so as to ensure that they are not regarded as a drain or millstone by management seeking to reach targets. Certainly, a great deal can be done and although safety hazards must not be ignored, these are not always insuperable obstacles. There is no substitute for a careful assessment of the nature of the work, the risks associated with it and a measured judgment based on an investigation into the nature of the disability matched against the risks involved.

7.39 Clearly, disabled persons will always pose special problems so far as health and safety matters are concerned. Deaf persons will not always be able to hear fire alarms or warning cries, blind persons will not find their way to escape routes, physically disabled persons will not be able to react with the necessary speed to emergency situations, and so on. Since the duties owed by an employer to his employees are personal to each employee, special attention should be paid to these problems when disabled persons are involved.

7.40 Even so, there must come a point in time when safety factors will override all other considerations, although the duty of the employer is to act reasonably when handling employees who have any type of disability. Usually this will mean taking medical advice and looking round for suitable employment. In *McCall v Post Office*, the applicant, unknown to his employers, suffered from epilepsy. He was employed as a cleaner, but had several fits which were of short duration. The personnel department took medical advice and were told that he should be employed in a "no risk" area. Unfortunately there was no suitable vacancy and he was dismissed. This was held to be fair. On medical advice the employee had to be moved to a safe area, and as there was none available it was in his interests and in the interests of other employees that he be dismissed.

7.41 Several years ago, the Manpower Commission (now dissolved) produced a *Code of Good Practice on the Employment of Disabled Persons*, which although purely voluntary sets out the aims and objectives of a desirable policy on the employment and training of disabled persons.

7.42 Employers who are willing to support and apply the principles and practices laid down in the Code are permitted to use a special symbol in their recruitment advertisements. Such employers undertake:

(a) to welcome applications for vacant posts from disabled persons
(b) offer training to secure integration into the workplace
(c) seek to utilise sources of help in providing any special equipment required to carry out the job
(d) offer equal opportunities for career development
(e) involve employees with disabilities in developing good practice.

7.43 A number of companies have banded together to form an Employers' Forum on Disability (EFD). They have defined a disabled person as "anyone who has a physical disability, learning difficulty or mental health problem and is thereby significantly disadvantaged in the jobs market". The aim of the organisation is to exchange information on ways to improve their ability to recruit, retain and develop the careers of disabled persons.

Vibration White Finger

7.44 This disorder is caused by a constriction of the blood supply to the fingers, due to working with vibrating tools, such as pneumatic drills, hammers, etc. In the vast majority of cases it does not prevent a person from continuing to work, although it may cause considerable discomfort, particularly in cold conditions. The precise causes of the injury are not clear and thus it is not possible to lay down specific safe exposure limits.

7.45 The first recorded civil action for damages in respect of VWF was in 1946 (*Fitzsimmons v Ford Motor Co. Ltd*) where a successful claim was brought under the Workmens Compensation Act. Later claims floundered because it could not be shown that the employer had been in breach of a duty to take reasonable care or because the trivial nature of the problem did not warrant preventative measures (eg see *Joseph v Ministry of Defence*). Employers were entitled to follow the recognised and generally accepted practice, and there was nothing in the literature to make them aware of any danger. Further, even if an employee had been warned of the risk, he would still have continued to work. However, more recently, a number of claims for damages have succeeded for the illness is now widely recognised and appropriate precautionary measures can be taken (see *Shepherd v Firth Brown Ltd*).

7.46 A useful summary of the legal and medical background of VWF, with a guide on the assessment of compensation, can be found in a decision of the Northern Ireland High Court in the case of *Bowman v Harland & Wolffe plc*.

7.47 Vibration White Finger is now a prescribed disease for certain categories of workers under the Social Security (Industrial Injuries) (Prescribed Diseases) Regulations.

AIDS

7.48 Acquired Immune Deficiency Syndrome (AIDS) is caused by a virus which attacks the body's natural defence system, thus leaving it vulnerable to a number of infections and cancer. However, not all those who have the virus (HIV) develop AIDS, although medical statistics on the extent of the disease are still in their infancy. At the present time there is no known cure. The HIV virus can only be transmitted through sexual intercourse with an infected person, by being inoculated with infected blood or (possibly) by drinking breast milk from an infected person. There is no evidence at present to suggest that the virus can be transmitted in any other way and certainly not by other physical contact with an infected person. As a result, the Department of Employment together with HSE, have issued a booklet *AIDS and Employment* which stresses that employees are not at risk from an infected person unless they have direct contact with the blood, semen or other body fluids of that person. This means that there is no grounds for refusing employment to a person who has the virus and the fact of infection is not a ground for dismissal.

7.49 However, there are some groups who are clearly at risk. These include doctors, nurses, dentists and others who, by the nature of their work, could come into contact with blood, etc and face the possibility of infection through a cut or accidental injection. These persons must take additional precautions in order to reduce the risk. HSC's Health Services Advisory Committee has issued a leaflet *AIDS; the prevention of infection in the health services*, which outlines the practical steps which should be taken. Many employers have issued policy statements which as well as indicating a refusal to discriminate against someone who has the virus, state the counselling services and other support which will be available.

Smoking at work

7.50 There are a number of specific prohibitions on smoking whilst at work, usually when there is a health or safety hazard (see para 9.14). In the absence of a legal requirement to prohibit smoking the topic is somewhat emotive, there being a conflict between an individual's "right" to smoke, and the equal "right" of non-smokers to breathe unpolluted air. There is some evidence that it is possible for people to be affected by passive smoking, but there is no legal decision in this country which takes the matter very far. It has been suggested that the employer's duty under s.2 of HSWA includes a duty to protect workers from the effects of passive smoking, but again there is no legal authority on the point.

7.51 There is an industrial tribunal decision to the effect that an employee who was forbidden to smoke was entitled to resign and claim constructive dismissal (*Watson v Cooke, Webb & Holton Ltd*) but there appear to be special facts in the case which led the industrial tribunal to hold that the employers had broken a fundamental term of Mrs Watson's contract of employment by imposing a new term without any discussion and consultation. Another industrial tribunal held that an employee does not have a contractual right to smoke (*Rogers v Wicks and Wilson Ltd*), and it is suggested that this is the correct approach. It would be unusual for there to be an express contractual term to this effect and to imply a contractual term that an employee has the right to smoke is stretching the implied term theory too far.

7.52 This view was confirmed by the Employment Appeal Tribunal in the recent case of *Dryden v Greater Glasgow Health Board*. Here, the Board operated a "no smoking" policy in all areas except a "smoking" coffee room and a smoking area in the canteen. After extensive consultations it was decided to ban smoking altogether in all the Board's premises, and three months' notice of the ban was given to all employees. Counselling and support was offered to those employees who wished to give up smoking. The applicant, who was a lifelong smoker, found that she could only smoke if she left the Board's premises, but this was difficult for her to do in view of the time constraints. Three days after the commencement of the ban, she resigned and claimed constructive dismissal. It was held that the right to smoke was not a contractual term, but a personal habit. The fact that the Board had, in the past, provided her with facilities for smoking did not imply that those facilities were needed by her to enable her to perform her contractual duties, and therefore the withdrawal of the facility did not break an implied term of the contract that it was necessary to give business efficacy to the contract. Further, the Board had not broken the implied term of trust and confidence which must exist between employer and employee, for they had handled the matter as sympathetically as possible with full consultation.

7.53 The problem can be handled by tactful consultations, education and agreement. Due notice of a "no smoking" ban should be given and prospective employees informed of the employer's policies. If possible, special smoking areas may be created away from the workplace, smokers and non-smokers could be segregated, counselling and medical advice/assistance provided for inveterate smokers and non-smokers recruited for vacant posts.

7.54 To date, there does not appear to have been any reported case of a non-smoker bringing a claim for constructive dismissal on the ground of being forced to work in an area where there are smokers, but in appropriate circumstances such a claim is not impossible. There is an implied term that an employee shall not be required to work in unreasonable conditions (*Concord Lighting v Willis*), and to require an employee to work in a confined space with habitual smokers may be regarded as being unhealthy as well as unpleasant. It could further be argued that by permitting a smoker to work in an area where non-smokers work, the employer is in breach of his duty under s.2(1) of HSWA, for there is some evidence to suggest that passive smoking can be a cause of illness.

7.55 In a recent decision (R(I) 6/91), a Social Security Commissioner held that a woman who was obliged to inhale smoke from fellow workers' cigarettes was entitled to a declaration that she had suffered an accident arising out of and in the course of her employment (see para 8.89). It was stated that in the ordinary case an injury caused by "passive smoking" would not constitute an "accident", but in this particular case the claimant suffered from asthma and she was able to document six occasions when the sudden inhalation of cigarette smoke caused her a sharp pain in her lungs and severe breathlessness for several days. Thus, on each of those days she had suffered personal injury within the meaning of the Social Security Act 1975.

Drug abuse

7.56 Generally, it is not the concern of an employer what an employee does outside working hours, but this rule may not necessarily apply if those actions have some effect or impact on work activities. Thus if an employee is taking drugs, it may result in changes in behaviour which become noticeable and which may cause a potential health or safety hazard to arise. Since the employer is under a duty to ensure the health and safety at work of all employees, the actions of someone known or suspected of taking drugs must be watched carefully and appropriate measures taken to ensure no safety or health hazard arises. In cases of minor infringements of the company's rules on the taking or possession of drugs, the disciplinary procedure should be invoked and warnings, etc given, but in serious cases, stronger measures should be taken.

7.57 Thus, in *Mathewson v RB Wilson Dental Laboratories Ltd*, the applicant, during his lunch break, purchased a small amount of cannabis for his own use, but was arrested by the police. His employers dismissed him because they felt that they could no longer employ a person who was using drugs. They also thought that he might adversely influence younger members of staff. An industrial tribunal held that his dismissal was fair, and this was upheld on appeal. The decision to dismiss fell within the range of reasonable responses of a reasonable employer.

7.58 It is an offence under the Misuse of Drugs Act 1971 for an occupier knowingly to permit the possession of certain controlled drugs on his premises. Thus, if an employee is known to possess drugs on his person, it may be a ground for dismissal (*Mathewson v RB Wilson Ltd* above). An employer may decide to offer medical assistance, counselling, etc to an employee who has this problem.

Alcohol at work

7.59 Similar considerations apply to alcohol abuse. These matters are best dealt with by a clearly defined policy statement or in the works/staff rules.

Working in agriculture

7.60 The HSC Annual Report for 1991–92 states that there were seventeen fatal injuries to employees working in agriculture, and five members of the public were also killed. There were thousands of non-fatal accidents, but it is suspected that there is considerable under-reporting in the industry.

7.61 Agricultural workers frequently work alone in remote places where immediate attention is not readily available. Supervision is minimal. The industry is highly mechanised, yet the general working environment is far from ideal and many dangerous substances are used. These facts illustrate the need for strong protective legislative measures and a greater need for educating workers in safe practices and procedures. The annual reports from HSE's Agricultural Inspectorate discuss many of the hazards which arise whilst working on farms and considers some of the special problems. The Agricultural Industry Advisory Committee is engaged in a wide programme of work in looking at improvements which can be made to increase safety in the industry generally. A new permanent office and a Health and Safety Information Centre has been established at Stoneleigh in Warwickshire, which aims to provide up-to-the minute advice and information on a wide range of health and safety problems.

Agriculture (Safety, Health and Welfare Provisions) Act 1956

7.62 This Act was designed to provide for the health, safety and welfare of persons employed in agriculture, and the avoidance of accidents to children arising out of the use of vehicles, machinery or implements used in connection with agriculture. The Act will apply to existing workplaces until 31 December 1995, and to existing work equipment until 31 December 1996 (see chapter 4). A Code of Practice and Guidance Notes have been issued by HSE on preventing accidents to children in agriculture.

Lifting heavy weights (s.2)

7.63 This section (and the Agriculture (Lifting of Heavy Weights) Regulations

1959) has been repealed from 1 January 1993 by the Manual Handling Operations Regulations 1992 (see chapter 4).

Sanitary conveniences and washing facilities (s.3)

7.64 If HSE considers that any agricultural unit is without suitable and sufficient sanitary conveniences, or suitable and sufficient washing facilities, the inspector may serve a notice on the appropriate person (which may be the landlord or occupier, as the circumstances dictate) requiring him within the specified time to execute such works or take other such steps as may be specified for the purpose of providing suitable and sufficient conveniences or facilities. In making this judgment, the inspector shall have regard to the number and sex of the persons employed, the location and duration of the work, and all relevant circumstances. In addition to a notice under this section, there is also the power of the inspector to issue an improvement notice under HSWA. One distinction between these two procedures is that under HSWA, appeals against an improvement notice must go to the industrial tribunals, whereas under the Agriculture (Safety etc Provisions) Act an appeal will lie to the magistrates' court within 28 days, with a further appeal to the Crown Court.

7.65 Facilities cannot be regarded as being suitable if they are some distance away. For example, in *Fairhurst v Luke*, an improvement notice was served requiring a farmer to provide accessible toilet facilities. To reach the nearest lavatories, it would have taken workmen four-and-a-half minutes by tractor, eight minutes by bicycle or 90 seconds in a car. It was held by the industrial tribunal that in view of the isolated nature of the farm, the improvement notice would be upheld and the farmer was ordered to provide additional facilities. Otherwise, it was quite clear that rather than make such a long journey, farm workers would tend to relieve themselves on the spot and this would create a health hazard (one may query whether this would create any greater risk than that which stemmed from animals, but the provision of additional facilities would certainly make body functions more comfortable).

Cleanliness of sanitary conveniences (s.5)

7.66 If an HSE inspector considers that sanitary conveniences are not being properly maintained or kept clean he shall serve a notice requiring the occupier of the unit to take such steps as may be specified to secure the proper maintenance or to cleanse it.

First aid

7.67 The provisions of the Act relating to first aid have been repealed and replaced by the Health and Safety (First-Aid) Regulations 1981 (see para 6.74).

Avoidance of accidents to children (s.7)

7.68 It is an offence to cause or permit a child to ride on or to drive a vehicle or machine or agricultural implement in contravention of the Agriculture (Avoidance of Accidents to Children) Regulations 1958. These provide that no child (ie a person below the age of thirteen) shall ride on certain agricultural vehicles while they are being used in the course of agricultural operations. The vehicles in question are tractors, self-propelled agricultural machines, trailers, trailers into which a conveyor mechanism is built, machines mounted on or towed by tractors, binders or mowers drawn by animals. A child may ride on the floor of a trailer or on any load carried by a trailer, provided it has four sides each of which is higher than the load. A child shall not drive a tractor or self-propelled vehicle or machine while it is being used in the course of agricultural operations, or ride on agricultural implements.

Regulations relating to agriculture

7.69 There are a number of regulations which relate to agriculture and the following is a summary of the relevant provisions which remain in force until 31 December 1996 in respect of work equipment provided before 31 December 1992 and 31 December 1995 in respect of those premises first used before 31 December.

Agriculture (Ladders) Regulations 1957

7.70 These require every employer to ensure that employees do not use ladders in the course of their employment unless the ladders are of good construction and sound material and properly maintained. Neither the employer nor the employee shall use a ladder if it is not strong enough for the purpose and manner of use or if any rung is missing. Every employee shall report any defects in ladders to his employer.

Agricultural (Power Take-Off) Regulations 1957, 1991

7.71 These provide that an employer shall not cause or permit a worker to use any tractor with a power take-off while the engine is in motion, unless it is guarded by a shield to protect the worker (or his clothes) from coming into contact with the power take-off, or it is not in use and is completely enclosed by a cover. The entire length of the take-off shaft shall be wholly enclosed by a guard while in motion.

7.72 A number of EC Directives (see chapter 10) require Member States to grant "type approval" to tractors and tractor components which satisfy the relevant tests as to construction and safety set out in the Directives. Once the type approval mark has been granted there must be no barrier on sale or use within the Community. The Agriculture (Power Take-Off) Amendment Regulations 1991 allow certain exemptions from the requirements of regulation 3(1) where tractors have type approval for their power take-off in accordance with EC Directive 86/297/EEC.

Agriculture (Circular Saws) Regulations 1959

7.73 These regulations lay down provisions in relation to agriculture which are similar to the Woodworking Machine Regulations 1974. Part I of Schedule 1 to the regulations lays down obligations on employers to ensure that circular saws shall be substantially constructed and properly maintained. Adequate artificial or natural light shall be provided when circular saws are being used and defective blades must be replaced. Top guards which are rigid shall be provided and bottom guards installed below the bench table. There are special provisions for circular saws with swing tables.

7.74 Part II of Schedule 1 places obligations on workers. They must keep in position and make use of riving knives and guards and report any defect to their employer. Both employer and worker must ensure that the floor around a circular saw is unobstructed and push sticks to push blocks shall be used whenever a risk of injury would be reduced. No adjustment shall be made while the saw blade is in motion. Schedule 3 of the regulations provides that a worker shall not operate a circular saw unless its workings have been demonstrated by an experienced person who is over the age of eighteen. A worker who is over the age of sixteen but below the age of eighteen shall not use a circular saw except under the supervision of a person who is over the age of eighteen and who has a knowledge of how it operates. A worker under the age of sixteen is prohibited from using a circular saw altogether.

Agriculture (Safeguarding of Workplaces) Regulations 1959

7.75 These provide that floors and stairways shall be as safe as is reasonably practicable. There are special requirements in relation to handrails for stairways and secure handholds for steep stairways. Apertures in floors and walls must be guarded by a cover or fence or guardrail, as must grain pits, stokeholds and furnace pits. Defects in steps, handrails, covers, fences and guardrails which are discovered by a worker must be reported to his employer.

Agriculture (Stationary Machinery) Regulations 1959

7.76 These lay down the precautions which must be taken in respect of stationary machines. Every component shall be so situated or guarded as to protect a worker from coming into contact with it and similar requirements are laid down with respect to primary driving belts, feeding inlets and discharge outlets. Prime movers and stationary machinery must have a device by which they can be quickly stopped, belts must be properly maintained, and there must be adequate natural or artificial lighting provided. Workers must use safety appliances and damaged guards must be reported to the employer.

Agriculture (Threshers and Balers) Regulations 1960

7.77 These state that the drum feeding mouth of a thresher shall be guarded to prevent a worker from coming into contact with the drum, or covered, as appropriate. The deck of every thresher shall be fitted with a guardrail, or rope, chain or fence if a worker is liable to fall more than five feet. Pointed hooks and spikes must not be used for the attachment of a sack or bag to the thresher. Balers and trussers shall also be guarded. Threshers and balers shall be of sound construction and properly maintained, components shall be adequately guarded, provision must be made for a device which will stop the machinery quickly, and there shall be adequate natural or artificial light provided when these machines are being used. Workers shall use all safety precautions and damaged guards must be reported to the employer.

Agriculture (Field Machinery) Regulations 1962

7.78 These regulations apply to those machines which are used for agriculture other than a machine which is stationary (excluding self-propelled vehicles which are primarily designed to carry persons or loads, and aircraft). All components driven by any ground wheel or which are driven by power must be guarded, or situated so as to prevent the worker from coming into contact with them. If the machine has rotating knives, tines, flails, etc (excluding cylinder mowers, hedge cutters, etc) the guard must cover the operative parts as near as is practicable, and if the parts rotate, the guard must cover the top and as near to the ground as is possible on a vertical rotation, and extend at least one foot beyond the periphery where the rotation is horizontal. There are provisions which relate to the guarding of power driven potato spinners, chains saws, rotary hedge cutters, and pick-up balers. Stopping devices shall be fitted on prime movers, and differential locks shall indicate to the driver whether or not the gear is locked. Valves and cocks shall indicate the effect of movement, draw-bar jacks shall be fitted, standing platforms shall have toeboards and guardrails. If the field machine has seats, these must be of adequate strength, with a backrest and footrest, and mounting devices shall be provided to enable a worker to mount or dismount safely. All field machines shall be maintained in a safe condition and safety devices shall be of adequate strength. Workers shall use safety devices and report any defect to their employer.

Agriculture (Tractor Cabs) Regulations 1974, 1990

7.79 These enable HSE to approve a safety cab for use with a tractor by issuing a certificate of approval. HSE must be satisfied that the model conforms to BS 4063 (1973), and that the noise levels inside the cab do not exceed 90dB(A) if tested in accordance with BS 4063 (1973). It is a condition of approval that the manufacturer to whom the approval is issued shall ensure that the approval mark is on every cab sold or let on hire, and he must make available for inspection any safety cab manufactured, and submit to any tests. By the Agriculture (Tractor Cabs) (Amendment) Regulations 1990 tractor cabs of a type approved by the European Communities are acceptable as an alternative to British Standards, and a CE mark is deemed to satisfy the regulations.

7.80 A person shall not sell a new tractor or let one on hire, unless it is properly fitted with an approved safety cab and is marked with the appropriate approval mark. Every employer shall ensure that every tractor driven by a worker in the course of his employment is properly fitted with a safety cab marked with the appropriate approval mark, and, so far as is reasonably practicable, ensure that every safety cab fitted to a tractor is approved for use with that tractor. No worker shall drive a tractor fitted with a safety cab which he knows is not approved for use with the tractor. He must report to his employer any occasion when the tractor overturns, or when there is damage to the cab or to its fittings, or when there is any defect with the windscreen wiper.

Health and Safety (Agriculture) (Poisonous Substances) Regulations 1975

7.81 These regulations, which laid down detailed provisions for safety precautions to be taken when dangerous or poisonous substances were being used were repealed by the COSHH Regulations (see para 6.135).

Agriculture (Poisonous Substances) Act 1952

7.82 Section 6 empowers a HSE inspector to take for analysis any substance which he finds on agricultural premises and, if practicable, give notice of his intention to do so to the employer of any person working there. He shall divide the sample into three parts, and:

(a) if required to do so by the employer, give one part to him
(b) retain one part for future comparison
(c) submit one part to an approved analyst.

7.83 If it is not practicable for him to inform the employer of his intention and he proposes to have the sample analysed, then he will forward one part of the sample to the employer (if he can ascertain his name and address) by registered post or otherwise, together with a notice informing him of the intention to have the sample analysed.

Construction industry

7.84 Section 127 of the Factories Act 1961 applies many of the provisions of that Act to building operations and works of engineering construction undertaken by way of trade or business, or for the purpose of any industrial or commercial undertaking and to any line or siding used in connection therewith which is not part of a railway. The relevant provisions are:

(a) Part I with respect to sanitary conveniences (s.7)
(b) Part II with respect to steam boilers and air receiver (ss.31–34, 37, 38)
(c) Part V (formal investigation of accidents and cases of disease)
(d) Part X with respect to notices, special regulations, general registers and the preservation of records and registers (ss.138, 140, 141)
(e) Part XI relating to certain duties of local authorities (s.153)
(f) Part XII relating to offences (ss.155–171)

(g) Part XIII (ss.172, 174)
(h) Part XIV (ss.175, 176).

7.85 However, the main source of legal rules relating to health and safety in the industry is the five principal sets of regulations which are in force. These are:

(a) Construction (General Provisions) Regulations 1961
(b) Construction (Lifting Operations) Regulations 1961
(c) Construction (Working Places) Regulations 1966
(d) Construction (Health and Welfare) Regulations 1966
(e) Construction (Head Protection) Regulations 1989.

These regulations apply to those premises which come within the scope of s.127 of the Factories Act (above).

7.86 In addition, there are a number of relevant regulations which were passed in order to comply with EC Directives on type examination certificates of approval. These include:

(a) Construction Plant and Equipment (Harmonisation of Noise Emission Standards) Regulations 1988
(b) Falling Object Protective Structure for Construction Plant (EC Requirements) Regulations 1988
(c) Roll-over Protective Structures for Construction Plant (EC Requirements) Regulations 1988.

7.87 Currently being considered are proposals for a new Construction (Design and Management) Regulations, designed to bring about effective management on construction sites. The proposals are in accord with a proposed EC Directive on temporary or mobile worksites.

Obligations

7.88 The first three sets of regulations mentioned (ie General Provision, Lifting Operations and Working Places) impose three general duties on every contractor and every employer of workmen. These are:

7.89 (a) To comply with those regulations as affect him or any workman employed by him. The workmen referred to are not only those who are engaged on the building work, but others employed, eg a nightwatchman (*Field v Perry (Ealing) Ltd*). A main contractor owes the duty towards workmen who are employed by him, but not to those employed by a subcontractor (*Claydon v Lindsay Parkinson Ltd*), nor to the workmen employed by the building owner (*Wingrove v Prestige & Co. Ltd*), nor to an independent contractor (*Herbert v Harold Shaw Ltd*). However, the insertion in the 1961 regulations of the words "him or" meant that an independent subcontractor owes a duty to ensure his own safety (*Smith v George Wimpey*

Ltd), and that if he failed to do so he could be prosecuted for an offence (obviously, if he injured himself through a breach of his own duty, he could not sue himself for damages!). Although the main contractor thus owes no statutory duty to the employees of the subcontractor, this in no way weakens the obligations owed by the main contractor at common law to ensure that the work is organised in a safe way (*McArdle v Andmac Roofing Ltd*).

7.90 The contractor's obligations do not apply to workmen if their presence in any place is not in the course of performing any work on behalf of the employer and is not expressly or impliedly authorised or permitted by the employer.

7.91 (b) To comply with such requirements of the regulations as relate to any act or operation performed by any such contractor or employer of workmen. Work is performed by the main contractor if it is being done by the subcontractor as long as the main contractor has not divested himself of control over the execution of the work, but if he has so divested himself, he is not performing the work within the meaning of the regulations *(Donaghey v Boulton Paul Ltd*).

7.92 (c) Every contractor and every employer of workmen who erects, installs, works or uses any plant or equipment, or who erects or alters any scaffolding, shall do so in a manner which complies with the regulations.

7.93 Additionally, the regulations impose a duty on every person employed to comply with the legal requirements as relates to the performance of or to the refraining of an act by him, to cooperate in carrying out these regulations and if he discovers any defect in any plant or equipment, to report such defect without unreasonable delay to his employer or foreman, or to a person appointed as a safety supervisor.

Construction (General Provisions) Regulations

7.94 The following is an outline of the main provisions of these regulations.

Safety supervisor

7.95 Every contractor and every employer of workmen who undertakes building or construction work and who normally employs more than twenty persons thereon at any one time (whether or not all those persons are employed on the same site or are all at work at the same time) shall appoint in writing a safety supervisor, who shall be experienced in such operations or works and suitably qualified for the purpose. He shall advise the contractor or employer as to the observance of the requirements for the safety or protection of persons employed which may be imposed by the Factories Act, and exercise a general supervision of the observance of the statutory requirements and of promoting the safe conduct of the work generally. The name of the safety supervisor shall be entered on the abstract of the regulations which must be displayed. There is no requirement that the safety supervisor shall be a full-time appointment, but any other duties assigned to him shall not be such as to prevent him from discharging with reasonable efficiency the duties assigned to him under those regulations. The same person may be appointed for a group of sites and two or more contractors or employers may jointly appoint the same person to be responsible for a particular site.

Supply and use of timber

7.96 An adequate supply of timber of suitable quality (or other suitable support) shall, where necessary, be provided and used to prevent, so far as is reasonably practicable, danger to any person employed from a fall or dislodgement of earth, rock or any other material forming a side or the roof of or adjacent to any excavation, shaft, earthwork or tunnel.

Inspections and examinations of excavations

7.97 Every part of any excavation, shaft, earthwork or tunnel where persons are employed shall be inspected by a competent person at least once every day during which persons are employed therein, and tunnels and trenches more than 2m (6 feet 6 inches) deep shall be inspected at the commencement of each shift. .

Supervision of timbering

7.98 No timbering or other support for any part of an excavation, shaft, earthwork or tunnel shall be erected, substantially added to, altered or dismantled except under the direction of a competent person, and, so far as possible, by competent workmen possessing adequate experience of such work.

Means of exit in case of flooding

7.99 If there is any reason to apprehend danger to persons employed therein from rising water or from an eruption of water, there shall be provided, so far as is reasonably practicable, means to enable such persons to reach positions of safety. If the work is likely to reduce the stability or security of any part of the structure (whether temporary or permanent) work shall not be commenced or continued unless adequate steps are taken before or during the progress of the work to prevent danger to any person employed from collapse of the structure or a fall of part of it. Materials shall not be placed or stacked near the edge of an excavation, etc so as to endanger persons employed below. Cofferdams and cassions must be of good construction, of suitable and sound material free from patent defect, of adequate strength and properly maintained. They shall not be placed into position, or added to, or altered or dismantled except under the immediate supervision of a competent person. No person shall be employed in them unless they have been inspected at least once on the same or preceding day.

Explosives

7.100 Explosives shall not be handled or used except by or under the immediate control of a competent person with adequate knowledge of the dangers. Steps must be taken to ensure that when a charge is fired, persons employed are not exposed to the risk of injury from the explosion or from flying materials.

Dangerous or unhealthy atmospheres

7.101 Ventilation must be secured and maintained in any excavation, pit, hole, adit, tunnel, shaft, cassion or other enclosed or confined space.

7.102 The provisions dealing with the prevention of inhalation of dust and fumes were repealed by the COSHH Regulations (see para 6.135).

Work adjacent to water

7.103 If a person is being carried to or from work by water, proper measures shall be taken to provide for his safe transport. If work is being carried on adjacent to water and there is a risk of drowning if an employee falls in, suitable rescue equipment shall be provided.

Transport

7.104 Rails and tracks on which locomotives, trucks or wagons have to move shall have an even running surface, securely fastened, supported so as to prevent undue movement, laid in straight lines or curves on which they can travel without danger of derailment and provided with a stop or buffer at each end of the track. Locomotives, trucks and wagons shall be of good construction, sound material, adequate strength, free from patent defect and properly maintained. There shall be adequate clearance so that persons are not liable to be trapped or crushed by passing locomotives, etc and suitable recesses where appropriate. If there is no such adequate clearance, effective warnings must be given of approaching locomotives, etc. Gantries must be provided with suitable and adequate footways, locomotives must have effective brakes and suitable arrangements made for dealing with derailments. Locomotives shall be fitted with a whistle or other warning device, and only a competent and trained person over the age of eighteen may drive or operate them. Power driven capstans or haulage winches shall have sufficient space for safe working, and sound or visual signals given by the operator to any person who may be endangered by their operation. Mechanically-propelled vehicles used for the conveyance of workmen, goods or materials shall be kept in an efficient state, efficient working order and good repair, and may not be used in an improper manner, or loaded so as to interfere with the safe driving. No person shall be permitted to ride in an insecure position, or remain on such a vehicle during the loading of loose materials by means of a grab excavator or similar appliance, and when the vehicle is being used for tipping materials, measures shall be taken to prevent it overrunning the edge of any excavation, pit, embankment or earthwork.

Demolition work

7.105 Every contractor undertaking demolition operation shall appoint a competent person to supervise the work, and before the work is commenced and during the work all practicable steps shall be taken to prevent danger to persons employed from risk of fire, explosion or leakage or accumulation of gas or vapour, and from the risk of flooding. No part of a building or structure shall be so overloaded with debris or materials as to render it unsafe, and certain types of work may only be done under the immediate supervision of a competent foreman or chargehand with adequate experience of the particular kind of work. All practicable precautions must be taken to avoid danger from collapse of buildings or structures and adequate shoring shall be undertaken.

Other matters

7.106 Flywheels, moving parts of prime movers, transmission machinery and every dangerous part of other machinery (whether or not driven by mechanical power) shall be securely fenced, and prime movers and mechanically driven machines constructed after the commencement of the regulations in 1962 must have certain specific parts securely fenced. Measures shall be taken to prevent steam, smoke or other vapour generated from the site from obscuring the work, scaffolding, machinery or other plant or equipment where any person is employed. Steps shall be taken to prevent any person who is working from being struck by any falling material or article. Every workplace and its approaches shall be adequately and suitably lit. No timber or materials with projecting nails shall be used, and loose materials shall not be left so as to unduly restrict the passage of persons, but shall be removed and stacked or stored. Materials shall not be insecurely stacked in a place where they may be dangerous. Temporary structures shall be of good construction and adequate strength and stability. All practicable steps shall be taken to prevent danger from the collapse of any building or structure during its temporary weakness. Iron or steelwork which has been painted or cement washed shall not be moved or manipulated unless the paint or cement is dry. Helmets or crowns used for pile-driving shall be of good construction, of sound and suitable material of adequate strength and free from patent defect. Form 91 (report of examination of excavations and of cofferdam or cassion) shall be kept on the site, and all other reports or documents required to be kept shall at reasonable times be open to inspection by HSE inspectors.

7.107 The use of electricity in building operations is now governed by the Electricity at Work Regulations 1989 (see para 6.114).

Construction (Lifting Operations) Regulations 1961

7.108 The following is an outline of the main provisions of these regulations.

Lifting appliances

7.109 Every lifting appliance and all appliances which support lifting appliances shall be of good mechanical construction, sound material, adequate strength free from patent defect, properly maintained, and as far as the construction permits be inspected at least once in every week by the driver or other competent person. The result shall be recorded on Form 91. If the lifting appliance has a travelling or slewing movement there shall be an unobstructed passageway of not less than two feet wide between the moving parts and any guardrails, unless all reasonable steps are taken to prevent the access of any person to such place. Where a platform is provided, it shall be of sufficient area, close planked and provided with a safe means of access, with sides provided with suitable guardrails. The driver of every power driven lifting appliance shall be provided with a suitable cabin which shall afford him adequate protection from the weather and have ready access to parts which need periodic inspection or maintenance, and shall not prevent him from having a clear and unrestricted view. Drums and pulleys shall be of suitable diameter, and every crane, grab and winch shall have efficient brakes or other safety device which will prevent the fall of the load when suspended. A safe means of access to and egress from any place where a person has to work on examination, repair or lubrication shall so far as is reasonably practicable be provided and maintained. Poles or beams which support pulley blocks and gin wheels shall be of adequate strength and adequately and properly secured. Appropriate precautions shall be taken to ensure the stability of lifting appliances used on a soft or uneven surface or on a slope. Before a crane is erected, the anchorage must be examined by a competent person, and after erection there will be a further test involving a load which is 25 per cent above the maximum load to be lifted by the crane. A report of such tests and the results shall be made.

7.110 Rail mounted cranes shall be supported on a firm and even surface jointed by fish plates or double chairs, securely fastened, laid in straight lines or curves which will not cause derailment, and provided with stops or buffers at each end. Bogeys, trolleys or wheeled carriages on which a crane is mounted shall be of good construction, adequate strength, suitable, made from sound material free from patent defect and properly maintained. Cranes with derricking jibs shall have effective interlocking arrangements to prevent the disengagement. A crane shall not be used for any purpose other than the raising or lowering of a load vertically unless no undue stress is imposed and the use is supervised by a competent person. Cranes shall not have any timber structure and shall be erected under the supervision of a competent person.

7.111 Lifting appliances shall not be operated except by a trained and competent person (unless under the direction of a qualified person for the purpose of training) and no person under the age of eighteen (other than as a trainee) shall be employed to operate the appliance or give signals to the operator. If the operator does not have a clear and unrestricted view, one or more competent persons shall be appointed and suitably stationed to give the necessary signals. Every signal given shall be distinctive in character, and if devices are used for giving sound, colour or light signals, these shall be properly maintained. Cranes, crabs and winches shall not be used unless tested by a competent person within the previous four years, and a further test shall take place if they have been subject to any substantial alteration or repair affecting its strength or stability.

7.112 No crane, crab, winch, pulley block or gin wheel shall be used unless a test certificate has been obtained stating (a) the safe working load, (b) the safe radii or maximum radii. Jib cranes shall have an automatic safe load indicator which has been tested before the crane is taken into use, and inspected once each week it is being used. Lifting appliances generally shall not be loaded beyond the safe working load, and where more than one lifting appliance is required to raise a load, the equipment shall be so arranged that no appliance shall be loaded beyond it safe working load or be rendered unstable. Such operations must be conducted under the supervision of a competent person.

7.113 Chains, ropes or lifting gear must be of good construction, sound materials, adequate strength, suitable quality, free from patent defect, tested and examined before use, and marked with its safe working load and means of identification. There are further provisions designed to ensure safety when using chains, rings, hooks, etc. Part V of the regulations deals with hoistways, platforms and cages, which must have substantial enclosures, gates, safety devices, and safe working loads. Hoists must be thoroughly examined by a competent person every six months, and a report sent to the district inspector within 28 days where the test or examination reveals that certain repairs are required.

Construction (Working Places) Regulations 1966

7.114 The following is an outline of the main provisions of these regulations.

7.115 So far as is reasonably practicable, there shall be a suitable and sufficiently safe means of access to and egress from every place at which any person at any time works and every place where a person works shall also be kept safe. No scaffold shall be erected or substantially added to or altered or be dismantled unless under the immediate supervision of a competent person with adequate experience of such work. Materials used for scaffolding shall be inspected each time they are used. Every scaffold shall be of good construction, of suitable and sound material and of adequate strength. Sufficient material shall be provided, timber which is used shall not be painted so that defects cannot be seen and metal parts must be free from corrosion. Defective materials shall not be used.

7.116 There are a number of provisions relating to the erection and dismantling of scaffolding, the materials which may or may not be used, supervision by competent persons, maintenance, stability, slung scaffolds, cantilever jibs and suspended scaffolds, cages, skips, trestle scaffolds, etc. There are also detailed requirements relating to working platforms, gangways and runs, with provisions for guardrails and toeboards. If any person is liable to fall a distance of more than 2m (6 feet 6 inches), guardrails must be provided. Ladders must be of good construction, of suitable and sound material and of adequate strength, securely fixed near to its upper resting place, or, if that is impracticable, at or near the lower end. Work on sloping roofs may only be carried out by suitable workmen, using crawling boards or crawling ladders. In certain circumstances, safety nets or safety sheets must be provided.

Construction (Health and Welfare) Regulations 1966

Obligations

7.117 Except as otherwise provided, it is the duty of every contractor to comply with such requirements as affect any person employed by him (compare this with the obligations imposed by the other three sets of regulations, above). If the contractor makes effective arrangements with another contractor on the site, or similar arrangements with another person for enabling persons employed to have adequate access to and use of facilities and which are reasonably accessible, then the contractor will have fulfilled his obligations in respect of those stated matters.

7.118 The following is an outline of the requirements of the regulations.

First aid

7.119 The regulations dealing with first aid have been revoked and replaced by the Health and Safety (First-Aid) Regulations 1981 (see para 6.74).

Shelters, etc

7.120 At or in the immediate vicinity of every site there shall be conveniently accessible for the use of persons employed adequate and suitable accommodation for taking shelter during interruptions of work owing to bad weather, and for depositing clothing not worn during working hours. If there are more than five persons employed on the site, there must be adequate and suitable means for enabling persons employed to warm themselves and to dry their clothing, and if there are five or less so employed, such arrangements must be made as are reasonably practicable for these purposes. Similar accommodation and drying facilities must be provided for protective clothing used for work. Dry facilities for taking meals and for boiling water must be provided and, if more than ten persons are employed and heated food is not available on site, adequate facilities for heating food. Wholesome drinking water must also be provided. All accommodation must be kept in a clean and orderly condition and not used for the storage of materials or plant.

Washing facilities

7.121 If an employee works on site for more than four consecutive hours, there must be adequate and suitable washing facilities, and if more than twenty employees are likely to be working on site for more than six weeks there shall be provided adequate troughs, basins or buckets, adequate means of cleaning and drying and a sufficient supply of hot and cold or warm water. If there are more than 100 likely to be employed on site for more than twelve months a minimum scale for these facilities is laid down. Suitable sanitary conveniences which are conveniently accessible shall be provided if there are more than 25 persons employed on site, which shall be ventilated, under cover, partitioned off so as to ensure privacy, and screened off with a proper door and fastening. Adequate and suitable protective clothing shall be provided for any person who by the reason of the nature of the work is required to continue working in the open air during rain, snow, sleet or hail. All the above facilities shall so far as is reasonably practicable have a safe means of access or egress, and every such place shall equally be made and kept safe.

Examinations and inspections

7.122 The following is a summary of the examinations and inspections which are required under the construction regulations generally.

	Nature of examination or inspection	*When undertaken*	*By whom*
(1)	Every part of any excavation, shaft, earthwork or tunnel	at least once on every day during which persons are employed therein	competent person
(2)	Face of every tunnel and the working end of every trench more than 2 m (6 feet 6 inches) deep, and the base or crown of every shaft	commencement of every shift	competent person
(3)	Thorough examination of parts of any excavation, shaft, earthwork or tunnel in the region of a blast	(a) after explosives have been used nearby in a manner likely to affect the strength or stability of timbering or other support; (b) since timbering or other support has been substantially damaged; (c) in the region of any unexpected fall of rock, earth or other material; (d) every part within the immediately preceding 7 days	competent person

	Nature of examination or inspection	*When undertaken*	*By whom*
(4)	Timbering or support material used for excavation, shaft, earthwork or tunnels	each occasion before use	competent person
(5)	Materials used for the construction of a cofferdam or cassion	each occasion before use	competent person
(6)	Cofferdams or cassions must be inspected	(a) on the day or day before a person is employed therein; (b) since explosives have been used in a manner likely to affect the strength or stability; (c) since the cofferdam or cassion has been substantially damaged; (d) in the 7 days immediately preceding persons working therein	competent person
(7)	Suitable testing of the atmosphere in an excavation, pit, hole, adit, tunnel shaft, cassion or other enclosed or confined space	where there is reason to apprehend that the atmosphere is poisonous or asphyxiating	by or under the immediate supervision of a competent person
(8)	Periodic examination of hoists forming part of permanent equipment	before use for carrying persons	competent firm of lift engineers
(9)	Every part of lifting appliances, all working gear, plant or equipment used for anchoring or fixing	as far as the construction permits inspection	by the driver (if competent) otherwise by a competent person
(10)	The whole of the appliances for the anchorage or ballasting of a crane	each occasion before the crane is erected	competent person
(11)	Securing of the anchorage or adequacy of the ballasting of cranes	before use, after each erection, removal or adjustment	competent person

	Nature of examination or inspection	*When undertaken*	*By whom*
(12)	Anchorage arrangements and ballast of cranes	after exposure to weather conditions likely to affect stability	competent person
(13)	Thorough examination of crane, grab or winch	within four years prior to use	competent person
(14)	Thorough examination of pulley block, gin wheel, or sheer legs	if used to raise or lower a load weighing more than 1 ton	competent person
(15)	Thorough examination of crane, grab or winch, pulley block, gin wheel, sheer legs	after any substantial alteration	competent person
(16)	Thorough examination of lifting appliances	within previous 14 months, or since undergone any substantial alteration or repair	competent person
(17)	Approved type of automatic safe load indicators on jib cranes	tested after erection or installation and before use	competent person (other than the crane driver)
(18)	Approved type of automatic safe load indicators on jib cranes	inspected once a week when crane is in use	driver (if competent) or competent person
(19)	Approved type of automatic safe load indicators on mobile cranes	tested before use	competent person
(20)	Approved type of automatic safe load indicators on jib cranes	inspected once a week when crane is in use	competent person
(21)	Chains, ropes, lifting gear used in raising or lowering or as a means of suspension	tested and examined before use	competent person
(22)	Chains, ring, link, hooks, plate clamps, shackle, swivel or eye-bolt which has been lengthened, altered, or repaired by welding	tested and thoroughly examined before use	competent person
(23)	Chains, ropes and lifting gear in regular use	thorough examination at least once in 6 months	competent person

	Nature of examination or inspection	*When undertaken*	*By whom*
(24)	Thorough examination of hoists which have been manufactured or substantially altered or repaired after March 1962	before being used	competent person
(25)	Thorough examination of hoists used for carrying persons	since erected or height altered	competent person
(26)	Thorough examination of hoists	at least once each 6 months	competent person
(27)	All material used for any scaffold	before taken into use	competent person
(28)	Scaffolds (including boatswain's chair, cage, skip or similar plant or equipment)	inspected within 7 days prior to use	competent person

Head protection

7.123 The Construction (Head Protection) Regulations 1989 are designed to give protection to persons who work on construction sites, which are defined as being works of building operations and engineering construction. Employers must provide and maintain head protection and replace it whenever necessary. An identical obligation lies on self-employed persons. The head protection must be suitable, ie conform to British Standard 5240 (or equivalent) and be compatible with the work or activity. Head protection must be worn at all times during construction work unless there is no risk of injury to the head from falling objects. Employers, self-employed persons and employees who control others (eg foremen) must ensure that the head protectors are worn. A person who has control of a site may make rules governing when and where helmets shall be worn. Such rules shall be in writing, and brought to the attention of those affected by them.

7.124 Sikhs are exempted from the requirements of the regulations at any time when they are wearing their turban and thus they cannot be required to wear safety helmets in such circumstances (Employment Act 1989, s.11). In consequence, an employer will not be liable to tort in respect of any injury or damage caused because he failed to comply with the statutory duty. A Sikh who is injured because of a failure to wear the safety helmet will only be able to recover damages to the extent the injury or damage would still have occurred had he been wearing a safety helmet.

7.125 Employees shall take reasonable care of head protection provided, and report to the employer any loss or obvious defect.

8

Compensation for injuries at work

8.1 Inevitably, an employee who is injured in the course of employment will seek some form of compensation from the person (if any) who was responsible for those injuries, or look to the state to provide some assistance. If an employee is killed, his dependants will also be seeking some form of financial recompense for themselves. It is this area of the law which in the past has tended to dominate all other considerations of health and safety, as compensation, rather than prevention, became the main function of the law. This attitude prompted the Robens Committee to attempt some shift in the impact of the legislation.

8.2 It is truism to say that legal decisions reflect the current social and economic forces of the day and this explains some of the changes in judicial attitudes which have taken place from time to time. Further, the impact of state and private insurance schemes (especially employers' liability insurance) has cast a powerful shadow over strict legal reasoning, for there is a natural tendency to seek some way in which the injured employee can be assisted financially, and, after all, if an insurance company had to foot the bill, this could easily be recouped by a minute increase in general premiums. This benevolent attitude even reached employers, and there are many cases where liability is admitted or where valiant attempts were made to admit their own negligence so as to enable an injured employee to obtain compensation (eg see *Hilton v Thomas Burton (Rhodes) Ltd*). But there were limits, too, on judicial credulity, which compelled some judges to hold that they could no longer equate the relationship between employer and employee with that of nurse and imbecile child (Lord Simmonds in *Smith v Austin Lifts Ltd*) or that of schoolmaster and pupil (Devlin LJ in *Withers v Perry Chain Ltd*).

8.3 The basis of the employer's duty towards his employees stems from the existence of a contract of employment. It is an implied term of that contract that the employer will take reasonable care to ensure the safety of his employees (*Matthews v Kuwait Bechtel Corporation*), and an employer who fails to fulfil that duty is in breach of that contract (*British Aircraft Corporation v Austin*). The express terms of the contract must be capable of co-existing with the implied terms. In *Johnson v Bloomsbury Health Authority*, Dr Johnson was required by his contract of employment to work a basic 40 hour week, and to be "on call" for a further 48 hours each week. He claimed that the number of hours he had to work were intolerable, depriving him of sleep, with consequent depression, stress and anxiety, which could result in the risk of mistakes or inefficient treatment of patients. He sought a declaration that he could not lawfully be required to work for so many hours in excess of his standard working week as would foreseeably injure his health. At a preliminary hearing, the Court of Appeal held that he had established an arguable case to warrant a full trial of the issues. The Court, however, were not unanimous in their views, but it appears that the employer's right to require Dr Johnson to work up to 48 hours work "on call" was subject to the implied duty of the employer to take care that the employee's health was not damaged as a result. Further, it was held that it was arguable that the term (that he should work for up to 88 hours per week) was void under the Unfair Contract Terms Act 1977, which prohibits a contract term which excludes or restricts liability for personal injury caused by negligence. Since the offending term could be said to restrict or limit the ambit of the duty of care owed by the employers, the plaintiff was permitted to proceed with that aspect of his claim.

8.4 However, from the point of view of an injured employee there is little advantage in suing in contract. Practically all modern cases are brought under the law of tort, in particular for the tort of negligence which, since the famous case of *Donoghue v Stevenson* in 1932 consists of three general ingredients, namely (a) there is a general duty to take care not to injure someone whom one might reasonably foresee would be injured by acts or omissions, (b) that duty is broken if a person acts in a negligent manner, and (c) the breach of the duty must cause injury or damage. The existence of a duty-situation between employer and employee has been long recognised, and most of the cases turn on the second point, ie was the employer in fact negligent?

8.5 The liability of the employer may come about in two ways. First, he will be responsible for his own acts of negligence. These may be his personal failures or (since many employers nowadays are artificial legal entities, ie limited companies or other types of corporations) due to the wrongdoings of the various acts of management acting as the *alter ego* of the employer. Second, the employer may be liable vicariously for the wrongful acts of his employees which are committed in the scope of their employment and which cause injury or damage to others.

8.6 Compensation may be obtained under one or more of three headings. The first is for the injured employee (or his personal representatives, if he has died) to bring an action at common law. This will be for either (a) a breach by the employer of a duty laid down by statute, or (b) a breach of the duty owed by the employer at common law to ensure the health and safety of his employees. Frequently, a claim will be presented under both headings simultaneously. With two strings to his bow, it matters not if he wins under either heading, or both. (Of course, if he wins under both, he will only get one lot of damages.) It is regarded as a misfortune if he fails under both headings, for he has then lost his main financial solace. It was the uncertainties of litigation in this area of the law, the difficulties of establishing satisfactory evidential standards in court hearings held years after an incident had occurred, the legal expenses and complexities, and the social injustices caused, which were among the main reasons for the appointment of the Pearson Commission in 1974. Its report, however, did not recommend any major changes in the compensation system.

8.7 The second remedy for an injured employee is the automatic recourse to the National Insurance (Industrial Injuries) scheme operated by the State in one form or another since 1911 (see now the Social Security Contributions and Benefits Act 1992), which provide for a pension in respect of an injury at work or a prescribed disease which causes permanent disabilities. This scheme is in addition to the right to sue at common law, although benefits payable will be taken into account when fixing damages. However, the State scheme operates as of right, irrespective of the existence of fault or blame on the part of any person, including the injured worker.

8.8 Third, in appropriate circumstances, there are other schemes which may be resorted to, such as those operated by the Criminal Injuries Compensation Board, the Motorists Insurance Bureau or (rarely used), the power of the courts to award compensation.

Claims at common law

Breach of statutory duty

8.9 When Parliament lays down a duty for a person to perform, it will usually ensure that there is an appropriate sanction to enforce that duty. This sanction will normally take the form of some sort of punishment in the criminal courts. The further question will thus arise; can a person who has been injured by the failure of another to perform that statutory duty bring a civil action based on that failure? After some hesitation, British courts upheld an action for the tort of breach of statutory duty, although the full extent of legal liability is not entirely settled. There is no automatic presumption that all breaches of statutory duties are actionable in civil courts; it is necessary to examine the purposes and objects of the statute in question, seek the intentions of Parliament (it is now permissible to look at Hansard in order to ascertain those intentions, see *Pepper v Hart*, para 1.80), and ascertain the class of persons for whose benefit the Act was passed. If the injured party has suffered the type of harm the Act was designed to eliminate, it would not be unreasonable to grant him a remedy in respect of a breach of the statutory duty. The first case in which these propositions were accepted was *Groves v Lord Wimborne*, where a statute provided that an occupier of a factory who did not fence dangerous machinery was liable to a fine of up to £100. A boy employed in the factory was caught in an unfenced cog wheel, and his arm was amputated. It was held that the criminal penalty was irrelevant to civil liability, and the claim for a breach of statutory duty succeeded.

8.10 However, not every breach of statutory duty is actionable (*Cutler v Wandsworth Stadium Ltd*), and though the point appears to be well settled so far as health and safety legislation is concerned, there are one or two areas where there may still be an element of doubt. The real difficulty is encountered when dealing with some of the welfare provisions in the Factories Act, OSRPA, etc. For example in *Ebbs v James Whitson & Co. Ltd* the question arose as to whether the plaintiff could sue in respect of a breach of s.4(1) of the Factories Act (securing adequate ventilation, see chapter 5) and Denning LJ (as he then was) expressly reserved his opinion on this point. However, similar claims have succeeded in a number of cases since then, though the point was either conceded or not argued. For example, in *Nicholson v Atlas Steel Ltd* a worker contracted pneumoconiosis as a result of exposure to a silica dust, from which he subsequently died. It was held that his widow was entitled to recover damages based on a breach of s.4 of the Factories Act in respect of a failure to provide adequate ventilation. Civil remedies have also been granted in other cases dealing with Part I of the Factories Act (eg *Lane v Gloucestershire Engineering Co. Ltd*, a case under s.50) and it would appear that the doubts of Lord Denning are misplaced. However, the point is less clear when considering some of the welfare provisions of Part III of the Act (see chapter 5), although again, some actions have succeeded without argument on this point (eg *McCarthy v Daily Mirror*: s.59—suitable accommodation for clothing). Similar considerations will presumably apply to other health and safety legislation, eg OSRPA, but there does not appear to be any direct decision on the point. It would seem that the accepted view is that welfare provisions are of two distinct types; first, those which are concerned with health and safety and those which are dealing with welfare and comfort. It may well be that no civil action will lie in respect of a breach of the latter kind of statutory provisions. Thus, if an employer fails to provide adequate washing facilities (Factories Act, s.59) this duty cannot be enforced *per se* by an employee, only by the inspectorate. If, as a result of the failure by the employer to provide washing facilities an employee contracts dermatitis, he may be able to recover damages (*Reid v Westfield Paper Co. Ltd*). For a contrary viewpoint see *Clifford v Challen & Son Ltd.*

8.11 It will be recalled that s.47 of HSWA provides that no civil action may be brought in respect of a breach of the general duties and obligations contained in ss.2–8, but that a breach of health and safety regulations made under the Act shall be actionable except insofar as the regulations provide otherwise.

Elements of the tort of breach of statutory duty

8.12 The first requirement is that the plaintiff must show that he is within the class of persons for whose benefit the duty was imposed. This will depend entirely on the provision in question. Thus there are provisions in the Factories Act which are designed to protect all persons who work in a factory, whether or not they are the employees of the occupier and whether or not they are doing the employer's work or their own (*Uddin v Associated Portland Cement Ltd*). Other provisions may be more limited in their scope. Thus in *Hartly v Mayoh & Co.* a fireman was electrocuted whilst fighting a fire at the defendant's premises. The widow sued in respect of a breach by the defendant of a statutory regulation. Her claim failed. The provisions in question were designed to protect "persons employed" in the premises and the fireman was not within this class of person. In *Reid v Galbraith's Stores* it was held that the provisions of OSRPA did not apply to a customer who was visiting the shop as the Act was concerned with people who work on the premises.

8.13 Insofar as health and safety regulations are concerned, the right to bring a civil claim in respect of a breach is probably even more circumscribed. Sometimes these will be designed to protect a person who is performing a particular type of work, and a person who is not engaged on that process but who may be injured as a result of a breach of the regulation will not generally be entitled to compensation under this heading. The reason is that in the past it has been presumed that Parliament only intended that the power to make regulations shall be exercised within particular limits, and the courts will not therefore go outside those limits. However, the power to make regulations under s.15 of HSWA is not so restricted and thus they may include a wider category of affected persons, as appropriate. It is clear that when regulations are made for the benefit of a particular group of persons, only those who are in that group can take advantage of the statutory protections (*Canadian Pacific Steamships Ltd v Bryers*).

8.14 Second, the injury must be of a kind which the statute was designed to prevent. In *Close v Steel Co. of Wales* a workman was injured by a part of dangerous machinery which flew out of a machine. His claim, based on a breach of s.14 of the Factories Act (duty to fence dangerous parts of machinery, see chapter 5) failed. The object of s.14 is to prevent the worker from coming into contact with the machine, not to stop the parts of the machine from coming into contact with the worker. The purpose of fencing is not to keep the machine or its products inside the fence.

8.15 The third requirement of the tort is that the defendant must be in breach of that duty. This involves a consideration of the duty imposed, the person upon whom it is placed, and the steps taken to perform that duty. Thus in *Chipchase v British Titan Products Ltd*, regulations provided that every working platform from which a person is liable to fall more than 2 m (6 feet 6 inches) shall be at least 34 inches wide. A worker fell from a platform which was only 9 inches wide, but which was 6 feet from the ground. The plaintiffs case obviously failed, as there was no breach of duty by the defendant. If the statute or regulations imposes absolute duties, then these must be observed irrespective of the inconvenience caused (*Summers & Sons v Frost*), but if these are qualified, eg "so far as is reasonably practicable", etc it is a question of fact in each case as to whether or not the defendant has complied with that standard.

8.16 Finally, it must be shown that the breach of the duty caused the damage. This is the causation rule, which may be illustrated by the decision in *McWilliams v Sir William Arrol & Co. Ltd*. Here, the employers provided safety belts for steel erectors on a site. As the belts were not being used, they were taken to another site. A steel erector on the first site fell from a scaffolding and was killed. Although the employers were clearly in breach of their statutory duty to provide the safety belts, they were not liable for damages. Even if they had provided the belts, there is nothing to suggest that this workman (who had never used them before) would have worn them on the day he was killed. Thus, the breach of duty did not cause the damage; it would have occurred anyway.

8.17 But if an injury is caused by the act of the injured employee, which would not have occurred if the employer had performed his statutory duties, then the employer will be liable for damages unless the act of the employee was an unnatural and improbable consequence of the breach. For example, in *McGovern v British Steel Corporation*, the plaintiff was walking along a gangway made from scaffold boards. He saw a toe board which had fallen from the upright position and which was obstructing the walkway. He attempted to pick it up, but, because it was jammed, it "whiplashed" causing him to suffer from a slipped disc. It was held that the employer was liable. The injury was not caused by the employee tripping or falling over the obstruction, but by the employer's breach of duty in failing to remove it. It was natural that the employee should attempt to do this, and the injury was not unforeseeable. Thus the injury was a natural and probable cause of the breach and the conduct of the employee was not such as to break the chain of causation.

Negligence

8.18 At common law the employer is under a duty to take reasonable care for the health and safety of his employees. This duty is a particular aspect of the general law of negligence, which requires everyone to ensure that his activities do not cause injury or damage to another through some act of carelessness or inadvertence (see *Donoghue v Stevenson*, para 8.4).

The personal nature of the duty

8.19 The duty at common law is owed personally by the employer to his employee, and he does not escape that duty by showing that he has delegated the performance to some competent person. In *Wilsons and Clyde Coal Co. v English* the employer was compelled by law to employ a colliery agent who was responsible for safety in the mine. Nonetheless, when an accident occurred, the employer was held liable. Thus it can never be a defence for an employer to show that he has assigned the responsibility of securing and maintaining health and safety precautions to a safety officer or other person. He can delegate the performance, but not the responsibility.

8.20 Further, the duty is owed to each employee as an individual, not to employees collectively. Greater precautions must be taken when dealing with young or inexperienced workers and with new or untrained employees than one might take with more responsible staff. The former may require greater attention paid to their working methods or may need more supervision (*Byers v Head Wrightson & Co. Ltd*). In *Paris v Stepney Borough Council* the plaintiff was employed to scrape away rust and other superfluous rubbish which had accumulated underneath buses. It was not customary to provide goggles for this kind of work. However, the plaintiff had only one good eye, and he was totally blinded when a splinter entered his good eye. It was held that the employers were liable for damages. They should have foreseen that there was a risk of greater injury to this employee if he was not given adequate safety precautions and the fact that they may not have been under a duty to provide goggles to other employees was irrelevant.

8.21 A higher standard of care is also owed to employees whose command of English language is insufficient to understand or comply with safety instructions, to ensure that as a result they do not cause injuries to themselves or to others. In *James v Hepworth and Grandage Ltd* the employers put up large notices urging employees to wear spats for their personal protection. Unknown to them, one of their employees could not read, and when he was injured he claimed damages from his employer. His claim failed. He had observed other workers wearing spats and his failure to make any enquiries led the court to believe that even if he had been informed about the contents of the notice, he would still not have worn the spats. But with the growth of foreign labour in British factories, the problem is one for obvious concern, especially as immigrants tend to concentrate in those industries which are most likely to have serious safety hazards. The task of the safety officer to ensure the health and safety of such employees is likely to be very onerous in practice (see *Hawkins v Ian Ross (Castings) Ltd*).

8.22 The duty is owed by the employer to his employees, but this latter term is not one which is very precise, and a number of problems have arisen. In *Ferguson v John Dawson & Partners Ltd* a man agreed to work on the "lump", ie as a self-employed bricklayer, but when he was injured, he sued, claiming the employers owed a duty to him as an employee. By a majority, the Court of Appeal upheld his claim, holding that it was the substance of the relationship, not the form, which was the determining factor in deciding whether or not a person was an employee in the legal sense.

8.23 As a general rule, each employer must ensure the safety of his own employees, and is not responsible in his capacity as an employer for the safety of employees of other employers. However, where a number of employees from different firms are employed on one job, there is a duty to coordinate the work in a safe manner (*McArdle v Andmac Roofing Co.*).

8.24 In some circumstances, the employer may be liable for the safety of a loaned employee, ie one who has been seconded to work for him, or, conversely there are circumstances when the employer will still be responsible for the safety of his employee who has been seconded to someone else. The courts will look to see which of the two employers retains the right to control the workman (*Mersey Docks and Harbour Board v Coggins and Griffiths*). Thus if a workman is loaned (together with an expensive piece of equipment, such as a crane) or he is an expert in his job so that the second employer cannot exercise any control over the way the work is done, it will be rare that the courts will infer that the right of control vested in the first employer has been transferred to the second. But if an unskilled workman is loaned, it would be easier to infer that there has also been a transfer of the legal responsibility to the second employer (*Garrard v Southey & Co.*). Thus once the right to control has been transferred, the second employer must accept the duty of care to the transferred employee.

The extent of the duty

8.25 The standard of care which must be exercised by the employer is "The care which an ordinary prudent employer would take in all the circumstances" (*Paris v Stepney Borough Council*). The employer does not give an absolute guarantee of health or safety, he only undertakes to take reasonable care and will be liable if there is some lack of care on his part or in failing to foresee something which was reasonably foreseeable. The employee, for his part, must be prepared to take steps for his own safety and look after himself and not expect to be able to blame the employer for everything which happens. In *Vinnyey v Star Paper Mills Ltd*, the plaintiff was instructed by the foreman to clear and clean a floor area which had been made slippery by a viscous fluid. The foreman gave him proper equipment and clear instructions. The plaintiff was injured when he slipped on the floor while doing the work, and it was held that the employers were not liable. There was no reasonably foreseeable risk in performing such a simple task, and they had taken all due care. In *Lazarus v Firestone Tyre and Rubber Co. Ltd* the plaintiff was knocked down in the general rush to get to the canteen. It was held that this was not the sort of behaviour which could be protected against.

8.26 If an employer does not know of the danger and could not reasonably be expected to know, in the light of current knowledge available to him, or did not foresee that there was a potential hazard and could not reasonably be expected to foresee it, he will not be liable. In *Down v Dudley, Coles Long Ltd* an employee was partially deafened by the noise which came from a cartridge assisted hammer gun. At the then state of medical knowledge (ie in 1964) a reasonable employer would not have known of the potential danger in using this particular piece of equipment without providing adequate safety precautions and the employer was held to be not liable for the injury. Clearly, with the wide dissemination of literature on noise hazards nowadays, a different conclusion would be drawn on these facts although the general principle of law remains the same.

8.27 Once a danger has been perceived, the employer must take all reasonable steps to protect the employees from the consequences of those risks which have hitherto been unforeseeable. In *Wright Rubber Co. Ltd, Cassidy v Dunlop Rubber Co. Ltd* the employers used an anti-oxidant known as Nonox S from 1940 onwards. The manufacturers then discovered that the substance was capable of causing bladder cancer and informed the defendants that all employees should be screened and tested. This was not done for some time, and thus the employers, as well as the manufacturers, were held to be liable to the plaintiffs.

8.28 The matter was summarised by Swanwick J in *Stokes v GKN Ltd:*

(a) the employer must take positive steps to ensure the safety of his employees in the light of the knowledge which he has or ought to have
(b) the employer is entitled to follow current recognised practice unless in the light of common sense or new knowledge this is clearly unsound
(c) where there is developing knowledge, the employer must keep reasonably abreast with it, and not be too slow in applying it
(d) if he has greater than average knowledge of the risk, he must take more than average precautions

(e) he must weigh up the risk (in terms of the likelihood of the injury and possible consequences) against the effectiveness of the precautions to be taken to meet the risk and the cost and inconvenience.

8.29 Applying these tests, if the employer falls below the standards of a reasonable and prudent employer he will be liable.

The threefold nature of the duty

8.30 Recent cases have stressed that there is only one single duty on the part of the employer, namely to take reasonable care. However, we may conveniently analyse that duty under three categories.

8.31 *Safe plant, appliances, and premises.* First, all tools, equipment, machinery, plant which the employee uses or comes into contact with and all the employer's premises shall be reasonably safe for work. Thus a failure to provide the necessary equipment (*Williams v Birmingham Battery and Metal Co.*) or providing insufficient equipment (*Machray v Stewarts and Lloyds Ltd*) or providing defective equipment (*Bowater v Rowley Regis Corporation*) will amount to a breach of the duty. There must be a proper and adequate system of inspection and testing, so that defects can be discovered and reported (*Barkway v South Wales Transport Co.*) and then remedied (*Monaghan v Rhodes & Son*). In *Bradford v Robinson Rentals*, a driver was required to go on a 400 mile journey during a bitterly cold spell of weather in a van which was unheated and had cracked windows. He suffered frostbite and his employers were held liable for failing to provide suitable plant. Before putting secondhand machinery into use, it should be checked to make sure that it is serviceable (*Pearce v Round Oak Steel Works Ltd*). If unfenced machinery is liable to eject parts of the machine or materials used by the machine, then a failure to erect suitable and effective guards may well constitute negligence at common law (*Close v Steel Co. of Wales*) irrespective of any liability for a breach of s.14 of the Factories Act (*Kilgollan v Cooke & Co. Ltd*). If the equipment is inherently dangerous, extra precautions must be taken (*Naismith v London Film Productions Ltd*).

8.32 However, if an employer purchases tools or equipment from a reputable supplier and has no knowledge of any defect in them, he will have performed his duty to take care and cannot be held liable for negligence (see *Davie v New Merton Board Mills*). An employee who was injured in consequence could only pursue his remedy against the person responsible for the defect under the general law of negligence (*Donoghue v Stevenson*). In practice, this would frequently be difficult or impossible. The employee would not have the time or resources to do this; it may be that the negligence was due to the acts of a foreign manufacturer, or stevedores at the docks, etc. In view of these problems, the law was changed with the passing of the Employers Liability (Defective Equipment) Act 1969. This provides that if an employee suffers a personal injury in the course of his employment in consequence of a defect in equipment provided by his employer for the purposes of his employer's business, and the defect is attributable wholly or partly to the fault of a third party (whether identified or not), then the defect will be deemed to be attributable to the negligence of the employer. Thus, in such circumstances, the injured employee would sue the employer for his "deemed" negligence, and the latter, for his part, would attempt to recover the amount of damages he has paid out from the third party whose fault it really was. Since the insurance company is the real interested party in such matters, it is they, rather than the employer, who will attempt to make such recovery. The Employers Liability (Compulsory Insurance) Act was also passed in 1969 to ensure that all employers have valid insurance cover to meet personal injuries claims from their employees, and a certificate to this effect must be displayed at the employers' premises (see para 6.1).

The Employer's Liability (Defective Equipment) Act was considered by the Court of Appeal in *Knowles v Liverpool City Council*, where the plaintiff was employed as a "flagger" by the highway authority. He was injured when a flagstone he was handling broke. The flagstone had not been cured properly by the makers. He sued his employers, arguing that the flagstone was "equipment provided by the employer for the purpose of the employer's business", and his claim was upheld. The Court of Appeal refused to draw a distinction between "equipment" and materials, for to do so would create unjustifiable inconsistencies. There is little doubt that the decision represents a purposive construction of the Act.

8.33 If an employer is aware of any defect in tools, etc which have been purchased from outside he should withdraw them from circulation. In *Taylor v Rover Car Co. Ltd* a batch of chisels had been badly hardened by the manufacturers. One had, in fact, shattered without causing an injury, but the rest of the batch were still being used and another chisel shattered, injuring the plaintiff in his eye. The employers were held liable.

8.34 The employer must also ensure that the premises are reasonably safe for all persons who come on to the premises (under the Occupiers Liability Act 1957) as well as for his employees in particular. In *Paine v Colne Valley Electricity Supply Co. Ltd* an employee was electrocuted because a kiosk had not been properly insulated and the employers were held liable. However, it must be stressed that the employer need only take reasonable care, and this is a question of fact and degree in each case. In *Latimer v AEC Ltd* a factory floor was flooded after a heavy storm, and a mixture of oil and water made the floor slippery. The employers put down sand and sawdust, but there was not enough to treat the whole of the factory in this way, and the plaintiff was injured. The employers were held not liable. The danger was not grave enough to warrant closing down the whole factory (which would have been unreasonable, bearing in mind that the risk was fairly minimal). However, had there been dangers because the structure had been damaged, different considerations would have applied.

8.35 The employer cannot be responsible for the premises of other persons where his employees have to work, but as he still owes to them a duty of care, he must ensure that a safe system of work is laid down.

8.36 *Safe system of work.* Secondly, the employer is responsible for the overall planning of the work operations so that it can be carried out safely. This includes the layout of the work, the systems laid down, training and supervision, the provision of warnings, protective clothing, protective equipment, special instructions, etc. Regard must be had for the fact that the employee will be forgetful, careless, as well as inadvertent, but the employer cannot guard against outright stupidity or perversity.

8.37 A reasonable employer will frequently be expected to be aware of the existence of risks to health and safety even though they arise out of commonplace activities. In *Pape v Cumbria County Council* the plaintiff was employed as a part-time cleaner. During her work, she used various chemical cleaning agents. The employer made available rubber gloves, but never advised her to use them, or warned of the dangers of the risks of working without them. She contracted dermatitis and eczema on her hands, which then spread to other parts of her body, and she was forced to give up her employment. She sued for damages. It was held that the employer should have warned her of the dangers arising from the use of chemical cleaning agents, instructed her to use the rubber gloves provided, and taken reasonable steps to ensure that those instructions were carried out. The knowledge of the risk was not so well known to employees that the mere provision of rubber gloves was sufficient performance of the employer's duty of care.

8.38 Examples of a failure to provide a safe system of work abound. In *Barcock v Brighton Corporation*, the plaintiff was employed at an electric substation. A certain method of testing was in operation which was unsafe and in consequence the employee was injured. The employers were held liable. If there are safety precautions laid down, the employee must know about them; if safety equipment is provided, it must be available for use. In *Finch v Telegraph Construction and Maintenance Co. Ltd* the plaintiff was employed as a grinder. Goggles were provided for this work, but no one told him where to find them. The employers were held liable when he was injured by a piece of flying metal. Whether a system is safe in any particular case will be a question of fact, to be decided on the evidence available.

8.39 The more dangerous the process, the greater is the need to ensure that it is safe. On the other hand, the employer cannot be expected to take over-elaborate precautions when dealing with simple and obvious dangers (*Vinnyey v Star Paper Mills*). A situation which gives rise to some legal difficulties is where the employer provides safety precautions or equipment, but the employee fails or refuses to use or wear them. Is the duty a mere passive one, to provide and do no more? Or is it a more active one, to exhort or even compel their use? It is suggested that the answer to these questions can be summarised in four propositions.

8.40 (1) If the risk is an obvious one, and the injury which may result from the failure to use the precautions is not likely to be serious, then the employer's duty is a mere passive one of providing the necessary precautions, informing the employees of their presence, and leaving it to them to decide whether or not to use them. In *Qualcast (Wolverhampton) Ltd v Haynes* an experienced workman was splashed by molten metal on his legs. Spats were available, but the employers did nothing to ensure they were worn. The injury, though doubtless painful, was not of a serious nature, and the employers were held not liable.

8.41 Similarly, in *Smith v Scott Bowyers Ltd*, the plaintiff had been provided with wellington boots to protect against the risk of slipping on a wet floor. The soles of the boots had worn smooth, and he asked for and was given another pair. These also wore smooth but he did not seek a replacement pair. He then slipped on the wet floor and was injured. The trial judge held that the employers were liable, as they had taken no steps to emphasise to employees the importance of wearing boots with soles in good condition, but the decision was reversed on appeal. The employee knew why the boots were provided and he knew they would be replaced if the soles were worn. The Court of Appeal cited with approval a dictum from *Qualcast (Wolverhampton) Ltd v Haynes* that "there may be cases in which an employer does not discharge his duty of care towards his workmen merely by providing an article of safety equipment, but the courts should be circumspect in filling out that duty with the much vaguer obligation of encouraging, exhorting or instructing workmen or a particular workman to make regular use of what is provided."

8.42 However, it is submitted that the employer must not only provide the safety precautions, but also inform the employee of the relevant work risks involved. Thus in *Campbell v Lothian Health Board* the plaintiff was a cleaner in a hospital. She was provided with rubber gloves, but was not told about the risks from using detergents, or how these risks could be reduced by using the gloves provided. The employers were thus held liable when she contracted dermatitis.

8.43 (2) If the risk is that of a serious injury, then the duty of the employer is a higher one of doing all he can to ensure that the precautions are used. In *Nolan v Dental Manufacturing Co. Ltd* a toolsetter was injured when a chip flew off a grinding wheel. Because of the seriousness of the injury should one occur, it was held that the employers should have insisted that protective goggles should be worn.

8.44 (3) If the risk is an insidious one, or one the seriousness of which the employee would not readily appreciate, then again, it is the duty of the employer to do all he can by way of propaganda, constant reminders, exhortation, education, etc to try to get the employees to use the precautions. In *Berry v Stone Manganese* the plaintiff was working in an environment where the noise levels were dangerously high. Ear muffs had been provided, but little effort was made to ensure their use. It was held that the workmen would not readily appreciate the dangers of injury to their hearing if they did not use the ear muffs and the employers were liable for failing to take further steps to impress on the plaintiff the need to use the protective equipment.

8.45 (4) When the employer has done all he can do (and in the context of safety and health, this means doing a great deal), when he has laid down a safe system, provided the necessary safety precautions and equipment, instructed on their use, advised how they should be used properly, pointed out the risks involved if they are not used, and given constant reminders about their use, then he can do no more and he will be absolved from liability. Admittedly, this does not solve the problem, which is how to ensure that employees are protected from their own folly. Various ways of dealing with the enforcement of safety rules will be discussed in chapter 9.

8.46 If an employee is working on the premises of another, the employer must still take reasonable care for that employee's safety. There may well be some limits to what he can do, but this does not absolve him from doing what he can. In particular, he must ensure that a safe system of working is laid down, give clear instructions as to how to deal with obvious dangers, and tell him to refuse to work if there is an obvious hazard. In *Wilson v Tyneside Window Cleaning Co.* the plaintiff was a window cleaner who had, in the course of his employment over a period of ten years, cleaned certain windows at a brewery on a number of occasions. One day he pulled on a handle, which was rotten, and fell backwards, sustaining injuries. His claim against his employers failed. He knew the woodwork was rotten and he had been instructed not to clean windows if they were not safe. This may be contrasted with *General Cleaning Contractors Ltd v Christmas*, where in almost identical circumstances, the employee succeeded in his claim. The distinction appears to be that in *Christmas*, the employers provided safety belts, but there were certain premises where these could not be used and there was a failure to instruct the employees to test for defective sashes before the work could proceed. Further, the employers could have provided ladders or taken other steps to ensure that the work could be performed safely.

8.47 *Reasonably competent fellow employees.* Finally, if an employer engages an incompetent employee whose actions injure another employee, the employer will be liable for a failure to take reasonable care. In *Hudson v Ridge Manufacturing Co. Ltd* an employee was known for his habit of committing practical jokes. One day he carried one of his pranks too far and injured a fellow employee. The employer was held to be liable. The practical answer in such cases is, after due warning, to firmly dispense with the services of such a person, for he is a menace to himself and to others. On the other hand, an employer will not be liable if he has no reason to suspect that practical jokes are being played, for such acts are outside the scope of the employee's employment, and not done for the purpose of the employer's business (*Smith v Crossley Bros*). In *Coddington v International Harvester Co. of Great Britain Ltd* an employee, for a joke, kicked a tin of burning thinner in the direction of another employee. The latter was scorched with flames and in the agony of the moment kicked the tin away so that it enveloped the plaintiff, causing him severe burns. The employers were held not liable. There was nothing in the previous conduct of the guilty employee to suggest that he might be a danger to others and his act was totally unconnected with his employment.

8.48 If an employer appoints an inexperienced person to perform highly dangerous tasks, he may be liable if through lack of experience another employee is injured (*Butler v Fife Coal Co.*).

Proof of negligence

8.49 As a general rule, the burden is upon the plaintiff in an action to affirmatively prove his case. In other words, he must show that the defendant owed to him a duty to take care, that the defendant was in breach of that duty by being negligent and that as a result of that negligence the plaintiff suffered damage. To assist him in such an action, there are a number of rules of evidence and procedure, designed to enable each side to clarify the issues in dispute and to avoid surprises at the actual court of trial. Thus the court may make an order for inspection of the premises or machinery, it can order one party to disclose documents, records, etc to another, it can order that a party should make further and better particulars of his case, and so on. In *Waugh v British Railways Board* the plaintiff's widow sued for damages, alleging that the defendant's negligence caused the death of her husband. She sought the disclosure of an accident report which was prepared by the defendants partly for the purpose of establishing the cause of the accident and partly to assist their legal advisers to conduct the proceeding before the courts. The defendants resisted the disclosure on the ground of professional privilege, but it was held that the report should be disclosed. A document is only privileged if the dominant purpose of making it in the first place was for the purpose of legal proceedings. If the document had a dual purpose, it would not be covered by professional privilege. The implications of this case in practice can be very wide. Thus if an accident report is made as a result of an employee being away from work for more than three days because of an accident, it will not be privileged. If a safety officer makes a report of an accident, it will also not be privileged. However, once legal proceedings have been commenced, or are imminent, a report prepared for the exclusive use of the company's legal advisers would be privileged.

8.50 Further assistance can be obtained from the inspector under s.28(9) of HSWA which enables him to disclose any factual information about any accident to persons who are a party to any civil proceedings arising from the accident.

8.51 Another rule of evidence which may be of considerable assistance to a plaintiff is *res ipsa loquitor* (let the facts speak for themselves) (see chapter 1). This will apply when the circumstances are such that an accident would not have occurred unless there had been some want of care by the defendant. Thus if a barrel of flour fell out of a building and injured a person walking below, the latter would find it extremely difficult to show that someone was negligent (*Byrne v Boadle*). In practice, he would not need to do so. He would invoke the rule *res ipsa loquitor*; barrels of flour do not normally fall out of buildings unless someone was negligent, and thus the burden of proof is thrown back to the other party to show that he had, in fact, taken reasonable care. *Res ipsa loquitor* is a rule of evidence, not a rule of law. It creates a rebuttable presumption that there was negligence. If the presumption is rebutted by evidence then the burden of proof is thrown back to the plaintiff to prove his claim in the usual way.

Defences to a common law action

8.52 Only one action may be brought against an employer in respect of injuries which arise out of one incident. The plaintiff, therefore, must plead his case in such a manner that all possible legal headings are covered. Thus, where appropriate, he should claim in respect of a breach of statutory duty and common law negligence, for each is a separate cause of action. The defendant, for his part, must also be prepared to defend each heading where liability is claimed.

8.53 Since there is no automatic right to compensation, the following defences may be raised.

Denial of negligence

8.54 The employer may deny that he has failed to take reasonable care, or claim that he did everything which a reasonable employer would have done in the circumstances (see *Latimer v AEC Ltd*, above). For example, in *Brown v Rolls Royce Ltd* the plaintiff contracted dermatitis owing to the use of an industrial oil. The employers did not provide a barrier cream on the advice of their chief medical officer, who doubted its efficacy. The employers were held not to be negligent in failing to provide the barrier cream. They were entitled to rely on the skilled judgment of a competent adviser and no more could be expected. Indeed, the medical officer had instituted his own preventative methods, as a result of which the incidence of dermatitis in the factory had steadily decreased.

8.55 An employer can only take reasonable care within the limits of the knowledge which he has or ought reasonably to have. After all, not every firm (particularly the smaller employer) can have available the resources of specialist expertise. Nonetheless, they must pay attention to current literature which may be available, either from their trade or employers' associations or from other sources. In *Graham v CWS Ltd* the plaintiff worked in a furniture workshop where an electric sanding machine gave off a quantity of fine wood dust. This settled on his skin and caused dermatitis. No general precautions were taken against this, athough the manager received all the information which was commonly circulated in the trade. It was held that the employers were not liable. They had fulfilled their duty to take reasonable care by keeping up to date with current knowledge, and were not to blame for not knowing something which only a specialist adviser would have known.

8.56 An employer will not be liable for an injury if he does not owe a duty of care to the injured person. In *Hewett v Alf Brown's Transport Ltd*, the plaintiff's husband was a lorry driver. He was employed to drive a lorry which contained lead oxide. While working he wore overalls and boots. When he returned home, the plaintiff would bang the overalls against a garden wall and bang or wipe his boots. While doing this she either inhaled lead oxide powder or came into contact with it. She was subsequently diagnosed as suffering from lead poisoning and sued her husband's employers for personal injuries suffered.

8.57 It was held that the action would be dismissed. It was accepted that if there was a foreseeable risk to the families of an employee from clothing, etc worn by the employee at work which became contaminated, then the employers owed a duty of care to those family members. However, in the circumstances of this case, the plaintiff's husband had not been exposed to any risk while removing the lead oxide waste from the site, and therefore the employers were not in breach of their duty to the plaintiff's husband either under the Control of Lead at Work Regulations 1980 or at common law. Consequently, there was no breach of duty to the plaintiff.

The sole fault of the employee

8.58 If it can be shown that the injury was the sole fault of the employee, again the employer will not be liable. In *Jones v Lionite Specialities Ltd* a foreman became addicted to a chemical vapour from a tank. One weekend he was found dead, having fallen into the tank. The employers were not liable. In *Brophy v Bradfield* a lorry driver was found dead inside a boiler house, having been overcome by fumes. He had no reason to be there and the employers had no reason to suspect his presence. Again, they were not liable. And in *Horne v Lec Refrigeration* a toolsetter had been fully instructed on the safety precautions to be followed when operating a machine, but was killed when he failed to operate the safety drill. The employers were held not liable, even though they were in breach of their statutory duty to ensure secure fencing.

8.59 If the claim is based on a breach of statutory duty, the employee cannot, by his own actions, put his employer in breach and then try to blame the employer for that breach. Provided the employer has done all that the statute requires him to do, ie provided the proper equipment, given training, provided adequate supervision, laid down safe systems, and so on, there will come a point when the injured workman will only have himself to blame. In *Ginty v Belmont Building Supplies Ltd* the plaintiff was working on a roof. He knew that it was in a defective state and that he should not work without boards. The employer provided the boards for use, but the plaintiff failed to use them and fell through the roof. It was held that the employers were not liable for his injuries. They had done all they could do, and the accident was the sole fault of the plaintiff.

8.60 In the nineteenth century the courts were inclined to the view that a worker accepted the risks which were inherent in the occupation and had to rely on his own skill and care, but this view was firmly discounted in the leading case of *Smith v Baker & Sons* and the defence of *volenti non fit injuria* (a person consents to the risks of being injured) is no longer applicable. The fact that the employee knows that there is a risk in the occupation does not mean that he consents to that risk because the employer has been negligent in failing to guard against it. This must apply, *a fortiori*, if the employer is under a statutory duty to guard against the risk. However, if the statutory duty is placed on the employee, and he disregards it, the employer is entitled to raise the defence of *volenti*. In *ICI Ltd v Shatwell*, the Quarries (Explosives) Regulations 1959 provided that no testing of an electrical circuit for shotfiring should be done unless all persons in the vicinity had withdrawn to shelter. This duty, which was imposed in order to avoid risks from premature explosions, was laid on the employees. The employers had also prohibited such acts. Two employees were injured when they acted in breach of the regulations and the employers' instructions, and it was held that the employers could successfully raise the defence of *volenti*.

8.61 The payment of "danger money" to certain types of employees (eg stunt artistes) may indicate that there is an inherent risk in the occupation which cannot be adequately guarded against, but the real question to be asked is, was the employer negligent? Further, the Unfair Contract Terms Act 1977 states that a person cannot by reference to a contract term or prominently displayed notice exclude or restrict his liability for death or personal injury resulting from negligence.

Causation

8.62 Although the employer may be negligent, it must still be shown that the injury resulted from that negligence. If the injury would have happened had the employer not been negligent, then the breach of the duty to take care has not caused the damage (see *McWilliams v Sir William Arrol*, para 8.16). Where a breach of statutory duty is alleged, the same principles apply. In *Bonnington Castings Ltd v Wardlaw* the plaintiff was subjected to a silica dust in premises where there was inadequate ventilation. It was held that the fact that there was a breach of statutory duty (to provide ventilation, Factories Act, s.4) and the fact that the employee suffered from pneumoconiosis did not by itself lead to the conclusion that the breach caused the injury. There must be sufficient evidence to link the one with the other. However, a more liberal view was taken in *Gardiner v Motherwell Machinery and Scrap Co.* (see chapter 1) where the court took the view that evidential presumptions may arise in such cases.

Contributory negligence

8.63 This defence is based on the Law Reform (Contributory Negligence) Act 1945 which provides that if a person is injured, partly because of his own fault, and partly due to the fault of another, damages shall be reduced to the extent the court thinks fit, having regard to the claimant's share in the responsibility for the damage. This defence is successfully raised in many cases. The employer will argue that even if he were negligent, the employee failed to take care for his own safety, and the court may well decide to reduce the damages awarded. There is no scientific basis for determining the percentage reduction and appeal courts may well take a different view of the apportionment of the blame between the parties.

Limitations of actions

8.64 Any action for personal injury or death must be commenced within three years from the date of the accident (Limitation Act 1980, s.11). This means that the actual writ must be issued within the three-year period, although the date of the court hearing may be considerably delayed thereafter. In accident cases the date of the incident is usually ascertainable, but in some circumstances, where the injury is a result of a constant exposure to the hazard, eg noise which causes deafness (*Berry v Stone Manganese*) or exposure to dangerous substances which can cause cancer (*Wright v Dunlop Rubber Co. Ltd*) or pneumoconiosis (*Cartwright v GKN Sankey Ltd*) it is not possible to fix a date, or the plaintiff will be unaware of the date. In such circumstances, the Limitations Act 1980, s.14 provides that the three year period shall begin to run from the date on which the cause of action accrued or the date when the plaintiff had knowledge of the fact that the injury was significant and that this was due to the employer's negligence. Knowledge in this connection means actual or constructive knowledge, ie knowledge which the plaintiff had or ought to have had. For example, if he has received medical advice which indicated an injury, he should know of the likely cause. The Act permits the court to exercise its discretion and allow the action to proceed even though it is outside the limitation period, if it is equitable to do so, having regard to the factors which brought about the delay, the effect it may have on the credibility of witnesses after such a period of time, the disability suffered by the plaintiff, and whether he acted promptly once he realised that he may have a cause of action having regard to any expert advice he may have received.

Damages

8.65 If an employee is killed in the course of his employment, an action may be brought by his personal representatives for the benefit of the estate of the deceased, under the provisions of the Law Reform (Miscellaneous Provisions) Act 1934. Damages will be awarded under the following heads:

(a) loss of expectation of life (this is usually a fairly modest sum)
(b) pain and suffering (if any) up to the time of death
(c) loss of earnings up to the time of death.

8.66 A further action may be brought simultaneously by his dependants for their own benefit under the Fatal Accidents Act 1976 based on the loss of financial support suffered by, eg his wife, children or other dependants. Any other money due to the estate is not taken into account, eg personal insurances, pensions payable to the widow, etc but any award made under the 1934 Act will be taken into account. In other words, the one action is brought for the benefit of the deceased estate, the other for the benefit of his family dependants. The two claims are invariably settled together.

8.67 The quantum of damages awarded is frequently a matter of speculation. No amount of money can compensate for the loss of a faculty (arm, leg, eyesight, etc) but the courts must try to do their best and awards will take account of inflation, the permanency of the injury, the effect of earning capacity, additional expenses incurred, and so on.

Rights against insurers

8.68 In normal circumstances, any damages awarded to an injured employee would be paid by the employer's insurance company. If the employer is no longer in business (eg because he has died, gone bankrupt or gone into liquidation, etc) then, provided his liability has been established, it is possible to pursue a claim against the insurance company under the provisions of the Third Parties (Rights against Insurers) Act 1930. But if, at the time of the claim, the employer's liability has not been established, this is not possible. For example, in *Bradley v Eagle Star Insurance Co. Ltd*, the plaintiff claimed that she contracted byssinosis whilst working in a mill from 1933 to 1970. The employer company had been dissolved in 1976, but her claim was not made until 1984. It was not possible to resurrect the company in order to establish liability and hence her claim failed.

8.69 However, by s.141 of the Companies Act 1989 (which amends s.651 of the Companies Act 1985) it is possible to make an application to have a company re-registered and its dissolution declared void. Once this is done the action may be proceeded with in the normal way and if liability is shown, the insurance company (who will in any case be the real defendant) will be obliged to pay any damages awarded.

Vicarious liability

8.70 The tort of vicarious liability arises when one person (who has not committed a wrongful act) is legally liable for the acts of another person which cause injury or damage to a third person. Of course the actual wrongdoer is always personally liable, but in practice he is unlikely to have sufficient financial resources to meet any claim and so the injured party will seek to make the first person vicariously liable. There are two general circumstances to consider: (a) the liability of an employer for the wrongful acts of his employees which are committed in the course of their employment, and (b) the liability of the employer for the acts of an independent contractor.

8.71 The general principle is that an employer will be liable for the acts of his employee which injure a third party if the employee, when doing the act, was acting in the course of his employment, in the sense that he was doing that which he was employed to do. Thus in *Century Insurance Co. v Northern Ireland Road Transport Board*, an employee was the driver of a petrol tanker. While he was discharging petrol at a garage forecourt, he lit a cigarette and the subsequent explosion caused damage to the garage. It was held that the employer was liable. The act (of lighting a cigarette) was a negligent way of doing that which he was employed to do, namely discharge petrol from the tanker, and he was therefore still acting in the course of his employment.

8.72 The act can be in the course of employment even though the employee was not authorised to do it. In *Kay v ITW Ltd* a fork-lift truck driver found that the path was obstructed by a lorry. Although he was not authorised to do so, he drove it out of the way and in so doing injured a fellow employee. Again, the employer was held liable, for the act was for the purpose of the employer's business.

8.73 If the employer expressly prohibits an employee from doing something, this will not necessarily remove the act from the course of the employment. In *Rose v*

Plenty the employer prohibited milkmen from permitting children to ride on milk floats. In breach of this instruction, a milkman engaged a young boy to help him deliver and collect milk bottles and as a result of negligent driving by the milkman the boy was injured. It was held that the employer, nonetheless, was liable, for the act (of permitting a boy to ride on the vehicle) was done for the purpose of the employer's business, and hence was still within the scope of employment. But in *Conway v George Wimpey Ltd* the employers issued an instruction to their drivers that no person other than a fellow employee was to be permitted to ride as a passenger in their lorries. In breach of this instruction, a driver gave a lift to a hitchhiker, who was injured following an accident. It was held that the employers were not liable, for the express prohibition had taken the act (of giving lifts) outside the scope of the employment and it had nothing to do with the employers' business.

8.74 If an employee does an act which is unauthorised or prohibited, it has been suggested that the test may well be, would a reasonable man consider that the act was part and parcel of the employee's employment, or was it so divergent from it as to be alien from it? In the former case, the employer would be vicariously liable for the act, in the latter case he would not (see *Harrison v Michelin Tyre Co. Ltd*).

8.75 An employee may be acting in the course of his employment even if he is outside working hours or away from the employer's premises. In *Poland v Parr* an employee was going home from work when he saw a boy trying to steal property from the employer's lorry. The employee struck the boy a hard blow, causing serious injury. It was held that the employer was liable, for the employee was acting in what he believed to be the employer's interests by protecting his property, even though his methods were somewhat over-enthusiastic.

8.76 But excessive zeal or force may take the act outside the course of the employment. In *Warren v Henley's Garage Ltd* a garage forecourt attendant had a violent argument with a customer and committed an assault on him. The employers were held not liable, for this was not part of his duties and the employee was pursuing a personal vendetta. Similarly, in *Hilton v Thomas Burton (Rhodes) Ltd* some workers were driven to a building site in the firm's lorry. After working for a short time, they made a journey in the lorry to a nearby pub and this was repeated several times during the day. As they were being driven back from the pub the plaintiff's husband was killed following a road accident, caused by the fault of the driver of the lorry. The employer was held not liable, for it could not be said that while driving to and from the pub the driver was acting in the course of his employment.

8.77 If an employee is travelling to and from work in a vehicle (whether or not provided by his employer) he will be acting in the course of his employment if, at the material time, he is going about his employer's business. The duty to turn up to work must not be confused with being on duty while travelling to work. In *Smith v Stages and Darlington Insulation Co. Ltd*, the House of Lords laid down a series of propositions.

(1) An employee travelling to work is not generally in the course of his employment, but if he is obliged by his contract of employment to use the employer's transport he will normally be regarded as being in the course of his employment while doing so.
(2) Travelling in the employer's time between workplaces, or in the course of a peripatetic occupation will be in the course of employment.
(3) Receipt of wages (but not a travelling allowance) will indicate that the employee is travelling in the employer's time and for his benefit and will be in the course of employment, and the fact that the employee has a discretion as to the mode and time of travelling will not generally affect this.
(4) An employee travelling in his employer's time from his ordinary residence to a workplace other than his regular place of work or in the course of a peripatetic occupation or to the scene of an emergency will be acting in the course of his employment.
(5) A deviation or interruption of the journey (unless merely incidental to the journey) will, for the time being, take the employee out of the course of his employment. Thus if the employee is driving in the course of his employment, and then departs from his normal route, he will be engaged "on a frolic of his own" (*Storey v Ashton*), and once he seeks to rejoin his normal route, it is a question of fact and degree as to whether or not he is in the course of his employment.
(6) Return journeys are to be treated on the same footing as outward journeys.

8.78 These propositions are always subject to any express arrangements which may be made between the employer and employee, and do not always apply to salaried employees, with regard to whom the touchstone of payment made in the employee's time is not generally significant.

8.79 An employer is not generally liable for the wrongful acts of an independent contractor. The main difficulty here is to distinguish between an independent contractor and an employee—the former being employed under a contract *for* services, the latter employed under a contract *of* service. However, an employer may be liable (a) if he authorises the act, (b) if the independent contractor is carrying out a hazardous activity over which the employer has some control (see *Holliday v National Telephone Co.*) or (c) if he coordinates or controls the activities of a number of independent contractors (*McArdle v Andmac Roofing Co.*).

8.80 The reality of the situation is frequently to decide which insurance company is going to pay the damages. In road accidents, the dispute will usually be between one company holding the employers' liability insurance and another company holding the road traffic insurance; so far as independent contractors are concerned, the dispute will usually be between the insurance companies holding the respective employers' liability insurance. However, there are many situations which occur when one (or neither) of the parties will be insured and liability must be established in accordance with the above principles.

Liability of others

8.81 Hitherto we have considered the liability of an employer for his failure to take reasonable care for the health and safety of his employees. There are, additionally, a number of other people who are not employers, but who may, in the particular circumstances of the case, owe a duty of care to ensure that another person (including, for our purposes, the employees of an employer) is not injured or does not suffer damage. This is merely a further application of the general law of negligence. Sometimes, the injured party will sue the employer and the other alleged wrongdoer jointly, leaving it to the court to apportion blame and responsibility accordingly. For example, in *Driver v William Willett (Contractors) Ltd*, a building contractor engaged a firm of safety consultants to advise on safety requirements and compliance with the relevant regulations. They failed to advise the employers to discontinue the unsafe use of a hoist, with the result that an employee was injured. He sued his employers and the safety consultant. The former were held to be 40% to blame for the accident, the latter 60%. Further, the employers were entitled to recover from the safety consultants the sum which they were liable to pay the injured employee.

8.82 This principle can be extended to other circumstances, eg a main contractor who employs a number of subcontractors (*McArdle v Andmac Roofing*, see para 7.88), manufacturers who fail to provide adequate and meaningful information about the dangers associated with their products (*Cook v Englehard Industries Ltd*) occupiers of premises, and so on. As Lord McMillan stated in *Donoghue v Stevenson* "... the categories of negligence are never closed".

Occupiers' liability

8.83 At common law, an occupier of premises owed legal duties to those people who came on to his premises, but the extent of those duties varied in accordance with the legal status which was ascribed to them, ie contractual invitee, invitee, licencee, etc. Because of the unnecessary legal complications which arose, the common law rules were swept away by the Occupiers' Liability Act 1957, which introduced a common duty of care to all lawful visitors (see also Occupiers' Liability (Scotland) Act 1960).

8.84 The Act provides that an occupier is to take such care in all the circumstances as is reasonable to ensure that a visitor will be reasonably safe in using the premises for the purposes for which he was invited or permitted to be there.

8.85 However, it was recognised that a person exercising his calling would be expected to appreciate risks ordinarily incidental to the work (eg a window cleaner, see *General Cleaning Contractors v Christmas*, para 8.46). An occupier must expect children to be less careful than adults, and if he puts up some form of warning, this will not discharge his legal duty unless in all the circumstances it is sufficient. As a general rule, an occupier is not liable for the risks which have been created by an independent contractor.

8.86 The position with regard to trespassers was left unaltered by the Act, the common law rule being that the occupier owed no duty of care to such persons. However, in *British Railways Board v Herrington*, the House of Lords held that if an occupier knew that trespassers were on the land, and knew of physical facts in relation to the land which would constitute a serious risk to those trespassers, he would owe a duty to take reasonable steps to enable the trespasser to avoid the danger. Common humanity dictated that the occupier should not ignore the problem.

8.87 Following Herrington's case, Parliament passed the Occupiers' Liability Act 1984, which provides that an occupier of premises owes a duty to trespassers if:

(a) he knows there is a risk because of the state of the premises
(b) he knows the trespasser will be on the premises, and
(c) the risk was one which the occupier could reasonably be expected to provide some protection against.

State insurance benefits

8.88 An employed person who is injured at work may make a claim for financial assistance under the scheme which is now contained in the Social Security Contributions and Benefits Act 1992 and the regulations made thereunder. The right to claim is independent of any right of action which may or may not exist at common law for negligence or breach of statutory duty, or indeed any other remedy, for the State scheme is a form of insurance policy, paid for partly by contributions from the employer and employee. Further, questions of fault, blame, contributory conduct, etc are irrelevant to the issue of claiming benefits, provided the employee is within the scope of the relevant provisions.

8.89 The basic outline of the scheme is to provide compensation for a person who suffers a personal injury caused by accident arising out of and in the course of his employment (s.94), or a prescribed disease or personal injury due to the nature of that employment (s.108). Provided certain criteria are met, a claimant may be able to claim certain benefits.

Industrial injuries

8.90 The following criteria must be met.

8.91 There must be a personal injury. This can mean physical or mental injury, such as nervous shock (*Yates v South Kirkby etc Collieries*). However, physical damage to one's property (eg spectacles, clothing, etc) is not covered by the scheme.

8.92 The injury must have been caused by an accident. This word is not defined and a general common sense approach must be used. An accident may occur even though the injury was deliberately caused and intended, at least, if one looks at the incident from the point of view of the victim rather than the perpetrator. Thus, in *Trim Joint District School Board v Kelly* a schoolmaster was killed by the deliberate act of some pupils, and this was held to be an "accident". An accident is "an untoward event, which is not expected or designed" (*Fenton v Thorley & Co. Ltd*). This must be distinguished from a process which takes place over a period of time (which, though not an accident, may well be a prescribed industrial disease). Thus the gradual contraction of an illness is not an accident, as, for example, when a doctor contracts tuberculosis as a result of a series of penetrations, though a series of events taken together may constitute an accident, eg several minor burns which cumulatively produce a major injury. It will be clear that the borderline between some of the cases is extremely thin and undefined (see R(I)6/91, para 7.55).

8.93 The accident must have arisen out of, and in the course of, the employment. This phrase has also given rise to difficulty. "In the course of employment" refers to the elements of time, place of work and job contents. The accident must have occurred after the employment has commenced and before it has terminated, but it is not necessary that the injured person shall actually be working. Thus he is still in the course of his employment if he is having a meal break or making preparations to start or leave work. If an employee is injured whilst at his normal place of work, he is generally within the course of his employment, eg a safety representative performing his functions as such. Some difficulty is experienced with those cases where the employee works in a public place, for the object of the statute is not to compensate for risks common to the general public. Thus if a salesman is injured in a car accident while travelling around to make calls on customers, he would not be entitled to claim. A person is still within the course of his employment if he is doing something which is reasonably incidental to that employment, eg stopping to talk to a fellow worker. However, in *R v National Insurance Commissioner, ex parte Michael*, a policeman was injured while playing football for his local police force. Such activities, though not within his contractual obligations, were encouraged, but it was held that playing football was not part of his ordinary work, and was not reasonably incidental thereto.

8.94 The next requirement is that the accident must arise out of the employment. This represents the causal link between the two. "Was it part of the injured man's employment to hazard, suffer or to do that which caused his injury?" (*Lancashire and Yorkshire Rly Co. v Highley*). The decisions in this branch of the law are equally disparate, as each case will be determined on its own facts. Thus an injured employee is not disbarred from claiming in respect of his own negligence or misconduct, unless his action created a risk which was entirely different from that which was inherent in his employment in normal circumstances. Further, there is a statutory presumption that if an accident arises in the course of the employment, it is deemed to have arisen out of the employment in the absence of evidence to the contrary (s.94(3)).

8.95 In addition, the Act deals with four special situations.

8.96 (1) An accident shall be deemed to arise out of the course of the employment even though at the time of the accident he was acting contrary to a statutory provision or a regulation or orders given by his employer, or is acting without instructions from his employer, provided the accident would still have been deemed to arise out of his employment had he not been acting in contravention of the law or his employer's instructions and the act was done for the purpose of the employer's trade or business (s.98). Thus if a workman is doing something he was forbidden by law to do, or not authorised to do, he may still be entitled to benefit provided, in the absence of such legal rule or instruction, he was in the course of the employment and acted for the purpose of the employer's business.

8.97 (2) An accident which occurs while the employee is travelling to or from work (with the express or implied permission of the employer) as a passenger in a vehicle shall be deemed to arise out of and in the course of the employment, notwithstanding that the employee was under no obligation to use the transport, if the accident would have been deemed to have so arisen had he been under such an obligation and the vehicle is being operated by or on behalf of the employer (or some other person by arrangement with the employer) and it is not being operated in the ordinary course of public transport. In other words, the employee may be entitled to benefits if he is injured when using transport provided by his employer (s.99).

8.98 (3) An accident which happens while the employee is at any premises at which for the time being he is employed for the purpose of his employer's trade or business shall be deemed to arise out of and in the course of the employment if it happens while he is taking steps on an actual or supposed emergency, and he is trying to rescue, succour or protect persons who are in peril, or while he is trying to avert or minimise serious damage to property (s.100).

8.99 (4) An accident shall be treated as arising out of the employment if it arises in the course of the employment and it is caused by another person's misconduct, skylarking or negligence, or the behaviour or presence of any animal, or he is struck by lightning, and the employee did not directly or indirectly induce or contribute towards the happening (s.101).

Prescribed diseases and injuries

8.100 A person who suffers from a prescribed disease or injury, which is a disease or injury due to the nature of the employment, is also entitled to claim benefits under the Act. The disease or injury must be one which has been prescribed as such by the Secretary of State, if he is satisfied that it ought to be treated as a risk of the occupation (and not just a risk common to all employments) and that it is attributable to the nature of the employment (s.108).

8.101 There is a presumption that if the employee works in the prescribed employment and he contracts the prescribed disease or suffers the prescribed injury, the disease or injury will be regarded as being due to the nature of the employment unless the contrary is proved (s.109).

8.102 The Secretary of State may also make special provision by regulations for cases of pneumoconiosis which is accompanied by tuberculosis, emphysema and chronic bronchitis, and for occupational deafness and byssinosis.

Benefits under the Act

8.103 A considerable number of changes have been made to the industrial injuries benefits which were formerly payable under the Social Security Act 1975. Benefits which have been abolished include industrial injury benefit (replaced by sickness benefit), death benefit, unemployability supplement, and so on. Special hardship allowance was replaced by reduced earnings allowance and this too is no longer payable in respect of accidents or claims which occur after 1 October 1990. Certain benefits already granted will continue to be paid, but, so far as new claims are concerned, there are only three benefits payable, namely, disablement benefit, constant attendance allowance and exceptionally severe disablement allowance.

8.104 (a) Disablement benefit (s.103). This is payable as a pension if as a result of the relevant accident or prescribed disease there is a loss of a physical or mental faculty amounting to not less than 14%. The assessment of the extent of the disability, and questions as to whether the disability results from the relevant accident or employment are to be determined by the medical authorities. The pension is payable after 15 weeks from the date of the accident.

8.105 (b) Constant Attendance Allowance (s.104). If there is a 100% loss of a faculty, so that the claimant requires constant attendance, a constant attendance allowance is payable.

8.106 (c) If constant care allowance is paid at the maximum rate, and the claimant is likely to be permanently in need of attendance, then exceptionally severe disablement allowance is payable (s.105).

Claims for benefit

8.107 These will be dealt with initially by the local insurance officer. There is a right of appeal from his decision to the local appeal tribunal, to which matters may also be referred by the insurance officer. An appeal will then lie to the commissioner. Certain matters may be referred by the insurance officer direct to the Secretary of State or to the Attendance Allowance Board for a determination.

8.108 Questions which relate to disablement pensions, such as whether or not the applicant has lost a faculty or the degree of disability are referred to the medical board, with a right of appeal to a medical appeal tribunal.

Reporting accidents by employees

8.109 Under the Social Security (Claims and Payments) Regulations 1979 every employee is required to report an accident which results in a personal injury to himself and in respect of which he intends to claim industrial injuries benefits. The report may be made orally, or in writing, but must be made as soon as is practicable after the accident has occurred. The report may be made by the employee, or by someone acting on his behalf, and it may be given to the employer or some person acting on his behalf, or to his foreman or supervisor. Form B1 510 may be used for this purpose.

Other legal remedies

8.110 An employee who is injured by an act which amounts to a criminal offence on the part of some person may find that he is unable to sue his employer for compensation, for the employer will not have broken any legal duty towards him. However, in 1964 Parliament created the Criminal Injuries Compensation Board, which may make *ex gratia* payments in such circumstances. These arise when a person suffers personal injury directly attributable to a crime of violence or attempting to arrest an offender. The injury must be one for which compensation of more than £1,000 will be awarded, the circumstances of the incident must be reported to the police and the applicant has given all reasonable assistance to the Board, particularly in relation to any medical reports which may be required. Injuries caused by traffic offences are excluded from the scheme, unless there is a deliberate attempt to run the applicant down.

8.111 By way of example, we may cite the case of *Charlton v Forrest Printing Ink Co.*, where the plaintiff was a manager at the defendants' works. One of his duties was to collect the wages from the bank. In 1974 there was an unsuccessful attempt to snatch the wages and thus the managing director gave instructions to those who were to collect the wages that they should take precautions, such as varying the route taken each week, using different modes of transport and sending different people. Despite these instructions, a pattern of collection tended to develop. In 1977, when the plaintiff was returning from the bank, he was attacked by bandits who threw ammonia into his face, causing severe damage to his eyesight. He claimed damages from his employers, arguing that they had failed to take reasonable care for his safety. In the High Court, the judge accepted the argument that although the sum of money involved was only small (£1,500), in view of the previous robbery, it would have been reasonable to use a professional security firm for this task and hence the employers were in breach of their common law duty to take sensible precautions to protect employees who were involved in a hazardous task. This decision was reversed by the Court of Appeal. Proper steps had been taken to instruct the employees to vary their methods used for collecting the wages. It was unreasonable to expect the employers to guard against a possibility which would not influence the mind of a reasonable man. Statistics showed that the majority of firms of this size did not employ specialist security firms. Hence, the employers were not negligent. However, Lord Denning went on to point out that the applicant would no doubt have a good claim if he applied to the Criminal Injuries Compensation Board.

8.112 Another type of scheme is operated by the Motor Insurers' Bureau, which was set up in 1969 by an agreement between insurance companies and the Ministry of Transport. If a person suffers death or injury arising out of the use of a motor vehicle, and he is unable to trace the person responsible, or the person responsible is unable to pay compensation (usually because he is uninsured), then the board will accept the liability to compensate the injured party, the damages to be assessed in a like manner as a court applying the normal legal principles would assess. In practice, the bureau nominates an insurance company to accept the risk and the latter will then seek to recover the damages paid (insofar as they are able to do so) from the wrongdoer.

8.113 The Pneumoconiosis etc (Workers' Compensation) Act 1979 provides for lump sum payments to be made to persons who are disabled by industrial lung diseases (pneumoconiosis, byssinosis and diffuse mesothelioma). The conditions are that the claimant must be entitled to disablement benefit under the Social Security Contributions and Benefits Act 1992 (para 8.104), he must be unable to recover damages from his employer because the latter has gone out of business and no legal action has been brought or compromised. This scheme is an interesting example of the State providing compensation to injured workers in circumstances where tort liability claims would not be met. A similar scheme for victims of pneumoconiosis has been in force on a voluntary basis for coal miners since 1974 and is operated by the National Coal Board.

8.114 Finally, under the Powers of Criminal Courts Act 1973 the criminal courts (including magistrates' courts) are empowered to make an award of compensation to a person who has been injured or suffered any loss or damage as a result of the commission of a criminal offence. This is in addition to any other punishment which the court may impose. The maximum amount of compensation which may be awarded is (currently) £5,000. Thus, in strict theory, if an employer was prosecuted for an offence under HSWA or other legislation for an offence which caused personal injury or damage to an employee's property, the latter could apply to the court for a compensation order to be made at the same time. Indeed, the court can make such an order on its own volition. If the injured person subsequently brings civil proceedings, any compensation awarded in the criminal court will be taken into account. Although this is a useful provision for dealing with claims in respect of minor personal injuries, very little use appears to have been made of it.

9

Enforcing health and safety rules

9.1 The duty to ensure that health and safety policies are observed falls on all those who are involved in the work processes—on the employer, management, safety officer, shop steward, safety representative, supervisor, and employees generally. Each must play his own special role in ensuring that health and safety policies are laid down, adequately promulgated, and, perhaps the most important of all, carried out in practice.

9.2 The basis for these duties is the contract of employment, which is essentially mutual agreement. It follows that a breach of contract by either side entitles the other party to pursue whatever remedy is appropriate in the circumstances. Thus, on the one hand, if the employee commits a breach of contract, the employer may terminate the contract, and, in theory—at any rate—sue for any damage he has suffered. On the other hand, there is an implied term of the contract that the employer will take reasonable care to ensure the health and safety of his employees while at work (*Matthews v Kuwait Bechtel Corporation*), and if he is in breach of that term the employee may "accept" the breach and resign (this is the doctrine of constructive dismissal). If he has suffered damages, he may claim in respect of these. Additionally, if the employer's breach has caused injury, he may sue in tort for a breach of duty imposed by law (see chapter 8).

Appointment procedures

9.3 Health and safety policies begin with appointment procedures. In theory, the employer should ensure that all his employees are fit, healthy, with 100% vision and hearing capacity and not suffering from any disability which renders them liable to an accident or to make them a hazard to themselves or to others. To this aim, pre-employment medicals may be used. The policy is as foolish in practice as it is sound in theory. By the time pre-medical screening has eliminated all those who are not suffering or who have never suffered from some medical disability, either there will be no one left to employ or employment will be limited to a few Amazons!

9.4 Pre-medical screening must be related to a particular hazard. Judgment must be made on medical and safety grounds, not on the ground of general health. Epileptics can do a useful job of work, depending on the degree of their illness and the nature of the danger they face at work. Disabled employees can do work other than act as car park attendants, if the work is matched to their abilities and care is taken to ensure their safety. Dedication to health and safety does not mean the exclusion of a large section of the population from employment opportunities. Thus the object of pre-medical employment must not be to exclude certain people, but to place employees in the appropriate niche.

9.5 Nonetheless, critical situations may require extreme measures. In *Jeffries v BP Tankers Ltd* it was the company's policy not to employ people as radio operators on ships if they had had any history of cardiac disease. They dismissed a radio officer who had suffered a heart attack, even though he had made an excellent recovery. His dismissal was held to be fair, for the policy was one which had to be rigorously enforced for reasons which the employers were satisfied were necessary.

9.6 Health considerations are equally relevant. In *Panesar v Néstle Co. Ltd* the applicant, who was a Sikh, enquired about a job with the respondents. He was told that there was a company rule prohibiting beards, and since he was not prepared to shave off his beard he was not interviewed for the job. He claimed that he had been unlawfully discriminated against on grounds of race (see Race Relations Act 1976, s.4). It was conceded that he had been indirectly discriminated against, in that the proportion of applicants of his race who could comply with the requirement that they should not wear a beard was smaller than the proportion of applicants from other racial groups (Race Relations Act, s.1(1)(b)). However, the requirement or condition was capable of being justified on grounds other than race, namely hygiene considerations and his claim failed before the industrial tribunal, the EAT and the Court of Appeal. It should be noted that it would be discriminatory on grounds of race to refuse employment to (or to dismiss from employment) a Sikh who refuses to wear a head protection helmet on a building site, as long as he is wearing a turban (see para 7.123).

Works rules

9.7 A rule book is a valuable source of information and guidance, and should in particular lay down precise rules concerning all aspects of health, safety and welfare. The contents of the rule book should be incorporated into the contract of employment, they should be updated in accordance with developments and experience and should be contained in a booklet which can be retained by the employee. Somewhat strangely, s.1 of the Employment Protection (Consolidation) Act (which requires employers to give to their employees written particulars of their terms and conditions of employment) includes a requirement to provide information relating to disciplinary and grievance procedures, but specifically states that this does not apply to rules, disciplinary decisions, grievances or procedures relating to health or safety at work. This exclusion is even more surprising when it is realised that health and safety matters probably constitute the biggest single cause of disciplinary problems. It is to be hoped that this gap in the law is remedied in the near future. However, the Code of Practice issued by the Advisory, Conciliation and

Arbitration Service (ACAS) entitled *Disciplinary Practice and Procedures in Employment* states that "When drawing up rules the aim should be to specify clearly and concisely those necessary for the efficient and safe performance of work".

9.8 Particular attention should be paid to publicising the contents of the rule book to new employees on some form of induction course. Those rules which are mandatory can be highlighted and disciplinary procedures and sanctions which will follow a breach can be spelt out. Attention can be paid to ways of communicating the rules to immigrant employees and others whose command of English is less than perfect, so that they are unable to plead ignorance. Records can be kept of when and how the rules were communicated to each individual concerned.

9.9 Rules which relate to health and safety are designed to protect employees individually and collectively and should therefore contain sanctions in the event of a breach. The matter was expressed forcefully by Stephenson LJ in *Bux v Slough Metals Ltd*, when he said "The employer must make the law of the land the rule of the factory". In other words, the employee should be informed as to the legal requirements and warned that he is breaking the law if he fails to wear or use the precautions provided, for which he can be prosecuted. He can also be warned that he faces disciplinary action or even dismissal if he acts in breach of the safety rules or the legal requirements.

9.10 To achieve consistency in procedure, certain principles must be observed. First, the rules must be promulgated. This means that they must be brought to the attention of the employees in a suitable form. It is no longer regarded as being sufficient to post rules on a notice board or hide them in the personnel office. In *Pitts v Rivertex Ltd*, the employee was dismissed for breaking a works rule, a copy of which could be found on the notice board. It was held that if a rule was so important that a breach would be visited by instant dismissal, it should have been expressly communicated to all the employees concerned.

9.11 Second, rules must be reasonable. An employer may impose his own standards, but they must have a sound functional basis and not be old-fashioned, out-of-date or based on prejudice. In *Talbot v Hugh Fulton Ltd* the applicant was dismissed for having long hair in breach of the company's rules. The dismissal was held to be unfair. Management did not specify the length of hair which was acceptable, it was not shown that long hair was a safety hazard and the rule did not appear to apply to women with long hair. Clearly, it was an act of prejudice against the hair style of the day. By contrast, we can cite *Marsh v Judge International*, where a youth had hair which was two feet six inches long, reaching down to his waist. The factory inspector told the employers that they would be prosecuted if the youth caught his hair in any machinery and was injured, and so, after due warnings to cut his hair (which he ignored) the youth was dismissed. This was held to be fair. The rule, in the nature of an instruction, was perfectly reasonable and in the interests of safety. It follows that an employer can lay down suitable safety standards provided they are functional and reasonable (*Singh v Lyons Maid Ltd*).

9.12 Third, the rules must be consistently enforced. If a rule is generally disregarded, or no severe sanction is imposed for a breach, then it may be unfair to act on it without giving some indication that there was to be a change in enforcement policy. Thus in *Bendall v Paine and Betteridge* the applicant had been employed for fifteen years. From time to time he was told to put out a cigarette he was smoking, as there was a fire risk. One day, he was summarily dismissed for smoking and this was held to be unfair. In the past he had been warned without it being brought home to him that he was risking instant dismissal. He should have been given a final, written warning before he was dismissed.

9.13 Health and safety rules should therefore be drawn up in accordance with the hazards perceived. This requires a careful assessment of the likely risks, based on the nature of the firm, its processes, the workforce, and all other relevant considerations. The following are some examples of the more common rules which should be considered.

Smoking

9.14 If there is a risk of fire (*Bendall v Paine and Betteridge*) or a health hazard (*Unkles v Milanda Bread Co.*), clear rules should be laid down informing employees that anyone caught smoking in the prohibited area will be instantly dismissed. Areas where smoking is permitted should be clearly defined. Additionally, the employer must pay attention to the statutory provisions which prohibit smoking. These include:

(a)	Celluloid Regulations 1921	no person shall be allowed to smoke in any room in which celluloid is manufactured, manipulated or stored
(b)	Control of Lead at Work Regulations 1980	an employee shall not smoke in any place which he has reason to believe is contaminated by lead
(c)	Manufacture of Cinematograph Film Regulations 1928	no person shall take any smoking materials into any room in which cinematograph film is manufactured, repaired, manipulated or used
(d)	Cinematograph Film Stripping Regulations 1939	no smoking materials shall be allowed in any part of the premises
(e)	Highly Flammable Liquids and Liquified Petroleum Gases Regulations 1972	no smoking shall be permitted when flammable liquids are present. The occupier shall take all reasonable practicable steps to ensure compliance, including the display of a clear and bold notice
(f)	Factories (Testing of Aircraft Engines and Accessories) Special Regulations 1952	no smoking shall be allowed in any place where aircraft engines are being tested

(g)	Control of Asbestos at WorkRegulations 1987	employees should not smoke in any "designated asbestos area"
(h)	Magnesium (Grinding of Castings and other articles) Special Regulations 1946	no smoking shall be permitted within 20 feet of certain processes or in any room where magnesium dust is being kept, or smoke when handling magnesium dust
(i)	Petroleum Spirit (Conveyance by Road) Regulations 1957	
(j)	Organic Peroxides (Conveyance by Road) Regulations 1973	
(k)	Explosives Act 1875, s.10	

Several other relevant statutory provisions were repealed by the COSHH Regulations. For the introduction of a "No Smoking" policy, see para 7.50. Note also the Workplace (Health, Safety and Welfare) Regulations 1992 which require that rest rooms and rest areas shall include suitable arrangements to protect non-smokers from discomfort caused by tobacco smoke, see para 4.98).

Eating and drinking

9.15 The following provisions prohibiting the partaking of food or drink are in force:

(a)	Non-Ferrous Metals (Melting and Founding) Regulations 1962	no person shall be permitted to take a main meal in any indoor workroom where processes are being carried on
(b)	Control of Lead at Work Regulations 1980	an employee shall not eat or drink in any place which he has reason to believe to be contaminated by lead
(c)	Control of Asbestos at Work Regulations 1987	employees should not eat or drink in any "designated asbestos area"

Fighting

9.16 This can lead to a serious accident occurring, and the rule should lay down that anyone caught fighting will be subject to disciplinary proceedings. It cannot be right to state that fighting will lead to instant dismissal; after all, if two people are fighting, one may be merely defending himself, or the one who started the fight may have been provoked. A careful investigation of the circumstances is therefore called for. Further, two people may be fighting in a no-risk area, which may invoke a disciplinary sanction less than dismissal. The rule, therefore, should indicate the discretionary power of management. In *Taylor v Parsons Peebles Ltd*, the applicant had been employed for twenty years by the company before he was dismissed after he was involved in a fight. It was the company's policy to dismiss automatically any employee who deliberately struck another employee. The industrial tribunal held that the dismissal was fair, because the policy was applied consistently and the other employee who was fighting was also dismissed. On appeal, the decision was reversed by the EAT. In determining whether a decision to dismiss was reasonable, the proper test was not the employer's policy, but what the reaction would be of a reasonable employer in the circumstances. The employers' rules of conduct must be considered in the light of how it would be applied by a reasonable employer. Taking into account the fact that the employee had been employed for twenty years with no serious disciplinary record against him, a reasonable employer would not have applied the rigid sanction of automatic dismissal. In other words, the employer must be consistent in his procedures, but flexible in his punishment. He must consider the gravity of the offence, and the circumstances of the offender. The employee must always be given at least an opportunity to plead mitigating circumstances, although the weight to be attached to such a plea is for the employer to decide, bearing in mind the gravity of the incident. In *Taylor*'s case, because the employers had applied a policy consistently without taking into account relevant factors, the dismissal was unfair. However, it was also held that the employee had contributed towards his dismissal, and compensation was reduced by 25 per cent.

Drunkenness

9.17 If an employee is found to be drunk on the premises or to have been drinking alcohol, it may be good policy to escort him off the premises, for the fact of drinking *per se* may not be sufficient to warrant dismissal (*McGibbon v Gillespie Building Co.*). However, disciplinary proceedings should normally be instituted. If the drunkenness is such as to cause or constitute a serious safety hazard, different considerations would apply. In these circumstances, the matter should be dealt with as a serious disciplinary offence and the procedure should be activated immediately. In *Abercrombie v Alexander Thomson & Son* the applicant was found to be in an intoxicated state while in charge of a crane. A decision was taken to dismiss him, but this was not implemented until two weeks had elapsed, during which time he was permitted to carry on working. The dismissal was held to be unfair. By delaying the taking of action, the employers had condoned the offence.

9.18 A person who has symptoms of alchoholism should not be put through the disciplinary procedure immediately. Rather, his condition should be treated as an illness, and medical advice should be sought as to his condition and the likelihood of recovery or obtaining treatment. HSE has produced an occasional paper entitled *The Problem Drinker at Work* which discusses the benefits which can be obtained from a policy aimed at encouraging problem drinkers to seek assistance and treatment.

9.19 There are some statutory provisions which also need to be borne in mind. These include the Work in Compressed Air Special Regulations 1958 (no person employed shall consume alcohol whilst in compressed air). There are a number of regulations which prohibit the consumption of food and drink whilst engaged in certain processes, and these could certainly cover drinking alcohol (see above).

Skylarking

9.20 The dangers from employees who indulge in horseplay or skylarking have already been noted (see chapter 8 and see *Harrison v Michelin Tyre Co. Ltd*), and the rules should state that such conduct will not be tolerated. Employees, particularly the young or inexperienced, should be given final written warnings, indicating that any repetition will result in instant dismissal. In *Hudson v Ridge Manufacturing Co.* the plaintiff was injured as a result of a prank played upon him by an employee who was known for horseplay. The employers were held to be liable. It was stated that "If a fellow workman . . . by his habitual conduct is likely to prove a source of danger to his fellow employees, a duty lies fairly and squarely on the employer to remove the source of danger".

Breach of safety rules

9.21 Again, this will be dealt with in accordance with the hazard incurred. In *Martin v Yorkshire Imperial Metals* the applicant tied down a lever on an automatic lathe with a piece of wire. This had the effect of bypassing the safety device, for the machine could only be used if the operator used both hands. It was held that his dismissal was fair. He knew that he would be dismissed if he neglected to use the safety device. In *Ashworth v John Needham & Sons* the applicant acted in flagrant breach of safety rules by putting a fence around a hole in the ground instead of replacing a plate. After the matter had been discussed with the company's safety officer and a trade union official he was dismissed. This was held to be fair, as a serious accident could have happened.

Failure to use safety equipment

9.22 Again, the gravity of the consequences should be a factor which determines the severity of the sanction and the rules should be flexible enough to deal with this situation. Thus in *Frizzell v Flanders* the employee was provided with a gas mask while working in a tank. He was seen working without the mask and was dismissed. This was held to be fair. It was essential to enforce rigorously the use of safety equipment. On the other hand, in *Henry v Vauxhall Motors Ltd* the employee discovered that his safety helmet was missing. He was provided with another one which, he claimed, was uncomfortable. He therefore worked without the helmet and persisted in his refusal after being instructed to wear it by the foreman. He was dismissed, but this was held to be unfair. There was no proper enquiry into the reasons for his refusal. Nonetheless, the industrial tribunal thought that he had contributed substantially to his dismissal and reduced his compensation award by 60 per cent.

Hygiene observance

9.23 It may be necessary to enforce standards of hygiene because there is a risk of contamination to the product or a health hazard to employees. For example, in *Gill v*

Walls Meat Co., the applicant, who was a Sikh, was employed to work with open meat. He did not have a beard at the time he commenced employment, but at some later stage "he was converted to the paths of righteousness", donned a turban, and grew a beard. He was told that he could not be employed on that particular job whilst wearing his beard, but he refused to shave it off. He was offered alternative employment where he would be permitted to have his beard, but he refused and was dismissed. This was held to be fair. Similarly, the rules should provide that employees who have been suffering from or in contact with a contagious disease should be encouraged to report to the appropriate medical adviser before commencing work to ensure that they are "clear" and do not transmit the disease or illness to other employees or do not cause contamination of the product. Personal hygiene is also important. In *Singh v John Laing & Sons* a company rule provided that anyone misusing the toilet facilities would be liable to instant dismissal. The applicant was seen urinating in a room he had been instructed to clean and he was thus dismissed. This was held to be fair. He knew of the rule, had a good command of English and could offer little by way of explanation. After all, employers are legally bound to maintain toilet facilities in clean and proper condition and thus it is not wrong to enforce high standards of hygiene (*Singh v Elliotts Bricks*).

Health generally

9.24 In some circumstances, general ill health must be reported and noted, so as not to cause a hazard. In *Singh-Deu v Chloride Metals Ltd* the employee worked in a lead smelting factory where it was essential to remain alert in view of the dangerous processes which were being carried on. He was sent home by the works doctor after complaining of feeling unwell. He visited his own doctor who diagnosed paranoid schizophrenia. He was then examined by a specialist, after which he attempted to return to work. However, the works doctor would not allow him to return unless the specialist gave an assurance that there would be no recurrence of the illness. This assurance was not forthcoming and so he was dismissed, as the works manager, mindful of the inherently dangerous processes being carried on in the lead factory, was not prepared to take the responsibility of allowing him back at work. The dismissal was held to be fair. It was not reasonable to continue to employ him in a delicately balanced job which called for a high degree of concentration. The effect of a relapse on the applicant and on others could have been devastating had a mistake or error been made. A similar result was reached in *Balogun v Lucas Batteries Ltd* where the applicant, who was working with lead, suffered from hypertension. Medical evidence clearly indicated that this type of work can be harmful, especially to those who have an existing predisposition to certain types of illnesses, including hypertension. Efforts were made to find him alternative work, but there was no suitable job and he was dismissed. This was held to be fair. His continued employment constituted a risk to himself and to others.

Vandalism

9.25 An employee who misuses the company's property or interferes with anything provided for the use of employees generally can be disciplined. This is especially true if there is an interference or misuse of anything provided for health, safety and welfare, for there is also a breach of s.8 of HSWA. In *Ferodo Ltd v Barnes* an employee was dismissed after the company decided he had been committing an act of vandalism in the lavatories. The industrial tribunal decided that the dismissal was unfair, as they were not satisfied that in fact the employee had committed this act. This was reversed on appeal. It is not the duty of the industrial tribunal to re-try the case. It was their duty to see that management acted reasonably and as long as there had been a fair and proper investigation, the industrial tribunal should not substitute their judgment for that of management.

Neglect

9.26 An employee who is incompetent or neglectful in his work may cause some damage to the work processes and the matter should be regarded as a disciplinary problem. The first duty of management is to ensure that the employee has been trained properly, supervised adequately, has sufficient support staff and sufficient facilities to do the job in question. An employee who is suffering from irredeemable incompetence can be offered alternative employment, failing which a dismissal will be fair. If he is suffering from neglectful incompetence, he should be warned, in accordance with the gravity of the case. However, if the neglect is of such a dangerous nature that there is the likelihood of serious injury to persons or damage to property, then the matter becomes a health and safety issue and can be dealt with as such. This could result in a disciplinary sanction which is appropriate to the case, and even dismissal. In *Taylor v Alidair Ltd*, an airline pilot landed his aeroplane in a manner which caused some concern and consternation among the rest of the crew and passengers. After a full investigation it was decided that he had been negligent and he was dismissed. This was held to be fair. There are some activities the consequences of which are so serious and grave that it is not possible to risk a repetition. Nor does it matter if the neglect causes a risk of injury to fellow employees or to the public or customers of the employer. Thus if an employee fails to follow the prescribed safety checks (*Wilcox v HGS*) or the work is done in a negligent manner which creates a risk (*McGibbon v Gillespie*) he may be dismissed.

Sleeping on duty

9.27 Whatever may be the position in other work situations, it has always been recognised that safety considerations must be regarded as being paramount. In *Jenkins v British Gypsum Ltd* the applicant was employed on the night shift checking and taking the temperature of a gas-fired kiln. He was found asleep on duty and was dismissed, even though there was no specific rule to cover this situation. Nonetheless, his dismissal was held to be fair. It was essential for him to monitor the temperature regularly as a safeguard, and the fact that he had to be aroused in order to do his work constituted gross misconduct. "Alertness is essential from the safety angle", commented the industrial tribunal.

Training

9.28 Since the employer is under an obligation to train his employees in safety and health matters, and since also the employee is obliged to cooperate with the employer in the performance of the statutory duties, an employee who refuses to be trained may be fairly dismissed. In *Minter v Willingborough Foundries Ltd* the applicant was a nurse employed at the employer's factory. There were complaints about her standards of medical care and she was asked to go on a training course, but she refused. Subsequently, there were further complaints and she was again asked to undertake further training, and again she refused. Because the employers were concerned about their obligations under HSWA, she was dismissed. The EAT upheld the finding of the industrial tribunal that the dismissal was fair. The course would not have involved her in any expense or inconvenience and she did not give an adequate explanation for her refusal.

Other dangerous practices

9.29 No list of actions which are to be the subject of disciplinary sanctions can be exhaustive and each employer must try to complete the list in accordance with his own situation, as well as covering the unexpected. Thus, it should be fairly obvious that it is an extremely dangerous practice to light a bonfire near to flammable material (*Bussey v CSW Engineering Ltd*) or to fire air guns whilst at work, even though this is during the lunch hour (*Shipside (Ruthin) Ltd v T&GWU*). To smoke in a wood and paint shop (*Bendall v Paine*), to walk out, leaving a high pressure steam boiler on (*Gannon v Firth*), to drive a vehicle without being qualified to do so, or to drive a vehicle so badly that the brakes overheat (*Potter v Rich*) are all examples of conduct capable of attracting disciplinary sanctions, including dismissal. The list can be extended almost indefinitely.

Enforcing safety rules: action by the employee

9.30 If there is an actual injury to an employee, he can, of course, pursue whatever remedy is available to him at common law (see chapter 8). If there is a threatened injury, the situation is more delicate. Since it is an implied term of the contract of employment that the employer will ensure the health and safety of his employees, the employer will be in breach of contract if he fails to take the necessary steps. In these circumstances, the employee will accept the breach, and resign, but, in law, since he was entitled to resign by virtue of the employer's conduct, it is the employer who has "dismissed" the employee. In technical terms, even though the employee has resigned, he may bring a claim for "constructive dismissal", and, provided he has the requisite period of continuous employment (or not asserting a statutory right, for which no period of continuous employment is required), he can bring his claim before the industrial tribunal for compensation. For example, in *British Aircraft Corporation v Austin* the employee asked her supervisor for a pair of prescription safety glasses. After waiting several months, during which time she heard nothing further, she resigned and claimed constructive dismissal. Her claim succeeded. It was an implied term of the contract that the employers would ensure her safety, and by failing to investigate her request and provide the necessary safety precaution they had broken the contract. It will be noted at this stage that the inaction was the fault of the supervisor, yet it was the employer who was held responsible.

9.31 A constructive dismissal claim does not need to be based on an actual injury (see *Knight v Barra Shipping Co. Ltd*); the fear of the possibility is sufficient. In *Keys v Shoefayre Ltd* the employee worked in a shop which was robbed in day time by a gang of youths. The manager was asked by the employee to do something about the security of the premises, but he replied that there was nothing he could do. A further daytime robbery took place, and the employee resigned and claimed constructive dismissal on the ground that the premises were no longer safe to work in. Her claim succeeded. The employers were obliged to take reasonable steps to operate a safe system of work and to provide safe premises. The industrial tribunal thought that it might have been possible to install a telephone, or to employ a male assistant, etc. (It may be doubted whether the first suggestion would be effective, or whether the second would be lawful, but this merely illustrates the unworldliness of some industrial tribunals.)

9.32 However, the contractual obligation of the employer is no higher than the duty owed in tort, which is to take reasonable care only. The employer does not guarantee absolutely the safety of his employees. In *Buttars v Holo-Krome Ltd* the employee was injured when a blank flew out of a machine and struck his safety glasses. A lens broke and injured his eye. When he returned to work he asked for a guard to be fitted to the machine, but the employers claimed it was safe. He resigned and claimed constructive dismissal, but the claim was rejected. The accident had been reported to the factory inspector who agreed that the machine was safe and proposed to take no further action on the incident. There was no duty on the part of the employer to fence, for this duty does not apply to parts of the machine or materials used by the machine which fly out (*Nicholls v Austin*, see chapter 5). The accident was a freak one, it was not usual to fit guards on this type of machine. In these circumstances, the industrial tribunal thought that the employers had not broken the contract, and hence there was no constructive dismissal.

9.33 More difficult is the situation where the employee responds to the employer's breach by action other than resignation. In *Mariner v Domestic and Industrial Polythene Ltd*, some workers discovered that the temperature in the workplace was 53 degrees. There was no fuel left for heating, as the employer had allowed his supplies to run down in anticipation of the warmer weather. The workers therefore went home, and the following day, when they reported for work, they were dismissed for going on strike. In law, a complaint of unfair dismissal, brought about because a person is taking part in a strike or other industrial action cannot normally be entertained by the industrial tribunal (Employment Protection (Consolidated) Act 1978, s.62), but in this case, the industrial tribunal decided that the workers had not been on strike, for they had not withdrawn their labour in breach of their employment contracts. It was the employer who was in breach, for he had allowed the temperature to fall below the statutory minimum and there is an implied term in the contract of employment that the employer will perform his statutory obligations. If he fails to do so, the employees are merely responding to the breach, not acting themselves in breach.

9.34 It is sound practice for an employee to take matters up with the appropriate level of management before taking the drastic step of resignation, but there appears to be no legal reason why he should do so, for the fact that the employer is in breach of contract should be sufficient (*Seligman and Latz Ltd v McHugh*). Thus in *Graham Oxley Tool Steels Ltd v Firth*, the employee had to work in a small bay near to an open door. The only heating came from a radiant heater fixed to the ceiling. One day, when the weather was very cold, she was kept waiting outside the entrance to the premises and eventually she decided to go home. She subsequently resigned and claimed constructive dismissal. She had made no previous complaint about the cold working conditions, although a subsequent visit from the factory inspector revealed that the temperature was 49 degrees. Her claim for unfair dismissal succeeded. The employer was in breach of his obligation to provide a proper working environment and the failure to do so constituted a fundamental breach of contract which entitled her to resign.

9.35 Nonetheless, a well-drawn-up grievance procedure which is incorporated into the contract may prove to be a useful method of preventing claims of this nature, particularly in respect of those "innocent" breaches, about which the employer knows nothing, or which were accidental or unintentional. Thus an employee who fails or refuses to use that procedure may find that he is not entitled to claim constructive dismissal, or, if he does succeed, he may find that his compensation award is reduced, on the ground that by failing to adopt the grievance procedure, he contributed towards his own dismissal, or failed to mitigate against his loss.

9.36 A claim based on constructive dismissal must be tested by industrial tribunals in accordance with the principles of employment law relating to the reasonableness of the employer's conduct, not in accordance with the principles of health and safety law relating to the employer doing something so far as is reasonably practicable. In *Dutton & Clark Ltd v Daly* the employee worked in the office of a building society agency. The employers had installed protective safety devices, including screens, partitions and alarm buttons. However, the premises were subjected to two armed robberies in a space of two months and the employee resigned. She claimed that the safety measures were inadequate and that she was too frightened to work in the premises, and she alleged that by failing to provide adequate security the employers were in breach of a fundamental term of the contract which entitled her to resign and claim that she had been dismissed. An industrial tribunal upheld her claim, but on appeal the EAT remitted the case to another tribunal for further consideration. The test to be applied is whether the safety precautions which were taken were those which a reasonable employer would have taken. This duty is not as high as ensuring safety so far as is reasonably practicable.

9.37 It should finally be pointed out that some of the decisions of the industrial tribunals on constructive dismissal are among the weirdest and most unreliable in employment law generally, and care should be taken not to elevate them into principles of law. The original test formulated in *Western Excavating (EEC) Ltd v Sharp* by the Court of Appeal was, has the employer broken the contract? The more modern approach appears to be, did the employer evince an intention to break the contract? This is slightly different, and neurotic employees who imagine that every little thing which goes wrong in their daily employment automatically gives them a right to claim constructive dismissal should be cautioned about such a false assumption. Further, it must be borne in mind that while constructive dismissal is, in law, a "dismissal", it is not necessarily an unfair dismissal (*Industrial Rubber Products v Gillon*).

Employment protection in health and safety cases

9.38 The Offshore Safety (Protection against Victimisation) Act 1992 gave protection against dismissal (or action short of dismissal) to safety representatives and members of safety committees who worked on offshore installations, and it was intended that such protection should be extended throughout industry. However, the Act was defective, in that it only applied to safety representatives who were appointed by recognised trade unions, whereas EC Directive 89/391 (the Framework Directive, see chapter 4) requires that such protection should be given to all persons with health and safety responsibilities.

9.39 Consequently the Act was repealed by the Trade Union Reform and Employment Rights Act 1993, and new rights were inserted into the Employment Protection (Consolidation) Act 1978. This Act now provided that an employee has the right not to be subjected to any detriment (s.22A), or be dismissed (s.57A) on the grounds that:

(a) having been designated by the employer to carry out activities in connection with preventing or reducing risks to health and safety at work, he carried out (or proposed to carry out) any such activities, or
(b) being a representative of workers on matters of health and safety at work, or a member of a safety committee (whether under statutory or voluntary procedures) he performed (or proposed to perform) any functions as a representative or committee member.

9.40 The above provisions will clearly protect an employee who is a safety assistant (appointed under the Management of Health and Safety at Work Regulations, see Chapter 4) as well as safety representatives and safety committee members, whether appointed by independent trade unions, or elected by the workforce, or nominated or appointed by the employer in non-union situations.

9.41 In addition, every employee will have the right not to be subjected to any detriment, or be dismissed, if:

(a) being at a place where there was no safety representative or safety committee (or where there was, but it was not reasonably practicable to go through those channels) he brought to the employer's attention, by reasonable means, circumstances connected with his work which he reasonably believed were harmful (or potentially so) to health or safety, or
(b) in circumstances of danger which he reasonably believed to be serious and imminent and which he could not reasonably be expected to avert, he left (or proposed to leave) or refused to return to (while the danger persisted) his place of work or any dangerous part of his place of work, or
(c) in circumstances of danger which he reasonably believed to be serious and imminent, he took (or proposed to take) appropriate steps to protect himself or other persons from danger.

9.42 Whether the steps were appropriate is to be judged by reference to all the circumstances, including his knowledge and the facilities and advice he had at the time. But if it was negligent for the employee to act as he did, action taken against him by the employer would not be a detriment or unfair dismissal, as the case may be.

9.43 The aggrieved employee may bring a claim in an industrial tribunal within the usual period of three months. In addition, if he is dismissed, the interim relief procedures will be available, in which case a claim must be brought within seven days.

9.44 The unfair dismissal of a safety assistant or safety representative is an inadmissible reason; the employee does not have to have any period of continuous employment before he can bring his claim, and certain minimum compensation awards apply.

Enforcing safety rules: action by the employer

9.45 Safety rules can be enforced within the context of existing disciplinary procedures. These may be drawn up by management, in consultation with the trade unions or workforce if possible, without their cooperation or agreement if necessary. Details should be given to each employee explaining the steps to be followed, the sanctions which may be applied in accordance with the gravity of the case and the method of appeal. Further reference should be made to the ACAS Code of Practice on Disciplinary Procedure and Practice.

9.46 A disciplinary procedure should have five characteristics:

9.47 (1) There must be a full and proper investigation to the incident. This should be undertaken as soon as possible (*Abercrombie v Thomson & Son*), and consideration should be given to a short period of suspension (with or without pay, in accordance with the contract and/or procedure) pending such investigation.

9.48 (2) The offender must be told of the charge against him. It is no bad thing to put this in writing, particularly if his command of English is weak, or the charge is a serious one, so that he can obtain advice from any available source.

9.49 (3) He should be given an opportunity to state his case, to plead that he didn't do it, or if he did, it was not his fault, or if it was, there were mitigating circumstances which ought to be taken into consideration, etc.

9.50 (4) He should be given the opportunity to be represented, if he so wishes, by a trade union official or shop steward, by a fellow employee, or by anyone who is willing to speak on his behalf.

9.51 (5) He should be given the right of appeal, to a level of management not previously involved in the decision-making process.

9.52 Obviously, the nature of the disciplinary procedure will vary with the size and resources of the firm. One does not expect the same formalities in a small firm as might exist in a large firm. Equally, the sanction which will be imposed will depend on the nature and seriousness of the offence, the circumstances of the individual, and so forth. The purpose of disciplinary sanctions is to improve the conduct of the offender, to deter others from doing the same or similarly wrongful acts, and to protect the individual, other employees, the public and ultimately, the employer. Thus no simple pattern emerges; sometimes the sanction will be corrective in nature, sometimes it will be designed to encourage others not to break the rules. The gravity of the sanction will reflect the objectives to be achieved. In the case of a minor offence, a minor sanction will be imposed, such as a warning, which may be verbal. A repetition of the offence, or a different kind of offence, or a serious offence, would be dealt with by a written warning, which should detail the offence, warn as to the consequences which may flow from a repetition of the offence, or any other offence of a similar or dissimilar nature. A very serious offence should be dealt with by a final warning, or by dismissal.

9.53 Depending on the nature of the offence and the circumstances of the offender, other sanctions might be imposed. Thus, consideration could be given to a period of suspension without pay (provided the disciplinary procedure confers this power), a transfer to other work, or even a "fine" (eg if an employee is failing to use safety equipment), which has been agreed as a recognised type of punishment (perhaps with the proceeds going to an appropriate charity).

Dismissal

9.54 The final power left to the employer is to dismiss the employee. This may be done for a number of reasons.

9.55 First, the circumstances may be so serious that a dangerous situation was created which put the employee or others at risk of serious injury. There are some activities where the degree of safety required is so high, and the consequences of a failure to achieve those standards so potentially serious, that a single departure from them could warrant instant dismissal. For example, in *Taylor v Alidair Ltd* (see above) it would be totally unrealistic to give the pilot a final warning saying "If you land your aeroplane in such an incompetent manner again we will dismiss you", etc. The driver of an express train, the scientist in charge of a nuclear power station, the driver of a vehicle carrying a dangerous chemical, etc, must all display the highest standards of care. In *Wilcox v HGS*, the employee was employed as a converter, changing gas appliances from town gas to natural gas. He was instructed that before he left premises he had to undertake a mandatory safety check, but he failed to do so and was dismissed. The dismissal was held to be fair by the industrial tribunal, although on appeal the case was remitted for reconsideration. If, as he alleged, the employers had persistently ignored the safety regulations, then such acquiescence was a relevant factor to be taken into account in determining whether or not a final warning should have been given.

9.56 Second, an employee may be in serious risk of injury to himself. In *Finch v Betabake (Anglia) Ltd* an apprentice motor mechanic was found to have defective eyesight. A report from an ophthalmic surgeon stated that the lad could not be employed without undue danger to himself and to others and he was therefore dismissed. This was held to be fair. The fact that the employee is willing to take a risk that he may be injured is irrelevant, for the employer may expose himself to civil or criminal liabilities by continuing the employment (*Marsh v Judge International*).

9.57 Third, the situation may arise where the employee's physical condition is such that it amounts to a health or safety hazard. This must be handled carefully; there must be a full investigation, preferably backed with medical reports, there should be consultation with the employee and alternative employment should be considered. In *Spalding v Port of London Authority*, the employee failed a medical examination after it was discovered that he was suffering from deafness. It was recommended that he worked with a hearing aid, but this did not prove to be satisfactory and he was dismissed. This was held to be fair; the company's medical standards were not unnecessarily high, and were justified in order to ensure the safety of the employee and his fellow employees. In *Yarrow v QIS Ltd* the employee was dismissed after it was discovered that he was suffering from psoriasis. Because he had to work with radiography equipment, he was subject to the Ionising Radiation (Unsealed Sources) Regulations, which made it unsafe for him to be employed. This dismissal too was held to be fair. The employers were in danger of breaking the law if they continued to employ him. And in *Parsons v Fisons Ltd* the company's medical adviser noted that the employee had poor vision and only narrowly averted several possible accidents. After a full discussion with the group medical adviser and her general practitioner, she was dismissed. This too was held to be fair. There was no other suitable job for her, and it was not necessary to wait until an accident occurred before taking appropriate action.

9.58 It is important to bear in mind the health and safety of other employees as well as their general comfort and working environment. In *Kenna v Stewart Plastics Ltd* the employee had a series of epileptic fits in an open plan office. The dismissal was held to be fair. The employer had a duty to ensure that other employees could do their work in reasonable working conditions which were physically and mentally conducive to work.

9.59 Fourth, the employee may be dismissed if he refuses to observe the safety instructions or wear the appropriate safety equipment. In *Frizzell v Flanders* the employee was provided with a gas mask while working in a tank. He was seen working without the mask and was dismissed. This was held to be fair. It was essential to enforce the safety precautions rigorously both for his own sake and for the sake of others, and his dismissal would serve as a warning that flagrant breaches of the safety instructions would not be tolerated.

9.60 An overzealousness on the part of the employee to be cossetted against the risks of the employment can also result in his fair dismissal. In *Wood v Brita-Finish Ltd* the employee had been provided with acid-proof gloves, goggles, wellingtons and a protective apron, all of which had been approved by the Factory Inspectorate. He refused to work unless he was also provided with an overall and was dismissed. This was held to be fair. Overalls had proved to be ineffective in the past and contributed nothing to the safety of the employee. In *Howard v Overdale Engineering Ltd* the employee refused to work in a new factory because of dust caused by engineers drilling cables into the floor. The industrial tribunal found that the employers were not in breach of any statutory obligation to prevent impurities from getting into the air or to prevent employees from being subjected to harmful substances, and his dismissal was held to be fair for refusing to obey a lawful order.

9.61 Although an employer is entitled to dismiss if he genuinely and conscientiously believes that there is a health or safety hazard, such dismissals should only be carried out with a full investigation of all the relevant circumstances. A procedural failure is likely to result in a wrong decision being reached and hence an unfair dismissal. In *Milk Marketing Board v Grimes*, the employee was the driver of a milk float. He was almost completely deaf, and could only communicate with his employers by means of written questions and answers. Fearing that there may be an obvious safety hazard, the employee was sent for an examination by the company's occupational health adviser, who reported that the employee was unfit to drive whilst deaf and that a hearing aid would not materially improve matters. He was thus dismissed. Before the industrial tribunal, the employee produced a consultant's report who concluded that the use of a hearing aid would restore his hearing to a tolerable level, which would be adequate for safe driving. Further, he was able to show that he had been driving for 34 years without an accident. Because the employers had not given the employee an opportunity to deal with the question of his incapacity, and because the procedure leading to the dismissal was flawed, the dismissal was held to be unfair.

9.62 It is not the function of the industrial tribunal to determine whether or not the employer is in breach of his common law or statutory duties, as they would not always have sufficient evidence available on which to make such a finding. In *Lindsay v Dunlop Ltd*, workers in the tyre-curing department became concerned about the possible carcinogenic nature of fumes and dust. As a temporary measure, it was agreed to resume normal working with masks being provided. The applicant, however, refused to adopt this course, maintaining that his continued exposure to fumes would endanger his health. His subsequent dismissal was held to be fair. Whether or not the employers were in breach of their obligations under s.63 of the Factories Act was a matter which could only be determined by the courts and in the circumstances the employers had not acted unreasonably.

9.63 If the employee refuses to do the work unless he is provided with the necessary safety precautions, it is up to the employers to make a full and informed investigation into the reasons for the refusal, consideration of whether or not there is justification for the refusal and a communication of the results of the investigation to the employees before the decision to dismiss is taken. If employees make a complaint about the lack of safety precautions, which is sensible, *bona fide* and not frivolous, the employer must take all necessary steps to reassure the employees, and should not just treat the refusal to work as being *per se* a ground for dismissing from employment (see *Atlas Products & Services v Jones*).

9.64 To establish that it is fair to dismiss an employee for refusing to follow the safety rules, or to wear or use the precautions provided, it must be shown (a) the employee knew of the requirement, (b) the employer was consistent in his enforcement policies, and (c) the precautions were suitable for the employee and for the work he was doing. Again, a full investigation into the circumstances is called for. In *Mayhew v Anderson (Stoke Newington) Ltd* an insurance company recommended that the employee be asked to wear protective glasses, stating that the company's insurance cover would be withdrawn if she did not do so. The employers purchased a pair of safety goggles for 78p but she refused to wear them because they were not comfortable. She was warned that if she persisted with her refusal she would be dismissed, and ultimately the threat was carried out. Her dismissal was held to be unfair. She had never refused to wear reasonable eye protectors, only this particular type, which irritated her eyes and were uncomfortable. Custom-made eye protectors were available at a cost of £33, and the industrial tribunal thought that these should have been provided for her, even at the risk of creating a precedent.

9.65 Finally, other reasons prompted by a genuine concern for health and safety can justify dismissal. In *Wilson v Stephen Carter Ltd* the applicant was dismissed after refusing to go on a training course which involved staying away from home for a week and this was held to be fair.

9.66 If lesser disciplinary sanctions do not succeed, the employer may ultimately dismiss a recalcitrant employee, but some employers do not consider this to be a satisfactory solution, as they would rather have the workers working than have the problem of obtaining new staff and training them all over again. At this stage it may be possible to invoke the assistance of the HSE Inspectorate, who could issue a prohibition notice on the employee, which would effectively prevent him from working in contravention of the matters contained in the notice. A failure to comply with this is punishable by a fine or even imprisonment, and this may yet prove to be an effective way of dealing with the problem. At the same time, an employee could be warned that he is acting in breach of his duty under s.7 or 8 of HSWA, which again is a criminal offence.

Suspension on medical grounds

9.67 Section 19 of the Employment Protection (Consolidation) Act provides that where an employee is suspended from work on medical grounds in consequence of:

(a) any requirement imposed by or under the provision of any enactment, or
(b) any recommendation contained in a Code of Practice issued under HSWA,

which, in either case, is a provision specified in Schedule 1 of the Employment Protection (Consolidation) Act, then that employee shall be entitled to be paid during the suspension for a period of up to 26 weeks. The present provisions are as follows:

(1) Control of Lead at Work Regulations 1980
(2) Ionising Radiations Regulations 1985
(3) Control of Substances Hazardous to Health Regulations 1988.

9.68 It will be noted that there must be a suspension on medical grounds. This means the potential effect on the health of the employee, not the actual effect. In other words, the provisions of s.19 are not relevant if an employee is actually off work sick. Nor is the suspension on medical grounds if he is unable to work because a prohibition notice has been imposed. Medical suspension payments can only be claimed when there is a suspension from work in order to comply with a requirement in any of the above provisions, but if he is incapable of working because of any physical or mental disablement, he has no legal entitlement (s.20(1)). Further, if he is dismissed because of one of the above requirements, he can bring a claim for unfair dismissal as long as he has been employed for a period of four weeks, instead of the more usual period of two years. Whether such dismissal would be fair will obviously depend on the circumstances. For example, it may be shown that the employee's job became redundant, etc.

9.69 Medical suspension pay is not meant to be a top-up for, or a substitution for, statutory sick pay. It is designed to meet the situation where employees are fit for work, but are prevented from doing so because of a health hazard, in particular following a recommendation that they should cease work made by a doctor from the Employment Medical Advisory Service. In *Stallite Batteries Co. Ltd v Appleton*, an employee fell into a skip containing lead waste. In consequence, his lead/blood level rose dramatically to 93 μ/100 ml, which was in excess of the limits laid down under the Control of Lead at Work Regulations. The level decreased over the following months, but his own doctor certified that he was still unfit for work. Eight months after the incident he was dismissed and he claimed compensation for unfair dismissal and medical suspension pay. The Employment Appeal Tribunal held that as he was not available for work because of sickness, he was not entitled to medical suspension pay by virtue of the provisions of s.20(3).

9.70 If the employer still needs someone to do the work, he may decide to take on a temporary replacement. He should inform the latter in writing that his employment will be terminated at the end of the period of suspension. If, therefore, he has to dismiss the temporary employee in order to permit the first employee to return to work, the dismissal will be for "some other substantial reason", but without prejudice to the rule that the employer will still have to show that he acted reasonably in treating that reason as a sufficient ground for dismissal (EPCA, s.61). However, since the medical suspension period is unlikely to last long enough to enable the temporary employee to obtain a sufficient qualifying period of employment, this provision is somewhat otiose.

9.71 To qualify for medical suspension payments, the employee must have been employed for more than four weeks. Further, he will not be entitled to be paid if the employer has offered him suitable alternative work (whether or not the employee was contractually obliged to do that type of work) and he unreasonably refuses to perform that work. The employee must also comply with reasonable requirements imposed by the employer with a view to ensuring that his services are available. In other words, as the employer is paying the employee wages during the suspension, the employer may require the employee to do other work, or hold himself in readiness for work. The amount of pay to be made is calculated in accordance with Schedule 4 of EPCA, which depends on the contractual arrangements for pay.

9.72 An employee may complain to an industrial tribunal that the employer has failed to pay him in accordance with the above provisions. The complaint must be presented within three months of the failure, and if the complaint is upheld, the industrial tribunal will order the employer to pay the amount due.

9.73 An employee who does not work for more than sixteen hours per week (unless he works between eight and sixteen hours per week, and has done so for more than five years), or who works on a fixed-term contract for ten weeks or less, is not covered by the above provisions (EPCA, s.143(3)).

10

The impact of international obligations

European Communities

10.1 In 1951, by the Treaty of Paris, the European Coal and Steel Community (ECSC) was established, when six countries (France, West Germany, Italy, Belgium, Holland and Luxembourg) agreed to pool their coal and steel resources and create a common commercial market for their products. Subsequently, the Mines Safety and Health Commission was created to work for the elimination of occupational risks to health and safety in coalmines.

10.2 In 1957 the European Atomic Energy Commission (EURATOM) was established in order to coordinate and develop the peaceful uses of nuclear energy, and strong emphasis was placed on the need to ensure the protection of the health of workers as well as the community at large from dangers arising from radiation hazards.

10.3 Also in 1957, by the Treaty of Rome, the European Economic Community (EEC) was established. This has the wider objective of establishing a common market for its economic activities by the elimination of customs duties, creating common customs tariffs, permitting the free movement of capital and workers, laying down common agricultural and transport policies, and harmonising the laws of Member States to ensure that competition is not distorted and to facilitate the anticipated economic expansion.

10.4 In 1967 these three institutions were merged into the European Communities (EC), with the fusion of their executive institutions, and the result is that although the three organisations have a separate existence, they are all now under the one umbrella. By the European Communities Act 1972, the UK signified its accession to the Treaty of Rome, including its laws, which by s.2(1) of the Act are to be given legal effect without further enactment. Ireland and Denmark joined at the same time as the UK and Greece became a member in 1981. Spain and Portugal became full members in 1992.

The working of the Community

10.5 The nature of European law, and the structure of Community institutions have already been considered in chapter 1. As noted, initial proposals are made by the Commission, there is a consultative process with interested parties (including the European Parliament) and final approval is given by the Council of Ministers.

10.6 The Commission operates through twenty Directorates-General (DGs) with the addition of a number of other departments. In the main, Directorate-General V, which deals with employment and social affairs, has an overall responsibility for health and safety matters, although there is an overlap with other DGs where matters of common concern arise. Directorate E of DG V is the department most closely concerned with health and safety matters, and is based in Luxembourg. It has responsibilities for (a) toxicology, biology and health effects, (b) radioactive waste, accident prevention and safety measures in nuclear installations, (c) public health and radiation protection, (d) industrial medicine and hygiene, (e) industrial safety, and (f) Mines Safety and Health Commission.

10.7 In order to advise the Commission generally on all aspects of health and safety at work, an Advisory Committee on Safety, Hygiene and Health Protection was established in 1974. This consists of two members from governments, two from employers' associations, and two from trade unions, making a total of six from each Member State. This Committee assists the Commission in the preparation and implementation of activities in the field of safety, health and hygiene relating to work activities, with the exception of those areas which are dealt with by the Mines Health and Safety Commission and EURATOM.

10.8 The Advisory Committee's terms of reference are as follows:

(a) conducting, on the basis of information available to it, exchanges of views and experience regarding existing or planned regulations
(b) contributing towards the development of a common approach to problems which exist in the field of safety, hygiene and health protection at work, and towards the choice of Community priorities, as well as the measures necessary for implementing those priorities
(c) drawing the Commission's attention to areas in which there is an apparent need for the acquisition of new knowledge and for the implementation of appropriate educational and research projects
(d) defining, within the framework of Community action programmes, and in cooperation with the Mines Safety and Health Commission, the criteria and aims of the campaign against the risks of accidents at work and health hazards within the undertaking, and methods enabling undertakings and their employees to evaluate and to improve the level of protection.

Consultative bodies

10.9 Before EC legislation is passed, a tremendous amount of consultative work takes place. Proposals need to be supported by relevant scientific or technical data or surveys, national experts are consulted, advisory committees are asked for opinions and initial proposals will then be drawn up. These are then transmitted to the European Parliament, to the Economic and Social Committee and to the Council of Ministers. At all stages, representations can be made by national groups representing employers, trade unions and other interested parties.

10.10 When proposals reach the UK, a Government department (generally known as the "lead department") which is most closely concerned with the proposal, will take charge of the consultative process. Usually, on health and safety matters, this will be the Department of Employment, but it may be some other department which has a major interest in the proposals (eg Department of the Environment). Discussions will continue with the TUC, CBI, trade associations, etc and an explanatory memorandum will be prepared by the lead department and submitted to Parliament for consideration by the scrutiny committee of each House. These committees may call for written or oral evidence, make recommendations for change, or request a Parliamentary debate. Once the Government has formulated its views, the matter can be transmitted back to the Council of Ministers for consideration by a working group. Here, the respective views are collated, the text may be revised, and the final proposals formulated and ultimately adopted. Not surprisingly, it can take many years before an initial proposal is finally transformed into a binding directive.

10.11 Once a directive relating to health and safety at work has been adopted, HSC draws up the necessary legislative proposals in order to implement it. Again, it will engage in a series of consultations with interested parties, but since all concerned should have been involved in the earlier discussion, the subject matter will occasion little surprise, and the only problems which are likely to arise will stem from the detailed arrangements which may be necessary in order to ensure that the final legislative proposals (usually made by regulations) will meet the European standards. Indeed, HSC takes pride in considering that it already anticipates European legislation as part of its own ongoing programme, and is thus in a favourable position to influence the European standards. Indeed, "The Commission's aim in negotiations is to influence the shape of EC proposals during their embryonic stages and where practicable to advance UK policy and practice as a model for adoption across the Community" (Annual Report 1989/1990 p.1).

EC Directives

10.12 As already noted (see para 1.37) the Treaty of Rome was amended in 1986 by the Single European Act, which aimed to create a Europe without economic barriers by the end of 1992. One of the amendments was the inclusion of a new Article 118A, which reads as follows:

> 1. The Member States shall pay particular attention to encouraging improvements, especially in the working environment, as regards the health and safety of workers, and shall set as their objective the harmonisation of conditions in this area, while maintaining the improvements.
> 2. In order to help achieve the objective laid down in the first paragraph, the Council, acting by a qualified majority on a proposal from the Commission and after consulting with the European Parliament and the Economic and Social Committee, shall adopt, by means of directives, minimum requirements for gradual implementation, having regard to the conditions and technical rules obtaining in each of the Member States. Such Directives shall avoid imposing administrative, financial and legal constraints in a way

which would hold back the creation and development of small and medium-sized undertakings.
3. The provisions adopted pursuant to this Article shall not prevent each Member State from introducing more stringent measures for the protection of working conditions compatible with the Treaty.

10.13 The result was the adoption by the Council of a Directive on the introduction of measures to encourage improvements in the health and safety of workers at work, the so-called "Framework Directive" (89/391/EEC). Its provisions have been given effect to by the Management of Health and Safety at Work Regulations 1992 (see chapter 4). In addition, a number of "daughter" Directives were adopted, ie Workplace Directive (89/654/EEC), Use of Work Equipment Directive (89/655/EEC), Personal Protective Equipment Directive (89/656/EEC), Manual Handling of Loads Directive (90/269/EEC) and Display Screen Equipment Directive (90/270/EEC). The provisions of these Directives have been implemented by the respective Regulations outlined in chapter 4.

10.14 Several further Directives on health and safety at work have been adopted by the Council, which have either been implemented by respective Regulations, or are under active consideration. These include the following.

(1) Carcinogens Directive (90/394/EEC)

10.15 This Directive has been implemented by the Control of Substances Hazardous to Health (Amendment) Regulations 1992, together with a revision of the supporting Approved Codes of Practice.

The Directive applies to substances which may cause cancer, and to certain further substances and processes specified in Annex 1 of the Directive. Employers must make an assessment of the risk of exposure, and, dependent on that assessment, replace the substance with a less harmful or less dangerous substance or use the substance in a closed system. If this is not possible, exposure must be reduced to as low a level as is possible. There must be suitable procedures for dealing with situations of abnormal exposure and emergency conditions, monitoring and health surveillance must be adopted, and the employer must provide adequate training, information and instructions concerning the risks to the health of workers, the precautions to be taken, and the results provided of any health surveillance.

(2) Asbestos Worker Protection Directive (91/382/EEC)

10.16 This has been implemented by the Control of Asbestos at Work (Amendment) Regulations 1992 and the Asbestos (Prohibitions) Regulations 1992. The Directive amends and updates the EC Directive on the protection of workers from risks relating to exposure to asbestos at work (83/477/EEC). Generally it increases the protection afforded to workers using asbestos, and, in particular, it requires employers to draw up a plan of work before starting on the removal from buildings of asbestos-containing products. Specific essential features of the plan are to be communicated to the competent authority.

(3) Temporary Workers Directive (91/383/EEC)

10.17 This Directive has been implemented by the Management of Health and Safety at Work Regulations 1992. The Directive applies to all workers with fixed duration contracts, and also to those who are seconded from one employer to another. Employers must give appropriate training and information to temporary workers, and they must receive medical surveillance on the same basis as permanent employees. The transferee employer is to be responsible for the health and safety of workers who are seconded to him.

(4) Biological Agents Directive (90/679/EEC)

10.18 The Council have already adopted two Directives on genetically modified micro-organisms and the release into the environment of genetically modified organisms. The Biological Agents Directive deals with the protection of workers from the risks related to exposure to biological agents whilst at work, although it does draw a distinction between exposure which is incidental to work activity (eg health care, farming etc) and where there is a conscious decision to work with such agents, eg a micro-biological laboratory. Employers must make a risk assessment, reduce the risks of exposure, provide training, instruction and information to workers, provide health surveillance, notify their activities to competent authorities, and take special measures related to health care. The Directive is to be implemented by Member States by 26 November 1993, and is currently under consideration by HSC.

(5) Construction Sites Directive (92/57/EEC)

10.19 This Directive will apply to building and civil engineering works, and any site at which the construction, equipping, alteration, renovation, repair, upkeep, maintenance and demolition of all types of buildings or structures is taking place. A project manager will have to be appointed to ensure that health and safety is considered from the concept of the project to its completion. Work plans will be required, with particular reference to specific hazards. There will be duties on designers and developers to ensure that the work is done in a safe manner, with additional reference to the safety of the end users. A Consultative Document has been issued by HSC, and it is expected that new Regulations implementing the Directive will be in force by 31 December 1993.

(6) Safety Signs Directive (92/58/EEC)

10.20 This Directive will replace the existing Directive (77/576/EEC), which was given effect to in the UK by the Safety Signs Regulations 1980 (see para 6.44). The new Directive will require employers to use a safety sign whenever there is a risk which cannot be adequately controlled by other means, taking into account the risk assessments made. In addition, the term "safety sign" would include other means of communication, such as hand signals, coding of pipe-work, marking of traffic routes, acoustic signals (eg fire alarms) and luminous signs. The number of conventional signs have been increased (with particular reference to identifying fire-fighting equipment). It is expected that a Consultative Document containing draft regulations will be published some time in 1993, and the Directive is to be implemented by 24 June 1994.

(7) Pregnant Women Directive (92/85/EEC)

10.21 This Directive is designed to protect the health and safety of women workers who are pregnant, or who have recently given birth, or who are breast-feeding. An assessment will have to be made of the chemical, physical and biological agents and industrial processes which are considered to be hazardous for such workers. Reference will have to be made to movement and posture, mental and physical fatigue, and other types of stress connected with the work. An assessment will also have to be made of any risks to health and safety which could arise from an appended list of agents, processes or working condition, and pregnant women are to be informed of the result of the assessment. If it is revealed that there is a risk to health or safety, or that there would be an effect on pregnancy or breast-feeding, the employer will be required to avoid the risk either by making a temporary adjustment to the working conditions, or move the worker to another job. If such methods are not possible, the worker is to be given leave for the period necessary to ensure her health and safety. Pregnant women, or those who have recently given birth, must not be obliged to do night work if they produce a medical certificate stating that this would be detrimental to their health or safety.

10.22 The Directive contains further provisions concerning the employment rights of pregnant women, including maternity pay, maternity leave of absence, and protection from dismissal because of pregnancy. The Directive must be implemented by Member States by October 1994. Some of the employment rights aspects of the Directive have been met by various amendments to the law made in the Trade Union Reform and Employment Rights Act 1993 (see Para 7.4)

(8) Other Directives

10.23 Other Directives which have been adopted and thus due for implementation include Protection of Workers in mineral-extracting industries through drilling (92/91/EEC), Protection of Workers in surface and underground mineral extracting industries (92/104/EEC), Safety Data Sheets (91/155/EEC), Limit Values (91/322/EEC), Genetically Modified Organisms (90/219/EEC), and so on. An interesting argument arises over the Working Time Directive, recently agreed by the Council of Ministers. The view of the British Government is that this is not strictly a health and safety issue, and therefore should not have been passed under Article 118A (where the qualified majority voting system is used) but rather under the provisions of the Treaty which require a unanimous vote. The British Government is therefore seeking to have the validity of the Directive challenged before the European Court.

Product Safety Directives

10.24 In addition to directives under Article 118A, the EC is attempting to harmonise the laws of Member States on product safety and supporting standards. These directives are made under Article 100A of the Treaty—sometimes referred to as "New Approach" Directives. These will depend on the availability of harmonised European standards because different laws in the various Member States could cause technical barriers to trade.

10.25 Directive 83/189/EEC requires Member States to inform the Commission of any new technical regulation, which is then circulated to other Member States for comment. If it is thought that the proposed regulation would create a barrier to the free movement of goods, the State may not implement it for a period, and the Commission may then decide to propose or adopt a directive on the subject of notification.

10.26 "New Approach" Directives set out essential requirements (eg on safety) which must be complied with before products may be sold anywhere in the Community. They also state how manufacturers are to meet those essential requirements. Once these are complied with, the product may carry the "CE" mark, which means that they can be sold anywhere in the Community.

10.27 There are two European bodies which prepare European Standards. One is the European Committee for Standardisation (CEN), the other is the European Committee for Electrotechnical Standardisation (CENELEC). These bodies work with the national standards organisation in the respective States. In the UK, this body is the British Standards Institution (see para 2.128). The European Committees achieve an acceptable consensus, and the standard is then adopted by the weighted majority system (see para 1.37).

10.28 The following directives have a particular interest to those involved in health and safety matters:

10.29 (a) Personal Protective Equipment Directive (89/686/EEC). This directive covers any device or appliance designed to be worn or used or held by an individual for protection against one or more safety or health hazards. It also covers combined personal protective equipment and interchangeable components which are essential to its satisfactory functioning.

10.30 PPE must preserve the health and ensure the safety of users, must not harm other people, domestic animals or goods when properly maintained and used for its intended purpose.

10.31 (b) Machinery Safety Directive (89/392/EEC). Machinery must satisfy the essential health and safety requirements set out in the directive, including the materials used in the construction, lighting, design, controls, stability, hazards relating to moving parts, fire, noise, vibration, radiation, emission of dust and gases, maintenance, warnings and instruction handbooks. This Directive has been implemented by the Supply of Machinery (Safety) Regulations 1992.

10.32 Other "New Approach" Directives deal with such topics as mobile machinery and lifting equipment, non-automatic weighing instruments, gas appliances, medical devices, and so on.

European legislation on health and safety

10.33 A collection of all legislative material on occupational health and safety in the twelve Member States of the European Community is now held by HSE. There is also a Language Service Unit which provides a translation service to HSE staff, and a Translation Bulletin (available free of charge) indicating the topics translated, and the cost of providing these to interested parties.

International Labour Organisation (ILO)

10.34 The ILO was formed in 1919. It consists of representatives of national governments, employers' and workers' organisations and is now an agency of the United Nations. It has worked consistently to improve international labour standards relating to such matters as conditions of work, training, freedom of association, social security, industrial relations, and many other similar topics. It holds international conferences, provides technical advice and assistance to individual countries, and generally acts as an international forum for the promotion and improvement of standards throughout the world.

10.35 A major part of the work of the ILO consists of adopting conventions and recommendations. These are submitted to national governments for consideration, for they are not automatically binding. A convention may be ratified by a nation State, which amounts to a pledge to implement its provisions. However, any State is free to denounce a convention it has adopted, and is then free to ignore its provisions. A recommendation does not require ratification, but merely serves as a guide if national action is to be taken on a particular topic.

10.36 Since its inception, the ILO has passed over 150 Conventions, many relating to occupational health and safety matters. It has also passed over 160 recommendations covering similar topics, and has published a large number of reports and studies.

10.37 The ILO also produces research papers, suggests international classification standards, and issues Codes of Practice giving guidance on practical measures which may be taken to safeguard workers' health against occupational hazards.

Appendix A

Names and addresses

HEALTH AND SAFETY EXECUTIVE: Public Enquiry Points (Information Centre):

Broad Lane, Sheffield S3 7HQ
tel: 0742 892345; fax: 0742 892333

Free leaflet line tel: 0742 892346

Part 1: FACTORY, AGRICULTURAL AND QUARRIES INSPECTORATE

Note: HSE has reorganised its professional field staff to form a new Field Operations Division with seven regions and its headquarters in Bootle, Merseyside. Seven Regional Directors of Field Operations (RDFOs) manage the integrated regional teams. This inspectorate incorporates the factory, agricultural and quarries inspectorates, as well as the employment medical advisory service (EMAS).

Head Office:	Magdalen House Stanley Precinct BOOTLE L20 3QZ 051–951 4000	
HSE Area Office	**Address and Telephone Number**	**Local authorities within each area**
1. SOUTH WEST	Inter City House Mitchell Lane Bristol BS1 6AN 0272 290681	Avon, Cornwall, Devon, Gloucestershire, Somerset, Isles of Scilly
2. SOUTH	Priestley House Priestley Road Basingstoke RG24 9NW 0256 473181	Berkshire, Dorset, Hampshire, Isle of Wight, Wiltshire
3. SOUTH EAST	3 East Grinstead House London Road East Grinstead RH19 1RR 0342 326922	Kent, Surrey, East Sussex, West Sussex
4. (now merged with Area 5)		

Area	Address	Coverage
5. LONDON N (2 offices covering the same boroughs)	Maritime House 1 Linton Road Barking IG11 8HF 081–594 5522 Chancel House Neasden Lane London NW10 2UD 081–459 8855	Barking and Dagenham, Barnet, Brent, Camden, Ealing, Enfield, Hackney, Haringey, Harrow, Havering, Islington, Newham, Redbridge, Tower Hamlets, Waltham Forest
6. LONDON S	1 Long Lane London SE1 4PG 071–407 8911	Bexley, Bromley, City of London, Croydon, Greenwich, Hammersmith and Fulham, Hillingdon, Hounslow, Kensington and Chelsea, Kingston-upon-Thames, Lambeth, Lewisham, Merton, Richmond-upon-Thames, Southwark, Sutton, Wandsworth, Westminster
7. EAST ANGLIA	39 Baddow Road Chelmsford CM2 0HL 0245 284661	Essex except parts of Essex covered by Area 5, Norfolk, Suffolk
8. NORTHERN HOME COUNTIES	14 Cardiff Road Luton LU1 1PP 0582 34121	Bedfordshire, Buckinghamshire, Cambridgeshire, Hertfordshire
9. EAST MIDLANDS	5th Floor Belgrave House 1 Greyfriars Northampton NN1 2BS 0604 21233	Leicestershire, Northamptonshire, Oxfordshire, Warwickshire
10. WEST MIDLANDS	McLaren Building 2 Masshouse Circus Queensway Birmingham B4 7NP 021–200 2299	West Midlands
11. WALES	Brunel House 2 Fitzalan Road Cardiff CF2 1SH 0222 473777	Clwyd, Dyfed, Gwent, Gwynedd, Mid Glamorgan, Powys, South Glamorgan, West Glamorgan
12. MARCHES	Marches House Midway Newcastle-under-Lyme ST5 1DT 0782 717181	Hereford and Worcester, Shropshire, Staffordshire
13. NORTH MIDLANDS	Birkbeck House Trinity Square Nottingham NG1 4AU 0602 470712	Derbyshire, Lincolnshire, Nottinghamshire

14. SOUTH YORKSHIRE	Sovereign House 110 Queens Street Sheffield S1 2ES 0742 739081	Humberside, South Yorkshire
15. WEST & NORTH YORKSHIRE	8 St Paul's Street Leeds LS1 2LE 0532 446191	North Yorkshire, West Yorkshire
16. GREATER MANCHESTER	Quay House Quay Street Manchester M3 3JB 061–831 7111	Greater Manchester
17. MERSEYSIDE	The Triad Stanley Road Bootle L20 3PG 051–922 7211	Cheshire, Merseyside
18. NORTH WEST	Victoria House Ormskirk Road Preston PR1 1HH 0772 59321	Cumbria, Lancashire
19. NORTH EAST	Arden House Regent Centre Regent Farm Road Gosforth Newcastle upon Tyne NE3 3JN 091–284 8448	Cleveland, Durham, Northumberland, Tyne & Wear
20. SCOTLAND EAST	Belford House 59 Belford Road Edinburgh EH4 3UE 031–247 2000	Borders, Central, Fife, Grampian, Highland, Lothian, Tayside and the island areas of Orkney & Shetland
21. SCOTLAND WEST	314 St Vincent Street Glasgow G3 8XG 041–204 2646	Dumfries and Galloway, Strathclyde and the Western Isles

Communications should be addressed to the Area Executive of the area concerned.

Appendix B

Approved Codes of Practice

The following have been approved or authorised by the Health and Safety Commission. Copies are available from HMSO unless otherwise indicated. British Standards may be ordered from the British Standards Institution, Linford Wood, Milton Keynes MK14 6LE.

Dangerous substances:

COP 11 Operational provisions of the Dangerous Substances (Conveyance by Road in Road Tankers and Tank Containers) Regulations 1981
COP 14 Road tanker testing: Examination, testing and certification of the carrying tanks of road tankers and of tank containers used for the conveyance of dangerous substances by road
COP 19 Classification and labelling of dangerous substances for conveyance by road in tankers, tank containers and packages (revision 1)
COP 22 Classification and labelling of substances dangerous for supply
COP 40 Packaging and labelling of dangerous substances for conveyance by road (revision 2)
COP 17 Operational provisions of the Road Traffic (Carriage of Dangerous Substances in Packages etc) Regulations 1986
COP 18 Dangerous substances in harbour areas
COP 33 Transport of compressed gases in tube trailers and tube containers

Petroleum-Spirit:

COP 6 Plastic containers with nominal capacities up to 5 litres for petroleum-spirit: Requirements for testing and marking or labelling.

Control of Substances Hazardous to Health:

L5 Control of substances hazardous to health (general ACOP) and Control of carcinogenic substances (carcinogens ACOP) (second edition)—both ACOPs published as one document
COP 30 Control of substances hazardous to health in fumigation operations
COP 31 Control of vinyl chloride at work
COP 41 Control of substances hazardous to health in the production of pottery

New substances:

Annex to EC Directive 87/302/EEC (available in the Official Journal of the European Communities; L133, volume 31, 30.5.88, from HMSO (see page 110).

Lead:

COP 2 Control of lead at work

Asbestos:

COP 21 Control of asbestos at work
COP 3 Work with asbestos insulation, asbestos coating and asbestos insulating board

Safety Representatives and Committees:

COP 1 Safety representatives and safety committees
Time off for the training of safety representatives

Gas:

COP 20 Standards of training in safe gas installation

First-Aid:

COP 42 First-aid at work: Health and Safety (First-Aid) Regulations 1981 and guidance
COP 32 First-aid on offshore installations and pipeline works

Zoos:

COP 15 Zoos: Safety, health and welfare standards for employers and persons at work

Ionising radiation:

COP 16 The protection of persons against ionising radiation arising from any work activity
COP 23 Exposure to radon
L7 Dose limitation—restrictions of exposure: additional guidance on regulation 6 of the Ionising Radiations Regulations 1985

Agriculture:

COP 24 Preventing accidents to children in agriculture

Docks:

COP 25 Safety in docks

Pressure Systems:

COP 37 Safety of pressure systems
COP 38 Safety of transportable gas containers

Quarries:

COP 27 Explosives at quarries
COP 35 The use of electricity at quarries

Mines:

COP 28 Safety of exit from mines underground workings
COP 34 The use of electricity in mines

Lift Trucks:

COP 26 Rider operated lift trucks—operator training

Explosives:

COP 36 Carriage of explosives by road

Legionnaires' Disease:

L8 The prevention or control of legionellosis (including Legionnaires' disease)

Pesticides:

L9 The safe use of pesticides for non agricultural purposes
Code of practice for the safe use of pesticides on farms and holdings (HSE/MAFF)

Management:

L21 The management of health and safety at work

Workplace:

L24 Workplace health, safety and welfare

Subject Index

Table of Cases

Table of Statutes